I0095044

"Death, dying, and grief are inescapable experiences, yet we can often fall into the trap of avoiding and denying that these experiences will actually happen to us. The recent worldwide pandemic has thrust upon us the nature of our vulnerability and the intense grief that is experienced when we lose those we love. There is no way to 'cure' grief, but experiencing grief and dying in a landscape of compassion can be healing and transformative. In this book, Darcy Harris and Andy Ho bring together the sharpest minds in the world of compassion science and examine how a compassionate focus can be applied to grief, death, and dying. This is simply a must read for all clinicians wanting to improve their compassionate understanding and practice."

James N. Kirby, *PhD, senior lecturer, codirector, Compassionate Mind Research Group, School of Psychology, University of Queensland*

"A valuable book for those who bear witness to grief and as well for those traveling in the landscape of grief."

Roshi Joan Halifax, *PhD, founder and abbot, Upaya Zen Center*

"One of the only things that binds together all of the billions of people on this planet is that we will all experience grief and loss at various stages of our life. In this important and timely book, internationally renowned researchers and clinicians outline the central role that compassion has in working with grief and loss. Covering a comprehensive range of topics, this book provides essential reading for all of us, and in particular, anyone working with these painful experiences."

Chris Irons, *PhD, DClinPsy, clinical psychologist and director, Balanced Minds Compassion-Focused Psychological Services and Resources*

"As medicine becomes more technology focused, with ever increasing emphasis on biological aspects of healthcare delivery, what is often lost is recognition of the human side of medicine. Now more than ever, patients and their families—especially those who are facing loss and grief—crave approaches that recognize personhood and the need for compassion. Drs. Harris and Ho have assembled an impressive, international group of leading clinicians and researchers in the theory and practice of compassion-informed care. As the world continues to grapple with the tragedy of COVID-19, the timing for a book focused on compassion could not be better."

Harvey Max Chochinov, *OC, OM, MD, PhD, FRCPC, FRSC, distinguished professor of psychiatry, University of Manitoba, and senior scientist, CancerCare Manitoba Research Institute*

"Compassion is the wellspring we draw upon when confronted with suffering: It is the invisible thread that connects us to our fellow beings. This thoughtfully conceived and brilliantly executed volume fully explores what it means to bring compassion to the encounters we have with other people—clients, inhabitants of our community and our world—and to the relationship we have with ourselves. *Compassion-Based*

Approaches in Loss and Grief is an immensely practical book that reflects the contributors' commitment to inspiring compassionate action at every level of human interaction, from therapeutic relationships to community organizations to political structures, with abundant illustrations of how these goals can be advanced. Detailed examples of compassion-based approaches to grief support make the book one that clinicians will want to keep close at hand. *Compassion-Based Approaches in Loss and Grief* is truly a gift for helping professionals and for anyone who wants to be a healing presence in a world that is very much in need of healers."

Phyllis Kosminsky, *PhD, LCSW, FT, author of*
Attachment Informed Grief Therapy: A Clinician's Guide
to Foundations and Applications

"This landmark book bridges compassion-based approaches with current theory and practices in loss, grief, and bereavement. The reader is taken on a journey from foundational concepts in these two fields to a deep understanding of clinical applications of compassion focused grief therapy. Deftly edited by two leading researchers and clinicians with contributions from a list of international authors, *Compassion-Based Approaches in Loss and Grief* reviews the recent and burgeoning research in compassion and grief and invites the reader to consider how we can engage with suffering as we seek to relieve it within ourselves and those we care for. Notably, the book moves beyond an individual's perspective to consider broader social, organizational, and political structures and the place of compassion within them. This is a highly significant contribution to the fields of loss, grief, and compassion and fills a profound void in the literature. *Compassion-Based Approaches in Loss and Grief* is an essential read for those concerned with the understanding and relief of suffering and the development of skills to assist those we support."

Christopher Hall, *CEO, Australian Centre for Grief and Bereavement*

"Anchored in science and the wisdom of clinical practice, *Compassion-Based Approaches in Loss and Grief* is an invaluable resource for compassionate person-centered care. The rich offerings of this book—from self-compassion to counseling techniques and social perspectives—will inspire, empower, and guide you on your healing journey with those you care for."

Dale G. Larson, *PhD, professor of counseling psychology,
Santa Clara University, and author of* The Helper's Journey:
Empathy, Compassion, and the Challenge of Caring

COMPASSION-BASED APPROACHES IN LOSS AND GRIEF

Compassion-Based Approaches in Loss and Grief introduces clinicians to a wide array of strategies and frameworks for engaging clients throughout the loss experience, particularly when those experiences have a protracted course.

In the book, clinicians and researchers from around the world and from a variety of fields explore ways to cultivate compassion and how to implement compassion-based clinical practices specifically designed to address loss, grief, and bereavement.

Students, scholars, and mental health and healthcare professionals will come away from this important book with a deepened understanding of compassion-based approaches and strategies for enhancing distress tolerance, maintaining focus, and identifying clinical interventions best suited to clients' needs.

Darcy L. Harris is a professor of thanatology at King's University College in London, Canada, where she also maintains a private clinical practice specializing in issues related to change, loss, and transition.

Andy H. Y. Ho is an associate professor of psychology and medicine at Nanyang Technological University in Singapore. He is also the 2022–2023 president of the Association for Death Education and Counseling and a board director of the International Work Group on Death, Dying, and Bereavement.

THE SERIES IN DEATH, DYING, AND BEREAVEMENT

Volumes published in the Series in Death, Dying and Bereavement are representative of the multidisciplinary nature of the intersecting fields of death studies, suicidology, end-of-life care, and grief counseling. The series meets the needs of clinicians, researchers, paraprofessionals, pastoral counselors, and educators by providing cutting edge research, theory, and best practices on the most important topics in these fields—for today and for tomorrow.

Series Editors: Robert A. Neimeyer, PhD, Portland Institute for Loss and Transition, Oregon, USA, and Darcy L. Harris, PhD, Western University Canada, Ontario, Canada

Chronic Sorrow, 2nd Edition
A Living Loss
Susan Roos

Continuing Bonds in Bereavement
New Directions for Research and Practice
Edited by Dennis Klass and Edith Maria Steffen

Prescriptive Memories in Grief and Loss
The Art of Dreamscaping
Edited by Nancy Gershman and Barbara E. Thompson

Loss, Grief, and Attachment in Life Transitions
A Clinician's Guide to Secure Base Counseling
Jakob van Wielink, Leo Wilhelm, and Denise van Geelen-Merks

Non-Death Loss and Grief
Context and Clinical Implications
Edited by Darcy L. Harris

Superhero Grief
The Transformative Power of Loss
Edited by Jill A. Harrington and Robert A. Neimeyer

New Techniques of Grief Therapy
Bereavement and Beyond
Edited by Robert A. Neimeyer

Pediatric Palliative Care
A Model for Exemplary Practice
Betty Davies, Rose Steele, and Jennifer Baird

The Restorative Nature of Ongoing Connections with the Deceased
Exploring Presence Within Absence
Laurie A. Burke and Edward (Ted) Rynearson

Compassion-Based Approaches in Loss and Grief
Darcy L. Harris and Andy H. Y. Ho

For more information about this series, please visit https://www.routledge.com/Series-in-Death-Dying-and-Bereavement/book-series/SE0620

COMPASSION-BASED APPROACHES IN LOSS AND GRIEF

Edited by Darcy L. Harris and Andy H. Y. Ho

Routledge
Taylor & Francis Group

NEW YORK AND LONDON

Cover image taken by Darcy L. Harris and Andy H. Y. Ho

First published 2023
by Routledge
605 Third Avenue, New York, NY 10158

and by Routledge
4 Park Square, Milton Park, Abingdon, Oxon, OX14 4RN

Routledge is an imprint of the Taylor & Francis Group, an informa business

© 2023 selection and editorial matter, Darcy L. Harris and Andy H. Y. Ho; individual chapters, the contributors

The right of Darcy L. Harris and Andy H. Y. Ho to be identified as the authors of the editorial material, and of the authors for their individual chapters, has been asserted in accordance with sections 77 and 78 of the Copyright, Designs and Patents Act 1988.

All rights reserved. No part of this book may be reprinted or reproduced or utilised in any form or by any electronic, mechanical, or other means, now known or hereafter invented, including photocopying and recording, or in any information storage or retrieval system, without permission in writing from the publishers.

Trademark notice: Product or corporate names may be trademarks or registered trademarks, and are used only for identification and explanation without intent to infringe.

Library of Congress Cataloging-in-Publication Data
Names: Harris, Darcy, editor. | Ho, Andy H. Y., editor.
Title: Compassion-based approaches in loss and grief/edited by Darcy L. Harris and Andy H. Y. Ho.
Description: New York, NY: Routledge, 2023. |
Series: Death, dying, and bereavement | Includes bibliographical references and index. |
Identifiers: LCCN 2022026431 (print) | LCCN 2022026432 (ebook) |
ISBN 9781032068343 (paperback) | ISBN 9781032068367 (hardback) |
ISBN 9781003204121 (ebook)
Subjects: LCSH: Grief. | Bereavement–Psychological aspects. |
Death–Psychological aspects. | Loss (Psychology)
Classification: LCC BF575.G7 C6448 2023 (print) | LCC BF575.G7 (ebook) |
DDC 155.9/37–dc23/eng/20220623
LC record available at https://lccn.loc.gov/2022026431
LC ebook record available at https://lccn.loc.gov/2022026432

ISBN: 978-1-032-06836-7 (hbk)
ISBN: 978-1-032-06834-3 (pbk)
ISBN: 978-1-003-20412-1 (ebk)

DOI: 10.4324/9781003204121

Typeset in Baskerville
by Deanta Global Publishing Services, Chennai, India

It is with deep gratitude that we wish to thank all the contributors for their time and willingness to share their expertise in this volume. We hope that you share our joy in the publication of this book, which would not have been possible without each of you.

Darcy Harris:
I would like to dedicate this book to those who demonstrated compassion to me along this path, modeling how to live with intention and openness. I also express my deep gratitude for my clients and students, whose trust and sharing have taught me so much about presence, compassion, and engaged learning. But most of all, I am grateful beyond words for my beloved Brad, whose very being envelops me with kindness and compassion, and for Lauren, for inspiring me, believing in me, and filling my life with joy beyond words.

Andy Ho:
I would like to dedicate this book to all the patients and families whom I had the privilege to work with, for teaching me the virtue and meaning of compassion in their most precious and vulnerable moments. I would also like to honor the memories of my grandparents who raised me selflessly and showed me the path toward resilience and resolve. Finally, I would like to express my deepest gratitude and love to my family for supporting and believing in me, and especially to Geri and Austin, for being the inspirational pillars of my life, always.

CONTENTS

LIST OF FIGURES

LIST OF TABLES

LIST OF CONTRIBUTORS

June Allan, PhD, MAASW, has a long-held interest in social work, loss, grief, and bereavement particularly from social justice and structural perspectives. Currently an adjunct staff member in Social Work and Social Policy at La Trobe University in Melbourne, Australia, June established the Loss, Trauma and Grief courses in the Social Work programs at RMIT University Australia. She has co-edited two editions of the book *Critical Social Work*. Other publications include a chapter on women's contribution to sociology in the *Handbook of the Sociology of Death, Grief and Bereavement*, and a chapter on critical social work in action in the *Handbook of Social Justice in Loss and Grief*. A former board member and vice-president of the Australian Centre for Grief and Bereavement for several years, June is a member of the International Work Group on Death, Dying, and Bereavement.

Tobyn Bell, MSc, is a compassion-focused therapist and part of the training executive for the Compassionate Mind Foundation. He is a co-author of *Compassion Focused Therapy from the Inside Out*, a self-practice/self-reflection workbook for therapists. He is also a CBT trainer, supervisor, and program-lead at the Greater Manchester CBT Training Centre (NHS) which is associated with Manchester University. He has published research on compassion and is completing his doctoral research on CFT through Derby University. He currently runs a regional CFT peer supervision group, and he offers CFT supervision to individual therapists, as well as offering CFT in a Manchester clinic. He is a member of the British Association of Behavioural and Cognitive Psychotherapists and Nursing and Midwifery Council.

Chia-Ying Chou, PhD, is a San Francisco-based licensed psychologist in private practice. Dr. Chou is a UCSF-trained specialist in hoarding disorder. She has worked with over 200 individuals with hoarding disorder, applying cognitive behavioral therapy and compassion-focused therapy. As a scientist-practitioner, Chou's clinical work is closely informed by her active research involvement. Her scientific publications focus on the roles of self-relationship, emotion regulation, and trauma in hoarding disorder. Dr. Chou strives to investigate novel interventions for hoarding disorder. She has developed a compassion-focused therapy treatment protocol for hoarding disorder and conducted studies to examine the effect of this treatment.

Nathan S. Considine, PhD, is a health psychologist in the School of Medicine at the University of Auckland in New Zealand. His training is in emotion and emotion regulation, looking at how such factors may be linked to physical health including screening, symptoms, adherence, and adaptation to chronic disease. Current research foci include compassion in health, disgust in medical contexts, and mindfulness. After graduating from Canterbury in 2000 and spending ten years working on grants in New York, Nathan returned to New Zealand in 2009. In addition to teaching in health psychology and medical programs, he supervises numerous students examining compassion (and self-compassion) in health. Nathan has published more than 150 scientific works and is an associate editor and reviewer for numerous international journals. He enjoys fishing, playing tennis with his son, and listening to the sort of music that his colleagues dislike.

Gerry R. Cox, PhD, is a Professor Emeritus of Sociology at the University of Wisconsin–La Crosse. He served as the director of the Center for Death Education and Bioethics. His teaching focused upon theory/theory construction, deviance and criminology, death and dying, social psychology, and minority peoples. He has over 100 publications including over 30 books. He has served as editor of *Illness, Crisis, and Loss* and for *The Midwest Sociologist*, and is the author and editor of numerous chapters and books related to death, dying, and grief. He is a member of the International Work Group on Dying, Death, and Bereavement, the Midwest Sociological Society, the American Sociological Association, the International Sociological Association, Phi Kappa Phi, and the Great Plains Sociological Society. He has also served on the board of directors of the National Prison Hospice Association.

Oindrila Dutta, PhD, is an award-winning researcher, psychologist, and thanatologist who specializes in employing culturally sensitive and digitally savvy interventions for empowering patients and families facing illness, mortality, grief, and bereavement to take charge of their own health and well-being. Her scholarly contributions include proposing the Trauma to Transformation model of Asian parental bereavement and piloting the Narrative e-Writing Intervention (NeW-I) for advancing pediatric palliative care and grief support services in Singapore through an innovative digital mental health approach. Oindrila is presently immersed in understanding how smart technology can enhance autonomy and quality of life for community-dwelling older adults and addressing the feasibility, scalability, and sustainability of a European Union-standardized open platform for facilitating long-term healthy and active ageing in Europe. In recognition of her work, Oindrila has received numerous local and international commendations—the most recent one being the Edie Stark-Shirley Scott Early Career Award presented by the Association for Death Education and Counselling (ADEC) in 2022.

Ronald Epstein, MD, has conducted ground-breaking research into communication in medical settings and developed innovative educational programs that promote mindfulness, communication, and self-awareness. Dr. Epstein co-directs the Center for Communication and Disparities Research and Mindful Practice Programs at the University of Rochester, where he is Professor of Family Medicine, Oncology, and Medicine (Palliative Care). A graduate of Harvard Medical School, he has received numerous humanism awards and fellowships, and the American Cancer Society's highest award, the Clinical Research Professorship. He has authored over 300 articles and chapters. His book, *Attending: Medicine, Mindfulness and Humanity*, was released in 2017.

Shari Geller, PhD, is an author, clinical psychologist, and mindful self-compassion (MSC) teacher. Shari is passionate about training therapists in cultivating therapeutic presence. With over 25 years' experience weaving psychology and mindfulness, Shari co-authored the book, *Therapeutic Presence: A Mindful Approach to Effective Therapy*, with Dr. Leslie S. Greenberg (second edition to be released in 2022). Shari's recent book, *A Practical Guide for Cultivating Therapeutic Presence*, offers practical guidance for cultivating and strengthening therapeutic presence as a foundational approach. Shari serves on the teaching faculty in Health Psychology at York University and for the Applied Mindfulness Meditation (AMM) program at the University of Toronto, and is Adjunct Professor in the Faculty of Music at the University of Toronto, in association with Music and Health Research Collaboratory (MaHRC). She is on the steering committee and part of the core faculty of the Self-Compassion in Psychotherapy (SCIP) certificate program. Shari is the co-director of the Centre for MindBody Health, in Toronto, where she offers training, supervision, and therapy in emotion-focused therapy and mindfulness and self-compassion modalities for individuals and couples. She has had a personal twice daily mindfulness and self-compassion practice for over 30 years. http://www.sharigeller.ca; http://www.cmbh.space.

Paul Gilbert, OBE, PhD, is the founder of compassion-focused therapy (CFT) and compassionate mind training (CMT) and author of numerous books on the evolutionary development of compassion and the implementation of compassion-focused approaches. He is an internationally recognized author, presenter, and researcher in the field. He was made a fellow of the British Psychological Society for his contributions to psychological knowledge and was president of the British Association for Cognitive and Behavioural Psychotherapy. He served on the government's National Institute for Health Care Excellence (NICE) guidelines for depression. He has published and edited over 20 books, over 100 academic papers, and 50 book chapters. He currently sits on the Emotion, Personality and Altruism Research Group at the Wright Institute (1992–present) and is Visiting Professor at the University of Fribourg (Switzerland) and the University of Coimbra (Portugal).

Cesar Gonzales, RPN, RN, BSc, has over 30 years of experience working in both mental health center and community settings. As a community health nurse, he has been involved in providing grief support to individuals and groups for over 24 years. He was involved in the development and implementation of the "Taking Steps Bereavement Group," a literal walking grief support group. Since that time, he has co-adapted the program using mindfulness and self-compassion practices to meet the needs of individuals experiencing grief and loss. He is a trained teacher of mindful self-compassion for adults and teens through the University of California San Diego School of Medicine. Recently, he has supported caregivers of family members living with dementia, young adults living with Type 1 diabetes, individuals living with Type 2 diabetes, and individuals dealing with issues of grief and loss utilizing the practices of mindfulness and self-compassion.

Brad Hunter, BA, OHT, studied English and Existential Philosophy at the University of Toronto, while beginning his initial forays into the world of meditation. After 'taking a break' from studies, with the intention of returning to graduate school, he ended up beginning a career in cemeteries and crematoria. This career paralleled decades of Zen meditation training. Twenty years ago, he began teaching meditation at the same time as he was training in grief and trauma therapy. Since retiring from his day-job in 2014, Brad became a Buddhist chaplain, specializing in end-of-life issues, grief, and trauma, and teaches meditation from a Theravada perspective.

Allan Kellehear, PhD, FAcSS, has held chairs in Australia, Britain, and Japan. He founded the "new" public health movement in palliative care and is the past president of Public Health Palliative Care International (PHPCI). In 2021, he took up a new post as Clinical Professor in the College of Nursing and Health Sciences at the University of Vermont in the United States. He holds concurrent honorary appointments as Emeritus Professor at the University of Bradford, Visiting Professor of Theology and Religion at Durham University, and Honorary Professor at McMaster University Medical School. Among his 25 books, he is best known for *Compassionate Cities: Public Health and End of Life Care* (Routledge 2005), *A*

Social History of Dying (Cambridge University Press 2007), and *The Inner Life of the Dying Person* (Columbia University Press 2014). His most recent book is *Visitors at the End of Life: Finding Meaning and Purpose in Near-Death Phenomena* (Columbia University Press 2020).

Philip Larkin, PhD, is a full Professor at the University Hospital Centre (CHUV). He also directs the Master of Science in Advanced Nursing Practice at the Institute for Higher Education and Research in Healthcare (IUFRS), University of Lausanne.

An Irish national, Philip Larkin has over 30 years of experience in the palliative care sector, both clinically and academically. He has become an important figure in the field in Ireland and elsewhere: As Professor of Palliative Care at University College Dublin, he has led the development of the All Ireland Institute for Hospice and Palliative Care, a public health project bringing together the Republic of Ireland and Northern Ireland to improve palliative care outcomes for all citizens. He was President of the European Palliative Care Association (EAPC) from 2015 to 2019. His research has focused on access to palliative care for vulnerable populations, with a particular focus on patients with mental health issues, disability, children, and palliative care needs in rural isolation, groups often marginalized in accessing palliative care. The place of compassion in palliative care is also part of his academic scholarship. He currently leads a palliative care nursing research team at the CHUV and continues to lecture nationally and internationally on nursing care, palliative care, and compassion in care.

Michael Krasner, MD, FACP, is a Professor of Clinical Medicine at the University of Rochester School of Medicine and Dentistry, practicing primary care internal medicine and teaching mindfulness-based programs to patients, medical students, and health professionals for more than 20 years. He was the project director of Mindful Communication: Bringing Intention, Attention and Reflection to Clinical Practice with results in the *Journal of the American Medical Association* in September 2009, leading to the establishment of the Mindful Practice programs at the university which he co-directs. He has offered programs to health professionals nationally and internationally over the past ten years, including multi-year teacher training programs for future facilitators. Engaged in a variety of research projects, his investigation includes the effects of mindfulness on the immune system in the elderly, on chronic psoriasis, and on caregivers of Alzheimer's patients.

Eric Leung, MSSc (Psy Couns), MSSc (Behavioral Health), is an Honorary Lecturer at the Department of Social Work and Social Administration at the University of Hong Kong. With the background of Christianity, he encountered mindfulness in 1999. Since then, Eric has explored the practice of mindfulness and the four immeasurables and has integrated these into his psychological counseling and life coaching career for more than a decade. He is now a certified teacher of the Mindful Self-Compassion program, and consultant and trainer of several social work organizations and NGO platforms in Hong Kong. In recent years, Eric has focused on integrating traditional Chinese regimen philosophy, mindfulness, and compassion into his teaching and training, especially applying these in parental stress reduction, parenting education, and children's life education.

Claudia Dias Martins, BA, is pursuing a Master of Arts in Counselling Psychology at McGill University, and she holds a Bilingual Specialized Honours Bachelor of Arts in Psychology from York University. She is passionate about various mindfulness research endeavors, including mindfulness and compassion-based interventions; and therapeutic presence for the promotion of safe therapeutic environments and effective therapeutic relationships. She has volunteered as a crisis text line responder with Kids Help Phone and continues to be actively engaged in youth mental health advocacy at the local and national levels with Jack.org. Claudia also works closely with the co-directors of the Centre for MindBody Health in Toronto, where she supports clinical operations, as well as research and training initiatives in the fields of dialectical behavior therapy (DBT), emotion-focused therapy (EFT), mindfulness, and self-compassion. She is passionate about advancing research in the areas of child development, mindfulness-based interventions, and therapeutic presence.

Marcela Matos, PhD, is a clinical psychologist and research faculty member at the Center for Research in Neuropsychology and Cognitive and Behavioral Intervention (CINEICC), University of Coimbra, Portugal. For 15 years, Dr. Matos' research and clinical interests have related to evolutionary clinical psychology, third-wave cognitive and behavioral therapies, and contemplative approaches. She has extensively researched shame experiences and memories, their traumatic qualities and centrality to personal identity, and their association with mental health difficulties. Her current research involves developing, implementing, and trialing compassion-focused interventions for promoting well-being, and investigating their impact on epigenetic mechanisms and biophysiological markers of prosociality and stress.

Dr. Matos has published over 60 international peer-reviewed articles and book chapters on the topics of compassion, shame, self-criticism, emotional regulation, psychopathology, and well-being, covering a diverse host of clinical and non-clinical populations. She has also authored over 150 scientific communications presented at international scientific conferences and is an affiliate member of the Compassionate Mind Foundation and of the Portuguese Association for Mindfulness.

Paul Victor Patinadan, PhD, CT, is an interdisciplinary academic and mixed-methods researcher working in the field of health research. He is an Association for Death Education and Counselling (ADEC) Certified Thanatologist. Paul specializes in psychosocial interventions and therapies, the implementation science of such interventions, and holistic education across stakeholders in care ecosystems. He has worked on several projects with a focus on clinical outcomes for various illness trajectories, community and critical health psychology, mental well-being, cyberpsychology, and evaluative research for health organizations. These include investigating health behaviors of the chronically ill, co-developing a serious game for diabetic management, addressing healthcare professionals' psychosocial issues, and evaluating the Singaporean National Advance Care Planning (ACP) Programme. To date, he has participated in multiple international and local conferences, and has been awarded a number of honors.

Alina Pavlova, MA (Sociology and Economics), is a PhD candidate in the Department of Psychological Medicine at the University of Auckland, studying the transactional nature of compassion in healthcare. By investigating the relationships between physician-, organizational-, and patient-related factors, Alina's biggest commitment is to designing multilevel interventions to enhance care at patient, physician, and organizational levels. Adjacent to her PhD on compassion, Alina is also involved in a suite of Cochrane reviews related to clinicians' and patients' experiences of services following an episode of self-harm, and she collaborates with suicide prevention experts and lived-experience researchers worldwide.

Before her PhD, Alina completed two master's degrees (in sociology and economics) from the Erasmus University Rotterdam, where she studied stigma in the context of mental health. Alina is a Yoga Alliance Certified yoga instructor and teaches yoga and mindfulness in the community.

Matthew Pugh, PhD, is a clinical psychologist, cognitive behavioral psychotherapist, advanced schema therapist, and voice dialogue facilitator. He works with the Vincent Square Eating Disorders Service (Central and North West London Mental Health Foundation Trust), is a Clinical Lecturer with University College London, and is the co-director of Chairwork.co.uk: A leading provider of training, supervision, consultation, and research related to chair work. He is the author of *Cognitive Behavioural Chairwork: Distinctive Features* and has published widely on the applications of chair work in psychotherapy, coaching, and single-session treatments. He is also the creator of dialogical psychotherapy and dialogical coaching, both of which center on chair work as an integrative therapeutic modality.

Jo Storozinksi, RN, BN, has over 26 years of experience as a community health nurse, 10 years of which she spent as a palliative care nurse. She currently practices in Winnipeg, MB, Canada. She has over 20 years' experience co-facilitating grief groups, supporting individuals and families as they journey through loss and bereavement. The focus of her work has been on spiritual and mental health and well-being, with an emphasis on grief, change, loss, and transitions. Additionally, as a spiritual health specialist, she works in a major tertiary care center where trauma, end-of-life transitions, grief, loss, and change occur within the lives of individuals and families primarily in the Emergency, Resuscitation, Medical, Pediatric, and Surgical ICU units. Supporting individuals and families experiencing pain and suffering, Jo is a trained teacher of mindful self-compassion for both adults and teens with the University of California San Diego School of Medicine.

Stan Steindl, PhD, is a clinical psychologist in private practice at Psychology Consultants Pty Ltd, and an Adjunct Associate Professor at the School of Psychology, University of Queensland, Brisbane, Australia. He is co-director of the UQ Compassionate Mind Research Group. He has over 20 years' experience as a therapist, supervisor, and trainer, and works with clients from a compassion-focused therapy perspective. His doctoral research examined combat-related posttraumatic stress disorder and comorbid alcohol dependency, and he continues to work in the areas of trauma and addiction, as well as having a general clinical practice. His research interests are in the areas of motivation, compassion, and compassion-based interventions, and especially the role of cultivating compassion and self-compassion in the context of trauma, shame, self-criticism, and clinical disorders, as well as promoting psychological well-being.

Geraldine Tan Ho, MSSc (Couns), CT, is Senior Counselor and Research Associate of Psychology and Nanyang Technological University Singapore. She also serves as co-chair of the Community Engagement and Communication Committee of the Singapore Hospice Council. A passionate advocate for quality of life and quality of death, Geraldine has rich experience in community action and social change. She is the co-founder of Mindful-Compassion Art-based Therapy, and she has also co-developed a number of novel and evidence-based interventions for supporting terminally ill patients and their family caregivers, young children with chronic life-threatening illnesses and their parent caregivers, as well as professional healthcare workers immersed in the field of palliative and bereavement care, with the ultimate goal to address the culture-specific psycho-socio-spiritual needs of Asian populations facing loss and mortality.

Neil Thompson, PhD, DLitt, is an independent writer, educator, and adviser based in Wales. Formerly a university professor, he now helps individuals and organizations to achieve optimal results through effective leadership and professional development. He has published extensively in relation to loss and grief, focusing in particular on the oft-neglected sociological aspects of the subject. He has been a speaker at conferences and seminars in the UK, Ireland, Italy, Spain, Norway, Greece, the Netherlands, the Czech Republic, Portugal, Turkey, India, Hong Kong, Canada, Australia, and the United States. He is a longstanding member of the International Work Group on Death, Dying, and Bereavement. His recent books include *Promoting Resilience: Responding to Adversity, Vulnerability* and *Loss and Death and Dying: Sociological Perspectives* (both with Gerry Cox). His website is at www.NeilThompson.info.

Mary L. S. Vachon, PhD, RN, is a nurse, registered psychotherapist, sociologist, author, and cancer survivor who has given over 1,600 lectures around the world on issues related to occupational stress, cancer, bereavement, survivorship, spirituality, and compassion. She has authored over 200 publications including the chapter on the emotional care of the dying person for the *Oxford Textbook of Palliative Medicine* (editions 1–4) and has written chapters on occupational stress in oncology, supportive, and palliative care specialists in several leading international textbooks for physicians, nurses, and other health professionals.

She is the recipient of many awards including the Dorothy Ley Award for Excellence in Palliative Care from the Ontario Palliative Care Association in 1997; the National Hospice and Palliative Care, Distinguished Researcher Award, 2001, for her continued contribution to the field of palliative care from the beginning of the specialty until the present time; the Lifetime Achievement Award of 2008 of the *International Journal of Palliative Nursing*; and the Herman Feifel Award for 2018 of the International Workgroup in Death, Dying, and Bereavement for outstanding contributions to the field of thanatology.

Adrian Wan, PhD, MSW, is a post-doctoral researcher, teaching staff, and a social work practitioner at the Centre on Behavioral Health, the University of Hong Kong. DrWan's major research area covers the applications of mindfulness-based and compassion-focused interventions, and he has published in areas including psycho-oncology, adjustment to stress, caregiver stress, chronic illness management, and culturally sensitive holistic healthcare. As a mental health practitioner, he works with people suffering from mood disorders, trauma, and those with stress-related adjustment issues. Dr. Wan has received training in mindful self-compassion (MSC), mindfulness-based stress reduction (MBSR), cognitive behavioral therapy (CBT), and dialectic behavioral therapy (DBT).

Venus Wong, PhD, is a senior lecturer and currently serves as the acting program director of the MSocSc (Behavioral Health) program at the University of Hong Kong. Her academic interests are in mindfulness-based interventions, contemplative practices, lifestyle medicine, holistic healthcare, spirituality, and well-being for healthcare professionals. She has been actively involved in well-being training for medical students, healthcare practitioners, and other human service professionals for the past decade. She is currently a voluntary member of the Plum Village Mindfulness Academy, supporting the professional program development under the Plum Village tradition and the teaching of Zen Master Thich Nhat Hanh.

SERIES FOREWORD

It could be said that grief is the quintessential human emotion, being deeply woven into our highly evolved neurocircuitry of bonding and attachment, poignantly expressed in a range of emotion and behavior, and intricately shaped by our social and cultural conventions. Thus, at levels ranging from the biological and psychological to the sociological and spiritual, the grief that arises in response to tangible and intangible losses of all kinds pervades every level of our personal and collective organization, as we seek to identify, voice, perform, regulate, and dignify our individual responses to the countless unwelcome changes that life transitions entail. Simply put, it is hard to imagine what humanity might look like were we stripped of our capacity to be pierced by a loss, to grieve, and in concert or conflict with others of our kind, adapt to a changed world in its aftermath.

But the premise of the editors of this book is that compassion is equally a *sine qua non* of our humanity, as reflected in the nearly universal capacity to be moved by the suffering of others, to feel the empathic resonance of their pain in our own hearts, minds, and bodies, and to give expression to this in acts of kindness, care, and simple presence. Like grief itself, a compassionate response to the hurt or misfortune of another—particularly in the context of bereavement—has increasingly clear evolutionary and neurological underpinnings, confers the ability to offer a sense of security and safeness to another in distress, and gives rise to expressions of compassion in intimate relationships, including our relations to ourselves. But it also informs, or can inform, the responses of human collectives, in psychotherapeutic, healthcare, organizational, urban, and even overarching political contexts. The symmetry between grief and compassion naturally invites a multidimensional consideration of the inter-braiding of the two, something that has been insufficiently developed beyond a few focal domains, such as end-of-life care.

Until now. In *Compassion-Based Approaches to Loss and Grief,* editors Darcy L. Harris and Andy H. Y. Ho have brought together a cadre of capable colleagues from a host of disciplines to offer a satisfying treatment of compassion as a framework and practice for addressing the profound existential aloneness that often characterizes grieving. Beginning with the seminal work of Paul Gilbert in Compassion-Focused Therapy (CFT), various authors ground their contributions in their own evolution as persons and professionals, in the burgeoning research base regarding the process and outcome of compassionate practices in spiritual, sociological, and clinical dimensions of such work, and its relevance for bringing dignity and humanity to bear on lives and deaths characterized by chronic sorrow, prolonged grief, and shame. In the pages of this volume readers will encounter models and methods for understanding and augmenting compassion as a sustainable resource that couples the capacity to feel for another with an ability to "show up" fully and vulnerably in the face of suffering, motivated by the intention to relieve it, particularly in cases where "problem solving" is insufficient or a "cure" is infeasible. As will be eloquently argued, self-compassion is a requisite for sustaining this stance, just as overarching social and cultural systems can build a frame for carrying it to a broader world.

In short, Harris and Ho have accomplished something remarkable: They have offered a synthesis and extension of previously balkanized programs and practices in a way that builds a stronger foundation for their deployment in the fields of bereavement support and grief therapy. I hope that every reader will be edified and inspired by the richness of the resources that their contributing authors bring to bear on this project and will find their own capacity to offer a centering and validating presence with those they serve to be burnished in the process.

Robert A. Neimeyer, PhD
Director, Portland Institute for Loss and Transition, and
Co-Editor, Routledge Series in Death, Dying, and Bereavement

INTRODUCTION

Darcy L. Harris and Andy H. Y. Ho

INTRODUCTION

After attending a ten-day intensive session for care providers that introduced compassion training as the primary focus, I (D.H.) became intrigued. Through various activities that included guided imagery and meditation, didactic teaching sessions, group engagement, and role playing of different clinical scenarios, I could readily see the potential for the integration of compassion into my work with grieving clients. I later attended a concurrent session at an international bereavement conference where the speaker presented research that demonstrated the value of compassion training in creating a sense of sustainability for clinicians as they journeyed alongside patients and family members at the end of life. After these two experiences, I searched for literature and training materials that would integrate compassion into clinical work with individuals facing loss and grief, and I was surprised to find the search coming up with scant results. Since my original foray into compassion training, I have immersed myself into the burgeoning body of literature on compassion from many different sources and approaches. I have also continued to attend workshops and trainings that explore ways to integrate the components of compassion into clinical settings. The applicability for my client work, teaching, and the foundational support for me, both personally and professionally, has been remarkable.

Working with terminally ill patients and their caregivers during the early days of my (A.H.) academic career was an utmost rewarding and inspiring experience, yet one that was emotionally draining and spiritually taxing. Seeing firsthand the many forms of suffering related to mortality, I was deeply motivated to help ease the pain that I observed. Yet, despite all the counseling skills that I possessed, I was at a loss as to what I could do to offer comfort when patients were actively dying or when families were sobbing beside the death beds of their loved ones. About a decade and a half ago, I had the opportunity to attend a weekend mindfulness retreat run by the Plum Village and taught by Zen Master Thich Nhat Hanh. Through the practices of mindful breathing, eating, and walking together, accompanied by profound philosophical discourses (dharma talks), I was able to experience for the first time a form of love and compassion directed to the self that allowed healing to take place. After learning from and experiencing the benefits of numerous workshops and trainings on mindfulness and compassion, I developed several psychotherapeutic interventions that support patients' dignity, caregivers' well-being, and clinicians' resilience though sustainable compassionate actions. Compassion, to say the least without sounding cliché, has indeed been life changing for me.

Compassion-based approaches have been widely supported through recent research in the field with diverse populations. These approaches are of specific interest in situations of loss, grief, and bereavement due to their capacity-building effect for clinicians and clients alike. Training in compassion has been demonstrated to enhance the ability to tolerate distress, maintain focus, and discern clinical interventions that are appropriate in a variety of contexts. Cultivating a compassionate stance provides clinicians with the opportunity to engage clients with their full attention and presence, allowing openness and receptivity for both the painful and the adaptive aspects of the client's process.

DOI: 10.4324/9781003204121-1

To date, there have been no publications that have integrated compassion-based approaches with current theory and practices in loss, grief, and bereavement. The exploration and clinical implications of compassion have been studied through several well-known centers of research, and the results from these studies have become widely published and drawn a great deal of interest. The literature and research in compassion have blossomed in the last 15 years, with much of the material that will be described in this book being recently published as well. Likewise, the literature in loss, grief, and bereavement has evolved in the same time frame in ways that have led to a greater understanding of the grieving process, with a variety of modalities to enhance clinical practice with grieving individuals.

As an introduction to this book, we will first begin with a basic understanding about what compassion encompasses. Compassion is frequently misunderstood as being synonymous with other prosocial behaviors, such as empathy or kindness. It is also often associated with formal religious beliefs and spiritual practices, where teachings of compassion may be emphasized. In addition, it is believed to be, at times, the cause of distress, as in the use of the term compassion fatigue (Figley, 1995). Jazaieri et al. (2013) state that compassion is

> a multidimensional process comprised of four key components: (1) an awareness of suffering (cognitive/empathic awareness), 2) sympathetic concern related to being emotionally moved by suffering (affective component), (3) a wish to see the relief of that suffering (intention), and (4) a responsiveness or readiness to help relieve that suffering (motivational).
>
> *(pp. 1117–1118)*

Halifax's (2013) description of compassion is very closely aligned with these as well, adding the dimension of insight and discernment to recognize situations where the relief of suffering may not be possible, but human presence and comfort may still provide a positive benefit. Paul Gilbert, the founder of Compassion-Focused Therapy (CFT), defines compassion as *a sensitivity to the suffering of self and others, with a commitment to try to alleviate or prevent it* (Gilbert, 2009).

According to Gilbert, there are two important aspects of compassion. The first involves the ability to notice, turn toward, and engage with suffering (as opposed to avoiding or dissociating from it). It is normal to wish to avoid situations that are distressing or painful; however, a compassionate stance opens the door for a choice (and the courage) to face suffering directly without pulling back. The ability to stay fully present requires practice that, when cultivated, enhances a sense of sustainable well-being, even in situations of significant distress and profound difficulty (Gilbert & Choden, 2013). The second aspect of compassion involves the motivation to relieve or prevent the cause of suffering. A motivation is different from a feeling, implying intentionality and focused behavioral components. Compassion is rooted in the evolution of basic social motivational systems (e.g., mutual care, cooperation, and affiliation) and different functional systems (e.g., responding to threats, seeking out resources, and experiencing states of safeness and soothing; Gilbert, 2014). Thus, compassion is viewed as an evolved motivational system that is acted upon with intentionality rather than merely an emotion that is felt.

Compassion is often seen as interchangeable with empathy, kindness, and sympathy. The main difference between compassion and these prosocial behaviors lies in the attentional and motivational components of compassion. Specifically, like empathy, compassion includes the ability to attune to and understand another's feeling state, but empathy does not necessarily involve a motivation or intention to relieve pain or distress.

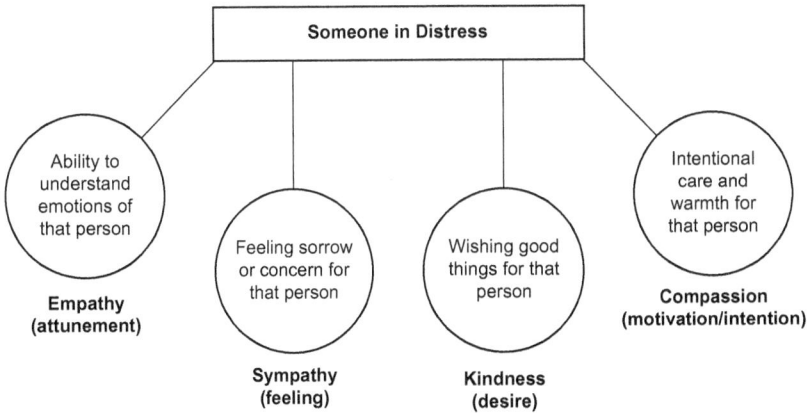

Figure 0.1 Differentiating Between Prosocial Behaviors and Compassion

Gilbert (2009) makes this point, stating that "the non-empathetic torturer puts a gun to your head, whereas the empathetic one puts a gun to your child's" (p. 203). Thus, empathy doesn't necessarily equate with a prosocial motivation. Likewise, kindness and sympathy are also viewed as similar predispositions, but there is no expectation that being kind or sympathetic includes the intention of directly addressing the source of the suffering in order to alleviate the accompanying distress (Figure 0.1).

The intention to relieve suffering is one of the main features that distinguishes compassion from other prosocial inclinations (Halifax, 2013). The term *compassion fatigue* is viewed as a misnomer, with the implied meaning of this phenomenon more closely resembling empathic overload or empathic distress fatigue. Most typically, this type of distress occurs in clinicians who are highly empathetic but who have not learned how to balance their experiences with insight, wisdom, and grounding, which are key components of compassion training. Throughout this book, the following understandings about compassion will provide a sense of continuity for the various topics that are covered:

1. Compassion is a motivation and intention to prevent and/or relieve suffering.
2. Compassion can be applied to individual, community, and global contexts.
3. The components of compassion can be trained to enhance the ability to respond in accordance with one's compassionate intention.
4. Compassion can serve as both a foundational component of helping professions as well as a guide for therapeutic interactions and interventions.

Since this book will integrate compassion with the experience of grief, we will also briefly discuss the foundational aspects of grief and bereavement that will make up the other core component of this book. Like the construct of compassion, grief has long been misunderstood despite its universality. We will draw upon the vast body of research that has been conducted to better understand the cause, nature, and impact of loss and grief. Perhaps one of the most common misconceptions of grief is that it is limited to a set of emotional responses (e.g., sadness, yearning, anxiety) experienced by individuals after the death of their loved ones. However, the early works of Lindemann (1944), who studied grief responses of 101 bereaved survivors of the Boston Coconut Grove Nightclub fire tragedy, which killed nearly 500 people, described complex and acute grief symptomatology such as somatic distress, preoccupation with the image of the deceased, guilt, hostile reactions, and the inability to function. Decades of research since that time have provided robust evidence that grief comprises multiple manifestations that go beyond emotions (Worden, 2018) to include physical sensations (e.g., breathlessness, weakness, depersonalization), cognitive symptoms (e.g., disbelief, preoccupation, confusion), and exhibited behaviors (e.g., sleep and eating disturbances, restlessness, social withdrawal).

While grief can potentially affect every aspect of our lives, its source is not limited to death-related losses, which is another common misconception. The seminal research by Bowlby (1969, 1973) on attachment theory provides a framework to better understand our responses to relational separation, which has been applied to comprehend how individuals cope with bereavement. Harris (2011, 2020) explored expanding the grief response to include non-death losses, such as the loss of trusted relationships, functional capacity, and cognitive acuity, which can potentially shatter one's views and challenge core aspects of the assumptive world.

With our relational attachments and assumptive world forming the core of our belief systems, how we come to terms with the significant losses in our lives is clearly unique and idiosyncratic. This conceptualization sheds light on two other common misconceptions of grief. The first concerns the view that we all go through grief in similar stages, made popular through the well-known but widely misunderstood Kübler-Ross' stages of dying (Kübler-Ross, 1970). The second relates to the view that we all need to process and share our grief with others in order to overcome it, a generally held misassumption based on Freud's grief work hypothesis, which postulates that successful adjustment to loss is derived from a total detachment from the deceased (Freud, 1917/1957). The reality is that grief is a subjectively appraised experience, and how well individuals adapt to their loss is influenced by a multitude of factors including, but not limited to the type of loss, the social context of the loss, and the worldview of the individual experiencing the loss, as well as how the individual makes sense of the loss. According to constructivist psychology, meaning making denotes the innate need of human beings to construct life narratives that are coherent with their everyday experiences and existing assumptive worlds. When individuals' existing assumptive worlds are crushed by a significant loss, they must undergo the process of recreating their meaning structures and cognitive schemas. This is done through narrating stories that situate the loss in their own life narratives, with the goal of restoring their identity and purpose for living via a renewed and coherent sense of self (Neimeyer et al., 2001).

Supporting dying patients and bereaved individuals through their end of life and grief journeys requires not only compassion, but also a clear grasp of the foundational knowledge of grief. The following understandings of grief will provide continuity for the various topics that are covered throughout this book:

1. Grief is not just an emotion, but also encompasses physical, cognitive, somatic, and behavioral responses.
2. Grief is applicable to all types of loss experiences, death and non-death related.
3. Grief is a subjectively appraised experience.
4. Grief is an adaptive response that fosters the process of meaning making after a significant loss experience.

CONTENTS OF THE BOOK

In this book, we have combined known clinicians and researchers from the field of various compassion-based models with clinicians and researchers from the field of grief and bereavement. The range of contributors' professional and academic backgrounds provides the book with a broad approach to practice in many different types of care settings. The book is also an international project, with contributors from many different places around the world. Thus, not only are we are bridging compassion-based approaches with grief/bereavement; we are also bridging many international perspectives and research in these areas as well. Each of the contributors to this volume has cultivated their work and practice in compassion as well as their clinical skills with those who have experienced significant losses. We feel greatly honored for their willingness to bring their expertise and thoughtful explorations to be included in this volume.

We start with the foundational section of the book, which includes basic understandings and the background for many of the concepts that will be presented. This section will include definitions of terms and an exploration of the intersection of compassion and grief through a merging of literature and common clinical approaches, starting with a personal reflection by Mary L. S. Vachon, a clinician who has trained in compassion. We then include a chapter that explores the concept of grief as yearning and how this yearning is also amenable to the lens of exploration through the theories and components of compassion. This section then explores current understandings about grief and bereavement, providing a review of research that unites the application of compassion in contexts of loss and grief, a review of sociological principles that underscore compassion and grief, and an exploration of compassion and grief at various levels (spheres) of social engagement.

The second section of the book will provide an overview of the various components of compassion, and how training in these components can support clinical skills in working with those who are grieving in various ways. Chapters in this section will describe the basic tenets of compassion training, including mindful awareness, the cultivation of therapeutic presence, enhanced awareness of the role of common humanity and interconnectedness related to compassion, as well as the practice of self-compassion for clinicians.

The third section of the book provides a plethora of practical applications of compassion for various grief-related scenarios, with the emphasis on clinical skill building and support for both clients and clinicians. Topics include models of clinical response that are based upon the principles of compassion, compassionate approaches to presenting issues that are related to loss and grief, and specific compassion-based techniques that have been adapted for use with grieving individuals.

The fourth section will examine macro-level issues that have an impact upon clinical practice, and how these issues may be approached with the principles of compassion. The chapters in this section will address organizational, systemic, and community-oriented structures and the way they influence attitudes, policies, and social messages that have a profound effect upon service providers and those who seek their support and care.

It is our deepest wish that this book will foster an important dialogue between those who have brought forward the important work of compassion training and research with those who have done the same in the field of grief/bereavement. Most importantly, we hope that this book will provide a new way of approaching deeply painful situations of loss and grief, while suggesting a path of sustainability to support those who provide care during a tremendously difficult time.

REFERENCES

Bowlby, J. (1969). *Attachment and loss: Attachment* (Vol. 1). London: Hogarth.

Bowlby, J. (1973). *Attachment and loss, vol. 2: Separation.* New York: Basic Books.

Figley, C. R. (1995). Compassion fatigue: Toward a new understanding of the costs of caring. In B. H. Stamm (Ed.), *Secondary traumatic stress: Self care issues for clinicians, researchers, and educators* (pp. 3–28). Sidran Press.

Freud, S. (1957). Mourning and melancholia. In J. Strachey (Ed.), *Standard edition of the complete psychological works of Sigmund Freud* (Vol. 14, pp. 237–258). Hogarth. (Original work published 1917)

Gilbert, P. (2009). *The compassionate mind: A new approach to the challenges of life.* Constable & Robinson.

Gilbert, P. (2014). The origins and nature of compassion focused therapy. *British Journal of Clinical Psychology, 53*(1), 6–41.

Gilbert, P., & Choden (2013). *Mindful compassion.* Constable-Robinson.

Halifax, J. (2013). Understanding and cultivating compassion in clinical settings: The A.B.I.D.E. compassion model. In T. Singer & M. Bolz (Eds.), *Compassion: Bridging practice and science* (pp. 208–226). Max Planck Institute for Human Cognitive and Brain Sciences.

Harris, D. L. (2011). *Counting our losses: Reflecting on change, loss, and transition in everyday life.* Routledge.

Harris, D. L. (2020). Non-death loss and grief: Laying the foundation. In D. L. Harris (Ed.), *Non-death loss and grief: Context and clinical implications* (pp. 7–160). Routledge.

Jazaieri, H., Jinpa, G. T., McGonigal, K., Rosenberg, E. L., Finkelstein, J., Simon-Thomas, E., Cullen, M., Doty, J. R., Gross, J. J., & Goldin, P. R. (2013). Enhancing compassion: A randomized controlled trial of a compassion cultivation training program. *Journal of Happiness Studies, 14*(4), 1113–1126.

Kübler-Ross, E. (1970). *On death and dying.* Collier Books/Macmillan Publishing Co.

Lindmann, E. (1944). Symptomatology and management of acute grief. *American Journal of Psychiatry, 101*(2), 141–148.

Neimeyer, R. A. (2001). The language of loss: Grief therapy as a process of meaning reconstruction. In R. A. Neimeyer (Ed.), *Meaning reconstruction and the experience of loss* (pp. 261–292). APA.

Worden, J. W. (2018). *Grief counseling and grief therapy* (5th ed.). Springer.

PART ONE
Foundations

CHAPTER 1

COMING TO COMPASSION

Mary L. S. Vachon

REFLECTIONS AND RETROSPECTIVE INTEGRATION FROM CHILDHOOD

My parents had multiple childhood deaths, which influenced them, my childhood, and life. My mother's father died when she was 12 and he was 45. Her 3 uncles also died at 45, leaving young children. Shortly before he died, my maternal grandfather told my mother, "and we never, ever, ever, that is hardly ever, ever cry."

My father's first brother, Richard Joseph, died before my father was born. He never discussed his father's death when he was 12. At 17 my father witnessed his mother dying in childbirth, giving birth to his stepsister, Mary Josephine. Mary and his sister Helen were put into an orphanage. At 17 my father was responsible for himself and his brother Ben, age 15.

My first memory is the day after my brother Richard Joseph's death when I was 3 1/2. On New Year's Eve Day, the family car was hit by a streetcar as we drove home from returning Mary to the orphanage after a Christmas visit prior to our adopting her.

I had two images of the next day, one of myself, my brother Walter, age two, and my sister Linda, age one, standing on the dining room table, waiting for the family doctor to examine us. My other memory was of my mother sitting in a rocking chair in front of the fireplace, wrapped in bandages.

While I knew I had done my work because of Richard's untimely death, in a meditation with Dr. Frank Anderson at an Internal Family Systems (IFS) course in 2020, I saw more clearly what happened that day. As I stood in front of my mother as a 3 1/2-year-old, I realized that her normally expressive face was flat. She was not crying. She was beyond tears. At a visceral level she had absorbed her father's admonition about hardly ever crying.

In the meditation, I realized in that moment I recognized my loving mother was not available to care for us. Someone needed to care for us. I became a compassionate caregiver that day. "Facing and accepting what is painful and difficult rather than turning from it" (Gilbert & Chodon, 2013, p. 104).

Reflecting on the working title for this chapter, I recognized that I came to compassion long before I knew the word. My meditation teacher Maria Gonzalez defines compassion as "recognizing the other person is suffering, wanting to alleviate that suffering, recognizing that I too am suffering, and wanting to alleviate my own suffering. We are all connected." Viscerally, and with my right brain, I saw my mother's suffering, recognized that I and my siblings were also suffering, and I wanted to alleviate that suffering. We were all connected. My first experience with compassion came from my first experience of grief at age 3 1/2.

Later meditating with Dr. Anderson about my role as a professional caregiver, I became aware of a tightening and discomfort in my stomach where I recently had emergency surgery. Interoceptively, I got the insight that in caring for others I needed to do some serious self-care. Using IFS, it was clear that my 3 1/2-year-old part was demanding that my then 74-year-old self (curious, compassionate, calm, clear, creative, courageous, confident, committed; Schwartz, 1995, in Fisher, 2008) pay attention. From the perspectives of

DOI: 10.4324/9781003204121-3

Siegel (2017) and Halifax (2012), this could be described as "visceral attunement," "known as interoceptivity, (which) activates the same brain circuits (e.g. within the insula cortex) as those of empathy" (Halifax, 2012, p. 230).

I remember Mary coming to live with us the next spring, standing quietly with her as she looked out the window onto the pond across the street in the new room that had been prepared for her. I was being a compassionate witness. By then I was a mature four years old. She was 14. Roshi Joan Halifax might call this attending (Halifax, 2018).

Another vivid memory is of walking several blocks to grade 1 at age 5 1/2 thinking, "this is great, for 5 hours a day all I need to do is to learn to read, write, spell, and do math. I do not need to take care of any kids, such freedom." By then Christine was born and mother was pregnant with Bob. The family grew to 13 children (12 of us grew up). I was conscious of self-compassion at age 5 1/2.

The second week of public school we were learning to spell. We had to think of a word and have the other kids guess the word by guessing the letters. No one guessed my word, God. I had just been to Sunday School. Obviously, a spiritual connection was present at an early age.

My siblings, Bob, Pat, and John, were born. I remember Uncle Leo visiting us. He was very handsome in his Massachusetts Maritime Academy uniform. He was with mother when she was in labor with Michael. He said, "I will never be with you when you are in labor again." He said to my father, "You helped me to go to college. I want to be able to help you put your kids through school. Just in case I am not alive to do so I have taken out a life insurance policy to help you."

At 22, Uncle Leo was killed in a car accident. I was ten. I remember going with Mary the next day to the back door of the convent as she told the nuns about Leo's death. Again, as a ten-year-old, being a compassionate witness and attending.

My next brother to be born after Michael was Leo Christopher. Tom and George came along after Leo. When George had a seizure one night and the ambulance was on the way, Mother woke me to be with her as she handled the seizure. My father was on the night shift as a policeman. Later she said, "I knew it was strange for me to wake a ten-year-old, but I knew I would feel better if you were with me." I was being acknowledged for providing compassionate witnessing and attending.

When my mother told me that she was expecting Beth, I was in high school. I thought, "I don't have time to raise another child. I have to get good marks." In retrospect, maybe this was self-compassion, as opposed to "being selfish." When mother was pregnant with Beth, her mother, my dearly loved grandmother, died suddenly the day after visiting each of her children and grandchildren.

At 17, I was accepted at a combined program between Massachusetts General Hospital (MGH) School of Nursing and Northeastern University. In an interview with the *Lynn Item*, announcing my scholarship and getting publicity for the innovative program, I was asked why I wanted to be a nurse and replied that I felt it was a Catholic woman's duty to serve mankind. The 17-year-old had the wisdom to understand my calling. Reflecting on this time, I am reminded that Roshi Joan Halifax associates wisdom with compassion (Halifax, 2013, 2018).

My professional life has been one of service. I have spoken around the world, done research, and received awards. However, many years ago, I realized that doing clinical work was what fed my soul. To be happy at work, I had to feed my soul. That insight came when I was 50. I went around announcing that I had found wisdom. At 51, I found stage 4 cancer and became even wiser.

REFLECTIONS AND RETROSPECTIVE INTEGRATION FROM MY PROFESSIONAL LIFE

My most important experience as a student at MGH involved working with "Mrs. Jones" on White 7. I cared for her prior to her endarterectomy and followed her after surgery. One day, I was learning to be a team leader. The first-year student caring for her came to tell me that Mrs. Jones had become upset when she got feces on her hands while using the bedpan and was crying. I told the student that unfortunately I had no time to speak with Mrs. Jones because I had to go to hear a lecture on grief by Dr. Tom Hackett.

I went to the lecture and heard how grief was "rediscovered" after Freud's *Mourning and Melancholia* (1917) by Dr. Erich Lindemann (1944) at MGH after the Coconut Grove Fire. I learned about various forms of grief. The next day I returned to the ward. Mrs. Jones was on cardiac precautions. I asked her what happened. She said "they think I had a heart attack. I don't think I had a heart attack. I don't know what is happening." I told her about the grief lecture and suggested that maybe she was experiencing delayed grief. She had stoically faced her surgery and recovery. Maybe now, in recovery, she was experiencing some of the grief that she might have faced if she had acknowledged the possibility of her death with the risky surgery. The flood gates opened. She sobbed as she recounted that 16 years ago on that day her husband had been returning from the War. While he was away, she realized that she no longer loved him and planned to ask for a divorce. The boat docked in Boston Harbor. He had a heart attack and died. She never grieved him. On the anniversary of his death, she appeared to have a heart attack.

I met with my instructor, Miss De Souza, to tell her I had finally decided the nursing specialty I would pursue. I was going into psychiatric nursing because I wanted to learn how to talk with and listen to people. If you really talk with and listen to them, you find many unexpected insights. I now understand that a part of me recognized then what I later learned to be Siegel's integration of awareness, bilateral, vertical, memory, narrative, state, interpersonal, and temporal integration (Siegel, 2017).

While at MGH I also learned about Weisman and Hackett's work (1961) on predilection to death. I came to understand Uncle Leo's comments about not being present when my mother was in labor in the future and his taking out the life insurance policy for our education, and perhaps my grandmother visiting all her kids and grandkids the day before her death. Dr. Hackett gave me my first lesson on grief and Dr. Weisman wrote the preface to my book (Vachon, 1987). Through them and their work, I had an initial introduction to how to listen, to integrate, and to be compassionate.

THE MOVE TO TORONTO

In 1969 we moved to Toronto as draft dodgers and for my husband Bruce to attend graduate school. Our son, Wolfgang Adeodatus, was born. I had a variety of positions before becoming a research scientist in a community-based program where we did both clinical and research work on prevention in psychiatry.

At the Newman Centre, the church we attended at the University of Toronto, we met a young couple, the Sidles, with 4 kids aged 4 to 12. Laurie, the mother, was diagnosed with metastatic melanoma at age 37. I told Bruce, "We should get close to these people. I think they are going to need help." I asked my boss, Dr. Stan Freeman, "What can I do to help these people? She is young, dying, and will be leaving four young kids and a husband."

He said, "I don't know, but if you are interested in these issues maybe you should go over to Princess Margaret Hospital. The nurses are looking for someone to work with them about their feelings about dying patients." That act of compassion led to my career, doing research and clinical care in the areas of cancer, bereavement, and occupational stress.

In 1992 I went to work at Sunnybrook Hospital and what is now the Odette Cancer Center, where I worked in psychiatry, oncology, and palliative care, and continued my research and clinical work.

AN OPENING TO A NEW AWARENESS

The opening to a new awareness began at the Terminal Care meeting in Montreal in 1996. As I walked the corridors of the meeting, I began to "get messages" that my life was going to be changing. I needed to go back to church on Sunday mornings instead of writing articles. I needed new topics for my research and lectures. I needed to do yoga and meditation at Wellspring, a community-based support program, of which I am a co-founder and where I am a clinical consultant.

At the same time, I began to get minor, but constant abdominal pain, 1–2/10. I returned to Toronto, told people I had an incredible spiritual experience, consulted my doctor when the pain continued, and had an abdominal ultrasound which showed six enlarged abdominal lymph nodes. I asked the radiologist if he thought that meant I had lymphoma. He said yes, either lymphoma or metastatic something else. We discussed who I should see as an oncologist. I went to Dr. Berenstein's office and said, "You don't know me, but I see a lot of your patients and they seem to like you. It looks like I have lymphoma. Will you be my oncologist? By the way, I am heading to Hong Kong and Shanghai with my husband, son, and daughter, Alexa Amadeus, to lecture in a few weeks and would like to be able to do that."

On a Monday, I was to have a bone marrow aspiration but had trouble breathing over the weekend so suggested they give me chemo after the aspiration, instead of waiting until Wednesday, as planned. On Thursday I headed with my family to lecture in Shanghai and Hong Kong. Because of my rapidly escalating symptoms, I assumed I would be dying soon. I was lecturing with my son for some of the lectures. If these were to be my last lectures, what could be better than to "pass on the torch" of my speaking?

In Shanghai, we attended the annual day of healing at the Buddhist Temple Garden. We were shown a statue and asked what we saw. I saw a beautiful woman. Bruce said she was smiling. We were told, "This is Quan Yin, the goddess of compassion. If you see that she is smiling, you will be granted whatever you wish for." Maybe Quan Yin is partly responsible for my cure and my coming to compassion.

When we went to Hong Kong, I had the first of several "manifesting" experiences. My supply of Neupogen, a drug I was on to keep my white blood cells up, had frozen. I explained my dilemma to the person at the display advertising Neupogen. The drug was not yet in Hong Kong but by the next day I had my supply. This began my experience of manifesting. Money, awards, and trips all began to appear. It seemed like the biblical "ask and you shall receive."

About the same time, I became aware that I was being walked through my experience with people, from the "other side." My "angels" went around my head and down to my shoulders. I did not say much about "my angels." This all sounded more than weird to me, even though I was experiencing it.

One Sunday the priest at church, Father Tom Rosica, spoke of his understanding of the Communion of Saints as being the scene in *Les Misérables* when Jean Valjean is dying.

He sees all the important people in his life who have predeceased him. I suddenly realized that not only were my deceased family and friends part of "my angels," so too were all the people I had worked with over the many years of my clinical practice, those who had died and those whose bereaved relatives I had seen.

I felt "spiritually transformed." I sought mentoring from Drs. John Rossiter-Thornton and Yvonne Kason. Dr. Kason (2000) speaks of spiritually transformative experiences (STEs) as being punctuations on life's spiritual journey that challenge "a person's entire world view and as a result, their ideas, values, priorities, and beliefs change. They think, feel, and see the world differently … perception of reality and their whole personality has been transformed and propelled in a far more spiritual direction" (Kason, 2000).

I wrote about being "spiritually transformed" (Vachon, 2001a, 2001b) and began to integrate spirituality into my clinical practice. This integration allowed me and my clients to develop insights, to make changes, to heal, and come to an acceptance of illness and death unlike anything I have seen before (Vachon, 2001b).

With Dr. Rossiter-Thornton I began to do A Self-Directed Inner Seeking Therapy (ASIST) meditation and the Prayer Wheel (Rossiter-Thornton, 1999). In my first ASIST meditation I found myself reciting familiar words but did not recognize the source. Dr. Rossiter-Thornton told me it was the Prayer of St. Francis. Since then, I have begun my day with that prayer plus a few others. In the meditation in which I asked how come I was having so many challenges in my work situation and what I needed to do to heal and move on with my life, I was taken from my personal paradise in Hawaii, Makena Beach in Maui, to the top of a waterfall in Kauai, Hawaii, and jumped into a glassy blue stream. The color of the stream was the background color of a picture of sunflowers I often looked at in the cancer clinic. As I was in the stream, whisps of gold began to come. I got the message that these whisps of gold would eventually become the beautiful image of sunflowers. I was told that I was having the problems at work because I "needed to." Later, I realized these were early messages that I was meant to move on.

COMING TO COMPASSION

Prior to a lecture I was giving on compassion fatigue in 2002, I received an email from a stranger, saying that, from what he understood, true compassion did not fatigue. I began to consciously ponder compassion. Previously, I wrote about and integrated the concept of the wounded healer into my practice. Henri Nouwen quotes from the Talmud, which asks the question how one might know the Messiah.

> He is sitting among the poor covered with wounds. The others unbind all their wounds at the same time and then bind them up again. But he unbinds one at a time and binds it up again, saying to himself, "Perhaps I shall be needed; if so, I must always be ready so as not to delay for a moment."
>
> *(Nouwen, 1972, p. 82, in Vachon, 2001a, p. 659)*

We learn from the Talmud the importance of self-compassion in the practice of compassion.

Kearney writes of the wounded healer as coming from Chiron, a centaur from Greek mythology. When he was wounded, the master of the healing arts could not heal himself. The concept of wounded healers evolved into universal shamanic stories of tribal priests, whose ability to heal others was directly linked to their having traveled into the depths of their own wounded selves (Kearney, 1996 in Vachon, 2001a). "The physician or nurse's own bleeding can become the source of their compassion, the healer's art. From the physician or nurse's own suffering can come the wine of fervent zeal and the oil of compassion" (Sulmasy, 1997, p. 48 in Vachon, 2001a, p. 659).

In 2000, when it became clear that I was going to live after my cancer treatment, I decided that I was going to have foot surgery so I could wear sandals. As I waited for surgery, I used the Mystic's Prayer Dr. Kason taught me, "Please heal in me what needs to be healed. Please teach me what I need to learn. I put my life in Your hands, Thy will be done" (source unknown). I awakened in recovery in the middle of that prayer. I meant to put up my feet and think about spirituality. I put up my feet; the message came to leave my job.

I left my job at the end of 2000 to focus my attention on my private practice, where I could integrate the concepts that seemed relevant and significant. Beginning my full-time private practice, I decorated my office around a print of the sunflowers. I commissioned a painting of my personal paradise and helpers from my ASIST meditation. Indeed, wonderful things have happened in that office.

FROM SPIRITUAL TRANSFORMATION TO COMPASSION

Gradually the shift began from a new-found spirituality to an increasing awareness of compassion. In 2000, one of the chaplains lent me Mathew Fox's book *Sins of the Spirit: Blessings of the Flesh* (Fox, 2000). I read about the image of the Man in Sapphire Blue by St. Hildegard of Bingen. Fox wrote of this man as being the image of compassion, a Christ-like figure with hands out-stretched. St. Hildegard was a mystic of the 11th century. Her theology was about veriditas, the green healing power of God in humans and nature, the greening power of nature as a metaphor for physical and spiritual health (Healthy Hildegard, 2020). Fox said that blue was the color of compassion, and compassion was taking the energy of the heart chakra, which is green, and putting it into the hands (Fox, 2000).

I had to have that image. I found Fox's book, *Illuminations of Hildegard of Bingen*, which had the Man in Sapphire Blue on the cover (Fox, 1985). In 2010, when I traveled to Germany to lecture, I 'hung out' with Hildegard. In the church of St. Hildegard, a mosaic of the Man in Sapphire Blue is the altar piece. The image is described as her depiction of the Trinity. The waves of energy around the man are described as the Holy Spirit, "who is always making waves." I bought the image of the Man in Sapphire Blue, which now faces me as I interview clients. It is beside a picture of St. Frances. The Prayer of St. Francis is on a radiator behind me, beneath a large silk screen of Quan Yin holding a sunflower and a bird. My office is filled with mementos from clients. I often say, "What I learned from that person I give to you. What I learn from you I give to someone else. I am but an instrument."

In my 60s, I did a walking meditation in which I was to identify one of my characteristics that gave me challenges and give it an amusing name. I called my anger "Willful Wally," since it came from my father. As I interviewed this aspect of myself, I came to recognize that my father's anger was a manifestation of all his unresolved grief. Another part of my "calling" was to help other families not live with unresolved grief.

THOSE FROM WHOM I HAVE LEARNED

In the early 2000s, Mary Pocock suggested that I get to know the work of Roshi Joan Halifax. I took my first course with Roshi Joan in 2005, shortly before Mary died. Since then, I have heard Roshi Joan lecture, taken courses with her, read her writing, invited her to do an article in which she first published her new insights on enactive compassion (Halifax, 2012), and synthesized her work into my writings (Vachon & Harris, 2016).

I began to study meditation in 2006 and, since 2010, have studied with Maria Gonzalez. Since I consciously started integrating compassion into my practice, I use Maria's simple definition. Maria reminds me that for true compassion, there must be action, not just feeling, and not acting. She says as well that there is no true compassion without self-compassion.

Our intention to help another in the way that we perceive we can help may not be realized. Maria says, "True compassion is deep caring without attachment" (Gonzalez, 2012, p, 164). Non-attachment is not detachment, which involves an arm's length relationship that does not touch you. Rather it is caring deeply but not being attached to the outcome (Gonzalez, 2012). Roshi Joan agrees on the need for "no attachment to outcome" (Halifax, 2012, p. 232) and refers to this as a 'therapeutic humility' (Halifax, 2012). She says compassion should be the basis of medical care, and kindness and equanimity are essential qualities in those who care for the dying (Halifax, 2013).

I began to attend meetings on spirituality. In 2008 I attended a meeting sponsored by Harvard on Spirituality and Healing in Medicine: The Resiliency Factor. I went to a session with Margaret (Peg) Bain. During a Tonglen Meditation, I imagined sending compassion energy to a client I saw before leaving. She was dying and was having trouble believing that there was anything beyond our present life. As I sent compassionate energy to her, it seemed that she was farther away than from Boston to Toronto. As my energy reached her, she began to send energy back to me. I saw incredibly beautiful colors. I thought, "I think she has gone to the other side and is sending me energy from where she is now." When I returned home, I learned that she had died the day before. Over time, the experiences of transforming spiritually and coming into an awareness of compassion began to coalesce, without my being particularly aware of it.

In 2013, Bruce gave me an article from *Science* describing the work of Dr. Tania Singer on kindness (Kupferschmidt, 2013). She had recently published an e-book with her colleagues incorporating the work on compassion with the world's experts (Singer & Bolz, 2013), including Roshi Joan and Dr. Paul Gilbert.

In 2013, I attended a Harvard meeting on attachment and listened to a couple of lectures by Dr. Dan Siegel. I became interested in his work on neurobiology, mental illness, chaos and rigidity, and mental health being about integration. He says, "*integration* made visible is kindness and compassion" (Siegel, 2015, 2017, p. 330).

In 2014, I attended a course with Dr. Paul Gilbert and began to integrate his concepts of compassion and Compassion-Focused Therapy (Gilbert & Chodon, 2013) into my work and writing (Vachon & Harris, 2016). Compassion involves more than just the alleviation of suffering. It also involves prevention of suffering and the desire for the *well-being* of others. "Alleviation and prevention are about creating the conditions for clear insight and change and that often means facing and accepting what is painful and difficult rather than turning from it" (Gilbert & Chodon, 2013, p. 104).

SUMMARY

This chapter describes how six decades of service to those with life-threatening illness and bereavement, and work in the field of occupational stress, evolved from a childhood involving significant grief. As a 17-year-old I said that a Catholic woman's duty was to serve mankind. In my 20s we befriended a young couple where the wife was dying, and my career path began. As a 50- year-old I went around announcing that I had found wisdom. As a 51-year-old, I found stage 4 Non-Hodgkin's lymphoma and became wiser and went through a spiritual transformation that led to an awakening into compassion. I began to integrate the concept of the wounded healer (Vachon, 2001a) into my writings.

At 55, a meditation led me to leave my job to better integrate spirituality and compassion into my practice. In my 60s a meditation on my anger led to a new awareness of how my father's anger reflected his long-standing unresolved grief. At 74, in a meditation I learned that my coming to compassion started with my brother Richard's death when I was 3 1/2, that self-compassion was essential, and that my coming to compassion is ever evolving.

REFERENCES

Fisher, J. (2008). *Psychoeducational flip chart.* https://janinafisher.com/flip-chart.html
Fox, M. (1985). *Illuminations of Hildegard of Bingen.* Bear & Co.
Fox, M. (2000). *Sins of the spirit, blessings of the flesh: Transforming evil in soul and society.* Harmony.
Freud, S. (1917). *Mourning and melancholia. The standard edition of the complete psychological works of Sigmund Freud, volume XIV (1914–1916): On the history of the psycho-analytic movement, Papers on metapsychology and other works* (pp. 237–258). Hogarth Press.
Gilbert, P., & Choden. (2013). *Mindful compassion.* Constable Robinson.
Gonzalez, M. (2012). *Mindful leadership: The 9 ways to self-awareness, transforming yourself and inspiring others.* Jossey-Bass.
Halifax, J. (2012). A heuristic model of enactive compassion. *Current Opinion in Supportive and Palliative Care, 6*(2), 228–235.
Halifax, J. (2013). Understanding and cultivating compassion in clinical settings: The A.B.I.D.E. Compassion model. In T. Singer & M. Bolz (Eds.), *Compassion: Bridging practice and science* (eBook). (pp. 209–228). Max Planck Society.
Halifax, J. (2018). *Standing at the edge: Finding freedom where fear and courage meet.* Flatiron Books.
Healthy Hildegard. (2020). *What is Hildegard's viriditas?* Retrieved May 15, 2021 https://www.healthyhildegard.com/hildegards-viriditas/.
Kason, Y. (2000). *Farther shores.* HarperCollins.
Kearney, M. (1996). *Mortally wounded.* Scribner.
Kupferschmidt, K. (2013). Concentrating on kindness. *Science, 341*(6152), 1336–1339.
Lindemann, E. (1944). Symptomatology and management of acute grief. *American Journal of Psychiatry, 101*(2), 141–148.
Nouwen, H. (1972). *The wounded healer.* Doubleday.
Rossiter Thornton, J. (1999). *The prayer wheel.* Rossiter Thornton Associates.
Schwartz, R. C. (1995). *Internal family systems.* Guilford.
Siegel, D. J. (2015). *The developing mind.* The Guilford Press.
Siegel, D. J. (2017). *Mind: A journey to the heart of being human.* WW Norton & Co.
Singer, T., & Bolz, M. (Eds.). *Compassion: Bridging practice and science.* eBook. Max Planck Society.
Sulmasy, D. P. (1997). *The Healer's calling.* Paulist Press.
Vachon, M. L. S. (1987). *Occupational stress in the care of the critically ill, dying and bereaved.* Hemisphere Publishing.
Vachon, M. L. S. (2001a). The nurse's role: The world of palliative care nursing. In B. R. Ferrell & N. Coyle (Eds.), *Textbook of palliative nursing* (pp. 647–662). Oxford University Press.

Vachon, M. L. S. (2001b, May). When the shrink gets cancer and gets spiritually transformed. *Hot Spot*, *3*(2), 2.

Vachon, M. L. S., & Harris, D. (2016). The liberating capacity of compassion. In D. Harris & T. Bordere (Eds.), *Handbook of social justice in loss and grief* (pp. 265–281). Routledge.

Weisman, A. D., & Hackett, T. (1961). Predilection to death: Death and dying as a psychiatric problem. *Psychosomatic Medicine*, *23*, 232–256.

CHAPTER 2

AN EVOLUTIONARY AND COMPASSION-BASED APPROACH TO YEARNING AND GRIEF

Paul Gilbert

INTRODUCTION

Grief is generally studied as a multifaceted response to death-loss, but there are many types of loss and grief (Harris, 2011, 2020). There is clear evidence that grief is an evolved reaction to losses, that animals show (at least) the behavioral signs of grief, and different grief processes can be understood with an evolutionary analysis (Archer, 2008). Humans are clearly different from other animals because of our new brain competencies for reasoning, insight, empathy, mindfulness, and knowing self-awareness (Gilbert, 2020). These enable us to understand the concept of a 'permanent ending' and living one's life 'without…,' with comparisons of what might have been against what is now *not* going to be. A loss of any *valued relationship* can give rise to anger, anxiety, sadness, and yearning as part of grief, and orient us to both conscious and unconscious 'seeking and searching.' Against the threat of permanent endings with loved ones, and our own ending, many religions offer the potential for the renewal of relationships and the continuation of some form of consciousness after death. Bereaved individuals may seek out mediums and spiritualist guides to get messages from the deceased, partly for reassurance of continuance and in the hope the dead person is now in a better place and is okay (Walter, 2008). This type of grief poses existential questions of "is this all that there is"?

We can also grieve the loss of objects to which we have become attached. When we had to give up our car of 15 years, that we had taught our children to drive in, and had been on many holidays with, we all felt sad. Crazy though it seems, we had anthropomorphic thoughts about that car, with one of us saying, "I hope the new owner will look after them." We can also grieve for the ways that we can be changed by injury, trauma, disease, or aging, realizing that in experiencing the loss of aspects of ourselves, we may never be able to experience ourselves like we were before (Harris, 2020). When I realized I had become too old (and incompetent) to play local competitive cricket, and that I would no longer (never) be able to play, be part of that life and team, I was very sad. For all of us, the challenge of aging and loss of function is how to live compassionately with that reality and find new sources of meaning. Some forms of yearning and grief set us on a course to try to recover from trauma or tragedy, whereas other forms (death) help us to come to terms with a permanent change and ending of what was but can't be again.

GRIEVING FOR THINGS WE HOPED FOR BUT WILL NEVER HAVE

The above relates to losses of what we had and then lost. However, another aspect of grief that is extremely important in psychotherapy is the grief and yearning for what *one did not have* rather than the loss of what one did. We can clearly grieve for the loss of plans, ideals, and fantasies; this is grief over the loss of hopes and dreams for the future (Harris, 2020).

DOI: 10.4324/9781003204121-4

For example, a young footballer, set for an international career, sustains a leg injury and will never play competitively again. A young woman, who from a young age looked forward to having a large family, discovers she is infertile. These losses focus on a future life that was literally created by internal plans, ideals, and fantasies. Hence, we are not just living in the moment, but living as actors that have a past, a history, and a future. In a way, of course, all grief is linked to our conceptualization of a future 'without,' but there is a clear difference of living without something that we had and valued, such as a relationship with a loved one or job, and grief from the loss of the potential life we desired based on our fantasies and dreams. It is the loss of these potential experiences in the future that we have not had, but we hoped we were going to have, that is the root of this form of grief and yearning. A person may come to terms with the reality of their infertility but continue to yearn for many years and be vulnerable to being triggered by seeing babies in prams. When our hopes and dreams for the future are dashed, we might have also lost a particular route for meeting the *archetypal needs* that all humans share to some degree, such as the need for connectedness, meaning, securing resources, status, sex, and security. Our grief may even take on feelings of envy linked to the fact that other people can live and have the life that we wanted to live.

If we think about the *loss of possible futures*, then the degree to which we are affected by that loss, and the grief journey afterwards, will depend upon the alternatives that exist for us, the support we have around us, and the ability to re-envision a life of alternative, one that can give new sources of meaning, joy, and social connectedness. Processes that can help us adjust to the 'dashing of hope' can be compassion toward ourselves, and compassion offered to us from others. These may help us deal with any sense of self-blame or criticism for the failure of our plans, offer us the foundation from which to cope with the complex emotions that can arise, and enable us to be open to others who may support us through these times. But we have to be open to it, turn toward it, be able to seek it out, and internalize it. Being fearful or avoidant of compassion is associated with elevated vulnerability to a variety of mental health problems and to a higher incidence of complicated grief (Kirby et al., 2019; Vara & Thimm, 2020).

THE ARCHETYPAL LOSS

While we can grieve and yearn for lost imagined and idealized futures, another type of grief, for what we never had, is more biological and archetypal (Stevens, 1982). From the day we are born we seek out and are responsive to the care of others and could not survive or mature without it. We have evolved needs—directed *care seeking* systems that search for and recognize and respond to signals of care from another (Banai et al., 2005; Bowlby, 1980). A childhood that lacks access to biological, need-satisfying inputs such as 'loving care' can have profound impacts on our physiological and psychological processes and maturational trajectories (Siegel, 2020). A child in this situation may have no clear conscious awareness of what their care seeking system is seeking and needing. Unlike the situation where we experience the loss of dreams and fantasies, here there is clearly no option to (simply) compassionately revise plans because there may be no alternatives. Evolved social motive systems will seek out, and yearn for, things that maintain their survival and flourishing. To put this another way, biological systems will seek out, and yearn for, things that maintain their survival and flourishing. This can be called motivational or archetypal need.

YEARNING AND GRIEF: THE NATURE OF SEEKING

At the center of grief is a form of *yearning*, a type of *desperate wanting* associated with a seeking of inputs that will satisfy certain wants and motivational needs. For example, when we are hungry, we may yearn to find food; when we are lonely, we may yearn for company; when we are overwhelmed with stress, we may yearn for solitude; when we are in pain, we may yearn to be free of pain, and we might yearn to go back in time and change something in our lives which had very negative consequences. The relationship between yearning and grief is complex because clearly the processes of wanting, yearning, and seeking are not a grief *process*, and yet grief will involve an experience of yearning for that which is absent/lost (Robinaugh et al., 2016). So, we can consider this issue of 'archetypal' grief and yearning from the perspective of having motivation systems within us that are seeking out certain types of input, that when experienced create psychophysiological well-being and positive affect (joy-satisfaction), but when they are absent do not simply go away but can leave us in a state of unresolved and even unconscious yearning. The question is: Can we yearn and "grieve" for a certain kind of bond/relationship that we have not experienced? Can we yearn to be loved even if we (feel we) have never experienced it? Can we yearn for a sense of belonging and connectedness when we have always felt an outsider? Can we yearn for something we are frightened of, as in yearning for closeness but also being frightened of it? Can relational yearning be unconscious? And to what degree can a compassionate approach, which seeks to directly stimulate and work with the care motivational systems (Gilbert, 2020), facilitate processes that address and resolve states of yearning for care-connectedness. I will suggest we can answer all of these in the affirmative, particularly when we hold the concept of yearning and grief as overlapping but also separate processes and related to our evolved biosocial needs.

ATTACHMENT, THREAT, SAFENESS, AND CARE MOTIVATIONAL SYSTEMS

It is well recognized that we come into the world with a range of motives, biosocial goals, and needs, and if those needs are not met, then we will suffer. Not only do human infants have a range of physical needs such as feeding and being kept warm, but one of the most important dimensions of caring is the degree to which the young grow up with experiences of *threat versus safeness* (Gilbert, 2014, 2020). Whereas *safety* is about the absence of and protection from threat and works through physiological systems evolved to detect threat and generate defensive behaviors (for example the amygdala and cortisol response), safe*ness* is about the presence of helpful encouraging or soothing others. Safeness 'stimuli' work through different physiological systems to the threat system (such as the vagus nerve; Gilbert, 2020; Music, 2017). A parent who can create a sense of safeness (who can encourage, soothe, develop confidence, and give a child a sense of being loved and wanted) has a phenomenal impact on the maturation of that child's mind and brain, whereas parents who are not able to provide that or are a threat themselves significantly compromise the child's maturation (Gilbert, 2020; Music 2017). Primatologist Harlow (1958) highlighted the fact that when under threat, young monkeys will not only seek to get away from the threat but *will also seek* out sources of physical comfort rather than food. In other words, the infant seeks *both safety (get away from) and (move toward soothing reassuring) safeness*. An absence of, or removal from threat by itself may not be enough to regulate the threat systems or build social confidence (Gilbert, 1989). One of the consequences is that if one is not able to experience physiological stimulation of the soothing system through attachment and caring connections, then the capacity to process emotional pain is compromised (Cassidy & Shaver, 2016; Gilbert, 2020; Music, 2017). Over the years attachment theorists have generated considerable research on the very serious consequences for mammalian young, and particularly humans, who do not receive adequate sources of safeness-fostering care (Cassidy & Shaver, 2016; Music, 2017).

Multiple physiological systems are coordinated through the micro interactions of mother and child (Hofer, 1984). For example, mother and infant synchronize and co-regulate each other's parasympathetic and neural systems and thereby set the tone for the maturation of those systems (Nguyen et al., 2020). Attachment theories highlight how the parent acts as a secure base that enables the child to face risks, guiding them on the journey of maturing the skills they need to function as a healthy adult (Cassidy & Shaver, 2016). Parents also act as 'safe havens,' providing sources of safe*ness*, soothing, and emotion regulation particularly, but not only, when the child is in a distressed state of mind. The early secure base provides protection, activation, encouragement, and guidance to the infant as well as a sense of being loved and wanted. This safe haven can offer a sense of slowing things down, providing a sense of calm for the infant, in addition to supporting play. It follows then that children have evolved motive systems for seeking protection, support, guidance, love, and encouragement, as well as sources of soothing (collectively called parental investment). If these seeking systems do not secure the appropriate inputs (e.g., a parent is neglectful or harmful) then children experience a *thwarting of evolved motivational needs* and are left in a position of *yearning without resolution*. This is similar to the concept of "thwarting of archetypal intent" (Stevens, 1982). The therapeutic question is what happens to the sorting of these motivational systems?

PROTEST AND DESPAIR

Given the enormous importance of the need for a secure base and safe haven that balance threat, infant and parent have what are called *proximity seeking and maintaining* motives such that if there is separation between them, they become distressed and seek re-connection. Attachment theory highlighted that disruptions in attachment connections generate two typical responses, called protest and despair (Bowlby, 1980; Cassidy & Shaver, 2016). In protest, the infant is activated in searching, moving around in the environment, and distress calling. The young infant is clearly in a state of yearning, and such displays can also be seen in the early stages of grief. However, if protest does not work, then continuing to wander in the environment unprotected, and without guidance, and calling out in distress would attract predators and other sources of harm. As in the learned helplessness paradigms when the *search* routines or efforts to control a situation fail, then the mind tends to start to shut down. In the attachment situation this shut down is called despair (Bowlby, 1980). Here the infant hides away and has to wait for the parent to find them and to be rescued. A key question then is what happens to these systems for people who have indeed not experienced appropriate inputs and have been traumatized or neglected (Music, 2017)? There is now considerable research to suggest that they go on to develop forms of insecure attachment (e.g., anxious and avoidant), which can impact the rest of their lives and the ways in which they seek and form social relationships.

YEARNING IN THE FACE OF DYSFUNCTIONAL ATTACHMENT

Mammals, and particularly humans, have evolved motives to be highly oriented to search and seek out forms of social connectedness. Not only in childhood, but as we grow beyond childhood, we seek to form relationships with caring others and to be part of caring communities. Experiences of rejection, exclusion by a community, or a sense of not belonging, can have profound effects on people's mental well-being and physiological states. But what happens if the parent (or community) is unresponsive (neglectful) and/or is the source of the threat itself (abusive)? The need for 'comfort from another' remains because that is a biologically evolved *seeking* system, but it becomes significantly inhibited by the threat system. Children who grow up in neglectful or abusive environments can't seek out and utilize their parents as a secure base or safe haven. Over time they may become anxious searchers, avoidant, have social distrust, or become compulsively self-reliant. There can be severe effects not only on the individual themselves but on their capacity for empathy and prosocial behavior (or lack of it), and harm to others.

In a major review of the neurophysiology of empathy, Shirtcliff et al. (2009) found evidence to support this view. They summarize their findings, saying:

> The review proposes neurobiological impairments in individuals who display little empathy are not necessarily due to a reduced ability to understand the emotions of others. Instead, evidence suggests individuals who show little arousal to the distress of others likewise show decreased physiological arousal to their own distress; one manifestation of reduced stress reactivity may be a dysfunction in empathy which supports psychopathic-like constructs (e.g., callousness).
>
> *(p.137)*

Some individuals may go on to become harmfully narcissistic as a way of dealing with social threat and resource acquisition (Banai et al., 2005). The effects of child neglect and abuse are well known in terms of the distortions of the self and emotional development (Music, 2017). While some individuals may go on to become harmfully narcissistic as a way of dealing with social threat and resource acquisition, others become vulnerable to harsh self-criticism, developing a sense of worthlessness, unlovability, and shame, resulting in a fear of emotions such as rage, and fear of others getting too close, discovering undesirable self-qualities, and then rejecting them (Music, 2017).

Empathic caring, therefore, is a resource that children really cannot do without if they are to mature into happy and healthy individuals. Given this basic understanding, can people yearn and grieve for the love (parental investment) and the parents they never had, even if they are not consciously searching for it? What determines the image or felt sense of the kind of person who represents their ideal caring other? Clearly, these images and fantasies differ from person to person (Stevens, 1982). Can some of their emotional difficulties be related to unresolved yearning? Further, can psychotherapy re-engage these (care-seeking) systems in such a way that they can facilitate a healing process of conscious grieving? If clients are helped to identify their 'yearning for archetypal unmet needs' as part of their difficulties, and guided through a grief process, can that be an important component of therapy? Equally we can ask: What are the consequences for individuals passing through therapy who do not have these archetypal systems of yearning and grieving acknowledged, brought into conscious experiencing, and addressed? Since this has not been systematically studied, there is no clear answer, although there are indicators that a grief process can be highly therapeutic (Gilbert & Simos, 2022; Holmes & Slade, 2017; Music, 2017; Stevens, 1982).

COMPASSION, YEARNING, AND GRIEF

There is now considerable evidence that caring connections, particularly but not only early in life, have profound physiological effects (Siegel, 2020). Moreover, the evolution of caring came with a range of specific physiological systems that link to processes that involve various aspects of our neurological system, including specific areas of our brain, autonomic nervous system, especially but not only the vagus nerve, hormonal agents, and neurotransmitters (Carter et al., 2017). Part of what Compassion-Focused Therapy (CFT) seeks to do is to (re)activate caring motivational systems, creating opportunities for these systems to be explored in terms of emotional memory, address and work through unmet yearnings within the caring system, and go on to cultivate the psychophysiological regulatory systems of caring, thereby building personal courage and wisdom to address suffering and promote well-being and prosocial behavior (Gilbert, 2014; Gilbert & Simos, 2022) . In (re)activating motivation-need based yearning and searching, we provide opportunities to find a secure base and safe haven for their resolution (Gilbert, 2008, 2020; Music, 2017).

To put this another way, we can define compassion as being like a good parent who is sensitive to the suffering/distress/need (in self and others) with a commitment to try to alleviate and prevent suffering (Gilbert, 2014, 2020). At the heart of compassion are courage and wisdom. Courage is essential because when we engage with compassion we are engaging with suffering, which can include feelings of threat and risk. The wisdom of compassion depends upon our capacity for empathic connectedness to others. If we are unsure about whether others are suffering or not or have little insight into the causes of their suffering, or what would help them, compassion will be difficult. When we are yearning for caring, we want to find individuals who have certain empathic competencies to connect with us and find wise solutions. When we develop compassion for ourselves, we are bringing our caring motivational system to our own minds, which requires courage and wisdom to work with frightening and, at times, overwhelming emotions.

The origins of CFT emerged from a combination of processes over many years relating to basic motivational systems, Buddhist practices, and also working with cognition (Gilbert, 2014). Cognitive-oriented therapy involves helping people identify unhelpful thoughts, then standing back and generating helpful alternative ones (Beck et al., 1979). However, we know that people can acknowledge the logic of such efforts to change their thinking, but this change in thinking does not affect them emotionally (Stott, 2007).

I was working with an individual that I will call Jane, who revealed a key issue about how we can change mental states by tapping into unprocessed grief and yearning that were also unconscious. Jane had strong beliefs that as a child who was adopted into a harsh family, she should not have been born and was not really wanted. As is common for people who have these difficulties, she had an underlying idea that she had to achieve things and try and be a nice person in order to earn other people's acceptance and affection. She had a good marriage, her children were affectionate and doing well at school, and she had friends. However, although she could hold these ideas in her mind, she still *felt* unlovable. One day, I invited her to speak out her alternative coping thoughts *as she actually heard them in her mind*. The coping thoughts were something like "although you feel you're a failure and unwanted, in fact you have twin son and daughter who you are proud of and close to, are

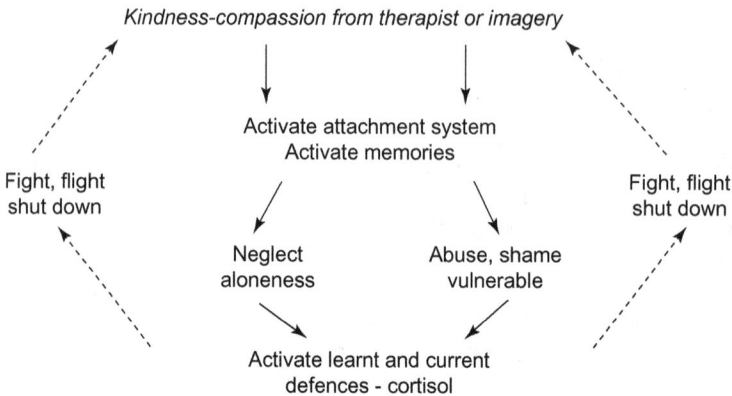

Figure 2.1 Fears, Blocks, and Resistances to Compassion. From Gilbert, 2008, with permission

doing very well at school, a husband who cares for you, and you were valued at work" etc. She was somewhat embarrassed, but when she spoke them out in the therapy room it was not with any genuinely kind, compassionate, supportive voice but one with hostility and contempt. There was an emotional texture of "come on, you're doing cognitive therapy! You know these thoughts are not accurate! What have you got to be depressed about?" The more I explored this discrepancy between thoughts and emotions with other clients, the more I found that the *emotional textures* of peoples' thinking were often cold, hostile, and did not match their supposed desire to generate helpful alternative thoughts. Clearly, the obvious intervention was to focus directly on the emotional textures of peoples' thinking and try to generate a felt sense of compassion, with a desire to be sensitive to suffering and working on the wisdom to be helpful.

An unexpected problem at the time was that clients did not want to be sensitive or empathic to their feelings, particularly of yearning, the sadness of which they often found overwhelming and sought to close down. Instead, they just wanted to get rid of or change them, not feel them more fully or accept them! Not only was this partly due to misunderstanding about the courage and wisdom of compassion and confusing it with kindness but trying to develop compassion motivation brought up many resistances. Some of these are depicted in Figure 2.1.

COMPASSION-FOCUSED THERAPY AND GRIEF

Jane was, at first, very resistant to the idea of developing empathic compassion for herself with the appropriate emotional textures, but gradually we explored her early life and the trauma associated with her adoption and subsequent upbringing. She revealed that she had spent her childhood yearning for her biological mother to find her and rescue her. When she first began therapy, she discussed these issues in a relatively matter of fact, detached way. However, as we explored more deeply, she began to experience emotions around these memories with increasingly intense sadness. Within a few weeks of beginning therapy, she began exploring *her grief for the mother she never had*. She acknowledged being very surprised at this depth of pain "that I never knew existed within me." As a chronically depressed and, at times, actively suicidal person, she had a lot of therapy beforehand, but felt that this Jane who was sobbing in the chair in my office was 'a different part of her.' The emergence of her memories was very powerful as she began to emotionally connect with how her adoptive mother would sometimes beat her and send her to her room, where she would then cry for her biological mother. Working with the yearning in her grief, the therapeutic relationship gave her a sense of a secure base and safe haven from which she could explore her feelings. She was then able to engage in a set of compassion-focused mind training exercises, which specifically focused on imagining receiving compassion. Doing these exercises enabled her to develop the courage and wisdom to engage with, tolerate, and work through her deep emotional pain of unmet yearning. Her ability for compassion emerged through sharing her grief and the yearning that she had not been fully conscious of previously.

CFT has always been particularly attentive to grief, forming the foundation of a secure base for grieving clients to begin to experience the depths of emotion and unprocessed yearning. In the previous example, Jane's yearning presented as a desire to be parentally rescued, loved, protected, and valued, which she felt she had not experienced up to the time of her therapy. However, at the beginning of therapy these were far from consciously recognized, but later in the therapy she began to see how they had textured her relationship seeking systems and the way she related to people. Toward the end of the therapy, she reflected, "I think most of my life I've been looking for some kind of parental figure that would love and protect me without really realizing that. I always just had the sense of being lost and waiting for someone to come and find me somehow."

COMPASSION AND CONNECTEDNESS

One exercise in CFT invites people to create images of an ideal compassionate other that they can practice relating to and imagine being present for them (Gilbert, 2010; Lee, 2005). It is their unique and "just for them" archetypal image. We explain what archetypal images are in the sense that when we work with them, they have the potential to stimulate a range of physiological systems. Just as when we imagine something sexual, we can stimulate our sexual system and are only interested in images that have that physiological effect. Or we can imagine or remember an angry encounter, and this will stimulate our threat/anger systems. Assuming that there are no fears, blocks, or resistances to work through, then imagining interacting with a compassionate other stimulates physiological systems that evolved as part of the caring system. Anecdotally, many people choose images that have parental-like functions; being cared for, protected, guided, and understood, but with affection—even love as well.

One of the roles of compassion, and other psychological approaches, is to help us to feel safe enough to become sensitive to our emotional needs, to recognize that our minds and our communities can be textured by a sense of yearning and (perhaps unconscious) sadness for the fast pace of life, the need to keep up rather than being able to develop a sense of safe enduring connectedness. Part of the compassionate agenda is therefore to orient individuals to safe social connectedness. Psychotherapy is not just about working with unconscious conflicts, living in alignment with our values or changing beliefs, but also working to understand what sustains us as *human beings*, including the pattern of our archetypal yearnings and how to address them helpfully rather than seek their suppression or avoidance.

CONCLUSION

This chapter suggests that we can yearn and grieve for what we never had but 'biologically' needed. There are conscious and unconscious ways this can happen. We can yearn for what was needed in the past or could have been in the future; we can feel envious yearning of those who have things we don't. But there is another level, which is yearning and grieving for what we were biologically designed to seek and need, particularly relationships, that would have a profound impact on the maturation of our brains and bodies. If we do not get those inputs from caring others, we might give up searching and seeking them and we may become socially distrustful or angry, yet this is a yearning ticking away in the background for a lifetime. These kinds of yearnings, and the cacophony of feelings that go with them, can be very difficult to acknowledge or understand and can be denied or dissociated from. Yet given enough opportunity, clients can indeed begin to recognize that some of their grief may be linked to both current crises in their lives as well as to the unresolved issues of yearning for absent archetypal relationships; those for a secure base, safe haven, and sense of loving connection (Holmes & Slade, 2017). Helping clients work through these processes, acknowledging and tolerating yearnings for certain types of caring connectedness particularly, but not only, parental-like, seems to be able to reset the care-compassion system and their sense of self. So, we come back to the idea that we are born with some inner guiding social motives and mentalities for what we need in order to grow and mature. These form the "archetypal search mechanisms" to connect with caring and others. If these systems are distorted, we end up overly relying on other motivational systems such as the competitive system and become easily overly self-reliant, narcissistic, and aggressive—or submissive, fearful, and depressed. Helping people work through the traumas of a neglectful or abusing parent does not necessarily address the yearning for a loving, protecting, admiring parent. We always have two parental forms inside of us: The one we were innately made to seek and respond to, and the one that we actually had. If they match reasonably okay, all may be well; however, if threat dominates these relationships, then the care system becomes toxic. Working through the emotions associated with grieving for the parent one did not have but wanted and needed, as well as recognizing that this was not the fault of oneself can have powerful therapeutic effects.

REFERENCES

Archer, J. (2008). Theories of grief: Past, present, and future perspectives. In M. S. Stroebe, R. O. Hansson, H. Schut, & W. Stroebe (Eds.), *Handbook of bereavement research and practice: Advances in theory and intervention* (pp. 45–65). American Psychological Association. https://doi.org/10.1037/14498-003

Banai, E., Mikulincer, M., & Shaver, P. R. (2005). "Selfobject" needs in Kohut's self psychology: Links with attachment, self-cohesion, affect regulation, and adjustment. *Psychoanalytic Psychology, 22*(2), 224–260.

Beck, A. T., Rush, A. J., Shaw, B. F., & Emery, G. (1979). *Cognitive therapy of depression.* New York: Guilford Press.

Bowlby, J. (1980). *Loss: Sadness and depression: Attachment and loss, vol. 3.* Hogarth Press.

Carter, S., Bartal, I. B., & Porges, E. (2017). The roots of compassion: An evolutionary and neurobiological perspective. In E. M. Seppälä, E. Simon-Thomas, S. L. Brown, & M. C. Worline (Eds.), *The Oxford handbook of compassion science* (pp. 178–188). Oxford University Press.

Cassidy, J., & Shaver, P. R. (2016). *Handbook of attachment: Theory, research and clinical applications* (3rd ed.). Guilford.

Gilbert, P. (2008). Developing a compassion focused approach in cognitive behavioural therapy. In G. Simos (Ed.), *Cognitive behaviour therapy: A guide to the practicing clinician* (Vol. 2, pp. 217–232). Routledge.

Gilbert, P. (2010). *Compassion focused therapy: The CBT distinctive features series*. Routledge.

Gilbert, P. (2014). The origins and nature of compassion focused therapy. *British Journal of Clinical Psychology, 53*(1), 6–41. https://doi.org/10.1111/bjc.12043

Gilbert, P. (2020). Compassion: From its evolution to a psychotherapy. *Frontiers in Psychology, 11*, 3123.

Gilbert, P., McEwan, K., Matos, M., & Rivis, A. (2011). Fears of compassion: Development of three self-report measures. *Psychology and Psychotherapy: Theory, Research and Practice, 84*(3), 239–255.

Gilbert, P., & Simos, G. (2022). *Compassion focused therapy: Clinical practice and applications*. Routledge.

Harlow, H. F. (1958). The nature of love. *American Psychologist, 13*(12), 673–685.

Harris, D. L. (Ed.). (2011). *Counting our losses: Reflecting on change, loss, and transition in everyday life*. Routledge.

Harris, D. L. (2020). Non-death loss and grief: Laying the foundation. In D. Harris (Ed.), *Non-death loss and grief: Context and clinical implications* (pp. 7–16). Routledge.

Hofer, M. A. (1984). Relationships is regulated: A psychobiologic perspective on bereavement. *Psychosomatic Medicine, 46*(3), 183–197.

Holmes, J., & Slade, A. (2017). *Attachment in therapeutic practice*. Sage.

Kirby, J. N., Day, J., & Sagar, V. (2019). The 'flow' of compassion: A meta-analysis of the fears of compassion scales and psychological functioning. *Clinical Psychology Review, 70*, 26–39.

Lee, D. A. (2005). The perfect nurturer: A model to develop a compassionate mind within the context of cognitive therapy. In P. Gilbert (Ed.), *Compassion: Conceptualizations, research and use in psychotherapy* (pp. 338–363). Routledge.

Music, G. (2017). *Nurturing natures: Attachment and children's emotional, sociocultural and brain development* (2nd ed.). Routledge.

Nguyen, T., Schleihauf, H., Kayhan, E., Matthes, D., Vrtička, P., & Hoehl, S. (2020). The effects of interaction quality on neural synchrony during mother-child problem solving. *Cortex, 124*, 235–249.

Robinaugh, D. J., Mauro, C., Bui, E., Stone, L., Shah, R., Wang, Y., Skritskaya, N. A., Reynolds, C. F., Zisook, S., O'Connor, M.-F., Shear, K., & Simon, N. M. (2016). Yearning and its measurement in complicated grief. *Journal of Loss and Trauma, 21*(5), 410–420.

Shirtcliff, E. A., Vitacco, M. J., Graf, A. R., Gostisha, A. J., Merz, J. L., & Zahn-Waxler, C. (2009). Neurobiology of empathy and callousness: Implications for the development of antisocial behavior. *Behavioral Sciences and the Law, 27*(2), 137–171.

Siegel, D. J. (2020). *The developing mind: How relationships and the brain interact to shape who we are*. Guilford.

Stevens, A. (1982). *Archetype: A natural history of the self*. Routledge.

Stott, R. (2007). When the head and heart do not agree: A theoretical and clinical analysis of rational-emotional dissociation (RED) in cognitive therapy. *Journal of Cognitive Psychotherapy: An International Quarterly, 21*(1), 37–50.

Vara, H., & Thimm, J. C. (2020). Associations between self-compassion and complicated grief symptoms in bereaved individuals: An exploratory study. *Nordic Psychology, 72*(3), 235–247.

Walter, T. (2008). Mourners and mediums. *Bereavement Care (RBER), 27*(3), 47–50.

CHAPTER 3

FOUNDATIONAL ASPECTS OF GRIEF

Darcy L. Harris

INTRODUCTION

Like compassion, there is a good deal of awareness in popular culture about grief. And similar to compassion, grief is often misunderstood in various ways. Perhaps the most ubiquitous misrepresentation of grief occurs with the application of neatly described stages or phases that are expected to unfold in a linear way, most commonly through the misinterpretation of Kubler-Ross' well-known stages of dying (Kubler-Ross, 1969). While the work of Kubler-Ross was important in fostering awareness and dialogue about death and dying, the stages that she described were not intended to be used in this way, and they have no resemblance to how grief is actually experienced. This chapter will provide an overview of current perspectives about grief and their implications for supporting grieving individuals.

THEORETICAL UNDERSTANDINGS ABOUT GRIEF

Grief can be defined simply as the normal and natural reaction to loss. However, the use of the word "normal" implies that there is a defined expectation of what normal grief should look like, and that is far from true. Although grief is a universal experience that is shared by all human beings, the actual grief response in each individual is very unique, and the expression of grief can vary greatly from one person to another. Many factors, such as personality traits, the presence of concurrent stressors and previous losses, the nature of the loss(es), and the social expectations and norms that are affixed onto grief, have a great deal of influence in shaping the course of grief for an individual. Grief is also not something that we strive to "overcome" or to which there is "recovery," as one might recover from an addiction or an illness. Therapists who work with grieving individuals understand that although the process may involve a tremendous amount of pain and adjustment, the goal of therapeutic support is to facilitate the unfolding of the healthy and adaptive aspects of the grieving process as it is manifest for each client, trusting that this unfolding will eventually help the re-entry back into life in a way that will be meaningful.

A key foundational component of grief is related to attachment. In humans, attachment is founded upon our most deeply rooted need for safety and security (Bowlby, 1969, 1973). 'Attachment' in this context refers to more than a relational bond. As stated in the previous chapter, attachment relationships are linked to our primary, instinctual need to be close to significant others in order to be safe and to feel a sense of "anchoring" in our world. In infants, the attachment system is formed around the primary caregiver who is present to meet the basic needs of the infant and who responds to the infant's cries and beginning attempts at social interaction. Later, we form attachments to individuals who tend to be closest to us, or to whom there is significance identified for us (Fraley & Shaver, 2021). It is important to note that the presence of an attachment bond in a relationship is not necessarily dependent on the quality of the relationship, the personality, or the temperament of

DOI: 10.4324/9781003204121-5

the individuals involved in the attachment bond. Attachment bonds form at an instinctual level, outside of our conscious awareness.

Attachment in humans was first described by John Bowlby, a psychoanalytically trained psychiatrist who worked with young children in postwar England. In his position at the Tavistock Clinic, Bowlby observed children who had been separated from their parents (their primary attachment figures), and he made note of some commonalities in the responses of these children, which he termed 'separation distress.' He also described specific behavioral elements of the response to separation as 'attachment behaviors,' and suggested that their function was to draw the primary caregiver back into close proximity with the dependent child (Cassidy, 1999). In situations where there is relative absence of threat/distress, attachment behaviors tend to exist in the background, out of conscious awareness. After consultation with colleagues who were conducting research with primates that demonstrated similar behavioral responses to separation, Bowlby proposed that the attachment system was instinctually mediated and passed on for survival purposes. Bowlby's later work, which is now known as *attachment theory*, became an eclectic model that incorporated elements of psychoanalysis, ethology, experimental psychology, learning theory, and family systems to describe the psychological and emotional development of the child (Bowlby, 1973).

Colin Murray Parkes, a psychiatrist based in London, UK, worked at the Tavistock Clinic with Bowlby. He postulated that the attachment behaviors observed in infants upon separation from their mothers were the same behaviors that grieving individuals display upon the loss of a loved one through death (Parkes & Weiss, 1983). Parkes (1996) conducted extensive longitudinal research with older widows, documenting their behaviors, thoughts, and feelings after the death of their spouses. He found common behaviors between the separated infants in Bowlby's research and the widows in his own studies. Examples of these common behaviors were searching, pining, and protest upon the disappearance/loss of the attachment figure. Weiss (1975) described similar attachment behaviors in the situation of divorce.

Later work that expanded upon attachment determined the existence of attachment styles that could be detected in children before the age of two. The attachment style that a child displayed was correlated with the experiences of the child with primary attachment figures in early life. Stable patterns of attachment style in children up to the age of ten were documented by Sroufe et al. (1990). Simpson and Rholes (2012) explored the role of attachment style in adult intimate relationships. These authors stated that adults tend to demonstrate the same types of attachment style in their current relationships with other adults that were originally present when they were much younger. More recent research into the relationship between attachment style and grief (Schenck et al., 2016; Stroebe et al., 2005) has provided insight into how grief might evolve and be experienced in specific individuals.

The "take home" message for this discussion is an understanding that:

- Grief is part of an instinctually mediated response that is based on our attachment system. The attachment system typically exists outside of our conscious awareness unless it is threatened.
- The loss of an attachment figure will be experienced as a threat to most individuals, creating a sense of distress and disequilibrium.
- An attachment relationship is one that is significant, but the attachment bond itself is not necessarily dependent on the quality of the relationship. Infants form attachments to mothers who are not attentive; however, the quality of the

attachment bond (often interpreted as attachment style) will certainly be affected
by the interaction between the two individuals.

- Attachment relationships are present throughout life and do not only involve
  parental figures from early life and development. That being said, patterns of
  attachment style/orientation that are established early in life tend to continue in
  similar ways in close relationships through adulthood.

THE ASSUMPTIVE WORLD AND GRIEF

As the attachment system is forming in infants, they also develop a sense of how to relate to
the world around them. The infant begins to learn about the predictability of their needs
being met, along with how to find safety and feel soothed when threatened or distressed.
Gradually, as there is more engagement with further life experiences, assumptions about
the world, others, and the self are established through patterns of interaction. Parkes (1971)
stated the assumptions that individuals form about how the world works are based upon
their early life experiences and attachments. He also emphasized that experiencing a significant loss can threaten one's assumptive world. In her extensive work that examined
the assumptive world in the context of traumatic experiences, Janoff-Bulman (1992) stated
that expectations about how the world should work are established earlier than language
in children, and that assumptions about the world are a result of the generalization and
application of early childhood experiences into adulthood. The assumptive world is an
organized schema reflecting all that a person assumes to be true about the world and the
self; it refers to the assumptions, or beliefs, that create a sense of security, predictability, and
meaning/purpose in life. This description resonates with Bowlby's accounts of the development of the attachment system to ensure a sense of safety in the individual. Thus, it can be
reasonably suggested that the attachment system and the assumptive world construct are
formed through similar mechanisms and are probably interrelated. The assumptive world
is most likely informed and shaped as part of the attachment system, and the assumptions
that are formed are deeply ingrained into the fabric of how individuals live their lives and
interpret life events.

In further exploration of the assumptive world construct in various scenarios, it could
be suggested that there may indeed be some overarching/main assumptions related to how
an individual has come to view the world, self, and others through formative experiences
that are modified through various experiences throughout one's life. Our assumptive world
includes basic/core assumptions centered around:

1. How we find safety in the world.
2. How we believe the world should work and why events happen.
3. Our view of ourselves and how we fit into our social circles (Harris, 2020).

In this version of the construct, there is allowance for individuals who have grown up in a
world where they may not have known safety, or where foundational individuals in a person's life were not well-intentioned, or the view of self has been mirrored in a way that is
distorted, or perhaps does not affirm the individual's worth, capacity, or value.

Janoff-Bulman (1992) stated that our basic assumptions about how the world should
work can be shattered by life experiences that do not fit into our view of ourselves and the
world around us. Neimeyer et al. (2008) discuss events that "disrupt the significance of the

coherence of one's life narrative" (p. 30), and the potential for erosion of the individual's life story and sense of self that may occur after such events. What is apparent is that the experience of a significant event that does not fit into our beliefs and expectations can throw us into a state of disequilibrium. Coping and accommodation after such experiences are part of a greater process that individuals undertake in an effort to "re-learn" their assumptions about the world in light of confrontation with a reality that does not match their existing expectations or assumptions (Attig, 1996). It is important to note that the assumptive world is more than a cognitive construct; these assumptions exist at the very core of what in life provides us with a sense of meaning, purpose, and security. Each aspect of the assumptive world will have cognitive aspects, but each will also incorporate social, spiritual, emotional, and psychological components as well.

Significant loss experiences challenge the core beliefs that comprise our assumptive world, and the entire structure that we have built our lives upon begins to crumble. The hopes, expectations, and predictions that were firmly in place are rendered irrelevant and useless in light of the reality that now presents itself to us. The assumptions which have kept us steady and have given coherence to our lives now seem like naïve illusions. The realization of how little control we have over what happens to us becomes glaringly evident. There is no going back; the way the world made sense before and the expectations and beliefs that we deeply held about ourselves and others are no longer salient. Losing one's assumptions about the world means the loss of safety, logic, clarity, power, and control (Beder, 2005). There is an overwhelming sense of loss and disorientation that occurs while we flounder, trying to navigate in a new, unfamiliar reality. In essence, we grieve the loss of our assumptive world, and our grief (although painful and disorienting) provides us with the process by which we will grapple with the assault on our most deeply held assumptions and beliefs to eventually rebuild a new assumptive world that will be able to take into account the lived experience that catapulted us into this uncharted territory.

A central concept to current grief theory is that grief is a process that is both adaptive and necessary in order to rebuild the assumptive world after its destruction from significant loss experiences (Harris, 2020). This understanding implies that loss of the assumptive world can occur from events that involve death as well as those that do not involve the death of a loved one. Not only can losses be death or non-death in orientation, they may also be tangible, intangible, or a combination of both. Sometimes, what dies may be inside the individual, such as the loss of hopes, dreams, identity, or beliefs (Harris, 2020).

In whatever way the assumptive world is rebuilt after a significant loss occurs, the revised assumptive world allows us to attach meaning to our experiences and provides us, once again, with a sense of safety and coherence in navigating through life. Rather than being a symptom of a disorder, the grief that accompanies the shattered assumptive world is a multifaceted attempt to adapt to the disorder and disorganization that can occur after our lives (and our assumptions about the world) have been upturned by a significant loss. Thus, instead of attempting to inhibit grief, it is important that grief be allowed to unfold without hindrance so that the loss experience can be assimilated into one's existing assumptive world or the assumptive world can be rebuilt in a way that makes sense of the loss that has occurred. It is this important principle that differentiates grief therapy and support from working with clients who present with clinical issues, such as depression, anxiety disorders, or other forms of mental distress. *Grief is, for the most part, an adaptive process to be supported rather than a diagnostic entity to be treated.*

We crave predictability and stability in our lives. In fact, most of us operate on the assumption that we have a lot of control over the events in our lives (Heckhausen et al.,

2010). In clinical work, it is common to work with individuals who experience profound anxiety because they can no longer live under the illusion that life will remain constant and unchanging, or that they can control the events in their lives. These realizations usually occur as a result of the experience of a significant loss or dramatic change. Even though we attempt to function as if there is certainty and stability in everyday life, the world around us, including our bodies, serves as a metaphor for the normalcy of loss, change, and transition. The seasons change. Living things are born, grow, reproduce, and die. Many of the cells that exist in our bodies today were not present a year ago and may not be present in our bodies in a month from now. This moment is gone and replaced by another moment in time. We cannot stop the changing nature of life, just as we cannot stop time in its place or change the course of events.

Weenolsen (1988) speaks of our innate resistance to change and our belief that things can remain the same as the *fundamental illusion*, functioning to allow us to feel safe and solid in the world. However, our clinging to this image creates great difficulty when the illusion cannot be maintained, such as when a major loss event does indeed occur or when we come to the realization that we have very little control over ourselves and the people, places, and things that matter very much to us. For many of the bereaved individuals who seek therapeutic support, the realization that (a) we really have very little control over the events in our lives, (b) there is very little predictability and stability in the world, and (c) we will never be the same again form the foundation of the work that occurs in the therapy process.

CURRENT UNDERSTANDINGS OF GRIEF

Grief can be experienced and expressed in many ways, which include thoughts, feelings, and emotions; however, it can also be experienced physically through bodily symptoms, socially through changes in interpersonal dynamics and social expectations for the bereaved individual, spiritually as a quest for meaning or as existential suffering, economically through changes in financial status and expenses incurred after a loss, and practically through the upheavals that occur in one's day-to-day routine as a result of a loss. One very important aspect of grief therapy is recognition of the complexity of the experience and the diverse factors that shape an individual's response to loss. For example, when there is a loss within a family system, each individual family member will experience grief depending on their relationship to the deceased person and other family members, the age and developmental stage of the family members, who provided the caregiving if needed, and the grieving styles of the members (Kissane, 2014).

Individuals tend to grieve in ways that are congruent with their age and developmental stage, and according to their personalities and attachment styles (Doka & Martin, 2010; Lai et al., 2014; Stroebe, 2002), in the context of social rules and expectations (Doka, 2002; Harris, 2016), with the influence of other factors and concurrent stressors at that time (Worden, 2018). Thus, therapists need to have a good understanding of how many different areas intersect in this one experience. For example, to explore only the feelings associated with a loss without understanding the social underpinnings and the impact of the concurrent stressors that shape these feelings would provide an inaccurate and overly simplistic account of the client's full experience.

Until recently, support of grieving individuals was dominated by the *grief work hypothesis*, which implied that the bereaved must do the "work" of grief by talking about their loss and their feelings in order to return back to life (Stroebe, W. et al., 2003). If a bereaved person did not do this, it was assumed that something was wrong with that individual or they were not grieving properly. Although many individuals do, indeed, talk about their loss and their feelings as part of their grieving process, others may not have this same need, and they will find their own ways to cope with loss. The grief work model also posited that the goal of grief was to help the bereaved individual to "let go" of their loved one in order to move forward in life (Stroebe, 2002). However, in the mid-1990s, research with diverse groups of bereaved individuals led to the proposal of the *Continuing Bonds Theory*, which normalizes an ongoing relationship with the deceased loved one, implying that the attachment bond is indeed not really broken after death (Klass et al., 2014). A common phrase that exemplifies this theory is that *death may end a life, but not a relationship.*

In their research with bereaved individuals, Stroebe et al. (2005) proposed the *Dual Process Model* of bereavement (see Figure 3.1), which allows for an understanding of diverse responses to separation and loss by examining the underlying attachment issues that are present in grieving individuals. This model posits that bereaved individuals will spend time in acute, active grief over the loss and its implications (loss orientation), and they also will spend time tending to their everyday life and returning to the world of the living that distracts them from their grief (restoration orientation). What this model implies is that grief is usually not continually on the surface at all times; rather, there tends to be cycles, or waves of grief that come and go, with a sense of oscillation between focus upon the loss and grief alternating with periods of time where daily life and even avoidance of grief are normal.

At this juncture, it is important to note that approximately 810% of all bereaved individuals lapse into a form of long-term, crippling grief that is highly disruptive to daily functioning. There has been a great deal of debate over the terminology and criteria to be used to describe this form of difficult grief, ranging from complicated grief, persistent complex bereavement disorder, to prolonged grief disorder. Most experts in the field tend to favor the use of prolonged grief disorder, and this entity is now listed in the International

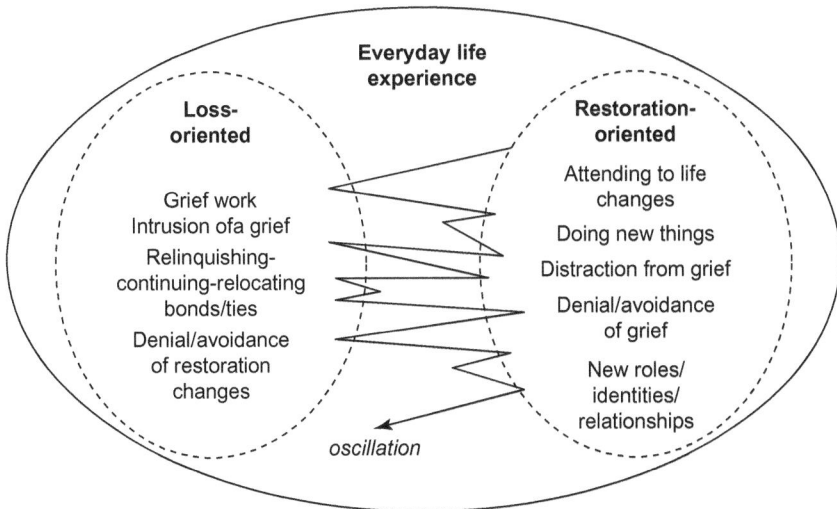

Figure 3.1 The Dual Process Model of Bereavement. Source: Stroebe, M., Schut, H., & Stroebe, W. (2005). Attachment in coping with bereavement: A theoretical integration. *Review of General Psychology, 9*(1), 48–66

Classification of Diseases, 11th Revision (ICD-11). In general, if a bereaved individual is still struggling with functioning and is continuing to experience grief that is overwhelming or even worsens after six months, consideration needs to be given to more intensive and structured support. It is beyond the scope of this chapter to provide a full delineation of this type of difficult grief and its treatment; readers are referred to the current literature and research that is widely available on this topic.

SOCIAL INFLUENCES AND CONTEXT

One of the difficulties in assessing grief is that it is subjectively appraised. Only the grieving individual can determine the meaning of the loss, the depth of the loss in terms of its impact upon their assumptive world, and the way that grief will be manifest and expressed in their lives. There is no one "right way" to grieve; grief is a universal human experience, but it is also highly personal and diverse in its presentation and impact upon an individual. This being said, grief responses are often stereotyped, reinforced by social messages and expectations, which may have nothing to do with the actual needs or response of a person who is grieving. Examples of unhelpful messages pertain to implicit social norms that fall along gender lines, with pressure upon males to take on a stoic, practical approach to grief and women expected to grieve through their emotions and to seek supportive others to share their feelings. In reality, these expectations are external to the inner workings of the grieving person's actual lived experience and way of expressing their grief. Other social rules that are frequently imposed upon grieving individuals include

- Whether the loss is seen as valid or not by others (such as in pet loss or miscarriage).
- How long grief should last (which is highly variable between individuals).
- Grief should be private and not affect productivity at work or public responsibilities (which is unrealistic and often not possible).

It may be the case that although the grieving process is normative and adaptive, if one's grief does not fit into a socially acceptable or recognized pattern, the grieving individual may be perceived as abnormal and referred for treatment, when in fact, the social norms that judge the expression of grief in such limited terms may be the real issue.

CONCLUSION

The following sections of this book will explore suggestions for assisting with the unfolding of the grieving process through various compassion-based approaches. Wolfelt (2005) suggests a model of 'companioning' the bereaved, emphasizing the relational component of therapeutic support, which may be especially helpful if the grieving individual does not have other supports available to 'walk alongside' them during the acute grieving process. When reading through this section, it is important to keep in mind the following:

- Grief is a healthy and adaptive response to loss, and not a disorder.
- Grief occurs after losses of all types, including both death and non-death losses, tangible and intangible losses, as well as loss experiences that may be ongoing in nature.

- What constitutes a loss is subjectively appraised by the individual, and the grief response to that loss will be unique for that individual.
- There are no stages, phases, or sense of linear progression through grief. Normal grief will last as long as there is a need to integrate the loss and its implications into one's assumptive world. For some, grief will remain a companion that accompanies them throughout their lives.
- When providing support to grieving individuals, the focus is upon facilitating the unfolding of the grieving process in the ways that the grieving individual needs that to occur.

An image that I like to use for grief is that of a shattered pane of glass. The shattered glass represents a point of no return. It would be impossible to go back and glue the pieces together to create a pane of glass that looked like the original one. Our assumptive world can be shattered by loss, similar to how glass shatters, leaving a mess of broken pieces and shards where there was once an intact window. However, this image also invites a lovely metaphor of stained glass, which is highly prized for its beauty and ability to direct light in ways that can be breathtaking. But we always remember that the glass was shattered before it became this magnificent piece of art.

REFERENCES

Attig, T. A. (1996). *How we grieve: Relearning the world*. Oxford University Press.

Beder, J. (2005). Loss of the assumptive world—How we deal with death and loss. *OMEGA: Journal of Death and Dying, 50*(4), 255–265.

Bowlby, J. (1969). *Attachment and loss: Attachment* (Vol. 1). Hogarth.

Bowlby, J. (1973). *Attachment and loss: Separation* (Vol. 2). Basic Books.

Cassidy, J. (1999). The nature of the child's ties. In J. Cassidy & P. R. Shaver (Eds.), *Handbook of attachment: Theory, research, and clinical applications* (pp. 3–20). Guilford.

Doka, K. J. (2002). *Disenfranchised grief: New directions, challenges, and strategies for practice*. Research Press.

Doka, K. J., & Martin, T. L. (2010). *Grieving beyond gender: Understanding the ways men and women mourn*. Routledge.

Fraley, R. C., & Shaver, P. R. (2021). Attachment theory and its place in contemporary personality theory and research. In O. P. John & R. W. Robins (Eds.), *Handbook of personality theory* (4th ed., pp. 642–666). Guilford.

Harris, D. L. (2016). Social expectations of the bereaved. In D. Harris & T. Bordere (Eds.), *Handbook of social justice in loss and grief: Exploring diversity, equity, and inclusion* (pp. 165–176). Routledge.

Harris, D. L. (2020). Non-death loss and grief: Laying the foundation. In D. Harris (Ed.), *Non-death loss and grief: Context and clinical implications* (pp. 7–16). Routledge.

Heckhausen, J., Wrosch, C., & Schulz, R. (2010). A motivational theory of life-span development. *Psychological Review, 117*(1), 32–60.

Janoff-Bulman, R. (1992). *Shattered assumptions: Towards a new psychology of trauma*. Free Press.

Kissane, D. (2014). Family grief. In D. Kissane & F. Parnes (Eds.), *Bereavement care for families* (pp. 3–16). Routledge.

Klass, D., Silverman, P. R., & Nickman, S. (Eds.). (2014). *Continuing bonds: New understandings of grief*. Taylor & Francis.

Kübler-Ross, E. (1969). *On death and dying*. Macmillan.

Lai, C., Luciani, M., Galli, F., Morelli, F., Cappelluti, R., Penco, I., Aceto, P., & Lombardo, L. (2014). Attachment style dimensions can affect prolonged grief risk in caregivers of terminally ill patients with cancer. *American Journal of Hospice and Palliative Medicine, 32*(8), 855–860.

Neimeyer, R. A., Laurie, A., Mehta, T., Hardison, H., & Currier, J. M. (2008). Lessons of loss: Meaning making in bereaved college students. *New Directions for Student Services, 121*(121), 27–39.

Parkes, C. M. (1971). Psycho-social transitions: A field for study. *Social Science and Medicine, 5*(2), 101–115.

Parkes, C. M. (1996). *Bereavement: Stories of grief in adult life*. Routledge.

Parkes, C. M., & Weiss, R. S. (1983). *Recovery from bereavement*. Basic Books.

Schenck, L. K., Eberle, K. M., & Rings, J. A. (2016). Insecure attachment styles and complicated grief severity: Applying what we know to inform future directions. *Omega: Journal of Death and Dying, 73*(3), 231–249.

Simpson, J. A., & Rholes, W. S. (2012). Adult attachment orientations, stress, and romantic relationships. *Advances in Experimental Social Psychology, 45*, 279–322.

Sroufe, L. A., Egeland, B., & Kreutzer, T. (1990). The fate of early experience following developmental change: Longitudinal approaches to individual adaptation in childhood. *Journal of Child Development, 61*(5), 1363–1373.

Stroebe, M., Schut, H., & Stroebe, W. (2005). Attachment in coping with bereavement: A theoretical integration. *Review of General Psychology, 9*(1), 48–66.

Stroebe, M. S. (2002). Paving the way: From early attachment theory to contemporary bereavement research. *Mortality, 7*(2), 127–138.

Stroebe, W., Stroebe, M., & Schut, H. (2003). Does 'grief work' work? *Bereavement Care, 22*(1), 3–5.

Weenolsen, P. (1988). *Transcendence of loss over the life span*. Hemisphere.

Weiss, R. (1975). *Marital separation*. Basic Books.

Wolfelt, A. (2005). *Companioning the bereaved: A soulful guide for counselors and caregivers*. Companion Press.

Worden, W. R. (2018). *Grief counseling and grief therapy* (5th ed.). Springer.

CHAPTER 4

A REVIEW AND SYNTHESIS OF CURRENT RESEARCH IN COMPASSION, LOSS, AND GRIEF

Oindrila Dutta, Paul Victor Patinadan,[1] and Andy H. Y. Ho

INTRODUCTION

Compassion is a watchword within numerous contemporary settings, extending across education, business, policy, civil, and community services. In no other aspect, however, is this humanistic value more enmeshed than in the sphere of healthcare, and more specifically within the context of palliation, grief, and loss. Compassion has been described as a flagship concept, a rallying call, and especially, an attribute to be nurtured when considered in the end-of-life health ecosystem (Jazaieri et al., 2013; Zaman et al., 2018). However, due to a lack of consensus in the definition and a shared understanding, classification of compassion's constituent elements remains nebulous. Issues of inadequacy may manifest for care providers where compassion is transformed into a romanticized, hyper-idealized vocational obligation (Hem & Heggen, 2004). The answers to what compassion (in relation to grief and loss) is made of and how might it be 'done' on a day-to-day basis in a way that facilitates rejuvenation for giver and recipient continue to be debated.

UNDERSTANDING COMPASSION THROUGH GRIEF AND LOSS LITERATURE

This chapter's objective is to comprehensively examine how compassion is defined and featured within the literature on grief and loss via a qualitative scoping review and thematic synthesis. Guided by the Preferred Reporting Items for Systematic Review and Meta-Analyses (PRISMA) framework (Moher et al., 2009), a search was performed in June 2021. The Sample, Phenomenon of Interest, Design, Evaluation, Research type (SPIDER) tool was used to design the strategy because of its efficacy with qualitative methods (Cooke et al., 2012).

SEARCH STRATEGY AND INCLUSION CRITERIA

Five major databases (MEDLINE (PubMed), PsycInfo, ERIC, ProQuest, and Web of Science Core Collection) were searched using the following Boolean search strategy: TI (grie* OR loss OR bereave* OR end-of-life OR pallia* OR mourn* OR death OR dying) AND TI (compassion*). Minor adjustments were made to the string in meeting the requirements of each database. Identified articles were included if: (a) the sample comprised professional or informal caregivers or individuals coping with illness, end of life, and impending death; (b) the phenomenon of interest was compassion as experienced by key stakeholders; (c) the study design involved the use of face-to-face or telephonic verbal interviews or focus groups; and (d) the research was qualitative in nature. Studies were excluded from the search if the sample comprised non-clinical populations, the psycho-socio-emotional

DOI: 10.4324/9781003204121-6

aspects of compassion were not discussed as a central theme in the article, or the article described a quantitative or mixed-methods study, case study, literature review, or commentary regarding published books, articles, and concepts. Only original research journal articles published in English during the period from 1980 to 2021 were included to provide an overview of relevant literature that had been published over the past four decades.

SCREENING PROCESS AND DATA EXTRACTION

In the initial stage of screening, the title and abstracts of all citations obtained through the search strategy were assessed by the first and second authors based on the inclusion criteria. Studies deemed fit by both authors were then carefully evaluated for appropriateness of inclusion via full text review. A study was included if both authors arrived at the same decision independently. In the event of a conflict regarding appropriateness for inclusion, a team meeting was held with the third author, concerns addressed, and a final decision reached. All excluded materials were also checked by a member of the authors' research lab to confirm exclusion. After all screening procedures, 11 articles were retained for data extraction and analysis. Details of the screening process are shown in Figure 4.1.

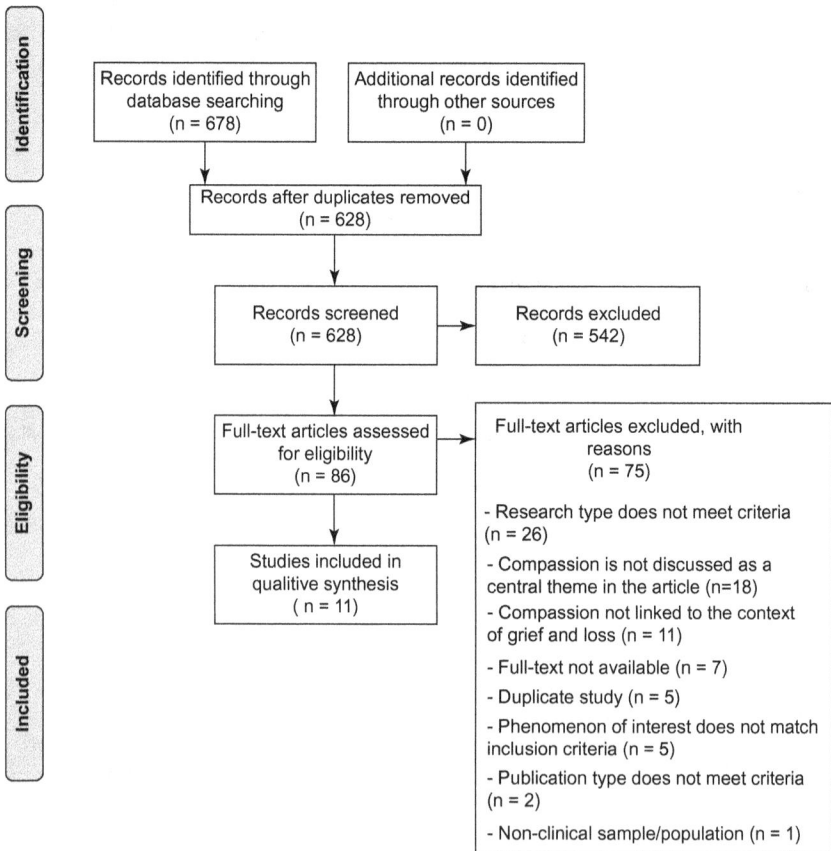

Figure 4.1 PRISMA Flow Diagram of the Screening Process

DATA ANALYSIS

Only first order constructs, quotations from respondents in the primary studies, were treated as data points. This allowed the elicitation of participants' voices in their purest form and eliminated the risk of the primary authors' interpretation of the data from confounding the analysis (Toye et al., 2014). Data was analyzed by employing thematic synthesis (Thomas & Harden, 2008). This involved three stages: (a) line-by-line coding of text to develop descriptive themes which construct new interpretations and explanations of the data; (b) inductive coding to capture the meaning and content of a cluster of similar quotes; and (c) classification of the inductive codes into three analytical categories which capture the delivery and experience of compassion within the context of grief and loss from the perspective of three major stakeholders: Care professionals, informal caregivers, and patients. Periodic coding and debriefing meetings occurred to maximize the credibility, criticality, and authenticity of the data analysis. The coding framework, data interpretation, and confirmation of themes and theme categories were agreed upon by all authors and compared to existing literature to ensure investigator and theory triangulation.

COMPASSION DEFINED VIA THE LENS OF EMPIRICAL RESEARCH

All 11 studies included in this review underwent appraisal using the SPIDER tool (Cooke et al., 2012), which was followed by a meticulous quality assessment (Thomas & Harden, 2008).

SCOPE AND QUALITY ASSESSMENT

The studies included in this review are representative of different regions including Australia (n = 1), Canada (n = 2), Hong Kong (n = 2), New Zealand (n = 1), Norway (n = 2), Spain (n = 1), the United Kingdom (n = 1), and the United States of America (n = 1). Although the literature search spanned the period from 1980 to 2021, the included studies dated back no further than 2012, indicating that interest in qualitatively studying compassion is a contemporary phenomenon. The majority examined experiences of compassion and compassionate care among active and bereaved informal caregivers (n = 6), followed by care professionals (n = 3), both informal caregivers and care professionals (n = 1), and patients (n = 1). Most studies recruited participants through hospitals, nursing homes, and medical centers within the community. Data collection methods included individual interviews as well as focus group discussions, while analytic methods varied across the extracted studies, ranging from thematic to framework analyses and grounded theory. These studies also took several ontological and epistemological stances (where defined), including constructivist, hermeneutic, and phenomenological. Detailed descriptions of the included studies are presented in Table 4.1.

Details of the data extracted from the included studies are shown in Table 4.2. Thematic synthesis of the extracted data revealed (a) *Micro-compassionate Action*, key acts of 'micro'-compassion that can be practiced by care professionals. These initially unassuming and micro acts, which range from having a coffee with a patient or taking precautions to ensure privacy when sharing news, are pivotal in enhancing patients' and informal caregivers'

Table 4.1 Overview of Articles Included in the Scoping Review

Author (Year)	Country Setting	Participant Description	Participants (n)	Research Paradigm (Ontological/ Epistemological Stances)	Research Methods	Language	Analytical Method
Cacciatore et al. (2017)	USA: Within the community: 9 states including a mix of rural and urban areas	Bereaved informal caregivers of children with terminal illness	n = 19 (13 mothers, 4 fathers, 2 grandparents) who talked about the deaths of 16 children	Qualitative descriptive methodology with phenomenological overtones	Open-ended interviews (phone, Skype, face to face)	English	Thematic analysis *not explicitly stated
Crowther et al. (2013)	United Kingdom: Urban, rural, and semi-rural areas of NW and NE England, Wales, and Scotland	Bereaved informal caregivers of persons with dementia	n = 40 (7 husbands, 17 wives, 3 sons, 10 daughters, 2 other family, 1 friend/ neighbor)	Grounded theory and phenomenology	Qualitative in-depth interviews *1 participant wrote about their experience	English	Thematic analysis *not explicitly stated

Study	Setting	Participants	Sample	Framework	Data collection	Language	Analysis
Devik et al. (2020)	Norway: Four community healthcare districts in a municipality	Care professionals, i.e., registered nurses (RNs) with experience in palliative care and terminal illness	n = 10 (5 specialist nurses—geriatric, cancer, or psychiatric nursing, 5 with nursing degrees)	Not defined	Narrative interviews *Secondary analysis of previous dataset	English	Hermeneutic circling based on 4 steps by Flemming et al. (2003)
Gott et al. (2019)	New Zealand: Hospitals	Bereaved informal caregivers of elderly patients	n = 58 (5 spouses, 12 sons/daughters, 1 son-/daughter-in-law, 1 other family, 1 friend/neighbor, 1 other) who talked about the deaths of 52 older adults	Social constructionist framework	Interviews (face-to-face, telephone, FaceTime)	English/Māori	Critical thematic analysis informed by social constructionist and Kaupapa Māori frameworks
Ho et al. (2012)	Hong Kong: Outpatient palliative care of a hospital	Active informal caregivers of terminally ill cancer patients	n=15 (12 daughters, 3 sons)	Grounded Theory approach	Meaning-oriented interview	Chinese (to reconfirm)	Qualitative Content Analysis

(Continued)

Table 4.1 Continued

Author (Year)	Country Setting	Participant Description	Participants (n)	Research Paradigm (Ontological/ Epistemological Stances)	Research Methods	Language	Analytical Method
Ho et al. (2015)	Hong Kong: Nursing home	Informal caregivers and care professionals involved in the EOL Integrated Care Pathway	n = 30 (9 medical professionals, 9 management administrators, 6 nursing home staff, 6 primary family caregivers of elderly nursing home residents)	Interpretive-systemic framework	Focus group discussions	Chinese (translated to English)	Framework analysis
Marsh et al. (2019)	Australia: Rural community in Tasmania	Active and bereaved informal caregivers of terminally ill patients	n = 19	Participatory research principles	Semi-structured, in-depth interviews (face-to-face, telephone)	English	Thematic analysis
Ortega-Galen et al. (2019)	Spain: 5 provinces of Spain	Bereaved informal caregivers who had lost a family member <2 months >2 years	n = 81 (19 spouses, 44 children, 3 parents, 15 others)	Hermeneutic phenomenology based on Van Manen (2003)	In-depth interview (41) and group discussions (5 with 40 participants)	Not specified	Protocol developed by Giorgi (1997)

Roze des Ordons et al. (2019)	Canada: 4 ICUs and 3 palliative care sites	Care professionals, i.e., clinicians working in intensive care units and palliative care services	n = 5 (1 nurse clinician, 1 nurse practitioner, 3 physicians)	Inductive inquiry/ activity theory/ realist inquiry/ phenomenology/ autoethnography	Participant field notes, focus groups (3), individual interview (2)	English	Constructivist grounded theory
Sinclair et al. (2017)	Canada: Urban hospital	Patients with terminal cancer diagnosis	n = 53	Grounded theory approach	Semi-structured interview	English	Straussian grounded theory
Tarberg et al. (2020)	Norway: Primary care, nursing homes in urban and rural settings	Professional caregivers, i.e., RNs with experience in palliative care	n = 21 (7 homecare exp only, 9 community institution exp only, exp in both)	Hermeneutic approach	Focus group discussion	Norwegian	Hermeneutic circle

Table 4.2 Extracted Data from the Included Studies

Author (Year)	Summary of Themes	Context of Grief/Loss	Study Employed Definition of Compassion (if any)	Compassionate Insight
Cacciatore et al. (2017)	1) Warmth/engagement of HCP versus objectification/detachment 2) Honesty and disclosure from HCP versus withholding and misrepresentation 3) Egalitarian rapport with HCP versus paternalism/coercion 4) Flexibility and individualized attention from HCP versus inflexibility and rule-bound uniformity 5) Maintaining contact and trust with HCP versus isolation/mistrust 6) Perceived competence of HCP (efficiency, promptness, and familiarity with care needs) versus incompetence	Terminal illness and death of children or grandchildren	Not defined.	Compassion described in terms of communication regarding bad news, noting sensitivity and empathy. Compassion was also mindful care, challenging institutional constraints, and showcasing integrity (owning decisions, mistakes, or uncertainty).
Crowther et al. (2013)	1) Compassion, kindness, and humanity from care professionals existed along a continuum across care settings ranging from compassionate care to poor-quality care due to practical challenges 2) Compassion, kindness, and humanity from strangers who were willing to help in times of need—both at the time of caregiving and after the death of the patient	Dementia caregiving and death of family member	The ability to understand the emotional state of another person, i.e., "putting oneself in another's shoes"; feeling that urges a person to do something to alleviate or reduce the suffering of another; having compassion leads a person to show kindness.	Formal carers and others did not need in-depth knowledge of a disease and trajectory to incorporate acts of kindness and care with compassion. Compassion is paramount in the funeral industry. Target-driven care is a necessity but cannot be at the expense of compassion.

(Continued)

Study		Context	Definition	Findings
Devik et al. (2020)	Nurses' experiences of compassion in delivering home-based palliative care were illuminated by one overarching theme: valuing caring interactions as positive (+), negative (–), or neutral (=), which entailed three themes: 1) Perceiving the patient's plea [patient needs me (+), patient is demanding (–), patient does not plead (=)] 2) Interpreting feelings [feeling amazed and curious (+), feeling disappointed and repelled (–), feeling balanced (=)] 3) Reasoning about accountability and action [patient is my responsibility (+), patient is our responsibility (–), patient is system's responsibility (=)]	Caregiving for patients with serious illness and palliative needs	Compassion as characterized by two main components: the affective feeling of caring for one who is suffering and the motivation to relieve that suffering. As a modality, compassion is intentional and targeted but coincidental because it involves action and choice.	Nurses' vulnerability may activate a self-defense that counteracts compassion (unless patient vulnerability exceeds their own). Findings observe categories of compassion "deserving" (modest, trusting, pose no conditions on care) and "undeserving" (assertive, suspicious, etc.) patient groups, with deserving patients awakening compassion readily and easily in nurses. Neutral care interactions saw lack of compassion as normalized (time pressure, low patient expectations). Compassion is inactive until under the presence of a will.
Gott et al. (2019)	1) A relationship based on empathy: He ngākau aroha—relationships that express care, kind-heartedness, benevolence, consideration for others, compassion, and empathy 2) Effective interactions between participants over time and across settings: Whakawhanaungatanga—establishing good relationships and nurturing ongoing connections by relating well to others 3) Contextualized knowledge of patient and family: Te tuakiri o ngā tangata Māori—adaptation of practice to the person's views on the world (Te Ao Māori), beliefs, spirituality, personality, and other important qualities of self and of others 4) Staff, patients, and families being active participants in their care: Manaakitanga—a reciprocal process for sharing and caring for one another and showing mutual respect	Death of elderly family member	Dewar and Nolan's (2013) definition of compassion—an awareness of another's feelings, an appreciation of how they are affected by their experiences and interacting with them in a meaningful way.	Western models can be adapted to include the worldview of other cultures. Māori conceptualization of compassion includes foregrounding of actions to achieve a compassionate outcome. In explicitly framing compassion as a verb, the onus is placed on these actions, rather than the emotion itself.

Table 4.2 Continued

Author (Year)	Summary of Themes	Context of Grief/Loss	Study Employed Definition of Compassion (if any)	Compassionate Insight
Ho et al. (2012)	1) Reciprocal relationships: Being able to discuss and share caregiving needs and concerns between dying parents and adult children 2) Mutual support: Garner support from their dying parents and other family members in caregiving 3) Compassionate duty: Need to understand the pain and suffering of their dying parents so as to care for them wholeheartedly with love and compassion 4) Emotional connections: Desire for emotional connection with their dying parents 5) Appreciation and forgiveness: Desired to ask for forgiveness and achieve reconciliation with their dying parents	Caregiving for dying parents	Not defined.	Compassion informs contemporary filial caregiving, where a true understanding of pain and suffering of mortality fuels care and devotion for parents.
Ho et al. (2015)	1) Regulatory empowerment • Interdisciplinary teamwork • Resource allocation • Knowledge Cultivation • Collaborative policymaking 2) Family-centered care • Continuity of care • Family conference • Care partnership 3) Collective compassion • Devotion in care • Empathic understanding • Compassionate action	Caregiving for elderly nursing home residents	Not defined.	Compassion is a critical thread woven through the many layers of systemic boundaries, mobilizing all stakeholders through a collective consciousness of shared meaning, compelling them to work tirelessly to alleviate the suffering of the dying and the bereaved. Compassion can enhance clinicians' levels of energy and effectiveness in working with dying patients.

Marsh et al. (2019)	Compassion is expressed in relational and innovative ways during EOL caring in a rural community. Challenges experienced: Transport into the city for treatment, and access to basic and specialized services. Positive aspects of formal and informal palliative care: Personable, expert, flexible, and innovative caregiving	Life-limiting illness or death of family member	A human and tender response to the distress and suffering of others; key component of HPPC as well as an ethical imperative which drives much of EOL care; a virtuous response that seeks to address the suffering and need of a person through relational understanding and action.	Compassionate caregiving (formal and informal) went beyond what was required. Compassion in rural areas was expressed by chopping wood, cooking meals, filling the freezer with food, or providing transport. Other more innovative ways expounded on cohesion and togetherness. These were creative individually tailored compassionate expressions such as moving a dying man's bed into the living room so he could feel part of the family. Compassion was also demonstrated even though a relationship was violent or dysfunctional.
Ortega-Galán et al. (2019)	1) Technical competence: Control of symptoms and continuity of care 2) Compassion: Effective/affective communication, attitudes of kindness and closeness toward the patient and the family, and generosity and personalized flexibility of care	EOL caregiving and death of a loved one	Sense of caring, sensitivity, and openness to one's own suffering and towards others, and the genuine intention to try and prevent it; includes elements such as kindness, empathy, generosity, and acceptance; the ability to open oneself to the reality of suffering and aspire to its healing.	Communication and the reception of attention, affection, and encouragement by professionals were important. Closeness, commitment, flexibility, understanding, listening, and presence humanize and dignify the dying process. Professionals must synthesize their own reflections and care toward the dying.

(Continued)

Table 4.2 Continued

Author (Year)	Summary of Themes	Context of Grief/Loss	Study Employed Definition of Compassion (if any)	Compassionate Insight
Roze des Ordons et al. (2019)	Compassion was conceptualized, observed, or expressed in different ways, depending on context and the observer's perspective. 1) Relational—acts, experiences of compassion toward patients and staff; connection; a kind caring attitude; integrative in nature and facilitated through self-awareness and reflection 2) Dispositional—a feeling that emerged between people; a way of being; requiring honesty by expressing vulnerability and acceptance without judgment without attempting to placate suffering 3) Activity-related—expressed through action; is a developable skill; is also an art and can be learned from abstraction 4) Situational—emergent through interaction and recursive presence over time	Dying and loss in the palliative setting	Multiple definitions: A virtuous response that seeks to address suffering and facilitate healing through relational understanding and action; caring, shared understanding or empathy, and a way of alleviating both emotional and physical distress.	Expressions of compassion were responsive to emerging needs and circumstances, including clinical, social, cultural, procedural, and institutional. They were reflected both in the states of mind of those involved, and in their actions, and included both practical skills and the intuitive expression and application of those skills within a given interaction. Expressions of compassion required being present to others' experiences, connectedness, honesty, and accepting of them. Compassion does not yield well to taxonomic definitions.
Sinclair et al. (2017)	Although the constructs of sympathy, empathy, and compassion are used interchangeably in healthcare literature, patients distinguish and experience them uniquely Sympathy: Unwanted, pity-based response to a distressing situation, characterized by a lack of understanding and self-preservation of the observer Empathy: Affective response that acknowledges and attempts to understand an individual's suffering through emotional resonance Compassion: Enhances the key facets of empathy while adding distinct features of being motivated by love, the altruistic role of the responder, action, and small, supererogatory acts of kindness	Terminal cancer diagnosis with a life expectancy of maximum 6 months	Awareness of the suffering of another coupled with the wish to relieve it; virtuous response that seeks to address the suffering and needs of a person through relational understanding and action (emergent from study).	Compassion is better for patients and healthcare teams, and there should be a reconceptualization of compassion fatigue into "empathic distress."

		Caregiving for patients with palliative needs	Awareness of or sensitivity to the pain or suffering of others that results in taking verbal, nonverbal, or physical action to remove, reduce, or alleviate the impact of such affliction.	Compassionate care is contextual. In the first phase, information and dialogue with patients and family caregivers are crucial. In the second phase, creating a space for the dying is important. In the third phase, family caregivers' acceptance of the patients' death is important.

Tarberg et al. (2020)	1) Information and dialogue
	  • Early involvement of primary care nurses
	  • Advance care planning
	  • Family caregivers as a part of the team
	2) Creating a space for dying
	  • Trust
	  • Balance conflict of interest
	  • Emotional reciprocity
	3) Family caregivers' acceptance of death
	  • Common understanding of the treatment
	  • Routine of bereavement counseling after death
	  • Communication about the process of dying			

experience of illness and care. The analysis also highlighted (b) *Discernable Humanity*, perceptions of micro-compassionate care emphasizing relational naturality which informal caregivers believe augmented the professional care experience for themselves or their ill loved ones. Furthermore, several patient-related factors emerged from the data that could result in (c) *Patient Connectedness* or (d) *Patient Dissension* with care professionals, thereby transforming the care teams' actions and decisions for micro-compassionate actions. Finally, (e) *Institutional Compassion Facilitators* and (f) *Institutional Compassion Deterrents* were identified, which impact the extent to which acts of micro-compassion can be exhibited by care providers. The themes were integrated into the Relational Model of Micro-ompassionate Agency, highlighting the attributional actions of compassion as witnessed by practitioners, patients, and family, and how the system they are embedded in influences them. These themes of the model are elaborated in greater detail below.

THEME 1: MICRO-COMPASSIONATE ACTION

Simple compassionate acts performed by care professionals communicate to patients that they can step into their shoes, see things from their perspective, understand what is meaningful and purposeful in their lives, and engage in actions that support personhood. Micro-compassionate action involves deep empathy as well as compassionate listening and presence in supporting patients and their families at the end of life.

> It is about entering the worlds of our patients and the family that we care for, seeing things from their perspectives … and somehow I begin to see myself, and understand how I want to be treated when I reach the end of my life.
>
> *(Ho et al., 2016)*

Compassion, according to care professionals, was defined as the ability to be:

> present to people. Being present to their suffering. It (compassion) is embedded in just the way we are with them … what is important and meaningful and purposeful in their lives. What their experiences have been.
>
> *(Roze des Ordons et al., 2019)*

Care professionals explained that compassion could be expressed through uncomplicated acts such as leaving a note letting the person know that they are being thought of (Roze des Ordons et al., 2019) or bringing food the patient wishes to eat but which the kitchen is unable to provide (Ho et al., 2016). The key element of this micro-compassionate act was to illustrate that care professionals were actively and attentively listening to patients as they performed their duties.

> There was a mother with small children who said she hoped to recover. The nurse then replied, "yes, I hope so too; but we must have an alternate plan." This way of responding to the patient illustrates that the nurse is listening to the patient in a way that conveys both hope and realism.
>
> *(Tarberg et al., 2020)*

THEME 2: DISCERNABLE HUMANITY

This refers to informal caregivers' views about acts of micro-compassion through which care professionals demonstrate their humanity and commitment to reducing the suffering of patients and families. Informal caregivers explained that it was the *little acts of kindness* that made a meaningful difference.

> I bought my husband new jogging bottoms and a top … the nurse didn't put it on until just before he was going to see the oncologist … so he wouldn't make a mess of it … I just thought … they are so busy there … little acts of kindness like that are very important, aren't they?
>
> *(Crowther et al., 2013)*

Informal caregivers highlighted that alternative compassion expression was through truthful and open sharing of information, without using medical jargon or incomprehensible terminology.

> He (doctor) did not say, "He won't die…" He said, "Childhood cancer is highly treatable … I'm going to do everything in my power to make sure you get the best of care … We'll try to treat the symptoms the best we can." By saying it gently like that … it was so much easier on us.
>
> *(Cacciatore et al., 2019)*

Finally, informal caregivers shared that they valued the ability of care professionals to put themselves in their position and demonstrate that their wishes and well-being mattered. Compassionate care professionals were observed to ensure this in a sensitive and respectful manner.

> The doctor took me for a cup of tea, and he said, "is there anyone you want to call because your father's not going to make it?" I said, "oh my son and daughter", and he said, "he won't get here in time" and that was when we realized that it was really serious.
>
> *(Gott et al., 2019)*

THEME 3: PATIENT CONNECTEDNESS

This refers to the internal dialogue that is elicited in care professionals during the process of providing compassionate care to patients. This dialogue exists as negotiations between patient expression and the care professional's own feelings toward the patient, with the outcome determining the extent to which caregiving interactions are interpreted as positive. This encourages the proliferation of micro-compassionate actions.

> It is easier to feel good about patients the less they request for themselves … Patients who do not ask for more than your presence … It is easier to give, then.
>
> *(Devik et al., 2020)*

Similarly, interactions with patients also elicited an inner negotiation in informal caregivers which determined the degree to which caregiving was interpreted as a positive experience.

> I would not be able to take care of her (mother) at home. I had a great deal of regret because I knew that she didn't want to live in a nursing home, but she told me that it was fine and I was already doing the best that I could … I felt somewhat relieved knowing that she understood my situation and that I wasn't abandoning her.
>
> *(Chan et al., 2012)*

THEME 4: PATIENT DISSENSION

This refers to unreasonable expectations of care that some patients have, or their open expression of mistrust or dissatisfaction with regards to the care received. Such 'demanding' patients were often negatively perceived by care professionals.

Some just have this mentality: "I am entitled to it" – or "Society owes me this". I really dislike this attitude.

(Devik et al., 2020)

Care professionals explained that they found it challenging to go the extra mile for such patients and their caregiving would usually be standardized and brief.

One day he (patient) could be pleasant and nice, but the other day he was angry and called me names ... I just delivered his medicines and took the blood samples as ordered. I didn't have to go there every day ... Some of the days he was on my colleague's list.

(Devik et al., 2020)

THEME 5: INSTITUTIONAL COMPASSION FACILITATORS

This theme refers to systemic processes that promote and assist the provision of micro-compassionate care to patients. Care professionals suggested that when the institution had standard operating procedures that were mindful of patients' needs and well-being during the most vulnerable moments of their lives, such care could routinely and seamlessly be provided.

When a patient is reaching the end-of-life, we try our best to provide them with a single room with a consistent personal care team so that they can be with their family in a private and familiar context to say their final goodbyes and farewells.

(Ho et al., 2016)

The same sentiment was echoed by informal caregivers from a very different context:

Everything my father needed he had ... everything worked very well, equipment, medicines ... I think that he died with the satisfaction of being cared for.

(Ortega-Galán et al., 2019)

THEME 6: INSTITUTIONAL COMPASSION DETERRENTS

This theme refers to systemic processes that obstruct the delivery of micro-compassionate action toward patients. When care professionals were compelled to check on multiple patients within a short timeframe, it adversely impacted their ability to be compassionately present with each and tune in to their unique suffering and needs.

It has to do with the setting and the timing. In order to manage a long list of patients you can't ask everybody how they really are ... We have to take care of the tasks that are expected from us.

(Devik et al., 2020)

Participants also explained that to be compassionately present with the patient, care professionals needed to journey with the patient over time, which was difficult because of the setup of hospitals and the division of care between departments.

The manner of some doctors – they're coming in, they've got a clipboard and they've got a million patients to see in one time and they're busy and it's not as if they've spent the day before with [Sam], they don't know me, whereas the nurses did, and we got to know them really well.

(Gott et al., 2019)

DISCUSSION

This chapter situates the humanistic value of compassion and its expression within the context of grief and loss through a rigorous, comprehensive review spanning existing literature over the past four decades. Data analysis revealed that several aspects of compassion were common across the extracted studies; these themes were consolidated into the Relational Model of Micro-Compassionate Agency (see Figure 4.2). Through the themes, the model considers compassionate actions within the grief and loss ecosystem, detailing what care professionals define such acts to be, what strikes family members as memorable, how patients can encourage or discourage such behaviors, and what institutions can do to help or hinder such practice.

The 11 extracted studies highlighted compassion as defined by small actions that breathed great significance. These acts of 'micro-compassion' were seen and held in a position of reverence for both recipients and providers of compassion. Sinclair et al. (2017), for example, found "small supererogatory acts of kindness" to be a cornerstone in the care relationship between patients and professionals. These subtle acts allowed for the nature and intentions of providers to become salient and appreciated (Sinclair et al., 2017). Similarly, Crowther (2013) found that 'small things' were often most meaningful. Likewise, Gott et al.'s (2019) theme of *He ngākau aroha* embedded within the Māori bi-cultural model showcased how a cup of tea held great significance given the context of impending death. The international findings also reflect how micro-compassionate actions bisect cultures, extolling the agentic phenomenon of common humanity within care settings. Though these acts are miniscule behaviors, encouraging them requires knowledge and navigation of interpersonal factors, learning that can be supported by systems of care that professionals are embedded in. Micro-compassionate actions are the outward expression of inner values that contribute to an understanding of and connection to human suffering; such values are core competencies of the healthcare profession that can be successfully taught (Halldorsdottir, 2012; Watson, 2007). Institutions can benefit from promoting this form of training, as with sustained practice and engagement, care professionals' compassionate competence can become intrinsic behaviors, in turn generating environments of respect, sensitivity, and human connectedness, complete with its myriad benefits.

IMPLICATIONS

Implications of the findings and model are manifold. Understanding compassionate action manifest through modest effort not requiring grandiose care endeavors promotes integration of the value into key encounters. Through micro-compassionate action, patients and families feel cared for, respected, and heard, with care providers allaying personal feelings of burnout by not overextending their socio-emotional capacities. These actions can also draw from the cultural nuances of the system they are embedded in, with gestures focusing on what is unique to the patients and families. As such, the Relational Model of Micro-Compassionate Agency can provide a foundational impetus for training healthcare providers for the sensitive incorporation of compassion in their work. The training of humanistic values for health providers has seen success across various methodologies. A systematic review found that compassion-directed curricula increased patient perceptions of physician compassion/empathy, aiding in posture and

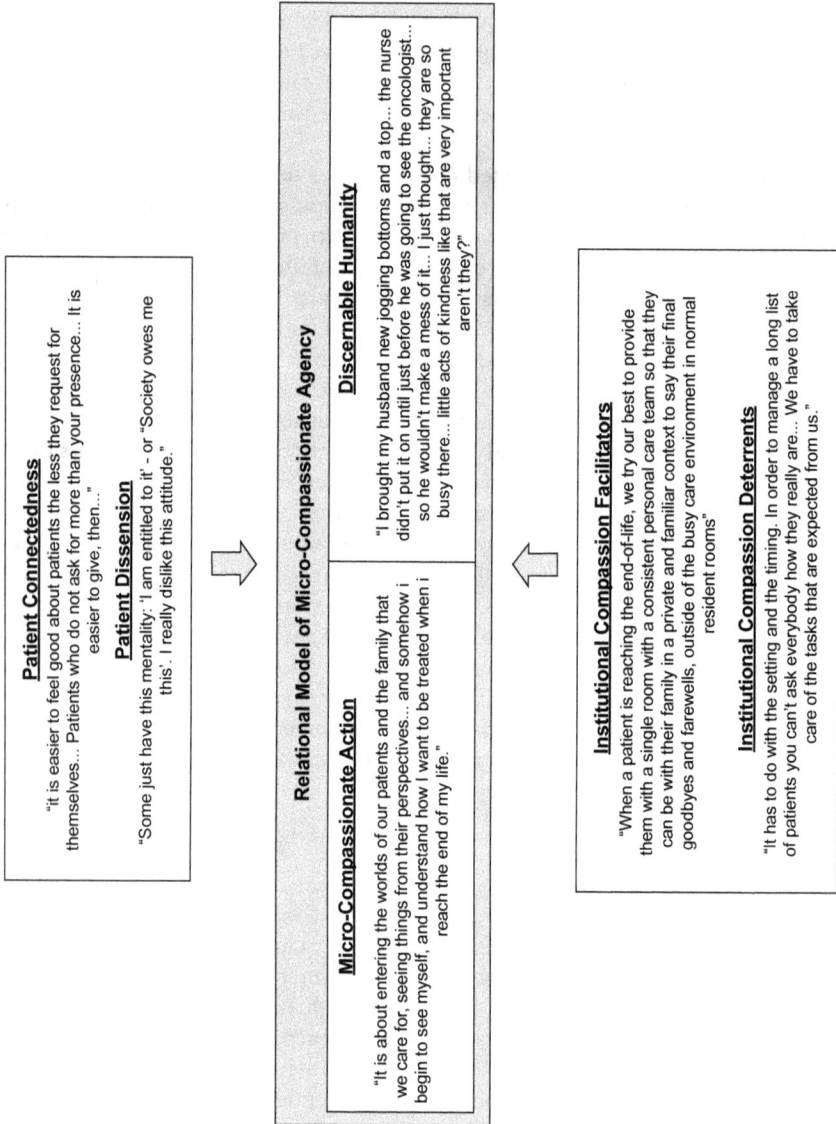

Relational Model of Micro-Compassionate Agency

Patient Connectedness

"it is easier to feel good about patients the less they request for themselves... Patients who do not ask for more than your presence... It is easier to give, then..."

Patient Dissension

"Some just have this mentality: 'I am entitled to it' - or "Society owes me this'. I really dislike this attitude."

Discernable Humanity

"I brought my husband new jogging bottoms and a top.... the nurse didn't put it on until just before he was going to see the oncologist... so he wouldn't make a mess of it... I just thought... they are so busy there... little acts of kindness like that are very important aren't they?"

Micro-Compassionate Action

"It is about entering the worlds of our patients and the family that we care for, seeing things from their perspectives... and somehow i begin to see myself, and understand how I want to be treated when i reach the end of my life."

Institutional Compassion Facilitators

"When a patient is reaching the end-of-life, we try our best to provide them with a single room with a consistent personal care team so that they can be with their family in a private and familiar context to say their final goodbyes and farewells, outside of the busy care environment in normal resident rooms"

Institutional Compassion Deterrents

"It has to do with the setting and the timing. In order to manage a long list of patients you can't ask everybody how they really are... We have to take care of the tasks that are expected from us."

Figure 4.2 Relational Model of Micro-Compassionate Agency

body language, non-verbal cue detection for emotions, identifying and using opportunities for compassion, and non-verbal/verbal validation (Patel et al., 2019). More recently, a video-based training for healthcare professionals focusing on scenarios of common humanity saw increased connection, concern, and compassion for patients (Ling et al., 2021). Focus on shared human or cultural experiences can provide a scaffold for the more nuanced development of compassion-based training. Patinadan et al. (2021a) observed that food remained an integral part of Singaporeans' personal and national identity, even up to the end of life. The authors introduced the Food for Life and Palliation (FLiP) model, which delineated the various aspects of food experiences present for terminally ill individuals and their families. This model was employed as a reference in the teaching of humanistic values and the provision of dignified care to junior nurses via a novel, half-day virtual applied-drama workshop (Patinadan et al., 2021b). Participants, through facilitated discourse and dramatic methods, learned to incorporate innocuous food-based dialogue into patient interactions. Findings observed a pre-post increase in empathy as well as compassionate competence, the active practice of compassion. Similarly, the current model may be extended into relevant training pedagogies that provide culturally sensitive information and training on how micro-compassionate acts can be practiced within institutional settings. Reflective journaling, mindful-meditation practice, and other reflexive practices may also be modularized into such training for everyday utilization. Ensuring pedagogy that leverages on instilling compassion can lead to micro-compassionate practice becoming second-nature for care professionals.

LIMITATIONS AND FUTURE DIRECTIONS

Although the authors practiced a structured search/screening strategy, working through a large number (n = 678) of articles, a chance remains that key studies were overlooked. Moreover, in order to direct methods to focus on compassion, the strategy did not include ancillary terms such as 'empathy,' 'kindness,' and 'humanity,' though these prosocial terminologies began to surface as paralleling components as the search narrowed. Additionally, only studies published in English were included, which may limit generalizability. With regard to the developed model, attributional studies focusing on qualitative inquiry that directly consider micro-compassion can be conducted for the development of future, more sensitive iterations.

This chapter provided an empirical observation on the nature of compassion within the context of grief and loss in care settings. As the term gains interest in healthcare with its value as an expected trait and obligatory actionable care interactions, holistic understanding and facilitation of compassion are imperative for patients, families, and the care team. Through this shared humanity that is best expressed through simple, micro-compassionate gestures, the pain and suffering of grief and loss can be soothed, and the illness journey made more bearable.

ACKNOWLEDGMENTS

The authors are deeply grateful to Shaik Muhammad Amin and all our wonderful friends and colleagues at ARCH Lab at Nanyang Technological University, Singapore, for supporting us in our research endeavors.

NOTE

1 Oindrila Dutta and Paul Patinadan share first authorship for this chapter.

REFERENCES

Cacciatore, J., Thieleman, K., Lieber, A. S., Blood, C., & Goldman, R. (2019). The long road to farewell: The needs of families with dying children. *Omega*, *78*(4), 404–420. https://doi.org /10.1177/0030222817697418

Chan, C. L. W., Ho, A. H. Y., Leung, P. P. Y., Chochinov, H. M., Neimeyer, R. A., Pang, S. M. C., & Tse, D. M. W. (2012). The blessings and the curses of filial piety on dignity at the end of life: Lived experience of Hong Kong Chinese adult children caregivers. *Journal of Ethnic and Cultural Diversity in Social Work*, *21*(4), 277–296. https://doi.org/10.1080/15313204.2012.729177

Cooke, A., Smith, D., & Booth, A. (2012). Beyond PICO. *Qualitative Health Research*, *22*(10), 1435–1443. https://doi.org/10.1177/1049732312452938

Crowther, J., Wilson, K. C. M., Horton, S., & Lloyd-Williams, M. (2013). Compassion in healthcare – Lessons from a qualitative study of the end of life care of people with dementia. *Journal of the Royal Society of Medicine*, *106*(12), 492–497. https://doi.org/10.1177 /0141076813503593

Devik, S. A., Enmarker, I., & Hellzen, O. (2020). Nurses' experiences of compassion when giving palliative care at home. *Nursing Ethics*, *27*(1), 194–205. https://doi.org/10.1177 /0969733019839218

Giorgi, A. (1997). The theory, practice, and evaluation of the phenomenological method as a qualitative research procedure. *Journal of Phenomenological Psychology*, *28*(2), 235–260.

Gott, M., Robinson, J., Moeke-Maxwell, T., Black, S., Williams, L., Wharemate, R., & Wiles, J. (2019). "It was peaceful, it was beautiful": A qualitative study of family understandings of good end-of-life care in hospital for people dying in advanced age. *Palliative Medicine*, *33*(7), 793–801. https://doi.org/10.1177/0269216319843026

Halldorsdottir, S. (2012). Nursing as compassionate competence: A theory on professional nursing care based on the patient's perspective. *International Journal for Human Caring*, *16*(2), 7–19. https://doi.org/10.20467/1091-5710.16.2.7

Hem, M. H., & Heggen, K. (2004). Is compassion essential to nursing practice? *Contemporary Nurse*, *17*(1–2), 19–31. https://doi.org/10.5172/conu.17.1-2.19

Ho, A. H. Y., Luk, J. K. H., Chan, F. H. W., Chun Ng, W., Kwok, C. K. K., Yuen, J. H. L., Tam, M. Y. J., Kan, W. W. S., & Chan, C. L. W. (2016). Dignified palliative long-term care: An interpretive systemic framework of end-of-life integrated care pathway for terminally ill Chinese older adults. *American Journal of Hospice and Palliative Care*, *33*(5), 439–447. https://doi .org/10.1177/1049909114565789

Jazaieri, H., Jinpa, G. T., McGonigal, K., Rosenberg, E. L., Finkelstein, J., Simon-Thomas, E., Cullen, M., Doty, J. R., Gross, J. J., & Goldin, P. R. (2013). Enhancing compassion: A randomized controlled trial of a compassion cultivation training program. *Journal of Happiness Studies*, *14*(4), 1113–1126. https://doi.org/10.1007/s10902-012-9373-z

Ling, D., Petrakis, M., & Olver, J. H. (2021). The use of common humanity scenarios to promote compassion in healthcare workers. *Australian Social Work*, *74*(1), 110–121. https://doi.org/10 .1080/0312407X.2020.1808031

Marsh, P., Thompson, S., & Mond, J. (2019). Living, loving, dying: Insights into rural compassion. *Australian Journal of Rural Health*, *27*(4), 328–335.

Moher, D., Liberati, A., Tetzlaff, J., Altman, D. G., & PRISMA Group. (2009). Preferred reporting items for systematic reviews and meta-analyses: The PRISMA statement. *PLOS Medicine*, *6*(7), e1000097.

9999999999999

Ortega-Galán, Á. M., Ruiz-Fernández, M. D., Carmona-Rega, M. I., Cabrera-Troya, J., Ortíz-Amo, R., & Ibáñez-Masero, O. (2019). Competence and compassion: Key elements of professional care at the end of life from caregiver's perspective. *American Journal of Hospice and Palliative Care, 36*(6), 485–491. https://doi.org/10.1177/1049909118816662

Patel, S., Pelletier-Bui, A., Smith, S., Roberts, M. B., Kilgannon, H., Trzeciak, S., & Roberts, B. W. (2019). Curricula for empathy and compassion training in medical education: A systematic review. *PLOS ONE, 14*(8), e0221412. https://doi.org/10.1371/journal.pone.0221412

Patinadan, P. V., Tan-Ho, G., Choo, P. Y., & Ho, A. H. Y. (2021b). "I Am not eating this!" Understanding identity, psycho-socio-cultural meaning and dignity expressed in patient food voices: An applied drama intervention for student nurses. Presented at the *Singapore Drama Educators Association Theatre Arts Conference 2021 – Creative Disruption: Exploring New Ground. Singapore.* 22–30 May 2021 (Conference Paper) *Today.*

Patinadan, P. V., Tan-Ho, G., Choo, P. Y., Low, C. X., & Ho, A. H. Y. (2021a). "Food for life and palliation (FLiP)": A qualitative study for understanding and empowering dignity and identity for terminally ill patients in Asia. *BMJ Open, 11*(4), e038914. https://doi.org/10.1136/bmjopen-2020-038914

Roze des Ordons, A. L., MacIsaac, L., Everson, J., Hui, J., & Ellaway, R. H. (2019). A pattern language of compassion in intensive care and palliative care contexts. *BMC Palliative Care, 18*(1), 15. https://doi.org/10.1186/s12904-019-0402-0

Sinclair, S., Beamer, K., Hack, T. F., McClement, S., Raffin Bouchal, S., Chochinov, H. M., & Hagen, N. A. (2017). Sympathy, empathy, and compassion: A grounded theory study of palliative care patients' understandings, experiences, and preferences. *Palliative Medicine, 31*(5), 437–447. https://doi.org/10.1177/0269216316663499

Tarberg, A. S., Landstad, B. J., Hole, T., Thronæs, M., & Kvangarsnes, M. (2020). Nurses' experiences of compassionate care in the palliative pathway. *Journal of Clinical Nursing, 29*(23–24), 4818–4826. https://doi.org/10.1111/jocn.15528

Thomas, J. D., & Harden, A. D. (2008). Methods for the thematic synthesis of qualitative research in systematic reviews. *BMC Medical Research Methodology, 8*(45), 1–10. https://doi.org/10.1186/1471-2288-8-45

Toye, F., Seers, K., Allcock, N., Briggs, M., Carr, E., & Barker, K. (2014). Meta-ethnography 25 years on: Challenges and insights for synthesizing a large number of qualitative studies. *BMC Medical Research Methodology, 14*, 80. https://doi.org/10.1186/1471-2288-14-80

Van Manen, M. (2003). *Educational research and lived experience: Human science for a pedagogy of action and sensitivity.* Barcelona, Spain: Idea Books.

Watson, J. (2007). Watson's theory of human caring and subjective living experiences: Carative factors/caritas processes as a disciplinary guide to the professional nursing practice. *Texto & E Contexto Enfermagem, 16*(1), 129–135. https://doi.org/10.1590/s0104-07072007000100016

Zaman, S., Whitelaw, A., Richards, N., Inbadas, H., & Clark, D. (2018). A moment for compassion: Emerging rhetorics in end-of-life care. *Medical Humanities, 44*(2), 140–143. https://doi.org/10.1080/medhum-2017-011329

CHAPTER 5

COMPASSION VIEWED THROUGH A SOCIOLOGICAL LENS

Neil Thompson and Gerry R. Cox

INTRODUCTION

Sociology as an academic discipline helps make sense of how people are able to manage the incredible power of social structures, processes, institutions, discourses, expectations, and relations that they cannot see; how we are able to develop meaning in our lives in the face of massive social differences that we encounter; and how we are able to find our place in society as positive contributors to the well-being of others (or as people who make life more difficult for others). As humans we give and take; whether it be taking through actions involving stealing, robbing, selling drugs, murder, or scams, or giving, such as through charitable contributions, helping homeless people, showing kindness to strangers, and caring about starvation in other countries. Humans can be cruel or kind.

Sociology gives us a basis for understanding the many cultures and societies that make up our world; to better understand the differences of the people of Zimbabwe, Japan, Chile, or Wales while also recognizing how similar they all really are; and to better understand why some are so violent, taking and using others, while some people are so giving, sharing, and concerned about the well-being of others. Traditionally, such matters have been addressed from a psychological point of view, with a focus on the inner workings of the mind. Sociology counterbalances this by considering the wider social context and its role in promoting (or preventing) compassion.

In this chapter we therefore consider what applying a "sociological lens" tells us about compassion and the role it plays in society and how social forces play a part in promoting and obstructing compassion.

THE SOCIOLOGICAL IMAGINATION

The concept of the sociological imagination (Mills, 1959) is at the heart of the sociological enterprise. Focusing narrowly on the individual level ("atomism," as it is technically known) presents us with a distorted picture, as it fails to take account of the fact that:

> everything we say, do, think and feel happens in a social context. It is as if the social milieu becomes invisible to us and we see the individual(s), but not the other side of the coin, the social factors that are such a significant set of influences and constraints on such individuals.
>
> *(Thompson, 2018a, p. 25)*

If we move beyond atomism and make use of the sociological imagination, what do we see? That is what we shall focus on here. We begin by looking at the important role of socialization, the process by which people internalize social mores, norms, values, and expectations, initially as part of their upbringing.

DOI: 10.4324/9781003204121-7

SOCIALIZATION

An atomistic focus largely obscures the powerful influences and constraints that contribute so strongly to our experience, our outlook, and even our identity. This social dimension will apply also to compassion, in the sense that its prevalence or otherwise will owe much to the wider social values that are passed from generation to generation through socialization. For example, a society that values competitiveness, emotional toughness, and rugged individualism is likely to produce a different approach to—or even understanding of—compassion than, say, a society that values a strong sense of community, emotional intelligence, altruism, and shared endeavor.

This is not a simple deterministic process whereby social values create personal values. The reality is much more complex than that, but it remains the case that the wider social values are highly significant and influential. To develop an adequate understanding of compassion we therefore need to ensure that wider social values are taken into consideration. For example, Ricard (2015) makes the important point that the materialist values of consumerism lead to extreme self-centeredness and a lack of empathy.

Part of this will be the media and their role in promoting certain worldviews and obscuring others. This includes the traditional media and now social media, with the latter sadly incorporating the modern phenomenon of "trolling," which in some ways is the opposite of compassion. Such media are powerful influences in contemporary society, but they can do considerable harm. They are an example of what Bauman calls "liquid evil," by which he means something which is regarded as a social good and benefit to society, but which actually does harm not only to individuals, but also to the fabric of society (Bauman & Donskis, 2016).

In terms of socialization, Freud regarded the first five years of life as the formative years and thus key in terms of how each of us learns to become a member of our society. However, sociology teaches us that, while the first five years may well be highly significant, socialization is a lifelong process. Consequently, changes in society can and do bring about changes in individuals in terms of attitudes and actions. Consider, for example, how different political regimes can encourage or discourage compassion—such as in relation to immigrants, religious minorities, and vulnerable groups. As social circumstances change so too can levels of compassion. The socializing influences of wider society are continuous and inevitable.

C. Wright Mills argued that the benefit of the sociological imagination is that comparing ourselves with others in similar circumstances helps us to recognize our life chances and understand our place in historical time (Mills, 1959)—that is, it gives us a sense of location in space and time, which are important factors in terms of identity formation. It helps us to develop a meaningful picture of how individuals and wider society interact and how social forces place certain expectations on us. To what extent an expectation of compassion will be to the fore will vary from society to society, epoch to epoch.

A COMPASSIONATE SOCIETY?

What causes people to be caring or uncaring toward others? The traditional, atomistic view of compassion concerns itself largely with the characteristics of individuals, but, as we are now beginning to see, that is only part of the story. The social context also brings a major set of factors into play. This raises the question of what role social factors play in nurturing or obstructing compassion. In an earlier work (Thompson & Cox, 2020), we argued that it is misleading to see resilience as simply an individual characteristic (and thus a lack of resilience as a character flaw). Resilience is more accurately seen as a complex multidimensional phenomenon that owes much to the social circumstances. The same argument can be made in terms of compassion. To do justice to the complexities involved, we need to adopt a holistic approach and that means taking account of sociological aspects.

One example of this is the role of ritual. Sociologist Emile Durkheim (1915) suggested that ritual played a major role in developing concern for others. He argued that, without language, the arts, science, and moral beliefs, humans would drop to the ranks of animals (Durkheim, 1915). Rituals play a part in bonding members of a culture together, giving them a sense of shared identity and interests. Many such rituals are generative of compassion—for example, funerals and memorial services. Other rituals, by contrast, can be highly detrimental in terms of compassion—for example, human sacrifices or, in a less extreme sense, gang rituals that generate hostility to others and encourage anti-social behavior. Such rituals are generally manifestations of social values. For example, ancient China is noted for developing "filial piety," where people are expected to view following the wishes of their parents, serving their families, and bringing them honor as a moral good and a social obligation. Many American Indian tribes, such as the Apache, honor those who give their possessions, money, and even their life to benefit others. The Lakota honor those who give rather than take from others. The story of the first American Thanksgiving is an example of giving to the less fortunate by the Wampanoag tribe. In addition, one of the five pillars of Islam is "zakat" (almsgiving), while "seva" (selfless giving) is a fundamental part of Sikhism.

On the other hand, however, it is unfortunate that there are many aspects of social life that are antithetical to compassion. Certainly not all people, nor all groups of people exhibit empathic feelings toward others, as is evidenced by the very existence of prejudice, genocide, wars, oppression, and ill will toward others that belie the notion that compassion is inborn or "natural." The Nazis' use of mass gassing and cremation of the millions of Jews, Poles, and others that they considered unworthy of human life can be seen as an immoral form of destruction. In addition, the massacres of American Indians rival those of the Nazis, to name a few: Tenochtitlan massacre—100,000 to 240,000 dead; Acoma—800; Sandia Mountains—900; Yontoket—450; Sand Creek—160; Wounded Knee—130 to 250; Washita—150 to 220; Massacre Cave—115 (Waldman, 2009). The Mayans, Aztecs, and Incas have a history of sacrificing their enemies, but their numbers are far less than those of the Nazis and the Europeans who came to the Americas and their attempts to destroy the Indian population. The attempts to destroy the Aboriginal population in Australia offer a similar example of unsympathetic feelings toward another group. As there are cultural examples of the lack of sympathetic feelings toward other groups, there are also examples of groups showing supportive feelings toward other groups (Treuer, 2019).

The stories of genocide across time and place are sadly a recurring feature of social life. The complete absence of compassion that they entail is tragically not an isolated incident. The picture, though, is complex. For example, American Indians have a history of compassion and caring for others, yet there is also a history of human sacrifice and eating those who were sacrificed. Positive and negative contributions to compassion can and do occur side by side in society. This social ambivalence in terms of compassion is widespread. Concern for orphans, those living in poverty, or those suffering from illness is based upon social values. As a member of various social groups, each individual will have many shared as well as many conflicting values that will influence their choices and behavior. Consequently, the same individual can show compassion for members of groups that share their values, while at the same time showing great disdain for those who have quite different values.

THERAPY CULTURE

Furedi (2004) comments on what he calls "therapy culture," by which he means the tendency to address problems on an individual basis without taking account of social circumstances. He refers to the work of Beck (2002) in stating that:

> Through the language of psychology, therapeutic culture frames the way that problems are perceived. The result is that social problems are increasingly perceived in terms of psychological dispositions: As personal inadequacies, guilt feelings, anxieties, conflicts, and neuroses.
>
> *(p. 25)*

Similarly, Illouz (2008) bemoans the therapeutic emphasis on the individual and thus the neglect of community relations and more holistic approaches to life's problems and challenges. This echoes Mills' classic work on "private troubles and public issues" (Mills, 1959) and the tendency to reduce the latter to the former (for example, stress being seen as the sign of a weak individual, rather than the result of the interplay of a complex array of social and organizational factors; Thompson, 2019). When it comes to compassion, therefore, it is important that we look at the broader sociological situation and address our efforts to make a positive difference to the full picture and not just to the individual aspects. Misplaced compassion could potentially play a role in reinforcing therapy culture and thereby contribute to keeping wider sociopolitical factors hidden and unaddressed.

DIFFERENCE, DIVERSITY, AND DISCRIMINATION

Discriminating against people simply because they are different in terms of ethnicity, nationality, religion, gender, age, or other such social factors is clearly not compatible with a commitment to compassion. The widespread presence of discrimination and inequality (Dorling, 2018; Thompson, 2018b) is therefore clearly an obstacle to developing compassion-based approaches to human relations and social problems. Mustering compassion toward people who are "like us" is a far easier undertaking, it would seem, than showing compassion toward people who differ from us in one or more socially significant ways.

This is where compassion needs to connect with the wider framework of social justice, a moral-political commitment to reducing inequalities and promoting a fairer and more humane society. In this regard, the work of Wilkinson and Pickett (2011) is very relevant. In an important study of the impact of inequality, they highlighted the huge social and human costs of economic inequality (defined as the gap between the richest and the poorest in any given society). They found that all manner of social problems were linked to inequality—the higher the level of inequality in a society, the greater the incidence of problems. In a follow up work (Wilkinson & Pickett, 2019), they focused specifically on the impact of inequality on mental health and well-being, again showing a high level of correspondence between levels of inequality and levels of mental health problems.

If we are to take compassion seriously, then, we need to see it as part of a broader commitment to social justice and the lessening of inequality. Compassionate actions that leave inequality, discrimination, and injustice untouched will only scratch the surface of what is needed if compassion is to achieve its potential.

COMPASSIONATE ORGANIZATIONS?

Finally, we come to the topic of compassion in an organizational context. The topic of workplace well-being has been receiving considerable attention in recent years. It seems that more and more employers are recognizing the benefits for all concerned of taking employee health and well-being seriously. The healthier and happier employees are, the more productive and problem free they will be, so win-win all round (van Veldhoven & Peccei, 2015). A compassionate approach to employees is therefore not only of moral value, but also good business sense.

In their study of healthcare, Ballat and Campling (2011) introduce the notion of "intelligent kindness." They point out how proceduralized, target-driven approaches can leave staff feeling alienated and disempowered. The book's basic message would appear to be that a more compassionate approach to staff will assure and motivate a more compassionate practice:

> It is really very simple: the safer people feel in their role, the more they will be able to look with curiosity at their own attitudes and prejudices and be more open to the emotional experience of their patients.
>
> *(p. 66)*

Their focus is on healthcare, but no doubt the same logic could be applied to a much wider range of workplace settings.

Finch and Aranda-Mena (2020) add an extra dimension to this when they discuss the significance of emotion in the workplace. They argue that, for too long, approaches to working life have focused too much on cognitive and behavioral aspects and thereby neglected the emotional elements. Compassion, of course, needs to fit into this more accurate and realistic understanding of social life within organizations. Neglecting emotional issues will necessarily push compassion out of the picture.

Again, we see that compassion needs to be understood not simply as an individual phenomenon, but a part of a wider multidimensional social context, one that incorporates the organizational context.

CONCLUSION

Illouz (2012) sums up the situation well:

> Precisely because we live in a time where the idea of individual responsibility reigns supreme, the vocation of sociology remains vital. In the same way that at the end of the nineteenth century it was radical to claim that poverty was the result not of dubious morality or weak character, but of systematic economic exploitation, it is now urgent to claim not that the failures of our private lives are the result of weak psyches, but rather that the vagaries and miseries of our emotional life are shaped by institutional arrangements.
>
> *(p. 4)*

Sociology can therefore be understood as offering a message of hope. If current social problems (and the "personal troubles" they give rise to) are a result of social processes and arrangements, then there is also potential to achieve solutions and alleviation through social processes and arrangements. Sociology encourages us—and enables us—to think in those wider, more holistic terms, thereby providing the basis of a compassion rooted in social solidarity and social justice, rather than atomized approaches that distort understanding by failing to see the big picture.

REFERENCES

Ballat, J., & Campling, P. (2011). *Intelligent kindness: Reforming the culture of healthcare.* RCPsych Publications.

Bauman, Z., & Donskis, L. (2016). *Liquid evil: Living with TINA.* Polity.

Beck, U. (2002). Beyond status and class. In U. Beck & E. Beck-Gernsheim (Eds.), *Individualization* (pp. 30–41). Sage.

Dorling, D. (2018). *Peak inequality: Britain's ticking time bomb.* Policy Press.

Durkheim, E. (1915). *The elementary forms of the religious life.* Free Press.

Finch, E., & Aranda-Mena, G. (2020). *Creating emotionally intelligent workspaces: A design guide to office chemistry.* Routledge.

Furedi, F. (2004). *Therapy culture: Cultivating insecurity in an uncertain age.* Routledge.

Illouz, E. (2008). *Saving the modern soul: Therapy, emotions and the culture of self-help.* University of California Press.

Illouz, E. (2012). *Why love hurts: A sociological explanation.* Polity.

Mills, C. W. (1959). *The sociological imagination.* Oxford University Press.

Ricard, M. (2015). *Altruism: The power of compassion to change yourself and the world.* Little, Brown.

Thompson, N. (2018a). *Applied sociology.* Routledge.

Thompson, N. (2018b). *Promoting equality: Working with diversity and difference* (4th ed.). Red Globe Press.

Thompson, N. (2019). *The managing stress practice manual.* Avenue Media Solutions.

Thompson, N., & Cox, G. R. (Eds.). (2020). *Promoting resilience: Responding to adversity, vulnerability and loss.* Routledge.

Treuer, D. (2019). *The heartbeat of Wounded Knee: Native America from 1890 to the present.* Corsair.

Van Veldhoven, M., & Peccei, R. (2015). *Well-being and performance at work: The role of context.* Psychology Press.

Waldman, C. (2009). *Atlas of the North American Indian.* Checkmark Books.

Wilkinson, R., & Pickett, K. (2011). *The spirit level: Why equality is better for everyone.* Penguin.

Wilkinson, R., & Pickett, K. (2019). *The inner level: How more equal societies reduce stress, restore sanity and improve everyone's well-being.* Penguin.

CHAPTER 6

SPHERES OF COMPASSIONATE
ENGAGEMENT AND RESPONSE

Darcy L. Harris

INTRODUCTION

When we think of compassion, what comes to mind are probably times when we have reached out to someone with a desire to somehow address difficulties or pain that the person was experiencing. This is, perhaps, the most common image of compassionate responding, and working with grieving clients probably supports this image well. But compassion goes way beyond this singular view of client work. As we continue in our growth and awareness of compassion, it becomes readily apparent that we begin to see and experience the world through a lens that opens our hearts and challenges our perceptions and previous ways of thinking. These moments are not limited to one-on-one interactions with others; indeed, sometimes we cultivate a deeper awareness and understanding of ourselves, and our compassionate base helps us to re-establish a different way of being with our self-talk and inner world. In essence, developing our compassionate self is more about a way of being and responding that encompasses not just our clients, but ourselves, and all of the contexts where we are engaged. Gilbert (2014) alludes to these different levels of response as the "flows of compassion," which incorporate three aspects: (a) compassion for self, (b) compassion extended to others, and (c) compassion received from others.

As the competencies for developing a compassionate self are cultivated, the potential to extend compassion to others and to receive compassion from others is enhanced. Expanding upon this idea is the concept of the spheres of compassion, recognizing that compassion is a multitiered concept that can include the intention to relieve suffering in one's self, others, and at the macro level of communities, governments, and the environment. It is important to keep in mind that the tendency to focus strictly upon the individual runs the risk of assuming that individuals are responsible for controlling things that may truly be outside of their ability to direct. Likewise, our compassionate motivation and intention can flow between all of these spheres quite readily. This concept is presented in Figure 6.1.

LEVELS OF HUMAN EXPERIENCE

Most clinicians are trained to work with clients at the interpersonal level, usually in one-on-one sessions, and sometimes with a partner or a family. However, education and training for clinical work often neglect the intrapersonal experience of the clinician, and the social context that determines much of the client's concerns. It is very important to view the client holistically, as a member of many spheres of social engagement and interaction, all of which will have an impact on the experience of loss and the grief response. Our daily experiences incorporate events that happen at the micro (intrapersonal), the mezzo (intrapersonal), and the macro (structural) levels. These levels are applicable to how grief is experienced as well as how compassionate action can be directed (see Figure 6.2).

DOI: 10.4324/9781003204121-8

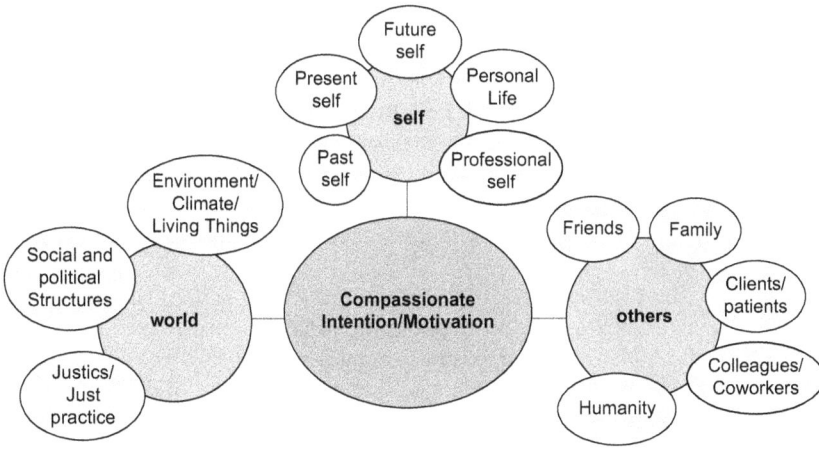

Figure 6.1 Spheres of Compassionate Engagement and Response. Harris, D. (2021). Compassion-focused grief therapy. *British Journal of Guidance and Counselling*, *49*(6), 780–790

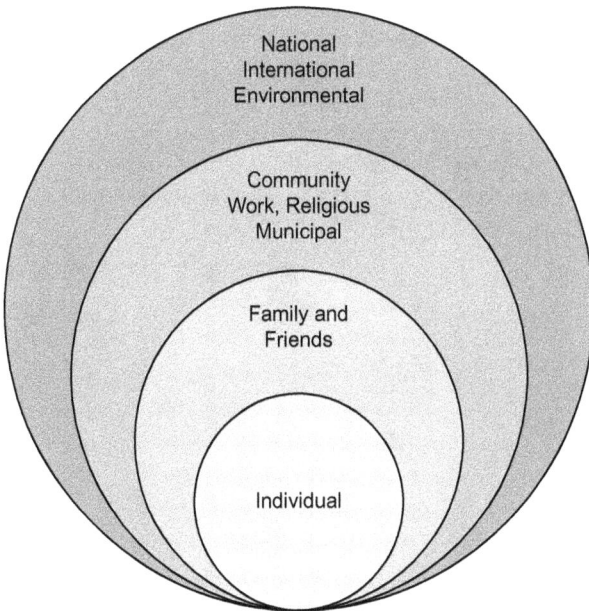

Figure 6.2 Layers of Human Experience and Influence. Harris, D. L. (2021). Political grief. *Illness, Crisis, & Loss*, doi-org.proxy1.lib.uwo.ca/10.1177/10541373219 99793

INTRAPERSONAL EXPERIENCE

The intrapersonal experience refers to the internal workings of a person's thoughts, feelings, and inner world. As referenced in Chapter three, the concept of the assumptive world is descriptive of our intrapersonal world, being initially formulated when we are very young, most likely alongside the developing attachment system. Our assumptive world reflects the way that we view ourselves, how we find safety and soothing, and our understandings of how things should work—and why they work in the ways that they do (Harris, 2020). The assumptive world (Figure 6.3) provides a sense of predictability and a way to navigate through daily life.

The assumptive world is a core part of our sense of self. When we encounter experiences that bump up against these core assumptions, we usually find ways to assimilate or accommodate these experiences into our existing assumptive world. However, experiences that truly shatter our assumptive world launch us into a painful sense of disequilibrium, triggering the grief response, which helps us to rebuild our assumptive world in a new way that is able to integrate the loss experience so that we are able to re-enter life in a way that is coherent, but different from before the loss. If each person's assumptive world has been uniquely shaped by their earlier experiences, then the appraisal of what a loss means will be different for each person. This is where the importance of the subjective interpretation of a loss occurs. What might be a profound loss for one person may not be as significant for someone else who shares the same experience.

Losses that originate intrapersonally are often intangible in nature. These are losses that are not readily identified outwardly and finding words to describe these losses is often difficult. Examples might be loss of identity, loss of innocence, or loss of hope or dreams (Harris, 2020). The concept of inner safety is also important to consider, as significant loss experiences often underscore our vulnerability and powerlessness. At the intrapersonal level, the concept of safety refers to the inner world, and how individuals feel about themselves. This inner sense of safety is often reflected in a person's self-talk, or what they say to themselves

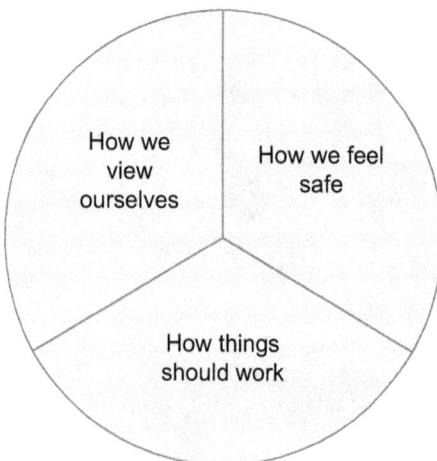

Figure 6.3 The Assumptive World. Harris, D. L. (2021). Political grief. *Illness, Crisis, & Loss*, doi-org.proxy1.lib.uwo.ca/10.1177/1054137321999793

during these times. Internalized messages that are negative, shame-based, or focused upon self-deprecation can be paralyzing, adding salt to the wound of an already painful loss.

Obviously, self-compassion will be more difficult for someone who experiences fears, blocks, or resistance to compassion. These hindrances to compassion need to be acknowledged and respected as boundaries that the client has in place, often protecting a vulnerable or fragile sense of self below the surface. The therapist can offer gentle compassionate re-frames to a client's self-derogatory expressions, which may open the possibility for the client to better understand what compassion entails by the way it is modeled by the therapist. Research in self-compassion indicates that having a compassionate base from which to draw upon is a self-sustaining capacity (Klimecki et al., 2014). It is also interesting to consider the possibility that self-compassion may be a core area of competency for clinicians to enact toward themselves (Kolts et al., 2018).

INTERPERSONAL EXPERIENCE

In Gilbert's (2014) work related to the flows of compassion, the interpersonal dimension is explored through the ability to receive compassion from others and to offer compassion to others. For many people, especially those in the helping professions, offering compassion to others comes much more readily than receiving compassion for oneself. Individuals may struggle with receiving compassion through fears, resistance, and blocks. For some, the fear of compassion relates to concerns about being overwhelmed by distress or feeling undeserving of compassion. Some clients may also fear compassion that counters their critical self-talk if they feel these negative internalized messages are what keep them accountable on the 'correct' life path. Blocks can be due to lack of knowledge or misunderstandings about compassion. External blocks can occur in environments and contexts where compassion is difficult. For example, some work environments may be toxic or critical, making compassionate responses very difficult. A common hindrance to compassion is feeling rushed or overworked, reducing the time and ability to reflect and interact with others in a meaningful way. Resistance is manifest when individuals are not frightened or blocked, but they simply aren't interested in compassion, or they may feel that compassion is not worth the time and trouble expended. Some may mistakenly believe that compassion is a passive state and will open them up to more pain and hurt. Others may express that compassion is simply a way to avoid responsibility for actions or that it bypasses being held accountable for wrongs that they may have done in the past. Not feeling worthy or deserving is also a common form of resistance to compassion (Gilbert, 2019).

The interpersonal layer of experience explores the relationships that we have with others in various levels of relating, including family, friends, co-workers, and others at the community level. Perhaps the most common presentation for grief counseling/therapy is loss of someone who was a part of the tapestry of the client's life. Social messaging about grief is a prominent force with people who have lost a loved one. For example, the loss itself may not be socially recognized (as in the loss of one's married lover), or the way the person is grieving may not be according to accepted social norms for gender expectations. Grief that is not socially recognized or validated, or that falls outside of socially acceptable norms is said to be disenfranchised (Doka, 2002). Disenfranchised grief usually carries a message that the person who is grieving does not have a right to grieve, or there is a problem with the way that they are grieving. When grief is disenfranchised, the grieving individual is isolated in their grief, usually without access to the social support that they need.

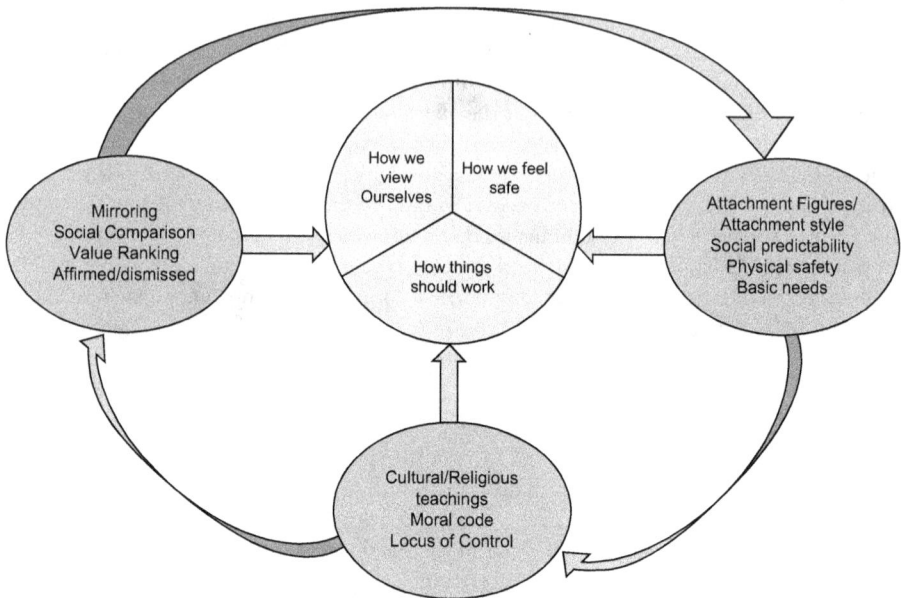

Figure 6.4 Mapping the Social Spheres of the Assumptive World. Harris, D. L. (2021). Political grief. *Illness, Crisis, & Loss*, doi-org.proxy1.lib.uwo.ca/10.1177/1054 137321999793

It is important to keep in mind that clients' experiences are embedded into their social system, much of which exists outside of their control. Likewise, while grief is often described as an individual's unique response to loss, it is shaped and molded to a great extent by the social context in which the grieving individual identifies and resides. These contextual factors have a profound influence on how loss and grief are viewed, including expectations about how grief should be expressed and experienced, as well as the supports and resources that may or may not be available to grieving individuals. Figure 6.4 shows the interrelationship between the assumptive world and the social context of the individual.

Core concepts related to the social context of grief include:

- We are basically social creatures, innately programmed to attach, with a need to belong.
- It is impossible to separate out individuals from the family, society, and culture in which they reside and identify.
- We are innately sensitive to social cues, which develop, guide, and shape our experiences.
- We feel pain when we are rejected, shamed, or ostracized by our social group (Harris & Winokuer, 2021; MacDonald & Leary, 2005).

Compassion extended to others is probably the most familiar image of compassion that people have. We think of people who are involved in selfless charity work or who volunteer their time to assist dying patients and their families as the "truest" expression of compassion. Most faith traditions extoll the virtues of the compassionate person, and so familiarity with this concept may have first occurred in this context. It is important to keep in mind that compassion relates back to intention and not to outward appearance or outcome. The relief of suffering may occur in singular small acts as well as in global outreach programs. Compassion that is extended to others needs to come from a place of balance and discernment in order for it to be self-sufficient rather than depleting, and the ways to cultivate these traits are discussed in the next section on compassion training.

NATIONAL, INTERNATIONAL, AND ENVIRONMENTAL EXPERIENCES

Grief that originates in the outer bands of the layers of experience tends to be political, international, structural, and/or environmental in origin. This form of sociopolitical grief can be experienced both individually and collectively. Collective grief may occur when the loss relates to a group where commonly shared assumptions are shattered. Examples of grief that may originate at this level are political grief and environmental grief. Political grief may be understood in two different ways. The first aspect occurs as a poignant sense of assault to the assumptive world of those who struggle with the ideology and practices of their governing bodies and those who hold political power or are imbued with authority by the state. The second aspect relates to direct losses that are experienced by individuals as a result of political policies, ideologies, and/or oppression enacted and/or empowered at the sociopolitical levels (Harris, 2021). Environmental grief is the reaction stemming from the loss of ecosystems caused by either natural or man-made events. An example of environmental grief is the response to the changes in weather patterns and resulting natural disasters that have increased in occurrence as a result of global warming (Kevorkian, 2020). Exploring grief at this level is a new area of interest and study.

Losses that occur at this level often provoke strong emotions that lead to action, and sometimes this action is violent. For example, a case could be made that the storming of the United States Capitol on January 6, 2021, by Trump supporters who felt the election had been stolen from them could be reframed as a form of political grief, especially when considering that the Latin root of the word bereavement comes from the word *rabir*, which means to snatch, grab, or take away (Harris, 2021). Interestingly, the response of many Democrats to the election of Donald Trump in the 2016 United States presidential election was seen in public demonstrations of disbelief, grief, and moral outrage, again expressing profound grief as well.[1]

Responding to these types of losses and their grief reactions is associated with what could be termed *structural compassion*, which involves choosing a response to a sociopolitical loss that is informed by wisdom, and discernment. There may be both reflective responses as well as actively engaged compassionate responses. These are outlined using the yin/yang symbol in Figure 6.5 as a representation of the different aspects of these processes.

Structural Compassion in Response to Socio-Political Grief

Reflection
- Big picture perspective
- Respond vs. react
- Appreciating human value
- Compassionate intention
- Understanding threat responses
- Recognizing common humanity

Engagement
- Principled activism
- Speaking truth with care
- Being an ally
- Engaged citizenship
- Educating oneself about many perspectives
- Conscious, intentioned dialogue

Figure 6.5 Compassionately Responding to Socio-Political Grief

Advocacy, activism, and protest can be powerful forces for compassionate meaning making in the wake of socio-political losses. However, it is important that these activities arise from a sense of clarity, that they are consciously chosen responses coming from a place of compassionate intention rather than knee-jerk reactivity, and that they include ethical resolve and consideration of all who are affected rather than a force used to channel vengeful anger and retaliation at "the other."

SUMMARY

To summarize, all individual experiences are influenced and perceived through lenses that are uniquely social, cultural, and political in nature. It is important to be able to understand and appreciate the social context of all loss experiences, recognizing the interconnectedness between individuals and their contextual elements. There also needs to be an awareness that while a loss itself may be subjectively appraised by the individual, the origin of a loss may be from any level of human experience, including the intrapersonal, interpersonal, and/or the sociopolitical contextual layers. Finally, grief may be experienced individually as well as collectively; collective grief may occur when the loss relates to a group where commonly shared assumptions are shattered. This chapter has attempted to provide an integrative model for mapping the different layers of experience related to loss and grief with a corresponding pathway for compassionate responses to these different layers. For example, we are currently seeing much collective grief in response to the global COVID-19 pandemic. Likewise, compassion is not limited to the interpersonal dimension alone. Self-compassion directs compassionate intentions toward one's self, treating ourselves as if we are our own best friend (Bluth & Neff, 2018). Structural compassion carries the compassionate intention to the macro level, helping us to carefully choose a response to people and experiences that involve positions of authority, power, and decision-making that have a more global impact, as summarized in Table 6.1.

Table 6.1 Grief and Compassion at the Different Levels of Human Experience

Level	Perspective	Examples of Grief Experiences	Examples of Compassionate Response
Micro	Intrapersonal	Loss of self Intangible losses Internalized disenfranchisement	Self-compassion Shame reduction
Mezzo	Interpersonal	Loss of another Disenfranchised grief	Reaching out to others Receiving from others Balance and healthy boundaries
Macro	Structural	Loss of environment Moral outrage Collective grief Displacement Oppression	Principled action "Big picture" perspective Wisdom and discernment

NOTE

1 For further exploration of the concept of political grief, see Harris, 2021.

REFERENCES

Bluth, K., & Neff, K. D. (2018). New frontiers in understanding the benefits of self-compassion. *Self and Identity, 17*(6), 605–608.

Doka, K. J. (2002). *Disenfranchised grief: New directions, challenges, and strategies for practice.* Research Press.

Gilbert, P. (2014). The origins and nature of compassion focused therapy. *British Journal of Clinical Psychology, 53*(1), 6–41.

Gilbert, P. (2019). Explorations into the nature and function of compassion. *Current Opinion in Psychology, 28,* 108–114.

Harris, D. L. (2020). *Non-death loss and grief: Context and clinical implications.* Routledge.

Harris, D. L. (2021). Political grief. *Illness, Crisis, and Loss.* https://doi.org/1054137321999793

Harris, D. L., & Winokuer, H. R. (2021). *Principles and practice of grief counseling.* Springer.

Kevorkian, K. (2020). Environmental grief. In D. Harris (Ed.), *Non-death loss and grief: Context and clinical implications* (pp. 216–226). Routledge.

Klimecki, O. M., Leiberg, S., Ricard, M., & Singer, T. (2014). Differential pattern of functional brain plasticity after compassion and empathy training. *Social Cognitive and Affective Neuroscience, 9*(6), 873–879.

Kolts, R., Bell, T., Bennett-Levy, J., & Irons, C. (2018). *Exploring compassion focused therapy from the inside out: A self-practice/self-reflection workbook for therapists.* Guilford.

MacDonald, G., & Leary, M. R. (2005). Why does social exclusion hurt? The relationship between social and physical pain. *Psychological Bulletin, 131*(2), 202.

PART TWO

Training in the Components of Compassion

CHAPTER 7

WHAT IS COMPASSION TRAINING?

Andy H. Y. Ho and Darcy L. Harris

INTRODUCTION

Compassion provides a sustainable base from which to relieve the suffering that is around us, as well as inside us. If we truly desire to respond in ways that are grounded in compassion, how do we cultivate that compassion? You can't just wish yourself to be more compassionate. Compassion itself cannot be cultivated or increased; however, it can be enhanced by the acquisition of knowledge, skills, and competencies that strengthen the ability to follow through on the motivation to relieve suffering. The process of further developing these components of compassion is often referred to as compassion training. Training in compassion allows for an increased ability to tolerate distress, maintain focus, and discern appropriate responses in a variety of contexts (Gilbert, 2014; Halifax, 2014; Kirby, 2017). Cultivating a compassionate stance provides clinicians with the opportunity to engage clients with their full attention and presence, allowing for greater openness and receptivity for both the painful and the potentially transformative aspects of difficult and painful situations. Compassion training can lead to significant changes in emotional experiencing, emotion regulation, and cognitive re-framing, which can deepen connections with others, while also reducing symptoms of stress, anxiety, and depression (Jazaieri et al., 2013; Brito-Pons et al., 2018). This chapter will provide an overview of what compassion training involves, drawing from some of the compassion training programs that are currently available.

COMPONENTS OF COMPASSION

SKILLS AND ATTRIBUTES

In order to enhance compassion, the focus needs to be upon developing the building blocks of compassion and strengthening the foundation from which specific compassion-oriented responses extend. Halifax (2008) refers to being able to respond to distress from the position of a strong back (courage), while at the same time having a soft belly (openness and tenderness). Compassion training focuses on relieving suffering in addition to supporting and encouraging compassion for the good of the self and others. The importance of self-compassion for both the therapist and the client is stressed as a foundational practice in this process. It is expected that clinicians who wish to utilize any compassion-enhancing exercises with clients should also engage in their own personal work with these same practices (Kolts et al., 2018). Training in the components of compassion can assist in the development of a strong compassionate base from which to engage with clients whose distress and suffering might otherwise be overwhelming. In a basic sense, the core components of compassion include:

- The ability to notice and attune to suffering/distress.
- Awareness of the "big picture" related to the nature of suffering in life.

DOI: 10.4324/9781003204121-10

- Understanding our interconnectedness and common human experience.
- Wisdom and discernment regarding the most appropriate response to distress.
- The ability to regulate one's own emotion.
- The ability to focus attention without distraction or avoidant response patterns.

According to Gilbert (2009), these components extend from the two psychologies of compassion, described earlier as the ability to approach and engage with suffering and the desire to relieve and prevent suffering. Compassionate Mind Training involves the use of specific skills that help to further develop the attributes of compassion. These are shown visually in Figure 7.1. In essence, engaging in compassion training strengthens our ability to attune and respond to suffering in ways that are helpful and sustainable.

ORIENTATIONS TO COMPASSION

The orientations to compassion include an awareness of how compassion flows within and between different relational contexts. There are three compassion orientations, which include compassion for others, compassion received from others, and compassion for one's self (Gilbert, 2009). Each of these orientations is important for sustainability in working with situations of intensity and distress. Compassion for others is probably the most familiar, as we innately understand a desire to reach out to others with the intention of helping. This type of compassion is universally acknowledged by most cultures and spiritual traditions and is often thought by some to be easier and more palatable than compassion

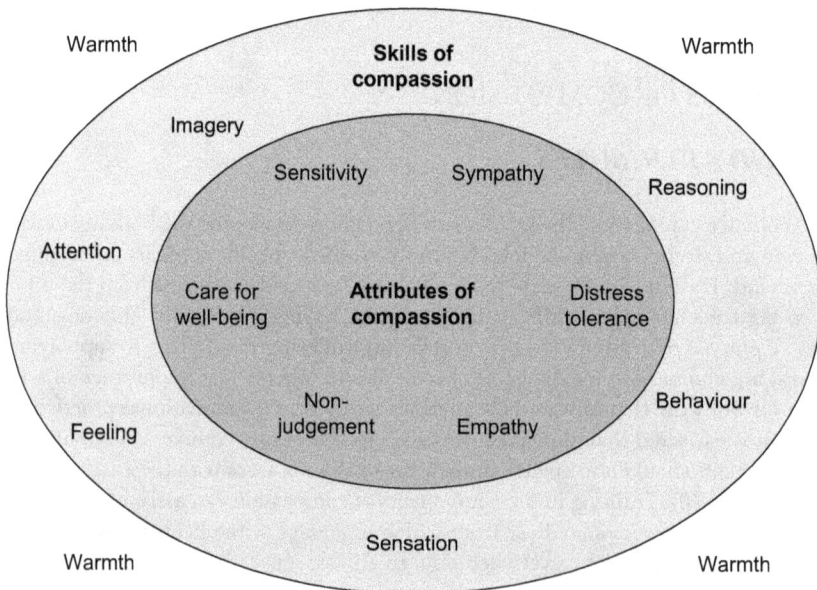

Figure 7.1 The Compassion Circle. Key Attributes of Compassion (Inner Ring) and the Skills Needed to Develop Them (Outer Ring). From P. Gilbert (2009). *The compassionate mind*. With Permission from Little, Brown Book Group

for oneself (Jazaieri et al., 2013). Some people are afraid of becoming more compassionate because they are worried that they could be overwhelmed by the distress that is present, or they mistakenly believe that being compassionate does not allow for healthy boundary-setting. Blocks to compassion can be related to internal processes, such as wanting to be compassionate but not knowing how, or a lack of understanding of what compassion actually entails. Sometimes, the blocks to compassion are external, such as certain types of work environments or political contexts that make compassion especially difficult. The second orientation includes receiving compassion from others. Many people find it hard to receive compassion. They may associate a compassionate response from someone as a sign of pity or indicative of a weakness within themselves. The reality, however, is that the ability to receive compassion is an acknowledgment of our true shared human experience and a recognition of our interconnectedness with each other.

Modeling compassion and gently addressing the blocks and resistance to compassion might comprise the primary work of the therapeutic relationship. The third orientation of compassion includes directing the flow of compassion to oneself. Self-compassion is often confused with narcissism or not accepting accountability for one's personal actions. Neff (2003) identifies the struggles that many people have being compassionate with themselves, finding it much easier to direct compassion outwardly to others. Exploring blocks and resistance to self-compassion is an incredibly important aspect of compassion training. The ability to acknowledge our personal flaws and shortcomings with compassion is an essential component of self-care in work that can be emotionally intense and layered with many different forms of individual, social, structural, and political grief.

WHAT DOES COMPASSION TRAINING INVOLVE?

The capacity to practice compassion as we offer support to individuals and families in their grief journey while attending to our own emotions requires a combination of skillset and mindset that can contain and attend to the suffering of others and self with openness and kindness. When clients feel heard and supported within the spaciousness of acceptance and non-judgment, they are empowered to approach their pain with tenderness and courage. This process requires the full attention of the clinician to stay engaged and focused without aversion (drawing upon mindful awareness), to offer a safe haven for the client to open up to their pain (modeling presence), and to discern in the present moment the best course of action that can help soothe the client's distress while attending to one's emotional resonance and response (shared humanity). As such, mindful awareness, presence, and shared humanity, together with a set of common theoretical underpinnings, have become the foundational core of most prominent compassion training programs.

THEORETICAL UNDERPINNINGS

Kirby (2017) reported at least six empirically supported interventions that focus on the cultivation of compassion through the gold standard of randomized controlled trials. These include Compassion-Focused Therapy (CFT; Gilbert, 2014), Compassion Cultivation Training (CCT; Jazaieri et al., 2013), Cognitive-Based Compassion Training (CBCT; Pace et al., 2009), Compassion Meditation and Loving Kindness Meditation (CM & LKM; Hoffmann et al., 2011), Cultivating Emotional Balance (CEB; Kemeny et al., 2012), and

Mindful Self-Compassion (MSC; Neff & Germer, 2013). Although adopting varied definitions of compassion that center on the cognitive, affective, intentional, and motivational
domains, all of these programs share a common denominator in their theoretical underpinnings—a secular approach to compassion. In spite of a non-religious emphasis, they
are guided by Eastern contemplative traditions including Buddhist psychology, Tibetan
Buddhist philosophy, traditional attention focus (*Shamata*), and contemplative practices (e.g.,
The Four Immeasurables). At the same time, their empirical bases are informed by Western
psychological science, including evolutionary psychology, applied research on social, emotion-focused, and cognitive psychology, attachment theory, as well as the neuroscience of
compassion and its impact on our parasympathetic system and physiological health (Kirby
& Gilbert, 2017). This integration of Eastern practices and Western sciences is uniquely
salient, forming the backbone for compassion-based training and therapies.

MINDFUL AWARENESS

A common feature across the various compassion training programs is an emphasis on
mindfulness training. As described earlier in this chapter, the practice of compassion
requires our ability to notice and become aware of the presence of suffering in others and
within ourselves. This awareness does not come naturally to the human brain, which has
been trained through millions of years of evolution to respond to potential threats, often
leading to preoccupation with intrusive thoughts and negative self-talk. In fact, Kanouse
and Hanson (1987) postulate that our brain has a built-in negativity bias, whereby we have
the tendency to pay more attention and give greater importance to negative experiences
than positive ones. This is due to our innate need for self-preservation in the face of constant environmental threats, such as wild predatory animals for our stone age ancestors
and ill-willed cyber bullies for our millennials and beyond. Because of this bias, our minds
are often filled with noise rather than clarity—regrets about the past or worries about the
future—leading us to never be fully here in the present moment with the clearest of intention and purpose.

An unfocused mind has little sensitivity toward the needs and sufferings of others and
self, as it cannot readily engender empathy, sympathy, and care for well-being, all of which
are important psychological attributes that make compassion possible (Gilbert, 2009). An
easily distracted mind fails at maintaining clear intentionality, non-judgment, and distress
tolerance, which again are essential for the rise of compassion. Epstein (1999) argues that *in
the context of clinical work, mindfulness allows the clinician to maintain a stance of clarity, nonreactivity,
and focused attention in the present moment without feeling overwhelmed*. Mindfulness practice further empowers the clinician to be fully attentive to the experiences of others and self with
curiosity, enabling them to let go of self-interest and positions of power, with the potential-
ity to discover what serves best under the circumstances with humility. As such, mindfulness is not a luxury but a clear necessity for all compassion-based approaches.

Gilbert (1998) argues that although the human mind is riddled with conflicts and complexities that lead to a persistent state of neediness, grasping, and holding on that ultimately results in suffering, human beings need to understand that they did not choose this;
rather, it is an outcome of 'glitches' in our evolution (Gilbert, 1998). To illustrate the causes
and effects of our tendency toward mindlessness versus mindfulness and negativity versus
positivity, psychoeducation about how our 'tricky' brain operates and its impact on our
physiological functioning and parasympathetic responses becomes a core cognitive feature

of mindfulness training (Kirby & Gilbert, 2017). To put theory into practice, to help train our mind to stay in the here and now, and to nurture its ability to remain focused in the immediacy of our experiences without judgment and aversion, experiential mindfulness practices are employed in compassion interventions. These involve grounding exercises that direct one's attention to one's surroundings and senses of touch, sight, hearing, smell, and taste. These exercises also teach about mindful breathing to bring attention to the present. Bodywork, such as yoga, movement, and body scan meditations, helps to cultivate the ability to focus on the immediacy of physical sensations and emotions. Other mindfulness-based meditative exercises activate the parasympathetic nervous system to help regulate emotions in situations of distress. These exercises are conducted during training and therapy sessions, as well as in at-home assignments to foster a sustainable practice.

PRESENCE

A third common feature of compassion training is the cultivation of presence for others and self. Presence builds upon our intention to "show up" and remain gently and carefully focused in situations that involve pain, trauma, and overwhelming feelings. Researchers have argued that compassion is an innate human motivation that is embedded into the folds of our brain to ensure the survival of our species, building upon the evolution of cooperation and affiliation within human relationships over time (Kirby et al., 2017). For example, through a series of observational studies, Warmenken and Tomasello (2009) reported that infants as young as 14–18 months can exhibit caring behaviors, show a desire to help others, and have a preference for toys that depict caring and helpful characteristics. Repeated functional MRI studies have also reported that when research participants are asked to recall and imagine a compassionate encounter, the regions of their brain that are associated with positive emotions light up with activity (Kim et al., 2020). Even though caring and prosocial behaviors may be hardwired into our brains, it is often not easy for our motivation for kindness to shine through the dark clouds of mindlessness and judgment. Thus, mindfulness training and the cultivation of presence go hand in hand in compassion-based interventions.

In the context of loss, presence is vital for creating a safe environment for clients to face their grief with open hearts and open minds, rather than turning away or suppressing their emotions. Humans engage in such defense mechanisms because grieving is a painful experience. When we lose someone close to us, our assumptive worlds shatter into a million little pieces containing fragments of our lost identities and belief systems. Making sense of the loss enables us to piece together our shattered lives and move toward healing. Within the therapeutic relationship, the full and unfettered presence of the clinician provides clients with the emotional safety net to examine the narratives behind their experiences of loss with new perspectives. This process helps to facilitate meaning making as well as restoration of their shattered identity and purpose for living via a renewed and coherent sense of self (Neimeyer et al., 2010). Therapeutic presence can be understood as a real relationship and alliance between clients and clinicians, where the former feels comfortable in sharing their utmost vulnerability with the latter having the capacity to contain it. Such a relationship necessitates authenticity, as compassion needs to be embodied for it to be heartfelt. In other words, therapeutic presence cannot be a pretense; clinicians need to be genuinely present and open in order to sustain their motivation to alleviate their client's suffering. Indeed, a study with oncology nurses working with end-of-life patients reported that presence with compassion requires one's ability to bear witness to suffering as well as to be comfortable in one's own skin in the presence of suffering (Sabo, 2011).

As presence requires clinicians to understand their own mental processes for activating their caring motivation systems, there is a need to nurture a 'self-enlightenment' for helping others—a compassionate intentionality (Gilbert, 2007). To achieve this, a common training module used in compassion interventions is building one's empathic capacity. Loving-kindness meditation and compassion meditation are widely adopted techniques in compassion training and therapy for nurturing presence. These meditations often incorporate imagery to envision being kind to others and oneself, as well as breathing training that engages the parasympathetic nervous system to help regulate one's emotion in situations of distress. Other common techniques include reflective practices for developing a compassionate inner-voice and an equanimity of the mind that is freed from judgment and unfazed by heavy emotions, active listening and empathic communication training, as well as body-focused exercises that train clinicians to develop appropriate expressions, postures, and tonalities that convey compassion.

COMMON HUMANITY

The fourth and final common feature of compassion-based interventions is the recognition of our common humanity. Common humanity involves the understanding that every human being is connected by our basic needs and desire to be free from suffering. Common humanity also acknowledges that suffering is a universal human experience (Strauss et al., 2016), with the recognition that we are not alone in our pain. It is common for us to immediately understand the pain of becoming sick just by seeing another person who is sick. We instinctively recognize the commonly shared experiences of loss, failure, having misfortunes, getting one's heart broken, and losing someone close to us. While there are idiosyncrasies in the circumstances and the personal narratives of these experiences, they are nonetheless the same experiences that we all share as a species. This understanding of interconnectedness forms the crux of our motivation for compassionate responding.

A growing body of research has found that our ability to perceive similarities with others can serve to minimize in-group and out-group differences (Sturmer et al., 2006), and foster empathy and compassionate behaviors (Penner et al., 2005). It is thus not surprising that when we view others being more akin to ourselves, we tend to put them in a more positive light and are more willing to offer help. But what makes common humanity so powerful as a conduit for compassion is that when we recognize that every one of us belongs in the same in-group of human beings, sharing similar weaknesses, inadequacies, losses, and tragedies, we begin to see each other as equal, and we then treat all others with dignity and respect. In clinical settings, the recognition of common humanity enables clinicians to let go of their egos, prejudice, and self-interest to offer complete support, acceptance, and unconditional positive regard for their clients. Moreover, it empowers clinicians to imagine being in the world of their clients, experiencing their emotions and pain, and to discern the best course of supportive engagement. Common humanity opens the clinician's eyes to recognize their own limitations and vulnerabilities in a therapeutic relationship, to be able to stop overidentification with their clients' emotions, and to respond with self-compassion in situations that are challenging and frustrating (Neff, 2012).

There is a wide spectrum of techniques and exercises used in compassion training and therapies that aim at enhancing common humanity. One common technique is the use of imagery to imagine ourselves in the position of the other, to see their world through their eyes, how we would feel as ourselves to be in such a situation, and what we would do to remedy the situation. Other commonly adopted techniques include reflective exercises that aim at developing and using the compassionate mind to address difficulties such as shame, self-criticism, and relational conflicts, through activities such as letter writing and journaling that focus on compassionate expressions, life appreciation, and gratitude. One very recent study by Ling et al. (2021) examined the use of common humanity scenarios—short videos that either depict a collective transcendence of stereotypes or a narrative interview that showcases human suffering and resilience to promote compassion in healthcare workers. The researchers found that simply viewing such videos had a positive effect on healthcare workers' feelings of care, concern, and compassion to others. New compassion training techniques like common humanity scenarios that use media, drama, and other creative mediums are currently being developed in other parts of the world as well (Koh et al., 2020; Shanmugan et al., 2021).

WHAT DOES COMPASSION TRAINING DO?

In 2015, Kirby et al. published the first meta-analysis that examined the effectiveness of compassion-based interventions that have undergone the rigorous evaluation of randomized controlled trials. This important research, which analyzed data from 1,285 participants who had undergone 21 trials, revealed significant and positive short-term effects on the mental health of people who had gone through 1 of the 6 major compassion interventions (i.e., CMT/CFT, CCT, CBCT, CM & LKM, CEB, and MSC) as compared to those who did not. Specifically, compassion-based interventions were found to be effective in elevating self-reported measures on compassion, self-compassion, mindfulness, and well-being, as well as reducing depression, anxiety, and psychological distress. The magnitude of change these interventions produced as calculated through the effect size of Cohen d were moderate, ranging from 0.47 to 0.64. Putting this into context, the overall effect size for one of the most prescribed antidepressants for the treatment of depression in the world, Prozac, was reported to range between 0.26 and 0.29 (Turner et al., 2008), while the reported effect size for physical activity for promoting psychological well-being ranged between 0.29 and 0.38 (Netz et al., 2005). These numbers reveal the robust effectiveness of compassion training and compassion-based therapies for wellness promotion as compared to other types of intervention.

New and innovative forms of compassion training and therapy are constantly emerging, with some integrating multiple modalities to support and empower individuals and families facing challenging life adversities. Examples include the Mindful-Compassion Art-based Therapy (MCAT; Ho et al., 2019) that integrates Mindful Self-Compassion Training with Expressive Arts (elaborated in Chapter 14 in the current volume), and the Mindfulness-Based Compassionate Living Course (MBCL; van den Brik & Koster, 2015) that integrates Compassion-Focused Therapy with Mindful Self-Compassion and intense mindfulness training. These newer models of intervention have shown great promise in reducing stress, burnout, and shame, while promoting resilience, self-esteem, well-being, and quality of life. While more research is needed to substantiate their clinical efficacy, it can be expected that the field of compassion-based intervention will continue to blossom in the foreseeable future.

CONCLUSION

While compassion itself is not amenable to enhancement on its own, the components of compassion can be reinforced and strengthened through the process of compassion training. There are several different trainings in compassion that are available around the world, with the common elements of most of these trainings being the cultivation of the components of compassion through engagement with mindful awareness, development of the ability to focus and remain fully present in the midst of challenging circumstances, and the recognition of our interconnectedness with each other through our shared humanity. Compassion training includes an understanding of the different "flows" of compassion, including compassion directed to others, compassion received from others, and self-compassion that we direct toward ourselves. Compassion training provides a foundation of discernment, wisdom, and kindness from which to offer ourselves as agents of healing to those whose lives have been broken by the pain of loss and grief.

REFERENCES

Brito-Pons, G., Campos, D., & Cebolla, A. (2018). Implicit of explicit compassion? Effects of compassion cultivation training and comparison with mindfulness-based stress reduction. *Mindfulness, 9,* 1494–1508.

Gilbert, P. (1998). Evolutionary psychopathology: Why isn't the mind better designed than it is? *British Journal of Medical Psychology, 71*(4), 353–373.

Gilbert, P. (2007). *Psychotherapy and counselling for depression* (3rd ed.). Sage.

Gilbert, P. (2009). *The compassionate mind: A new approach to life's challenges.* Constable-Robinson.

Gilbert, P. (2014). The origins and nature of compassion focused therapy. *British Journal of Clinical Psychology, 53*(1), 6–41.

Halifax, J. (2008). *Being with dying: Cultivating compassion and fearlessness in the presence of death.* Shambhala.

Ho, A. H. Y., Tan-Ho, G., Ngo, T. A., Ong, G., Cheng, P. H., Dignadice, D., & Potash, J. S. (2019). A novel mindful compassion art therapy (MCAT) for reducing burnout and promoting resilience for EoL care professionals: A waitlist RCT protocol. *Trials, 20*(1), 406.

Hoffmann, S. G., Grossman, P., & Hinton, D. E. (2011). Loving-kindness and compassion mediation: Potential for psychological intervention. *Clinical Psychology Review, 13,* 1126–1132.

Jazaieri, H., McGonigal, K., Jinpa, T., Doty, J. R., Gross, J. J., & Goldin, P. R. (2013). A randomized controlled trial of compassion cultivation training: Effects on mindfulness, affect, and emotion regulation. *Motivation and Emotion, 38*(1), 23–35.

Kanouse, D. E., & Hanson, L. R., Jr. (1987). Negativity in evaluations. In E. E. Jones, D. E. Kanouse, H. H. Kelley, R. E. Nisbett, S. Valins, & B. Weiner (Eds.), *Attribution: Perceiving the causes of behavior* (pp. 47–62). Lawrence Erlbaum Associates, Inc.

Kemeny, M. E., Foltz, C., Cavanagh, J. F., Cullen, M., Giese-Davis, J., Jennings, P., & Ekman, P. (2012). Contemplative/emotion training reduces negative emotional behavior and promotes prosocial responses. *Emotion, 12*(2), 338–350.

Kim, J. J., Cunnington, R., & Kirby, J. N. (2020). The neurophysiological basis of compassion: An fMRI meta-analysis of compassion and its related neural processes. *Neuroscience and Biobehavioral Review, 108,* 112–123.

Kirby, J. N. (2017). Compassion interventions: The programmes, the evidence, and implications for research and practice. *Psychology and Psychotherapy*, *90*(3), 432–455.

Kirby, J. N., & Gilbert, P. (2017). The emergence of the compassion focused therapies. In P. Gilbert (Ed.), *Compassion: Concepts, research and applications* (pp. 258–285). Routledge.

Koh, T. L. H., Chia, T. Y., & Ho, A. H. Y. (2020). *Movie reflection for junior doctors working in palliative care units*. Proposal to the Palliative Care Centre for Excellence in Research and Education. Singapore.

Kolts, R. L., Bell, T., Bennett-Ley, J., & Irons, C. (2018). *Experiencing compassion-focused therapy from the inside out: A self-practice/self-reflection workbook for therapists*. Guilford Press.

Ling, D., Petrakis, M., & Olver, J. H. (2021). The use of common humanity scenarios to promote compassion in healthcare workers. *Australian Social Work*, *74*(1), 110–121.

Neff, K. (2003). Self-compassion: An alternative conceptualization of a healthy attitude toward oneself. *Self and Identity*, *2*, 85–101.

Neff, K. D. (2012). The science of self-compassion. In C. Germer & R. Siegel (Eds.), *Compassion and wisdom in psychotherapy* (pp. 79–92). Guilford Press.

Neff, K., & Germer, C. K. (2013). A pilot study and randomized controlled trial of the mindful self-compassion program. *Journal of Clinical Psychology*, *69*(1), 28–44.

Neimeyer, R. A., Burke, L. A., Mackay, M. M., & Van Dyke Stringer, J. G. (2010). Grief therapy and the reconstruction of meaning: From principles to practice. *Journal of Contemporary Psychotherapy*, *40*(2), 73–83.

Netz, Y., Wu, M.-J., Becker, B. J., & Tenenbaum, G. (2005). Physical activity and psychological well-being in advanced age: A meta-analysis of intervention studies. *Psychology and Aging*, *20*(2), 272–284.

Oveis, C., Horberg, E. J., & Keltner, D. (2010). Compassion, pride, and social intuitions of self-other similarity. *Journal of Personality and Social Psychology*, *98*(4), 618–630.

Pace, T. W., Negi, L. T., Adame, D. D., Cole, S. P., Sivilli, T. L., Brown, T. D., Issa, M. J., & Raison, C. L. (2009). Effect of compassion meditation on neuroendocrine, innate immune and Behavioral responses to psychological stress. *Psychoneuroendocrinology*, *34*, 87–98.

Penner, L. A., Dovidio, J. F., Piliavin, J. A., & Schroeder, D. A. (2005). Prosocial behavior: multilevel perspectives. *Annual Reviews of Psychology*, *56*, 365–392.

Sabo, B. M. (2011). Compassionate presence: The meaning of hematopoietic stem cell transplant nursing. *European Journal of Oncology Nursing*, *15*(2), 103–111.

Shanmugam, R., Patinadan, P. V., Tan-Ho, G., Choo, P. Y., & Ho, A. H. Y. (2021). I am not eating this! Understanding identity, psycho-socio-cultural meaning and dignity expressed in patient food voices: An applied drama intervention for student nurses. *Paper presented at the Singapore Drama Educators Association Theatre Arts Conference, 2021 – Creative Disruption: Exploring New Ground. Singapore*. 22–30 May 2021.

Strauss, C., Taylor, B. L., Gu, J., Kuyken, W., Baer, R., Jones, F., & Cavanagh, K. (2016). What is compassion and how can we measure it? A review of definitions and measures. *Clinical Psychology Review*, *47*, 15–27.

Sturmer, S., Snyder, M., Kropp, A., & Siem, B. (2006). Empathy-motivated helping: The moderating role of group membership. *Personality and Social Psychology Bulletin*, *32*(7), 943–956.

Turner, E. H., Matthews, A. M., Linardatos, E., Tell, R. A., & Rosenthal, R. (2008). Selective publication of antidepressant trials and its influence on apparent efficacy. *New England Journal of Medicine*, *358*(3), 252–260.

van den Brik, E., & Koster, F. (2015). *Mindfulness-based compassionate living*. Routledge.

Warneken, F., & Tomasello, M. (2009). The roots of human altruism. *British Journal of Psychology*, *100*(3), 455–471.

CHAPTER 8

MINDFUL AWARENESS

A Cultivated Journey for Clinicians and Practitioners

Adrian Wan, Eric Leung, and Paul Victor Patinadan

INTRODUCTION TO MINDFUL AWARENESS: CONCEPTUAL UNDERPINNINGS

The last four decades have seen mindful awareness and contingent mindfulness-based practices flourish within the spheres of academic and clinical work (Bishop et al., 2004). A search of 'mindful awareness' and 'mindfulness' on Google Scholar seeking material within the last year (2020–2021) observes close to 20,000 and 30,000 hits respectively. However, despite exponential popularity as an interventional tool, universal definitions of what constitutes mindful awareness/mindfulness remain occluded. Often, the terms are employed interchangeably, circling Kabat-Zinn's (2013) description of a process that brings a quality of attention toward moment-to-moment experience. Though an attentional, observational, and correctional quality is enunciated with the use of 'mindful awareness,' both terms have been employed to describe a quality of attention, a mental mode, a psychological trait, specific or collective meditative techniques, or the outcome of the practice itself (Bishop et al., 2004; Segal et al., 2018). One certainty is that it is rooted within the spiritual practice of Buddhism, a tenet embedded within a system developed as a path, with the cessation of personal suffering its destination (Thera & Fromm, 2005). With aspirations of holistic healing, the integration of mindfulness within clinical practice seems a natural progression.

Within literature describing mindful treatments, a synthesis of definitions focuses on the cognitive and socio-emotional, with mindfulness being a non-elaborative, non-judgmental, present-centered awareness in which arising thoughts, feelings, or sensations are acknowledged and accepted 'as is,' fully within the moment (Bishop et al., 2004; Kabat-Zinn, 2013; Segal et al., 2018). From what is observed in the attentional field, there is no automatic, habitual patterned reactivity or overidentification; instead a space is created between perception and reaction, guiding reflective (rather than reflexive) response (Bishop et al., 2004).

To consolidate the experience of mindfulness, Bishop et al. (2004) proposed a two-component model with: (a) *self-regulation of attention* and maintenance upon the immediate experience allowing increased recognition of mental events and (b) *orientation to experience* within the present moment characterized by curiosity, openness, and acceptance. Siegel (2009) enunciates the integrative processes of mindful awareness, moving to hypothesize internal attunement as a catalyst for a coherent flow of energy and information through the brain, mind, and relationships, thus freeing one from associative memory and encouraging a resilient and vital self. Taken together, the cognitive, attentional, and biological mediating factors of mindfulness become apparent (Bishop et al., 2004).

Mindfulness seems to be the fountainhead for processes primary in the development of universal values such as empathy and compassion. Tirch (2010) details mindful practice

DOI: 10.4324/9781003204121-11

within prescientific Buddhist traditions as reaching toward training in compassion and loving-kindness toward the self and others. In empirically justifying this relationship, Tirch's (2010) consolidation of theoretical and neuroimaging data observed the interrelatedness of mindful awareness and compassion, an example being the thickening of the insula and prefrontal cortices of mindful meditators—areas of the brain linked to caregiving and compassionate behavior. Contemporary research seems affirming of Buddhist philosophy; that mindful awareness and arising compassion are correlates of self-experience as an interrelated part of ever-evolving interbeing.

The suite of universal interpersonal values that can be born from mindful awareness (altruism, empathy, interconnectedness, and compassion) is imperative for professional caregivers to cultivate, for the benefit of themselves and their charges. Due to the intensity of caregiving work, however, healthcare professionals supporting traumatized clients are consequently vulnerable to emotional and psychological distress (Newsome et al., 2012). Prolonged exposure to vocational stress may result in burnout, which is manifested in physical symptoms and emotional exhaustion (Maslach et al., 2001).

These findings of negative psychological and mental states due to vocational responsibilities are especially true among healthcare professionals working within the field of grief and end-of-life care (Dijxhoorn et al., 2021). Guided cultivation of mindful awareness and arising compassion as such can be an efficacious means in ensuring professionals contributing within the spheres of death, dying, grief, and bereavement are able to care not only for their charges but for themselves as well.

END-OF-LIFE CAREGIVING AND THE NEED FOR MINDFUL AWARENESS

End-of-life care can be the most psychologically and spiritually challenging healthcare setting. Care professionals are required to not only provide succor for painful experiences of others, but also embrace vulnerability in the face of death and dying, confronting their own existential fears and worries. Moreover, they are often distressed by the overwhelming uncertainty of the client's condition and ongoing disappointments, grievance, and anguish they encounter in their everyday work. As death becomes imminent, the foundation of how, even as a care specialist, one views the self can often be shaken, questioning the medical profession, faith in higher powers, and outlooks on life. The distressing nature of the work continues to be well-documented. A systematic review of 59 studies of end-of-life professionals saw burnout rates ranging from 3% to 66%. Emotional exhaustion, depersonalization, and low personal accomplishment were observed in the study samples (Dijxhoorn et al., 2021). Unresolved, burnout and ill-managed care values during practice are observed to cause *empathic distress fatigue*, a reconceptualization of the increasingly discarded 'compassion fatigue,' focusing on vicarious negative emotions overwhelming the empathizer and threatening the self with blurring of the self-other distinction (Oakley, 2012). Empathic distress as the physical exhaustion that predisposes one to the feelings of apathy and intra- and inter-personal disconnection is detrimental to the emotional, cognitive, behavioral, and interpersonal functioning of healthcare professionals (Pope & Vasquez, 2005). It is imperative for healthcare professionals to find balance where feelings for their charge's suffering do not reach the extent of becoming overwhelming, hampering caring for the other patients they serve.

The empathic response is a noble one, a natural outgrowth of the mammalian brain associated with human survival and occurring automatically without conscious awareness by the activation of neuro-cortical structures active in other experiencing the emotion (Singer & Lamm, 2009). Though this can be helpful in sympathizing and understanding the suffering of others in therapeutic relationships, it can be inimical in the long term. Instead, academic and clinical consensus has shifted toward the other-oriented focus of a more compassionate response, one that mediates the empathizer's identification with witnessed suffering (Oakley, 2012). Evidence suggests that compassion and loving-kindness can proffer health benefits to the empathizing carer to the advantage of both parties, with sufferers gaining from received aid and empathizers from the feelings of caring and warmth toward the self (Oakley, 2012). Mindful awareness and antecedent skills that allow healthcare professionals to reach a sustainable emotional and compassionate balance are thus a vital component in providing quality end-of-life service.

MINDFUL AWARENESS: A JOURNEY OF MANY PATHS

As in other fields, healthcare professionals are discovering that the practice of mindfulness can be utilized as a beneficial resource for themselves and their clients (Cacciatore & Flint, 2012). Mindful awareness practices have become popular in the healthcare community to manage stress, preserve well-being, and develop healthier ways to cater to the suffering of individuals and families being cared for. Observing the suffering of others becomes bearable if practitioners engage clients mindfully, with compassion; proper cultivation of the practice is the first vital step for holistic care. Meditation has long provided a foundational impetus in the achievement of a mindfully aware state, and has also been showcased in the prevention and mitigation of caregiver burnout (Bishop et al., 2004; Dijxhoorn et al., 2021). Shapiro's (1982) classic definition of meditation as "a family of techniques which have in common a conscious attempt to focus attention in a nonanalytical way and an attempt not to dwell on discursive, ruminating thought" (p. 268) is a useful catchall term focusing on the mental state that incorporates forms of stationary (traditional seated) and movement-based (yoga) approaches.

Kristeller and Johnson's (2005) *Two-Stage Model of Meditation* examines the relationship between mindfulness and well-being; it also describes how mindfulness practice helps to foster compassion. The model perceives mindfulness as not only a relaxation skill, but also an anchoring process that facilitates the cultivation of compassion, echoing the original intention of practicing mindfulness. The first stage involves awareness of habitual patterns and responses and a de-conditioning from usual preoccupation with self-reinforcing, self-defeating, or self-indulgent behaviors and reactions (Kristeller and Johnson, 2005). In order to facilitate compassion's requirement of engaging with the other, Loving-Kindness Meditation (LKM; a common form of Buddhist-inspired mindfulness) is suggested as the second step via focused engagement with one's own compassionate agency. Connection with the target of LKM (for example, the self in self-compassion, and the other in other-compassion) can be achieved through self-regulation practice, such as reciting a mantra, or eliciting a compassionate internal dialogue. Regardless of the meditative techniques employed, care practitioners can benefit from cultivating several key 'paths' to achieve their compassionate goals; namely, cultivating mindful awareness in attentional, emotional, and co-regulatory manners.

THE PATH TO ATTENTIONAL REGULATION

The practice of mindfulness emphasizes the cultivation of a non-judgmental, direct aware-ness of the present environment. The core of practicing mindful awareness is to cultivate an attitude of non-attachment, allowing experience to be what it is, noticing it moment by moment with a beginner's mind (Kabat-Zinn, 2013). Of such practice, Siegel (2007) char-acterizes the quality of attention as involving Curiosity, Openness, Acceptance, and Love (COAL). This attention is purposefully kept open in mindful practice attending to whatever enters the field of awareness sans analytic engagement or thinking about the object (which can be emotions, physical feeling, images, or external objects; Kristeller & Johnson, 2005). Direct perception and understanding of the world thus occur through actual experiences, not just through the lens of one's thoughts—which are representational and symbolic. The perceptual shift with attentional regulation would require awareness of the situation as it is and disengagement from the habitual, reactive coping strategies of fight-flight-freeze (e.g., resistance, avoidance, and numbing; Kristeller & Johnson, 2005; Neff & Germer, 2018). Thus, as healthcare providers are consistently in touch with suffering, instead of getting swept away by intense emotions through analytic rumination and reactivity, attentional de-centering and turning toward the suffering with mindfulness before response benefits both carer and charge.

THE PATH TO EMOTIONAL REGULATION

Salvarani et al. (2019) demonstrated a time-limited mindfulness training for nursing staff that was found effective in promoting emotional regulation, variability, flexibility, and enhanced cognitive empathy, buffering against professional distress. A recent systematic review revealed that mindfulness was effective at improving negative affect and empathy fatigue, with the cultivation of compassion improving positive affect (Conversano et al., 2020). The practice of mindfulness has been shown to be closely linked to the mechanisms of emotion regulation (Roemer et al., 2015), and appears to be a protective factor against professional burnout among healthcare professionals. Mindful practices were also found to be useful in promoting emotionality in spheres of balance, awareness, acceptance, recogni-tion, and expressive suppression (Jiménez-Picón et al., 2021).

For healthcare professionals working with vulnerable populations, the ability to regu-late one's emotions is important. Vocational responsibilities, such as management of pain and loss, and the emotional discomfort of supporting charges through the end-of-life pro-cess can contribute to a heightened emotional burden. A balance must be struck between emotional investment and detachment, allowing for effective response to the demands of the role and needs of those they serve. Mindful awareness can cut a path for this process.

THE PATH TO CO-REGULATION

Žvelc and Žvelc (2021) posit that effective therapy requires the therapist to keep them-selves regulated through mindful awareness, in turn co-regulating the state of the client in attendance to themselves; so too with mindful awareness and compassion. Hallett (2021) describes their client's appreciation for co-regulation during a session; that the author was "a steady presence even in the volatility of (their) emotions. Seeing someone unshaken by suffering but still there to talk" (p. 3). When a healthcare professional can mindfully receive bereaved or grieving individuals, they can begin to acknowledge that it is understandable to be in this difficult place despite the difficult emotions, thoughts, or sensations that arise in the journey. This way of being models a path for those who are grieving to eventually become more tolerant and welcoming to these experiences (Cacciatore & Flint, 2012; Siegel, 2009). This is especially important for those at the beginning of their grief journey, who feel like they have been thrown into an unknown characterized by anger, sadness, grief, and hopelessness. When healthcare practitioners are mindfully aware, co-regulation of emotional states can occur for their charges.

THE COMPASSIONATE WAY

Self-compassion entails being kind and understanding toward the self at times of suffering, perceiving experiences as part of the larger human experience, and holding suffering in mindful awareness. It has been described as a feeling of empathy/kindness toward one's failure or suffering, which encourages understanding rather than self-criticism and punishment (Germer & Neff, 2013). A compassionate attitude toward oneself emerges when clarity and perspective are gained through personal experience (Germer & Neff, 2019; Neff & Seppala, 2017). With mindful awareness, experience of these stories unfolds within the present moment; curiosity and openness pave the way for honest, compassionate introspection (Cacciatore & Flint, 2012). Newsome et al. (2012) reported that the practice of mindfulness reduced perceived stress, and improved self-compassion. Consequently, having compassion for others entails a sense of self-compassion. As mindful practice develops self-compassion for healthcare professionals, attitudes of concern for patients' feelings are promoted and lead to a more pronounced care tenor.

PROFESSIONAL WAYFINDING: CULTIVATING PATHS FOR HEALTHCARE PROFESSIONALS

A substantial amount of research has shown that mindfulness-based stress reduction (MBSR) training helps cultivate optimal levels of mindfulness and may even contribute to brain plasticity for functional and structural changes (Tang et al., 2020). Along with MBSR, Mindfulness-Based Cognitive Therapy (MBCT) has also demonstrated effectiveness in mitigating burnout for healthcare professionals vis-à-vis cultivating qualities of mindfulness (Ruths et al., 2013).

The adaptation of mindful awareness into clinical practice not only serves the purpose of being an evidence-based practice for the clients, but aids self-development, stress management, and prevention of burnout for practicing professionals. Various forms of mindfulness training programs have been adopted to help healthcare professionals cope with work-related stress, burnout, and empathic distress, including nurses (Mackenzie et al., 2006) and therapists in training (Shapiro et al., 2007). Accumulating research also supports the effectiveness of mindfulness-inspired programs, such as Compassion-Focused Therapy (CFT) (Beaumount et al., 2016) and Mindful Self-Compassion (Conversano et al., 2020) in cultivating mindfulness and promoting overall wellness of healthcare professionals.

The Mindful Self-Compassion (MSC) program, developed by Kristin Neff and Christopher Germer, debuted in 2010, and the first randomized controlled trial was conducted in 2012 (Germer & Neff, 2013; Neff & Germer, 2013). Effectively, the MSC program emphasizes the cultivation of self-compassion through the practice of mindfulness and other meditations, a feature not commonly shared by other mindfulness-inspired programs available. Instead of paying attention to here-and-now experiences and practicing mindfulness as a means of stress management, the MSC program places emphasis on the *experiencer* (one who is experiencing those here-and-now experiences), and the nurturance of the attitude of mindful awareness, self-kindness, and a sense of common humanity (Germer, 2009). The program comprises 3 core compassion-inspired practices, 4 meditations, and 18 informal practice methods (Germer & Neff, 2019). The program is available in various lengths and formats, including an 8-week foundational version and a 5-day intensive course, and more recently, the team at the Centre for Mindful Self-Compassion (CMSC) has also developed an accessible 'short course' for Mindful Self-Compassion which consists of 6 90-minute sessions especially for healthcare professionals.

As Certified Teachers in MSC, the current authors (A.W. and E.L.) have found that two brief mindful awareness-based practices can be particularly helpful for professionals: *Affectionate Breathing* and *Sole of Feet*. These practices are simple, short, and can be practiced anywhere, helping professionals to cultivate mindfulness awareness in everyday life.

The *Affectionate Breathing* practice—one of the core practices from the MSC program—aids in the immediate cultivation of mindful awareness. It is a common form of mindful breathing meditation with added suggestions that bring affection to the self during the process—adding warmth to one's mindful breathing practice (Neff & Germer, 2018). The practice invites the mind to be more focused and calmer. This can be done by finding a posture where our body is comfortable and feels supported. We then notice the breath in our body through the subtle movements of breathing, the rhythm of breathing, and the sensations in the body when breath is drawn, and allow the self to become part of the breath. A sample instruction for *Affectionate Breathing* is detailed in Table 8.1.

The informal *Sole of the Feet* is a mindfulness practice that helps to anchor ourselves at the present moment and to offer grounding when experiencing overwhelming emotions, facilitating emotional regulation (Neff & Germer, 2018). We can bring awareness to the sense of touch of the soles of our feet on the floor when we encounter difficult emotions, or when we want to cultivate our mindful awareness of the present moment. This practice can be done when we are seated, or we can also feel the changes in our sensations when we rock gently with our feet on the floor as we stand or walk slowly. A sample script of *Sole of the Feet* is presented in Table 8.1.

For most of the classes we (A.W. and E.L.) have taught, we notice that many beginners find mindful breathing practice challenging due to our wandering mind—the overdominance of the *default mode network*—the brain structures located right down the midline of the brain, from front to back. The default mode network becomes highly active when nothing in particular is occupying our attention; this neurological network creates a sense of self, and projects this self into the past or future while looking for problems, thus making us alert and resulting in our wandering mind (Grugerger et al., 2011). One alternative to help cultivate mindful awareness is by directing our attention to what is happening around us in the present moment using all five of our senses. We can integrate the practice of mindful awareness in our daily lives, such as allowing ourselves the time to close our eyes and listen to the sounds of the environment, letting the sounds come to us. We can also practice mindfulness by maintaining a soft, wide-angle gaze, noticing the visual impressions that we see. Additionally, we can practice mindfulness when we eat or drink, by allowing ourselves to notice the scents and the tastes of the refreshments we enjoy during the day.

Table 8.1 Scripts for Practice

Affectionate Breathing	Sole of the Feet	Mindfulness in Daily Life
Find a posture in which your body is comfortable and feels supported, and then gently close your eyes, partially or fully. Place your hand over your heart or any other soothing place to remind us that we are bringing affectionate awareness to our breathing and to ourselves. Begin to notice your breathing within your body… Notice how your body is nourished on the in-breath and relaxes with the out-breath. Notice the rhythm of your breathing, flowing in and out. Notice your body moving with the breath… Allow your whole body to be gently rocked and caressed by your breathing Gently release your attention on your breath, sitting quietly in your own experience, and allow yourself to feel whatever you are feeling and be just as you are. Slowly and gently open your eyes.	Place the soles of your feet on the floor, and gently close your eyes, fully or partially. Notice the sensations in the soles of your feet on the floor as you sit on the chair, or as you stand. To better feel sensations—the sense of touch—in the soles of the feet, try gently rocking forward and backward (or making small steps) on your feet (or if you are standing, you can walk slowly, too). Notice the changing sensations on your feet as you lift your foot as you are making the small step, and placing your foot on the floor. Feel how the ground supports your whole body. Now, returning to the resting position and expanding your awareness to your entire body, let yourself feel whatever you are feeling and let yourself be just as you are. Slowly and gently open your eyes.	Pick an ordinary activity, maybe something that you enjoy doing (you may wish to pick an activity that occurs early in the day before your mind gets distracted by your daily hassles). Pick one sensory experience to explore in this activity; maybe the sounds, the sensations, the smell, etc. Give yourself permission to fully immerse yourself in the experience through the sense you have chosen. Allow yourself to feel the experience to the fullest, gently bringing your attention back again and again when you notice your mind has wandered. Practice mindful awareness with this activity every day for a week.

These *Mindfulness in Daily Life* practices can be accomplished by following the instructions delineated in Table 8.1.

CONCLUSION

The practice of mindfulness is a cultivated journey for clinicians and practitioners in the field of healthcare. Mindful awareness is the foundation of self-compassion. While it is not extremely difficult for us to be mindful for a moment or two, it is challenging to maintain the state of mind due to natural tendencies of the *wandering brain*. Nevertheless, mindful awareness is a simple skill that can be learned through practice. This chapter considered the foundational conceptualizations of mindful awareness and how it progresses into compassion, along with the benefits they can bestow. Easy-to-use skills helpful for the helping professional to cultivate mindful awareness and self-care in their everyday life were proposed. It is hoped that this chapter encourages healthcare professionals to holistically serve those who are in need, and themselves, in ways that are congruent with the very intention of their devotion to entering the profession in the first place.

REFERENCES

Beaumount, E., Irons, C., Rayner, G., & Dagnall, N. (2016). Does compassion-focused therapy training for health care educators and providers increase self-compassion and reduce self-persecution and self-criticism? *Journal of Continuing Education in the Health Professions, 36*(1), 4–10.

Bishop, S. R., Lau, M., Shapiro, S. L., Carlson, L., Anderson, N. D., Carmody, J. (2004). Mindfulness: A proposed operational definition. *Clinical Psychology: Science and Practice, 11*(3), 230–241.

Cacciatore, J., & Flint, M. (2012). ATTEND: Towards a mindfulness-based bereavement care model. *Death Studies, 36*, 61–82.

Conversano, C., Ciacchini, R., Orru, G., Di Giuseppe, M., Gemignani, A., & Poli, A. (2020). Mindfulness, compassion, and self-compassion among health care professionals: What's new? A system review. *Froniters in Psychology, 11*, 1–21. https://doi.org/10.3389/fpsyg.2020.01683

Dijxhoorn, A.-F. Q., Brom, L., van der Linden, Y. M., Leget, C., & Raijmakers, N. J. (2021). Prevalence of burnout in healthcare professionals providing palliative care and the effect of interventions to reduce symptoms: A systematic literature review. *Palliative Medicine, 35*(1), 6–26. https://doi.org/10.1177/0269216320956825

Germer, C. K. (2009). *The mindful path to self-compassion: Freeing yourself from destructive thoughts and emotions.* Guildford Publications.

Germer, C. K., & Neff, K. D. (2013). Self-compassion in clinical practice. *Journal of Clinical Psychology, 69*(8), 856–867.

Germer, C. K., & Neff, K. D. (2019). *Teaching the mindful self-compassion program: A guide for professionals.* Guildford Press.

Grugerger, M., Ben-Simin, E., Levkovitz, Y., Zangen, A., & Henderly, T. (2011). Towards a neuroscience of mind-wandering. *Fronters in Human Neuroscience.* https://doi.org/10.3389/fnhum.2011.00056

Hallett, J. (2021). Review of integrative psychotherapy: A mindfulness-and compassion-oriented approach by Gregor Žvelc and maša Žvelc, Routledge, 2021. *International Journal of Integrative Psychotherapy, 11*(1), 1–7.

Thera, N., & Fromm, E. (2005). *The heart of Buddhist meditation: Satipaṭ ṭhāna: A handbook of mental training based on the Buddha's way of mindfulness, with an anthology of relevant texts translated from the Pali and Sanskrit.* Buddhist Publication Society.

Jimenez-Picon, N., Romero-Martin, M., Ponce-Blandon, J. A., Ramierz-Baena, L., Palomo-Lara, J. C., & Gomez-Salgado, J. (2021). The relationship between mindfulness and emotional intelligence as a protector factor for helathcare professionals: Systematic review. *International Journal of Enviromental Research and Public Health, 18*(10), 549. https://doi.org/10.3390/ijerph18105491

Kabat-Zinn, J. (2013). *Full catastrophe living, revised edition: How to cope with stress, pain and illness using mindfulness meditation.* Little Brown Book Group.

Kristeller, J. L., & Johnson, T. (2005). Cultivating loving-kindness: A two-stage model of the effects of meditation on empathy, compassion, and altruism. *Zygon, 40*(2), 391–407.

Mackenzie, C. S., Poulin, P. A., & Seidman-Carlson, R. (2006). A brief mindfulness-based stress reduction intervention for nurses and nurse aides. *Applied Nursing Research, 19*(2), 105–109.

Maslach, C., Schaufeli, W. B., & Leiter, M. P. (2001). Job burnout. *Annual Review of Psychology, 52*, 397–422. https://doi.org/10.1146/annurev.psych.52.1.397

Neff, K. D., & Germer, C. K. (2013). A pilot study and randomized controlled trial of the mindful self-compassion program. *Journal of Clinical Psychology, 69*(1), 28–44.

Neff, K. D., & Germer, C. K. (2018). *The mindful self-compassion workbook: A proven way to accept yourself, build inner strength, and thrive*. Guildford Publications.

Neff, K., & Seppala, E. (2017). Compassion, well-being, and the hypoegoic self. In K. W. Brown & M. R. Leary (Eds.), *The Oxford handbook of hypo-egoic phenomena* (pp. 189–203) . Oxford University Press.

Newsome, S., Waldo, M., & Gruszka, C. (2012). Mindfulness group work: Preventing stress and increasing self-compassion among helping professionals in training. *Journal for Specialists in Group Work*, 1–15. https://doi.org/10.1080/01933922.2012.690832

Oakley, B. A. (Ed.). (2012). *Pathological altruism*. Oxford University Press.

Pope, K. S., & Vasquez, M. J. (2005). *How to survive and thrive as a therapist: Information, ideas, and resources for psychologists in practice*. American Psychological Assoiation.

Roemer, L., Willston, S. K., & Rooline, L. G. (2015). Mindfulness and emotion regulation. *Current Opinions in Psychology, 3*, 52–57.

Ruths, F. A., de Zoysa, N., Frearson, S., Hutton, J., William, J. M. G., & Walsh, J. (2013). Mindfulness-based cognitive therapy for mental health professionals—A pilot study. *Mindfulness, 4*(4), 289–295. https://doi.org/10.1007/s12671-012-0127-0

Salvarani, V., Rampoldi, G., Ardenghi, S., Bani, M., Blasi, P., Ausili, D., Di Mauro, S., & Strepparava, M. G. (2019). Protecting emergency room nurses from burnout: The role of dispositional mindfulness, emotion regulation and empathy. *Journal of Nuring Management, 27*(4), 65–774. https://doi.org/10.1111/jonm.12771

Segal, Z. V., Williams, J. M. G., Teasdale, J. D., & Kabat-Zinn, J. (2018). *Mindfulness-based cognitive therapy for depression* (2nd ed., paperback ed.). The Guilford Press.

Shapiro, S. L., Brown, K. K., & Biegel, G. M. (2007). Teaching self-care to caregivers: Effects of mindfulness-based stress reducation on the mental health of therapists in training. *Training and Education in Professional Psychology, 1*(2), 105–115.

Siegel, D. (2009). Mindful awareness, mindight, and neural integration. *Humanistic Psychologist, 37*(2), 137–158.

Siegel, D. J. (2007). *The mindful brain: Reflection and attunement in the cultivation of well-being* (1st ed.). W.W. Norton.

Singer, T., & Lamm, C. (2009). The social neuroscience of empathy. *Annals of the New York Academy of Sciences, 1156*, 81–96. https://doi.org/10.1111/j.1749-6632.2009.04418.x

Tang, R., Friston, K. J., & Tang, Y. Y. (2020). Brief mindfulness meditation induces gray matter changes in brain hub. *Neural Plasticity*, 1–8. https://doi.org/10.1155/2020/8830005

Tirch, D. D. (2010). Mindfulness as a context for the cultivation of compassion. *International Journal of Cognitive Therapy, 3*(2), 113–123. https://doi.org/10.1521/ijct.2010.3.2.113

Žvelc, G., & Žvelc, M. (2021). *Integrative psychotherapy a mindfulness- and compassion-oriented approach*. Routledge.

CHAPTER 9

BEING WITH GRIEF AND LOSS

The Foundational Role of Therapeutic Presence

Shari Geller and Claudia Dias Martins

INTRODUCTION

Despite the universality of suffering, there exists a tendency in Western cultures toward a fear and avoidance of loss. Nonetheless, we all directly bear witness to grief and loss through our own lived experience, or through the disclosed narratives of others. Discomfort surrounding death and non-death related losses (e.g., relationships, jobs, functioning) can be a major hindrance to healing, especially when coupled with the perceived pressure to fix something that cannot be fixed. It is important to process major losses, and consciously transition between stages of this precious life (Geller & Greenberg, 2012, in press). Psychotherapists have the capacity to shape the course of healing by curating a compassionate and safe environment that is conducive for transformation and growth. This is done through the cultivation and embodiment of therapeutic presence.

Extensive research demonstrates that the therapeutic relationship and alliance are the most consistent predictors of therapeutic outcomes and therapeutic change (Norcross & Lambert, 2019). Yet contributions to the alliance are less understood. A growing body of evidence suggests therapeutic presence is a common factor integral to generating psychological and emotional safety, developing strong therapeutic alliances, and optimizing the effectiveness of therapy trans-theoretically (Friedberg et al., 2013; Geller, 2017; Geller & Greenberg, in press; Geller & Porges, 2014; Geller et al., 2010; Hayes & Vinca, 2011; Pos et al., 2011). This chapter will outline the components of therapeutic presence, followed by a discussion of its theoretical and empirical support, as well as practical applications within compassion-based approaches when working with clients who are struggling with grief and loss.

WHAT IS THERAPEUTIC PRESENCE?

Therapeutic presence is a way of *being* in the therapeutic encounter that elevates the quality of service or the *doing* of therapy. It is attained when therapists offer their whole self to clients, physically, emotionally, cognitively, relationally, and spiritually (Geller, 2017; Geller & Greenberg, 2002, in press). Therapists' presence includes being grounded in oneself, while receptively attuned to the verbal and bodily expression of clients' moment-to-moment experience (Geller, 2017). This inner receptive stance of attunement to therapists' own bodily experience enriches embodied knowledge, professional skill, and wisdom, as well as an embodied understanding about the client and the therapeutic process. This client- and self-attunement also allows therapists to recognize when they are not present, and to bring themselves back into contact with the client and the moment. Being fully present invites an attuned responsiveness that stems from sensing one's own and the other's affect and experience.

DOI: 10.4324/9781003204121-12

RESEARCH ON THERAPEUTIC PRESENCE: HOW DOES IT HELP?

Presence has been shown to positively predict the therapeutic alliance and session outcome across multiple modalities (Geller, 2017; Geller & Greenberg, in press; Geller et al., 2010; Pos et al., 2011). An empirically validated model of presence includes (a) **the preparation for presence**, in life and before sessions, (b) **the in-session process of presence**, which involves extending contact to be open, attuned, and receptive to the client's and one's own moment-to-moment experience, and finally (c) **the embodied experience** of groundedness within self, immersion in the moment with the client, connection to a vast sense of expansion, and commitment to being compassionately with and for the client and their healing process (Geller & Greenberg, 2002, in press).

Therapists' self-care is essential in the model of therapeutic presence as it supports therapists in remaining attuned within themselves, and responsive to their clients' moment-to-moment verbal and nonverbal experiences (Geller, 2017; Geller & Greenberg, 2002, in press). Especially in supporting clients with grief and loss, knowing it can touch the grief we carry as therapists, attunement to self and self-care are essential to remain present, compassionate, and closely attuned and in contact with clients' experience.

The expression of presence helps clients to feel safe and held, strengthening the therapeutic relationship and creating the ground for clients to share their vulnerabilities and fears. Porges' Polyvagal Theory (2011; Geller & Porges, 2014) delineates how this expression of presence is possible through vocal prosody, open body posture, soft facial expression, and attentive eye gaze. Clients receiving presence experience safety on a neurophysiological level as a result of bidirectional attunement, neuroception, and co-regulation (for more on the neurophysiological underpinnings of therapeutic presence, see Geller, 2018; Geller & Porges, 2014). They "feel felt" (Siegel, 2010), met, and understood, thereby optimizing their emotional expression and engagement in therapy (Geller, 2017).

ACCEPTANCE OF SUFFERING, GRIEF, AND LOSS

The Buddha's teachings emphasize how suffering is inevitable and a large part of life is spent in pain, stress, and confusion. Upon departure from his father's kingdom, Siddhartha Gautama (the Buddha) was shocked by the reality of aging, illness, and death. The unsatisfactoriness inherent to life influenced the First Noble Truth of Buddhism, dukkha, which is based on accepting that life is suffering. In fact, ignoring suffering is said to only perpetuate it. Despite our deep fear of suffering, the conception of life and death as inextricably connected and death as inevitable continues to be reiterated, and authors often affirm the importance of slowing down and attending to suffering with presence (e.g., Bonwitt, 2008; Cecil, 2020; Harris & Winokuer, 2019; Rapgay, 2006).

Accepting life and death as opposite ends of the same spectrum is particularly important because even in the face of death, memories of a loved one *live on* for those who remain. Cecil (2020) outlines an analogy of the elephant in the room which is generally something nobody wants to talk about until it becomes so large that it is unavoidable. Through this analogy, death is seen as a sort of elephant in the room, with therapists and clients feeling discomfort in navigating these painful experiences. Paradoxically, it is often these hidden parts of ourselves and our clients that require attention, tenderness, and care for transformation to occur. Teachings from Tibetan Buddhism are intended to make death and dying more manageable, while also inspiring wholehearted compassion toward all beings who will ultimately die at some point (Rapgay, 2006). Rapgay (2006) asserts that being in the presence of death and dying can help us activate constant presence in life; it can pour meaning into the lives we are living. The inner work and resilience of accepting grief, loss, and suffering would de-construct therapists' blocks to presence with grieving clients, empowering therapists to lean in with presence and compassion rather than hold back in fear.

PRESENCE AND COMPASSION FOR GRIEF AND LOSS: THE BENEFITS AND THE CHALLENGES

There is no more important place in psychotherapy for therapeutic presence than being with someone who has experienced loss (Geller & Greenberg, 2012). Being present and compassionate with the depths of grief people experience in this inevitable life stage, without trying to fix or change their experience, is necessary for healing, especially in a society where there is pressure to "get over" a loss, with messages such as two-day bereavement leaves from work setting the expectation that the loss of a loved one should be processed quickly and a return to daily life is easy.

Having said that, being there for a client who is experiencing grief from death or non-death related losses can be a major challenge to therapeutic presence. Our own feelings of helplessness, fear, overwhelm, and grief can get in the way of our ability to help someone whose heart has been wrung out and who is struggling to accept the reality of their loss. Everyone will experience death. Ensuring we have cared for our own grief is important so that we can stay open to the pain of our clients without shutting down. This also includes knowing our limitations when our own grief and pain are too raw to be able to stay open with others. This was apparent in a real way to the first author during the recent pandemic:

Vignette. I (first author) tragically lost my father after he spent almost ten weeks in the intensive care unit on a ventilator. Following several weeks off work prior to his death, I took another month off after his death. I was aware of the long hiatus and wanted to return to clients since they had been left without necessary support (they had a choice to see someone else yet chose not to). Upon my first week back, I realized how much I embody presence, and how important it was to have a readiness and inner stability to be with clients' pain. As I listened and attuned to my clients' pain and fear during the pandemic, I felt an emptiness and overwhelm in myself. I would drop into my body to be present with them, a core skill in therapeutic presence, and would quickly touch the overwhelming pain of my own grief from losing my beloved parent. I realized I was not ready to return and took an additional six weeks off so that I could care for myself and my own grief. This allowed the necessary time to heal "enough" so that I could be fully present with others without losing contact with myself.

Being present with others requires us to be fully open and in contact with clients' pain and our embodied presence. There is nothing to change or do, yet there is power in being fully present with clients in all their humanness as they navigate the painful experience. Harris and Winokuer (2019) emphasize the importance of sitting with client's grief as the client adjusts to their painful loss, considering we cannot make clients feel better or bring their loved one back. This requires courage, vulnerability, and skill when it comes to broaching a subject that a client may not feel comfortable discussing with others (i.e., the circumstances around their loved one's tragic death), as well as groundedness, stability, and deep listening so that clients can feel truly heard when they do open up.

In stark contrast to the enormous fear and avoidance of death and dying in the Western world, the compassionate care movement highlights how revolutionary it can be to bring presence into end-of-life care (Halifax, 2009). Roshi Bernie Glassman outlined three tenets of compassionate care, which include (a) *not knowing*, (b) *bearing witness*, and (c) *compassionate action* (Halifax, 2009). Building on these tenets, Frank Ostaseski (2019) teaches five invitations, which offer helpful guidelines and also reflect a presence stance to grief. These are (a) *don't wait*; (b) *welcome everything, push away nothing*; (c) *bring your whole self to the experience*; (d) *find a place of rest in the middle of things*; and (e) *cultivate don't-know mind*. When therapists carry the intention to stay grounded in themselves, trust in the process of attunement with others, and set the foundation for compassionate action, they will be better able to gauge what is needed for deeper therapeutic work.

Bonwitt (2008) explains the importance of balancing along the tightrope between life and death, making room for unfolding, and letting go of rigidity in therapeutic processes to allow for deeper resonance with the client experiencing grief in all its complexity and contradiction. From an Accelerated Experiential Dynamic Psychotherapy (AEDP) approach to death and dying, Cecil (2020) refers to therapeutic presence as a "quiet strength," which involves attunement, compassion, courage, and deeper wisdom. Presence replaces "fixing" with the genuine offering of ourselves to those in pain, so we are experiencing alongside them while also shining a light on their strengths. In this framework, presence and compassion allow for trust building and better understanding of the issue at hand and the needs of the client, which can help them feel safe and supported. Being there in this way is a practice of loving-kindness toward clients and therapists, whose work together is then optimized in session.

CULTIVATING AND TRAINING THERAPEUTIC PRESENCE AND COMPASSION

As a result of the COVID-19 pandemic, systemic racism, and widespread social inequities, there has been no shortage of grief and loss. Devastation has occurred at perpetually alarming rates, and simultaneously, the mourning process was completely transformed by public health regulations requiring physical distance. The cumulative and compacted grief caused by death and non-death related losses pervaded both individual and collective levels. In the context of helping professions, these experiences emerged for clients and similarly impacted the therapists who were extending themselves to support their clients through this difficult time. Aafjes-van Doorn et al. (2020) found that therapists reported moderate levels of vicarious traumatization, with higher levels among younger therapists with less clinical experience. The findings illustrate the importance of therapist training and support, which we believe could be enhanced by an increased focus on cultivating therapeutic presence. Even post-pandemic, training in therapeutic presence will help therapists feel more comfortable working with the universal experiences of grief and loss, and teach them how to be there for clients while also being in contact with and taking care of themselves (for more on therapeutic presence training and an extensive list of practices, see Geller & Greenberg, 2012; in press; Geller, 2017). Below we offer presence practices and specific clinical skills and guidelines aimed at cultivating safety and compassion before, during, and after sessions.

CULTIVATING PRESENCE IN LIFE

The importance of self-care extends to therapists' lives in between and outside of sessions. There is evidence that personal practices enhance attention, awareness, warmth, compassion, and sensitivity, which are foundational to attunement, understanding, and the development of positive therapeutic alliances (Geller & Greenberg, in press). Researchers also encourage integrating mindfulness practices in training programs and mindful self-compassion practices in life to help cultivate therapeutic presence and related qualities (Geller & Greenberg, in press; Germer, in press). Evidence shows that mindfulness training, loving-kindness meditation, and compassion practices can increase therapists' presence, compassion, empathy, and attunement with clients, as well as heighten their own sense of security in themselves and effectiveness in the therapeutic process, and reduce burnout (Boellinghaus et al., 2013; Tannen et al., 2017). Considering how compassion helps to mediate the positive influence of mindfulness in cultivating therapeutic presence (Bourgault & Dionne, 2018), it follows that compassion is not only an outcome of therapeutic presence but also a major contributor to its cultivation as well.

The following practices can be engaged with personally to help strengthen your presence in general and specifically with grief and loss.

Acceptance and saying yes (adapted from Brach, 2009). Relax into the moment by sitting or lying down comfortably and becoming aware of your breathing. Bring to mind an experience in your life that has caused you grief. For example, the death of a loved one, loss of a job, or diagnosis of a health condition. Now imagine how it would feel to fully accept the multitudes of that experience. Notice the sensations and feelings that emerge, imagine responding with a nod to yourself or a silent "yes," and notice how it feels to accept the experience wholeheartedly.

Self-compassion. Reflect on a particular loss you have experienced. See if you can contact the pain that still resides in relation to this loss. Notice where you feel that in your body. Name the sensations that arise in relation to this pain (i.e., tight burning in the stomach). Place a compassionate hand on the suffering, offering some compassionate touch or words of kindness ("I am here for you; I want to understand you"). Recognize your humanness and connection with others who have also experienced loss, a universal experience among all of us. Finally, ask this suffering, what does it need? Listen with presence and compassion to what arises.

CULTIVATING PRESENCE PRIOR TO SESSION

Preparing for presence and compassion requires therapists to intentionally set aside personal concerns, needs, preconceptions, expectations, beliefs, and theories while also taking care not to become enmeshed (Geller, 2017). This involves *clearing a space* by visualizing the emptying of your inner experience to welcome the experience of your client, as is similarly suggested in Gendlin's (1996) focusing process. Also important is putting aside plans about how sessions should go and opening to a more natural flow in service of the client, which can be conceptualized as *bracketing* (Geller & Greenberg, 2012). Engaging in a practice for even five minutes prior to session can support your presence in session as well as strengthen the therapeutic alliance and improve session outcomes (Dunn et al., 2013; Geller, 2017). This can include mindful breathing, long exhalations, listening to music, or engaging a practice such as the PRESENCE acronym below.

PRESENCE (from Geller, 2017). The following acronym encompasses all aspects of presence such as contact with self and other.

- **P**ause.
- **R**elax into this moment.
- **E**nhance awareness of your breath.
- **S**ense your inner body; bring awareness to your physical and emotional body.
- **E**xpand sensory awareness outwards (seeing, listening, touching, sensing what is around you).
- **N**otice what is true in this moment, both within you and around you. Notice the relationship between the internal and external.
- **C**enter and ground (in yourself and your body).
- **E**xtend and make contact (with client, or other).

CULTIVATING PRESENCE IN-SESSION

In-session techniques draw upon polyvagal theory, including leaning forward, mutual eye gaze, prosody of voice, and conveying sounds of care and compassion (Cecil, 2020; Geller, 2017, 2018). Also, bearing witness to clients' pain, with presence and acceptance for whatever arises, allowing clients to experience whatever they are experiencing and move through it without bypassing it (Cecil, 2020). Back et al. (2009) encourage silence to convey compassion and empathy, particularly when it is not necessarily being "used" as a technique. It is suggested that being there, rooted in presence, and sitting comfortably with compassionate silences as they emerge may be more healing than forcing alternate narratives. Generally, compassionate silences are more easily accessible in those with enhanced moment-to-moment awareness generated through contemplative practices and training (Back et al., 2009). This skill is especially relevant in the case of grief and loss, as therapists cannot fully understand the clients' experience or "fix" the circumstances. The skill of compassionate silence requires therapists to tolerate discomfort and uncertainty, to be present with clients' unfolding experience, and to allow clients the space to access their pain.

At times, bearing witness to the pain of others may elicit pain in our own body that becomes hard to sustain. A powerful practice comes from mindful self-compassion and involves breathing in compassion for self, while breathing out compassion for others (see Geller, 2017 for a detailed description of this practice). The following practice can also be helpful in moments of disconnection.

Pause, notice, and return (PNR; Geller, 2017). During experiences of overwhelm, helplessness, or disconnection in session, we recommend a simple yet profound PNR practice. This involves (a) pausing to ask yourself what is coming up for you, (b) non-judgmentally noticing what led to this feeling, and taking a moment to visualize yourself putting it aside for the time being, and (c) returning awareness to the present moment through intentional breathing, grounding, and directed focus back to the client from this place of inner stability. It is important to carve out time outside of session to care for your inner experience of being with grief and loss, and process the underlying emotional triggers to prevent future re-occurrences.

CONCLUSION

Therapeutic presence is a powerful stance in holding clients' grief and suffering while grounding and holding ourselves. As an empirically validated model, it guides therapists' attunement and is foundational to the cultivation of compassion and clients' safety in session. When therapeutic presence is conveyed by a therapist in a way that can be received by a client, it sets the foundation for growth and healing (Geller et al., 2010). The qualities of acceptance, openness, receptiveness, and warmth are particularly valuable when working with clients experiencing grief and loss (Halifax, 2009; Ostaseski, 2019). Presence requires practice and commitment to this way of being in ourselves, our personal relationships, and with our clients, so that we can attune to clients' pain, overwhelm, and shutdown, and stay in contact for all of it.

Based on the evidence that these qualities can be trained and applied across therapeutic approaches (see Geller, 2017 and Geller & Greenberg, in press; for an expanded literature review), researchers are expressing support and beginning to envision modules which could be integrated in training programs (Boellinghaus et al., 2013; Geller, 2017; Geller & Greenberg, in press; Tannen et al., 2017). As outlined in this chapter, we offer recommendations for presence practices that could be incorporated into training in working with grief and loss. These include self-care, practices based in mindfulness and compassion, as well as specific clinical skills intended to enhance presence, safety, and compassion. Above all, therapists must continue their own work in becoming comfortable with the uncertainty of life and death, processing their own grief and loss, embodying presence, and staying in contact with the moment-to-moment flow of life, death, and the between.

REFERENCES

Aafjes-van Doorn, K., Békés, V., Prout, T. A., & Hoffman, L. (2020). Psychotherapists' vicarious traumatization during the COVID-19 pandemic. *Psychological Trauma: Theory, Research, Practice, and Policy, 12*(S1), S148–S150. http://doi.org/10.1037/tra0000868

Back, A. L., Bauer-Wu, S., Rushton, C. H., & Halifax, J. (2009). Compassionate silence in the patient–clinician encounter: A contemplative approach. *Journal of Palliative Medicine, 12*(12), 1113–1117. http://doi.org/10.1089/jpm.2009.0175

Boellinghaus, I., Jones, F. W., & Hutton, J. (2013). Cultivating self-care and compassion in psychological therapists in training: The experience of practicing loving-kindness meditation. *Training and Education in Professional Psychology, 7*(4), 267–277. https://doi.org/10.1037/a0033092

Bonwitt, G. (2008). The seam between life and death and therapeutic presence. *American Journal of Psychoanalysis, 68*(3), 219–236. http://doi.org/10.1057/ajp.2008.24

Bourgault, M., & Dionne, F. (2018). Therapeutic presence and mindfulness: Mediating role of self-compassion and psychological distress among psychologists. *Mindfulness, 10*(1). https://doi.org/10.1007/s12671-018-1015-z

Brach, T. (2009, April). Practices and applications of mindfulness in psychotherapy. Symposium conducted at the Faces Conference, San Diego, CA.

Cecil, M. (2020). Finding the elephant in the room: An AEDP journey to the heart of loss, presence, and self. *Transformance: AEDP Journal, 10*(1). https://aedpinstitute.org/the-therapeutic-presence-issue-cecilfinding-the-elephant-in-the-room/

Dunn, R., Callahan, J. L., Swift, J. K., & Ivanovic, M. (2013). Effects of pre-session centering for therapists on session presence and effectiveness. *Psychotherapy Research, 23*(1), 78–85.

Friedberg, R. D., Tabbarah, S., & Poggesi, R. M. (2013). Therapeutic presence, immediacy, and transparency in CBT with youth: Carpe the moment! *Cognitive Behaviour Therapist, 6*(E12). https://doi.org/10.1017/S1754470X13000159

Geller, S. M. (2017). *A guide to cultivating therapeutic presence.* American Psychological Association.

Geller, S. M. (2018). Therapeutic presence and polyvagal theory: Principles and practices for cultivating effective therapeutic relationships. In S. Porges & D. Dana (Eds.), *Clinical applications of the polyvagal theory: The emergence of polyvagal-informed therapies* (pp. 106–126). W.W. Norton & Company.

Geller, S. M., & Greenberg, L. S. (2002). Therapeutic presence: Therapists' experience of presence in the psychotherapeutic encounter. *Person-Centered and Experiential Psychotherapies, 1*(1–2), 71–86.

Geller, S. M., & Greenberg, L. S. (2012). *Therapeutic presence: A mindful approach to effective therapy.* American Psychological Association.

Geller, S. M., & Greenberg, L. S. (in press). *Therapeutic presence: A mindful approach to effective therapeutic relationships* (2nd ed.). American Psychological Association.

Geller, S. M., Greenberg, L. S., & Watson, J. C. (2010). Therapist and client perceptions of therapeutic presence: The development of a measure. *Journal of Psychotherapy Research, 20*(5), 599–610.

Geller, S. M., & Porges, S. W. (2014). Therapeutic presence: Neurophysiological mechanisms mediating feeling safe in therapeutic relationships. *Journal of Psychotherapy Integration, 24*(3), 178–192. http://doi.org/10.1037/a0037511

Gendlin, E. T. (1996). *Focusing oriented psychotherapy: A manual of the experiential method.* Guilford Press.

Germer, C. (in press). Self-compassion in psychotherapy: Clinical integration, evidence base and mechanisms of change. In A. Finlay-Jones, K. Bluth, & K. Neff (Eds.), *Handbook of self-compassion.* Springer.

Halifax, J. (2009). *Being with dying: Cultivating compassion and fearlessness in the presence of death.* Shambhala.

Harris, D. L., & Winokuer, H. R. (2019). The practice of presence: Compassion and self-awareness in the grief counseling setting. In D. L. Harris & H. R. Winokuer (Eds.), *Principles and practice of grief counseling* (3rd ed.). Springer. http://doi.org/10.1891/9780826173331.0005

Hayes, J., & Vinca, J. (2011). Therapist presence and its relationship to empathy, session, depth, and symptom reduction. *Proceedings of the from the 42nd annual meeting for society for psychotherapy research,* Switzerland.

Norcross, J. C., & Lambert, M. J. (Eds.). (2019). *Psychotherapy relationships that work: Volume 1: Evidence-based therapist contributions.* Oxford University Press.

Ostaseski, F. (2019). *The five invitations: Discovering what death can teach us about iving fully.* Flatiron Books.

Porges, S. W. (2011). *The polyvagal theory: Neurophysiological foundations of emotions, attachment, communication, self-regulation.* Norton.

Pos, A., Geller, S., & Oghene, J. (2011). Therapist presence, empathy, and the working alliance in experiential treatment for depression. *Proceedings of the from the 42nd annual meeting for society for psychotherapy research,* Switzerland.

Rapgay, L. (2006). A Buddhist approach to end-of-life care. In C. M. Puchalski (Ed.), *A time for listening and caring: Spirituality and the care of the chronically ill and dying* (pp. 131–137). Oxford University Press. http://doi.org/10.1093/acprof:oso/9780195146820.003.0008

Siegel, D. J. (2010). *The mindful therapist: A clinician's guide to mindsight and neural integration.* Norton.

Tannen, T., Daniels, M., & Koro, M. (2017). Choosing to be present with clients: An evidence – based model for building trainees' counselling competence. *British Journal of Guidance and Counselling.* https://doi.org/10.1080/03069885.2017.1370694

CHAPTER 10

COMMON HUMANITY

Recognition of Interconnectivity among Health Professionals and Their Patients

Venus Wong, Ronald Epstein, and Michael Krasner

In the past decade, driven by emerging evidence in reducing burnout symptoms, improving practitioners' well-being, and enhancing the quality of medical care, mindfulness-based programs (MBP) have been gaining popularity among healthcare professionals (Dobkin et al., 2016; Martín-Asuero & García-Banda, 2010; Scheepers et al., 2020; Verweij et al., 2018). Apart from these pragmatic goals, various modifications have been adopted to meet the needs of different medical specialties and organizations (Duggan & Julliard, 2018; Slatyer et al., 2018; Stephen & Mehta, 2019). While these MBPs differ in format and focus, many converge on compassion and empathy as core components in their curricula, as well as emphasis on interconnectedness. A more compassionate healthcare system may be possible if the values of compassion, empathy, and interconnectedness are fully embraced by key stakeholders in the interdisciplinary practice environment. Hence, education and training in mindfulness-based approaches to cultivate these values may help to ensure their expression in medical care.

This chapter provides a review on the root of common humanity in medicine. Together with the illustration of mindfulness as a relational practice, the importance of interconnectedness in the provision of healthcare, and especially end-of-life care, is discussed. Finally, an elaboration on the training foundations of the Mindful Practice in Medicine (MPIM) program is presented as an example to illustrate the vital importance of emphasizing relational mindfulness and compassion in medical settings.

COMMON HUMANITY IN HEALTHCARE

Close contact with human suffering that stems from physical, emotional, mental, existential, and spiritual manifestations is an unavoidable element of medicine. The lack of awareness, as well as the incapacity to properly respond to these hidden struggles, can often trigger moral distress among healthcare practitioners, especially when institutional conditions limit the capacity for what are perceived to be the right actions (Jameton, 1984). The incongruence experienced through such encounters can rarely be explored amidst the hustle and bustle of medical settings. And while the need to uphold one's professional identity can be another barrier for healthcare practitioners to be fully in touch with their inner experiences, reflective practices such as narrative medicine provide a platform for physicians to examine the unspoken dilemmas behind the white coat (Baruch, 2007; MacGregor, 2014; Vegni et al., 2005). In a study that analyzed 158 physicians' narrative reflections on the practice of medicine published in leading medical journals, Moniz et al. (2017) discovered several lessons, with 'humanity matters' (a focus on physician and patient as 'person') being one of the most commonly articulated in nearly two-thirds of the

DOI: 10.4324/9781003204121-13

published narratives. Through the stories captured, humanity was most often narrated as the awakening "to be a compassionate healer," and the importance of human relationships in medicine (p. 124).

Yalom (2002) describes therapist and patient as fellow travelers in the therapeutic relationship. By honoring human qualities and honesty in relationships, the distinctions between the afflicted and the healers, and between those giving and receiving are abolished. In the teaching of mindful self-compassion, Germer (2019) describes common humanity as a way to remember that everyone suffers from time to time, while recognizing the connectedness within, instead of feeling trapped in isolation with one's perceived imperfection. This can be helpful in understanding the inner struggle triggered by feelings of incompetence. On the other hand, from a philosophical point of view, Gaita (2000) relates common humanity to morality. He states that the foundation of ethical life is love rather than reason—the recognition of an individual as an unconditionally precious fellow human being is important. He points out the central concern of common humanity is how human beings are sometimes invisible, or only partially visible, to one another. Although Gaita's conceptualization of common humanity is driven by historical and moral foundations, his ideas can serve as a reminder of the importance of humanity in medicine. It can be regarded as the way in which common humanity is being honored, or forgotten, in the most intimate encounters with human suffering.

The way in which one relates to their personal struggles and responds to human suffering forms the building blocks for the understanding of common humanity. The contemplation on how to acknowledge each individual as a precious fellow human being in clinical settings will thus be essential for the establishment of a compassionate practice environment that brings relational well-being into consideration for both healthcare practitioners and patients.

INTERCONNECTEDNESS IN MEDICAL PRACTICE

With a focus on treating and curing diseases, healthcare professionals are oriented toward relieving pain and liberating patients and their family members from suffering. Nevertheless, opportunities for exploration for healthcare professionals to liberate themselves from burnout and overidentification in therapeutic relationships with patients are rare. The distress triggered by the witnessing of disease progression and the provision of poor prognoses can be agonizing not only for patients and their families, but also for healthcare practitioners. The quest for healing, understanding, and relief is important for both patients and care workers. Thus, advocating for compassion to be more widely acknowledged and fully embraced in the healthcare system with a shared sense of vulnerability and narrowing the separation between healthcare professionals and patients in facing suffering can lead to healing and positive transformation. Clinical psychologist Dr. Christopher J. Mruk (2003) describes the liberating potential of compassion in therapeutic relationships; in the medical care environment, compassion can be liberating for both therapists and clients in every encounter. The Buddhist teacher Pema Chödrön (2003) describes how compassion is a courageous way to open up to suffering by being fully present within the wholeness of the experience. While being in touch with one's own suffering, the suffering of others can also be embraced. In a therapeutic context, this translates into a balanced and equitable relationship between the healers and the wounded, where both share responsibilities for healing. Compassion liberates when shared humanity is recognized and embodied.

Being genuinely open to human suffering requires courage. Referencing the teaching of meditation in the Buddhist tradition, the cultivation of the four immeasurable qualities, including love, compassion, joy, and equanimity, together with a fearless heart, is crucial for building deep human connections. In her description of interconnectedness, Chödrön (2003) mentioned the practice of Tonglen—breathing in painful and unwanted feelings and emotions allows the practitioner to surrender to the nature of suffering and fully embrace oneself with openness and kindness. Such deep connection nurtures an inner spaciousness that enables the practitioner to experience the full spectrum of human emotions without judgment and aversion. Similarly, if one can fully connect with what is inspiring and relieving of suffering, the same connection can be nurtured by cultivating the wish to send these qualities to all sentient beings. Being open and honest with sorrows and helplessness is the very essence of being human, courageous, and genuine.

With authenticity recognized and appreciated, the vulnerability experienced by healthcare practitioners becomes a part of our common humanity, rather than taboo and frowned upon within the medical community. Within this nurturing environment, interconnectedness can be remembered in every encounter and become the source of empowerment for healthcare practitioners. Discussions of such potentialities are still evolving in medical training. Continuous efforts are needed to provide the necessary platforms to enable healthcare practitioners to explore and examine their experiences, including their vulnerabilities, in a safe, accepting, and caring environment.

FROM CHALLENGES TO OPPORTUNITIES FOR GROWTH

Many challenges that emerge within the experience and practice of compassion in medicine relate to the care of patients facing the end of life. While palliative care professionals are prone to more specific and complex struggles with death and dying, stressful experiences with grief and loss can also be found among healthcare practitioners in all medical specialties. Roshi Joan Halifax (2008), a Zen priest who has over 30 years of experience in working with and teaching about the care of the dying, pinpoints numerous outcomes and impacts when supporting patients at life's end, including an amalgam of exhaustion, suspicion, resentment, guilt, and relief. The hidden struggles between heroism and the desire for reassurance, or the tendency to become the exhausted martyr who feels trapped between saying 'yes' to various demands and acknowledging resentment, can become a subtle battle within individual care workers. In facing these difficulties, Halifax (2008) suggests that there is a need for palliative care professionals to reflect on the notion "May I accept my own limits with compassion" (p. 116). This statement perfectly illustrates how the wounded healers can better cope with their feelings of helplessness as a result of the experience of loss and grief, which emerge in all aspects of medical practice.

Being in touch with one's inner feelings and learning how to embrace vulnerability are essential for developing compassion among healthcare practitioners. Thus, psychological care needs to be a core driver for the promotion of compassion and burnout prevention in medical settings, rather than being offered as a remedial intervention until problems emerge. Furthermore, maintaining positive morale among medical teams is critical for team members to continue their work with kindness and authenticity. In responding to these recognized challenges and needs, mindfulness training has become one of the key interventions to better support healthcare practitioners in coping with and working through their experiences of grief and loss.

COMPASSION IN MEDICAL CARE

Goetz et al. (2010) define compassion as the feeling that arises in witnessing another's suffering that motivates a subsequent desire to help. They suggested compassion should be regarded as an appraisal pattern. When an individual finds that available resources are enough to cope with a situation, compassion can be elicited. On the other hand, if an individual appraises oneself as unable to cope physically or psychologically, distress or anxiety might be triggered instead. This conclusion can be applied to the phenomenon of compassion in medical care, and how barriers commonly experienced by healthcare providers make it difficult to cope physically or psychologically. Although compassion is explicitly stated as a core element in most of the ethical guidelines for healthcare professionals, one wonders how difficult it is for this value to be present in frontline medical care. This multifactorial and complicated phenomenon cannot be resolved by focusing on any single facet of the medical system. Larson and Yao (2005) described emotional labor as an essential component of the patient-physician relationship in medical practice, which calls for regular training and commitment in developing patience, curiosity, and openness to understand the patients' world beyond their clinical symptoms, leading to the nurturance of common humanity, interconnectedness, and ultimately compassion. These attitudinal factors and psychological resources take time to grow by building on an intellectual understanding of ethical guidelines that point to shared goals.

In order to establish a compassionate healthcare environment, the understanding of the necessary work conditions and the nurturing of inner resources among team members are important. While agreeing on the need for a more compassionate practice environment, stakeholders find it difficult to determine where to begin. Can compassion be trained? Is it possible to help frontline medical staff feel more resourceful in responding to suffering? Lown's (2014) study of compassionate care emphasized that compassionate care should not be separated from other kinds of care, nor be limited to end-of-life care. Through the narratives of various stakeholders, including healthcare professionals, researchers, educators, administrators, healthcare policy makers, patients, and their family members, the following themes have been identified as the guiding commitments for compassionate care:

1. Commitment to compassionate healthcare leadership.
2. Commitment to teach compassion.
3. Commitment to value and reward compassion.
4. Commitment to support caregivers.
5. Commitment to partner with patients and families.
6. Commitment to build compassion into healthcare delivery.
7. Commitment to deepening our understanding of compassion.

These key areas illustrate the importance of a collective effort in nurturing a compassionate care system. Personal aspiration and efforts are essential but not enough. In his book, *Full Catastrophe Living,* Jon Kabat-Zinn (2013) described hospitals as magnets of 'dukkha,' which is often translated as 'suffering.' While Kabat-Zinn's Mindfulness-based Stress Reduction program is designed to address the suffering experienced by patients and the general public, the Mindful Practice in Medicine program focuses on the suffering experienced by the healthcare practitioners. Through properly guided exploration and reflection, distressful experiences can turn into powerful vehicles through which to cultivate compassion and common humanity in medical practice.

AN OVERVIEW OF MINDFUL PRACTICE IN MEDICINE

Among different mindfulness-based programs offered for healthcare professionals, emerging evidence reveals positive impacts of mindfulness practice on relieving stress and anxiety, as well as enhancing well-being. Although consistency in study outcomes is yet to be conclusive because of the differences in research design, the collective effort in establishing a more caring and compassionate medical culture deserves recognition (Elliott et al., 2021; Lomas et al., 2019; Ruiz-Fernández et al., 2020). Among different mindfulness trainings provided to healthcare professionals, Mindful Practice in Medicine is an evidence-based program that specifically addresses well-being and resilience, while emphasizing the exploration of meaning in healthcare and the relational components of therapeutic relationships.

Mindful Practice in Medicine (MPIM) training was developed by a group of physicians at the University of Rochester School of Medicine and Dentistry (Rochester, New York, USA). The program placed emphasis on three linked goals: (a) the enhancement of well-being and resilience among healthcare practitioners, (b) the advancement of quality of care, and (c) improvement in quality of caring, all through the cultivation of self-awareness, interpersonal awareness, and improved communication within the physician-patient relationship. Inspired by the teaching of George Engel (1997), an internist and psychoanalyst from the University of Rochester who proposed the biopsychosocial model of healthcare, the MPIM program adopted such principles in a mindfulness-based framework to promote holistic care for healthcare professionals and their patients. Although common humanity is not explicitly named in the training, it is embraced as the philosophical underpinning to acknowledge the interconnected nature and the bonding between professionals and patients.

The MPIM curriculum includes a spectrum of thematic learning modules related to clinical practice. For instance, topics on 'managing time,' 'teamwork,' and 'tackling medical errors and conflicts' are taught to support participants in working through pragmatic challenges in the daily clinical environment. Other topics like 'awareness,' 'self-care,' or 'challenges to professionalism' help the participants to reflect on subtler concerns of professional competence that might have been overlooked through their practice development. Furthermore, themes such as 'suffering,' 'working through uncertainties,' 'grief and loss,' and 'compassion' are topics that help participants explore their embedded and habitual behaviors, including how these are manifest within and outside of their professional lives, as well as examining how they utilize resources or face challenges to achieve professionalism (Epstein et al., 2021). All these topics are presented and explored to deepen the understanding and facilitate the flourishing of the unexplored potential among the participants outside of the challenging work environment they are engaged in.

The MPIM program's pedagogy focuses on promoting qualities of exemplary physicians, including attentive observation, critical curiosity, beginner's mind, and presence. These qualities are developed with specific relevance to the clinical setting and how they support the relational elements of the medical practice (Epstein et al., 2021). The other two core components of the Mindful Practice program, which are grounded in the notion of common humanity, narrative medicine and appreciative interviews, are intended to facilitate deeper understanding among the participants by reflection on, sharing of, and inquiring about clinical experiences through exploring their narrative qualities and discovering capacities of the health professional to manage even the most challenging events (Charon, 2001; Cooperrider & Whitney, 2005; Suchman et al., 2004). This process begins by inviting participants to write stories about their clinical experiences working with patients. Participants then share their narratives or engage in appreciative interviews in paired, small, and large groups. In the appreciative interviews, participants are guided to explore strengths and capacities of the interviewee. By focusing on these qualities, the participants begin to recognize, acknowledge, and anticipate positive potential. This strength-based approach counterbalances the prevailing culture of medical practice that emphasizes deficiencies rather than capacities, often leaving individuals feeling a lower sense of accomplishment, and contributing to the problem of burnout (Epstein & Krasner, 2017; Epstein et al., 2021). Those are seen as a precious opportunity for the participants of the group to explore and consolidate interconnectedness in the medical practice environment.

Clarity and compassion are the essential qualities adopted by exemplary mindful practitioners in their everyday tasks (Epstein, 1999). A particular theme is assigned within the curriculum to explore compassion in medical care. Different perspectives of compassion and empathy in medical care are reviewed. Participants are invited to share their experiences in witnessing compassion through the narrative exercises. The developers of the program believe that intellectual understanding is only one part of the foundation in establishing compassion in medical care. The recognition and sharing of personal experiences and appreciation of episodes in which compassion is incorporated into medical practice inspire participants, revealing the many practical ways to recognize and further nurture compassion in the workplace.

Originally developed in 2007, the MPIM program, influenced by Mindfulness-based Stress Reduction, Narrative Medicine, and Appreciative Inquiry, was delivered as a medical community experience for practicing physicians, medical students, and residents to address burnout and cultivate resilience through secular contemplative practices. In 2009, the results of a year-long pilot with practicing primary care physicians were published, demonstrating that participants exhibited enhanced mindfulness, empathy, and improvements in burnout and mood states, as well as changes in personality characteristics of conscientiousness and emotional stability (Krasner et al., 2009). Beckman et al. (2012) followed up with the same group through qualitative interviews to explore the participants' experiences. Three themes were generated, including the importance of (a) professional community to share individual experiences and reduce professional isolation, (b) mindfulness skills in listening to patients' concerns and responding more effectively, and (c) self-care. In a recently published study, participants who joined a four-day MPIM workshop between 2018 and 2019 in New York, Norway, and the Netherlands showed improvement in emotional exhaustion and depersonalization, the two burnout symptoms most commonly found among healthcare practitioners (Epstein et al., 2021). Other indicators of improvement in their personal well-being were also identified, including reduction in work-related distress, increase in job satisfaction, patient-centered compassionate care, work engagement and meaning, teamwork, well-being, positive emotions, mindfulness, somatic symptoms, and spirituality. All these components show the potential to turn challenges and difficulties into opportunities and sustenance for professional growth in the medical field despite the perceived limitations.

IGNITE COMPASSION AND COMMON HUMANITY WITH THE MINDFUL, INTENTIONAL PAUSE

Embracing the qualities of mindfulness in one's life and putting them into the work setting is a life-long journey. Mindfulness should not be taken as a designated state to be achieved, or as a prescription to fix certain problems at work. According to traditional teachings, the essence of mindfulness practice is about 'remembering,' which is a basic human capacity that can be cultivated through persistent practices. The incorporation of mindfulness can be attained through establishing a habit of an 'intentional brief pause' in the middle of a hectic schedule. These pauses can nurture moments of stillness and reflection. For instance, noticing the contact of the hand with the doorknob before stepping into the consultation room, or noticing the touch of the feet upon the floor while standing in the operation theatre are concrete ways to create intentional, brief pauses in the workplace. Experiencing the possibility and power of just a brief pause is good enough to kick start a new way of relating to daily life experiences.

The collective efforts and observations over the past decade have confirmed the importance of advocating for greater mindfulness in medicine. Inspiring greater awareness in our professional community, while cultivating the practice of mindful awareness and caring presence for self and others, and ultimately enhancing empathy, compassion, and common humanity in clinical settings are urgent and realistic goals to be achieved. The devastating impact of the COVID-19 pandemic and its lingering effects should be a wakeup call for radical change in the culture of medical care. A proactive approach with preventive measures is needed to better support all healthcare professionals. The development of a compassionate care environment, together with the recognition of interconnectedness among all stakeholders, is possible by cultivating mindful qualities in leadership, training, research, and education in the larger healthcare system.

REFERENCES

Baruch, J. (2007). *Fourteen stories doctors, patients, and other strangers.* Kent State University Press.

Beckman, H. B., Wendland, M., Mooney, C., Krasner, M. S., Quill, T. E., Suchman, A. L., & Epstein, R. M. (2012). The impact of a program in mindful communication on primary care physicians. *Academic Medicine, 87*(6), 815–819.

Charon, R. (2001). The patient-physician relationship. Narrative medicine: A model for empathy, reflection, profession, and trust. *JAMA, 286*(15), 1897–1902.

Chödrön, P. (2003). *Comfortable with uncertainty: 108 teachings on cultivating fearlessness and compassion.* Shambhala.

Cooperrider, D. L., & Whitney, D. K. (2005). *Appreciative inquiry: A positive revolution in change.* Berrett-Koehler.

Dobkin, P. L., Bernardi, N. F., & Bagnis, C. I. (2016). Enhancing clinicians' well-being and patient-centered care through mindfulness. *Journal of Continuing Education in the Health Professions, 36*(1), 11–16. https://doi.org/10.1097/ceh.0000000000000021

Duggan, K., & Julliard, K. (2018). Implementation of a mindfulness moment initiative for healthcare professionals: Perceptions of facilitators. *Explore (NY), 14*(1), 44–58. https://doi.org/10.1016/j.explore.2017.09.009

Elliott, K. A., Lamers, C., Owen, R., & Kriakous, S. A. (2021). The effectiveness of mindfulness-based stress reduction on the psychological functioning of healthcare professionals: A systematic review. *Mindfulness, 12*(1), 1–28. https://doi.org/10.1007/s12671-020-01500-9

Engel, G. L. (1997). From biomedical to biopsychosocial: Being scientific in the human domain. *Psychosomatics, 38*(6), 521–528. https://doi.org/10.1016/s0033-3182(97)71396-3

Epstein, R. (1999). Mindful practice. *JAMA, 282*(9), 833–839. https://doi.org/10.1001/jama.282.9.833

Epstein, R., & Krasner, M. (2017). *Mindful practice® workshop facilitator manual* (3rd ed.). University of Rochester School of Medicine and Dentistry.

Epstein, R., Marshall, F., Sanders, M., & Krasner, M. (2021). Effect of an intensive mindful practice workshop on patient-centered compassionate care, clinician well-being, work engagement and teamwork. *Journal of Continuing Education in the Health Professions*. https://doi .org/10.1097/ceh.0000000000000379

Gaita, R. (2000). *A common humanity: Thinking about love and truth and justice*. Routledge.

Germer, C. K. (2019). *Teaching the mindful self-compassion program: A guide for professionals*. Guilford Press.

Goetz, J. L., Keltner, D., & Simon-Thomas, E. (2010). Compassion: An evolutionary analysis and empirical review. *Psychological Bulletin, 136*(3), 351–374. https://doi.org/10.1037/a0018807

Halifax, J. (2008). *Being with dying: Cultivating compassion and fearlessness in the presence of death* (1st ed.). Shambhala.

Jameton, A. (1984). *Nursing practice: The ethical issues*. Prentice-Hall.

Kabat-Zinn, J. (2013). *Full catastrophe living: Using the wisdom of your body and mind to face stress, pain, and illness* (revised and updated ed.). Bantam Books.

Krasner, M. S., Epstein, R. M., Beckman, H., Suchman, A. L., Chapman, B., Mooney, C. J., & Quill, T. E. (2009). Association of an educational program in mindful communication with burnout, empathy, and attitudes among primary care physicians. *JAMA: the journal of the American Medical Association, 302*(12), 1284.

Larson, E. B., & Yao, X. (2005). Clinical empathy as emotional labor in the patient-physician relationship. *JAMA, 293*(9), 1100–1106. https://doi.org/10.1001/jama.293.9.1100

Lomas, T., Medina, J. C., Ivtzan, I., Rupprecht, S., & Eiroa-Orosa, F. J. (2019). A systematic review and meta-analysis of the impact of mindfulness-based interventions on the well-being of healthcare professionals. *Mindfulness, 10*(7), 1193–1216. https://doi.org/10.1007/s12671 -018-1062-5

Lown, B. A. (2014). Seven guiding commitments: Making the U.S. healthcare system more compassionate. *Journal of Patient Experience, 1*(2), 6–15. https://doi.org/10.1177 /237437431400100203

MacGregor, B. (2014). *In awe of being human: A doctor's stories from the edge of life and death*. Abiding Nowhere Press.

Martín-Asuero, A., & García-Banda, G. (2010). The mindfulness-based stress reduction program (MBSR) reduces stress-related psychological distress in healthcare professionals. *Spanish Journal of Psychology, 13*(2), 897–905. https://doi.org/10.1017/s1138741600002547

Mruk, C. J. (2003). *Zen and psychotherapy: Integrating traditional and nontraditional approaches*. Springer.

Ruiz-Fernández, M. D., Ortíz-Amo, R., Ortega-Galán, Á. M., Ibáñez-Masero, O., Rodríguez-Salvador, M. D. M., & Ramos-Pichardo, J. D. (2020). Mindfulness therapies on health professionals. *International Journal of Mental Health Nursing, 29*(2), 127–140. https://doi.org/10 .1111/inm.12652

Scheepers, R. A., Emke, H., Epstein, R. M., & Lombarts, K. M. J. M. H. (2020). The impact of mindfulness-based interventions on doctors' well-being and performance: A systematic review. *Medical Education, 54*(2), 138–149. https://doi.org/10.1111/medu.14020

Slatyer, S., Craigie, M., Rees, C., Davis, S., Dolan, T., & Hegney, D. (2018). Nurse experience of participation in a mindfulness-based self-care and resiliency intervention. *Mindfulness, 9*(2), 610–617. https://doi.org/10.1007/s12671-017-0802-2

Stephen, A. E., & Mehta, D. H. (2019). Mindfulness in surgery. *American Journal of Lifestyle Medicine, 13*(6), 552–555. https://doi.org/10.1177/1559827619870474

Suchman, A. L., Williamson, P. R., Litzelman, D. K., Frankel, R. M., Mossbarger, D. L., Inui, T. S., & Relationship-Centered Care Initiative Discovery Team. (2004). Toward an informal curriculum that teaches professionalism: Transforming the social environment of a medical school. *Journal of General Internal Medicine, 19*(5), 501–504. https://doi.org/10.1111 /j.1525-1497.2004.30157

Vegni, E., Mauri, E., & Moja, E. A. (2005). Stories from doctors of patients with pain. A qualitative research on the physicians' perspective. *Supportive Care in Cancer, 13*(1), 18–25. https://doi.org/10.1007/s00520-004-0714-2

Verweij, H., van Ravesteijn, H. J., van Hooff, M. L. M., Lagro-Janssen, A. L. M., & Speckens, A. E. M. (2018). Mindfulness-based stress reduction for residents: A randomized controlled trial. *Journal of General Internal Medicine, 33*(4), 429–436. https://doi.org/10.1007/s11606-017 -4249-x

CHAPTER 11

SELF-COMPASSION FOR CLINICIANS

Philip Larkin

CASE STUDY[1]

Clare, a community-based palliative care nurse/team leader, was a pioneer of her local service and, with 20 years' experience, widely acclaimed for her expertise, caring, and ability to give patients and families a sense of total presence and focus.

Clare advised her employer that she needed sick leave for a viral infection. After several weeks and despite repeated attempts by the team, Clare was uncontactable. She eventually met the team and in a distressing meeting for everyone, she shared her experience of physical exhaustion, a sense of burnout, feeling unable to function and guilt at having 'let the team down.' Clare was advised by her family physician to take a period of leave which she reluctantly agreed to do. She never returned to the service.

CASE STUDY

Martin, a physician working in children's palliative care, was widely sought after as clinician, mentor, and teacher. He was a source of inspiration to the staff and an immense support to the children and their parents. After one particularly challenging weekend, Martin disappeared. The team were informed that he had taken his own life. At the inquest, personal issues became apparent: Marital breakdown, alcohol dependency, and medical treatment for depression, none of which was known. Determined death by suicide, the pressure of work was cited as key to his death. The team struggled to come to terms with the loss of their colleague but moreover, a sense of failure as colleagues.

INTRODUCTION

Living through a global pandemic, our world is aware of how much we need to be cared for in loving and tender ways to help us make sense of life's transitions. The media has constructed images of professional caregivers as selfless heroes, saints, and sometimes martyrs, noting those who died from COVID-19 in their attempt to care for others. The invisibility of caregiving became public. The risks were seen in the tears and frustration of clinical staff, trying to make sense of the intangible and increasingly exposed to suffering, grief, and loss, precursors to fatigue and burnout. Less evident in the discourse is how those who choose to make caregiving their life's work find strategies to sustain and nourish them in their daily work. This is the focus of this chapter.

The main premise is that compassion toward others is only truly possible when it begins with compassion toward oneself. Within both academic and gray literature in psychology, mental wellness, and spiritual care, the wisdom of self-compassion as a basis for living a full and propitious life is extolled. There is a strong message from both Clare and Martin that we need to learn to appreciate our intuitive selves. Clare's experience of burnout evolved

DOI: 10.4324/9781003204121-14

over time. Martin's struggle with his mental health was, in hindsight, evident in his ability to function. As expressed by Karen Armstrong, we need to learn to love our enemies, both external and within (Armstrong, 2011). Internal enemies are often voiced through a sense of hopelessness, loss of self-worth, and loss of meaning and purpose. They speak to a constant drive to do one more thing, see one more patient, write one more report. External enemies include organizational systems which, implicitly or explicitly, foster those actions with little consideration for the impact on the person, or worse, transfer the responsibility onto the team and/or colleagues, who then experience guilt and distress in a perceived failure to care. It is common in organizational leadership that compassion is extolled as a virtue within mission statements and billboards advertising services. How that compassion is expressed in real terms or embedded in those organizational values is often less evident.

This chapter will firstly consider how self-compassion is described and understood and the value of developing intuitive practices which sustain and comfort with a specific focus on professional caregivers working in end-of-life care. Organizational responses to supporting self-compassion will be addressed through the work of the Schwartz Center for compassionate healthcare.[2]

The term end-of-life care is used as part of the spectrum of palliative care but focusing on the dying where compassionate caregiving and its consequences may be more pronounced. This does not mean that self-compassion is any more important to this group than others. However, notably in the United Kingdom, systematic failures in patient care at end of life defined clinicians as lacking compassion and the ability to care (Seymour & Clark, 2018). Nurses came under specific criticism, citing failures in their duty of care and the shift toward academia as having diminished the vocational (presumably more compassionate) aspects of practice. These public criticisms compound the self-perception of the practitioner as having failed in their duty and ultimately, having been failed by the system.

DEFINING AND UNDERSTANDING SELF-COMPASSION: AN END-OF-LIFE CARE PERSPECTIVE

Is self-compassion particularly difficult in end-of-life care? The early work of Kristin Neff (2003a, 2003b) defines self-compassion as a way to care for oneself without the de-valuing elements of negative self-worth and self-esteem. Self-compassion warrants the ability to be kind to oneself, to be mindful in how we approach our perceived weaknesses and failures, and to believe in our common humanity. As humans, we are part of a shared world, not separate from it. Elements of kindness, connectedness, and mindfulness shape our clinical activity with others. Subsequently, research-based interventions have supported the relationship between mindfulness and self-compassion, its impact on resilience and confidence, and the value of training (Neff et al., 2020, Rao et al., 2017, Olson & Kemper, 2014).

Interestingly in end -of-life care literature, a focus on Buddhist self-compassion perspectives, and in particular the work of Roshi Joan Halifax, has upheld the impact of real presence in the face of compassionate caregiving in dying (Halifax, 2009). Referring to the '*shadow side of care-giving*' (p. 115), she presents various personas expressed by clinicians and lay caregivers making sense of how to deal with their suffering in the face of suffering others; the Hero, Expert, Parent, Martyr, and Priest. Critically, the early modern hospice movement of Cicely Saunders (1918–2005) espoused a Christian tradition to express its practice, and although the fundament of compassion transcends faith and dogma (Barad, 2007), its roots reflect some of the challenges faced by clinicians in finding self-compassion hard to embrace. The description offered by Catholic theologian, Henri Nouwen, is particularly stark in its expectation: "Compassion asks us to go where it hurts, to enter into places of pain, to share in brokenness, fear, confusion and anguish … Compassion means full immersion in the condition of being human" (p. 4).

To ask this of a healthcare professional working in palliative and end-of-life care is both somewhat presumed and yet relatively unrealistic. The physicality of compassionate caregiving is evoked in Nouwen's description of feeling compelled to respond to suffering at a physical level within the gut (described in Greek as the *splanchizomai*). Without balance, the risk is too great and Halifax's personas become the way to survival. Germer and Neff (2019) propose an inverse version of the Golden Rule (do unto *yourself* as you would do unto others) as a precursor to understanding the challenges and risk of caregiving. This may be easier said than done.

THE COMPLEXITY OF VOCATION

Historical perspectives on the care of dying focused on the vocational approach to caregiving, a position particularly but not exclusively attributed to nursing. Indeed, the perceived loss of vocation has been used in the media to criticize the failure to provide sensitive and appropriate care. Of interest, a critique of theology-based nursing theories would contend that the idea of vocation, originally stigmatized for its focus on obedience, femininity, and subservience, has been replaced by a discussion on vocation as a motivational and support factor in caregiving (Lundmark, 2007). What is not known is the relationship between self-compassion and vocation and whether this is a predictive factor for better self-care. The action of compassion involves elements of presence and timely response to pain and suffering, which figure within the discourse on vocation, so it would be wrong to discount this as an influence for clinicians. In the absence of evidence, it is imprudent to discount or abandon the place of vocation, yet its language may challenge appropriate responses to suffering. Sometimes, the "depth" aspiration of Nouwen's compassion is not possible.

The palliative care pioneer, Dr. Mary Baines (1933–2020), argued that self-compassion was equally about knowing when compassion was not possible. Citing a clinical experience with a particularly challenging patient, she noted, "*I have nothing to give of myself to this patient. I am done in today. So I will for now simply be a doctor*" (Larkin, 2016, p. 27).

This important message re-defines self-compassion as having the capacity to move from times when deep engagement is possible to knowing when it is not and what is needed to replenish depleted resources. Considering Clare's case, the vocational zeal of the pioneer is a red flag, leading to questions about whether she was able to give herself permission to step back from her duties (a challenging word in itself), perhaps her dilemma would have been addressed sooner, and sustainable supportive solutions put in place. In a discipline where loss and grief play a significant factor in daily work, the loss of Clare to the service and her own loss of self and purpose speak to an imbalance toward perfection as opposed to the very best that is possible.

LISTENING TO THE INTUITIVE SELF

Martin's case is particularly tragic and extreme, but highlights the consequences when suffering remains unheard and unaddressed. Most striking in the support provided to the team afterwards were the reflections on what people had sensed or thought prior to his death:

> *I knew something was wrong but I couldn't put my finger on it…*
> *I should have said something, I was really worried about him…*
> *What did we miss … well, there was that one time…*

Undoubtedly, the need to explore the impact of this loss on the role and function of the team is critical to its survival. However, as expressed in these reflections, there is an intuitive response here to be considered.

Although the need for intuition to form part of clinical decision-making has been supported (Miller & Hill, 2018; Pearson, 2013), its value had been somewhat discredited in favor of an empirical science discourse valued as the source of evidence for best clinical practice. Palliative and end-of-life care respects that the transition from life to death is neither sequential nor predictable and the management of complex symptoms needs both the *art and science* of caregiving. Intuition probably frames decisions more visibly as patients move toward the last days of life. It relies on an ability to trust in the absence of fact, knowing the risk that a decision may not be correct but that, based on experience and practice, it is on balance the best option. One evocative biblical description, *"listening to the still small voice"* (Kings 1:22), suggests that there is something intuitive which can govern the choices we make. This is an English translation of Talmudic Hebrew text "the *voice of fragile silence"* (Comins, 2001). Such texts describe a depth of vulnerability and risk in being open to the intuitive self. Intuition may be fleeting and transient and, yet, a powerful tool if nurtured and used to care for self and others. Ostensibly, self-compassion comes from a connection with the intuitive self, able to discern one's needs and give voice to them so that others can hear and act on that need. Again, this touches the shared experience of common humanity and interconnection. If empathy may be the key to compassion, intuition may be a key to self-compassion.

CAN WE LEARN HOW TO BE MORE SELF-COMPASSIONATE?

Evidence suggests that healthcare practitioners can be taught be to be more compassionate toward others. Research by Riess et al. (2012) demonstrates that resident physicians can improve their compassionate care response through a neuroscience training program. A particularly rich and valuable self-compassion training program proposed by Germer and Neff (2019) incorporates exercises and practices that enable practitioners to not only explore, but to feel the enormity of their work and develop strategies for self-care. The development of the Self-Compassion Scale (SCS) by Neff (2003a, 2003b) is highly valued for utility in progressing the inter-related elements of self-compassion, strengthened by its use in a range of settings and further elaborations. The breadth of subsequent work identifies a growing body of evidence to support the science of self-compassion (see Germer & Neff, 2019, pp. 31–57 for a more comprehensive discussion).

The need to develop programs in palliative and end-of-life care that consider self-care and self-compassion has also been addressed (Watts et al., 2021; Orellana-Rios et al., 2018; Kim et al., 2013). Learning from such programs suggests the following elements may be beneficial in reinforcing the benefits of such education to palliative care practitioners:

- Can the practitioner exit the program with a range of skills or aptitudes adaptable for practice when need arises, at times of stress and suffering?
- Can elements of the program be incorporated into the daily work (i.e., on the job)?
- Is the program uni-professional or multi-disciplinary, and is the rationale for both clear?
- Is there a 'top-up' option provided, and is the organization supportive of this?
- Are trainers cognizant of and/or experts credible in the topic of self-compassion as it relates to end-of-life care and death and dying?

Morris et al. (2019) argue that a vital learning for palliative care practitioners is the art of remembrance. Describing bereavement rounds as a way to process the impact of working with dying patients, it is argued that remembrance "highlights the importance of saying 'goodbye' and acknowledges the range of emotions that doing so can evoke in us as clinicians" (p. 317). As well as discussing bereavement care needs, the program offers what are termed 'teachable moments' so that wider implications of caring for dying people can be addressed, such as team conflict or moral distress. Notably, these are brief interventions of 30 minutes. A structured space for the multi-professional team to share experiences appears more important than the length of time.

A final point is whether there are specific mediums of learning to instill greater self-compassion in practitioners. A body of literature supports the use of creative and visual arts in addressing issues of grief and loss, although there is surprisingly little work in the field of palliative and end-of-life care. One recent systematic review has supported the use of visual arts such as painting, drawing, and photography in creating positive outcomes in relation to grief and making meaning (Weiskittle & Gramling, 2018). One study with end-of-life care workers demonstrated that focused art-based supervised therapy led to a reduction in the antecedents of burnout, exhaustion fatigue, and death anxiety (Potash et al., 2015).Additionally, mindfulness programs as part of a range of health-orientated behaviors can protect against burnout in palliative care practitioners (Horn & Johnston, 2020). Bringing professionals together in an environment conducive to talking about the reality of caregiving has positive effects. Renzenbrink's use of expressive arts in grief work has salient messages and worked examples of how such programs may be developed and nurtured in professional caregiver teams (Renzenbrink, 2021).

ORGANIZATIONAL COMPASSION AND THE CARE OF THE DYING

The final part of this chapter refers to self-compassion at the organizational as well as individual level. After 30 years' experience in palliative care, time spent interviewing new clinicians shows the standard competence-based assessment of skills and aptitudes falls short of understanding capacity to face into suffering on a daily basis and survive.

Working with people at end of life requires the internal capacity to have a clear focus on the joy and beauty of living. Asking questions on how people fulfill their life expectations and dreams may give a better understanding of what nourishes the human spirit in caregiving and in doing so, sustain them in their professional work. However, self-compassion is not just an internal and personal activity on the part of the individual. Sustenance on the part of the organization is equally essential. In cases of burnout and fatigue practitioners often attribute this to a lack of being heard by leaders or working in an inflexible and defensive system. Over time, lack of organizational support leads to the erosion of self-compassion and is replaced by tactics of survival. Warning signs include phrases like '*I live for the weekend*,' or '*I just need to get the job done*.' The first questions how the practitioner is really living the other five days of their life, and the second suggests a lack of joy and passion in what they are doing. Critical to this is the fact that self-compassion speaks to the expression of our human relation to self and others.

In 2014, as part of a Fulbright scholarship, I spent a year working in the Dana Farber Cancer Center and I experienced the value of Schwartz rounds.[3] This international movement derived from one doctor's own cancer experience and the realization of the value of the human relationship between clinical and patient as an essential component of healing. Schwartz programs offer clinicians a venue to express the real impact of caregiving in a multi-professional and supportive environment. Regular scheduled meetings dedicate time for clinicians to engage in the challenges of care and gain insight into themselves and others in terms of roles and responsibilities. My sabbatical was shortly after the Boston Marathon Bombing. Because of its proximity to the route, the Dana Farber Cancer Center received patients at the hospital as an emergency, even though its focus was not acute care. Schwartz Rounds enabled those who had been involved to share their experience, their fears, anger, and pain—but also to listen to other stories and so develop a collective experience which shaped their global vision of this tragedy. In another example, a young nurse was able to discuss her challenges in bridging cultural diversity and her self-identity. There is a drive toward developing compassion-oriented organizations, such as the CCARE project,[4] which focus on the psycho-physiology of compassion, offering a range of research and education opportunities. They also act as a hub for a range of organizations demonstrating an openness for collaboration and sharing of knowledge and resources. This is key to strengthening self-compassion programs at an organizational level, advancing collaboration and making self-compassion a visible and tangible element of the organizational mission and vision.

CONCLUSION

A key skill in self-compassion is knowing where to find helpful resources. As discussed here, self-compassion is nurtured in environments where people feel safe to share their emotional self. There is a wealth of self-compassion literature, but the gap is how to translate this into real-world practice. Self-compassion is a strength that clinicians can draw upon in their everyday lives, providing a sustainable way to address the challenges that they face as they tend to those in their care. Self-compassion is also a practice with a foundation built upon the recognition of our shared common humanity. We are stronger when we are able to apply our compassionate caring to ourselves as well as others, in the acts of giving as well as receiving.

NOTES

1 The case studies in this chapter are based on real events, but, for anonymity, names and events have been changed.
2 www.theschwartzcenter.org
3 See http://theschwartzcenter.org for more information.
4 www.ccare.stanford.edu

REFERENCES

Armstrong, K. (2011). *12 steps to a compassionate life*. Vintage.

Barad, J. (2007). The understanding and experience of compassion: Aquinas and the Dalai Lama. *Buddhist–Christian Studies, 27*(1), 11–29.

Comins, M. (2001). https://www.rabbimikecomins.com/elijah-and-the-still-small-voice.html

Germer, C., & Neff, K. (2019). *Teaching the mindful self-compassion program: A guide for professionals.* Guilford Press.

Halifax, J. (2009). *Being with dying: Cultivating compassion and fearlessness in the presence of death.* Shambala.

Horn, D. J., & Johnston, C. B. (2020). Burnout and self care for palliative care practitioners. *Medical Clinics of North America, 104*(3), 561–572. https://doi.org/10.1016/j.mcna.2019.12.007

Kim, H. C., Rapp, E., Gill, A., & Myers, J. (2013). An innovative self-care module for palliative care medical learners. *Journal of Palliative Medicine, 16*(6), 603–608. https://doi.org/10.1089/jpm.2012.0351

Larkin, P. J. (2016). *Compassion: The essence of palliative and end-of-life care.* Oxford University Press.

Lundmark, M. (2007). Vocation in theology-based nursing theories. *Nursing Ethics, 14*(6), 767–780.

Miller, E. M., & Hill, P. D. (2018). Intuition in clinical decision making: Differences among practicing nurses. *Journal of Holistic Nursing, 36*(4), 318–329. https://doi.org/10.1177/0898010117725428

Morris, S. E., Kearns, J. P., Moment, A., Lee, K. A., & de Lima Thomas, J. (2019). "Remembrance": A self-care tool for clinicians. *Journal of Palliative Medicine, 22*(3), 316–318. https://doi.org/10.1089/jpm.2018.0395

Neff, K. D. (2003a). The development and validation of a scale to measure self-compassion. *Self and Identity, 2*(3), 223–250.

Neff, K. D. (2003b). Self-compassion: An alternative conceptualization of a healthy attitude toward oneself. *Self and Identity, 2*(2), 85–102.

Neff, K. D., Knox, M. C., Long, P., & Gregory, K. (2020). Caring for others without losing yourself: An adaptation of the mindful self-compassion program for healthcare communities. *Journal of Clinical Psychology, 76*(9), 1543–1562.

Nouwen, H. J., McNeill, M. D., & Morrison, D. (1982). *Compassion: A reflection on the Christian life.* Doubleday.

Olson, K., & Kemper, K. J. (2014). Factors associated with well-being and confidence in providing compassionate care. *Journal of Evidence-Based Complementary and Alternative Medicine, 19*(4), 292–296. https://doi.org/10.1177/2156587214539977

Orellana-Rios, C. L., Radbruch, L., Kern, M., Regel, Y. U., Anton, A., Sinclair, S., & Schmidt, S. (2018). Mindfulness and compassion-oriented practices at work reduce distress and enhance self-care of palliative care teams: A mixed-method evaluation of an "on the job" program. *BMC Palliative Care, 17*(1), 1–15.

Pearson, H. (2013). Science and intuition: Do both have a place in clinical decision making? *British Journal of Nursing, 22*(4), 212–215. https://doi.org/10.12968/bjon.2013.22.4.212

Potash, J. S., Chan, F., Ho, A. H., Wang, X. L., & Cheng, C. (2015). A model for art therapy-based supervision for end-of-life care workers in Hong Kong. *Death Studies, 39*(1–5), 44–51. https://doi.org/10.1080/07481187.2013.859187

Rao, N., & Kemper, K. J. (2017). Online training in specific meditation practices improves gratitude, well-being, self-compassion, and confidence in providing compassionate care among health professionals. *Journal of Evidence-Based Complementary and Alternative Medicine, 22*(2), 237–241. https://doi.org/10.1177/2156587216642102

Renzenbrink, I. (2021). *An expressive arts approach to healing loss and grief: Working across the spectrum of loss with individuals and communities.* Jessica Kingsley.

Riess, H., Kelley, J. M., Bailey, R. W., Dunn, E. J., & Phillips, M. (2012). Empathy training for resident physicians: A randomized controlled trial of a neuroscience-informed curriculum. *Journal of General Internal Medicine, 27*(10), 1280–1286. https://doi.org/10.1007/s11606-012 -2063-z

Seymour, J., & Clark, D. (2018). The Liverpool care pathway for the dying patient: A critical analysis of its rise, demise and legacy in England. *Wellcome Open Research, 3*, 15.

Watts, K. J., O'Connor, M., Johnson, C. E., Breen, L. J., Kane, R. T., Choules, K., Doyle, C., Buchanan, G., & Yuen, K. (2021). Mindfulness-based compassion training for health professionals providing end-of-life care: Impact, feasibility, and acceptability. *Journal of Palliative Medicine.* http://doi.org/10.1089/jpm.2020.0358

Weiskittle, R. E., & Gramling, S. E. (2018). The therapeutic effectiveness of using visual art modalities with the bereaved: A systematic review. *Psychology Research and Behavior Management, 11*, 9–24. https://doi.org/10.2147/PRBM.S131993

PART THREE

Clinical Applications

CHAPTER 12

COMPASSION-FOCUSED GRIEF THERAPY

Darcy L. Harris

INTRODUCTION

While this entire volume is dedicated to the exploration of compassion in various settings that pertain to loss and grief, we haven't so far delineated how compassion might form the base of therapy with grieving individuals. In his development of Compassion-Focused Therapy (CFT), Paul Gilbert states that rather than being a separate or distinct form of therapy, CFT is meant to serve as a base for the therapeutic work that clinicians provide to their clients. CFT is not meant to replace the approaches that clinicians already utilize in their practice; rather, the model emphasizes the potential for compassion to serve as a foundation for the clinician's stance and a running thread throughout the therapeutic work with clients.

Training in compassion allows the clinician to work from a place that is grounded, enabling greater distress tolerance and an enhanced ability to focus, thus allowing the clinician to remain fully present and available to clients as they share their experiences. Clinicians can also incorporate aspects of compassion training into their therapeutic work with grieving clients, providing them with a greater ability to be present and open to their own experiences and to allow their grief to unfold in the most adaptive way possible. Grief is a painful experience, often made even more so by self-disenfranchisement, shame, and negative social messaging, all of which can benefit from compassion-based approaches. This chapter will explore how the principles of compassion apply to the therapist's compassionate base in the therapeutic relationship, the client's work in developing self-compassion, and specific compassion-based techniques that can be useful in the process of grief therapy.

CULTIVATING THE THERAPIST'S COMPASSIONATE BASE

Chapter seven provides an exploration of compassion training, so that material will not be repeated here. As a recap, most compassion training programs incorporate the use of contemplative practices and specific exercises to enhance mindful awareness, allow greater attunement to our sense of shared humanity with others, increase our ability to be fully present in our encounters, and help us to nurture self-compassion. Much of what is involved in cultivating a compassionate base for working with grieving clients includes actively engaging in compassion training and continuing with ongoing practices that enhance and deepen the awareness of compassion and grief in various ways.

Compassion is not something that you necessarily 'do,' but is more akin to who you are and how you engage in the world around you. This way of being is similar to the Rogerian description of congruence. Therapists are human, relating to their clients in the context of their shared humanity. A sensitive therapist doesn't enact a role when with clients; rather, the therapist as a person fully engages with the client in a shared experience. There is no smoke and mirrors, nor is there a secret "code" that the therapist unlocks for the client. Likewise, the cultivation of compassion in your own daily life and way of being in the world

DOI: 10.4324/9781003204121-16

will naturally transfer to the way that you work with the clients in your practice (Greenberg & Geller, 2001).

Working with people who have experienced profound and painful losses requires the therapist to be able to remain present and fully open to experiences that can be incredibly painful, potentially activating, and seemingly meaningless. Thus, there is a need to develop a strong compassionate base from which to engage with clients whose distress and suffering might otherwise be overwhelming. Gilbert (2020) emphasizes that a core component of compassion is courage that gives us the strength to acknowledge and turn toward suffering and pain rather than turn away from it. Halifax (2009) refers to being able to respond to distress from the position of a strong back (courage and distress tolerance), while at the same time having a soft belly (openness and tenderness):

> All too often our so-called strength comes from fear, not love; instead of having a strong back, many of us have a defended front shielding a weak spine. In other words, we walk around brittle and defensive, trying to conceal our lack of confidence. If we strengthen our backs, metaphorically speaking, and develop a spine that's flexible but sturdy, then we can risk having a front that's soft and open, representing choiceless compassion. The place in your body where these two meet—strong back and soft front—is the brave, tender ground in which to root our caring deeply when we begin the process of being with dying.
>
> *(p. 17)*

Additionally, the importance of self-compassion for both the therapist and the client is stressed as a foundational practice in this process. In fact, it is expected that therapists who wish to utilize any compassion-enhancing exercises with clients will also be engaged in their own personal work with these same practices. (For more information about compassion practices for therapists, see Kolts et al., 2018.)

ABILITY TO FOCUS, ATTUNE, AND BE FULLY PRESENT

Working with clients who have experienced profound loss and grief requires the therapist to be able to hold attention (and intention), even as the stories, images, and emotions of clients can be intense and emotionally triggering. Mindfulness practice helps us to stay in the present moment, being aware of the sensations that arise and fall, with an ability to focus and be with our thoughts and feelings without becoming immersed in their ruminative or reactive content. Mindfulness also helps the therapist to gain a sense of perspective about the nature of life, including an understanding that suffering, pain, and distress are all a part of being alive. The practice of mindfulness can occur through many avenues; it is important for each person to find the best practice that helps them to feel grounded and focused, with the ability to return back to this foundational place readily.[1] Remaining present with clients in times of deep grief and distress requires familiarity with the sensation of being grounded, being able to find emotional balance and equanimity in situations of intensity, and the ability to remain focused on one's intention in the midst of competing distractions (Harris & Winokuer, 2021).

It would be impossible to adequately attune to a client's emotional state and needs if the therapist were unable to hold focus and attention in the present moment. Geller and Porges (2014) discuss the importance of presence in the therapeutic encounter. As discussed in Chapter eight, therapeutic presence involves the therapist's ability to be fully in the moment on several concurrently occurring dimensions, including physical, emotional, cognitive, and relational. Being fully present involves the therapist preparing for the encounter in advance, being able to remain focused and attuned during the session, and then being careful to observe and address any residual effects from the session afterward. The ability to stay fully present in situations where exposure to the client's distress and suffering could be potentially overwhelming requires practice that, when cultivated, enhances a sense of sustainable well-being even in the midst of potentially activating material (Gilbert & Choden, 2013). Presence requires practice to develop familiarity with being grounded and comfortable sitting with intense feelings and situations, while remaining focused on one's intention. Therapeutic presence is not a technique, but rather, a foundation for enhancing attunement, attention, engagement, and awareness within therapeutic encounters (Geller & Greenberg, 2012). According to Geller and Porges (2014), the experience of therapeutic presence involves:

- Being grounded and in contact with one's integrated and healthy self.
- Being open, receptive to, and immersed in what is poignant in the moment.
- Having a larger sense of spaciousness and expansion of awareness and perception.
- The intention of being with and for the client in service of their healing process (p. 180).

Working with the body can serve as a means to help the therapist to stay fully present when a client is sharing deeply intense emotions or traumatic material that might increase arousal. In very simple terms, threat and anxiety states activate the sympathetic nervous system, which directs the body into the fight/flight/freeze response as a protection, overriding other stimuli that may be present. The problem is that when in such a state of arousal, it is impossible to engage deeply and listen fully to what is being shared. In contrast to the sympathetic nervous system response to threat, stimulating the parasympathetic nervous system helps to slow the body down and enhance feelings of safety and receptivity (Gilbert, 2014). This can be done in several ways; a common exercise in CFT that is used to stimulate the parasympathetic system is soothing rhythm breathing practice.[2]

BIG PICTURE PERSPECTIVE

While the practice of grief therapy is aimed at the alleviation of suffering, this motivation needs to be balanced with the understanding that not all suffering can be relieved. Grief is an inevitable and painful part of the human condition; however, it is also an adaptive process that helps us to rebuild our assumptive world after a significant loss has shattered that world (Harris, 2020). Cultivating mindful awareness allows the therapist to understand this big picture perspective and work to support grieving clients in their pain rather than trying to move them away from their grief, which may also interfere with their ability to adapt and heal after a significant loss. It is important for clinicians to recognize that they cannot control outcomes, nor are they responsible for what is beyond their control. We all deeply desire to help our clients in whatever ways are possible, but we can't reverse a diagnosis, bring a loved one back to life, or make the painful grieving process any less painful than it is.

COMPASSION-BASED APPROACHES WITH GRIEVING CLIENTS

Compassion training is uniquely suited to equip the grief therapist with skills to effectively support clients in situations of deep grief and pain. Many of the stories that are shared by grieving clients involve scenarios of trauma, despair, and difficulty, with painful and intense feelings that are difficult for the client to process, and for others to hear without being profoundly affected. People who are grieving often find that others are unable to tolerate their pain and distress; many will blunt their emotions or suppress their grief in response to the reactions they receive from those closest to them (Harris, 2016). The grief therapist must be able to mindfully embrace their clients' experiences and feelings, being fully present to the distress without jumping in with a "fix it" mentality, and to discern how to best journey alongside clients in a way that allows the grief to unfold rather than be suppressed or misdirected.

EMOTION REGULATION

In addition to providing a compassionate base from which to engage clients, compassion-focused grief therapy uses various ways to balance the emotion regulation system after a significant loss, while providing clients with skills for cultivating self-compassion, especially in relation to their grieving process. An underlying premise of CFT is that our brains have evolved in ways to support social processing and emotion regulation that are linked to social roles, such as status, belonging, affiliation, cooperation, and caring (Gilbert, 2014). Our relationships and the need to belong are intricately tied to our responses in social situations. Emotions serve underlying motives, with the three dominant motives being harm avoidance (threat system), resource seeking (drive system), and rest, digest, and repair (soothe system). Ideally, these systems are in balance with each other, as each serves an important function in everyday life and overall survival. Figure 12.1 shows these three motivational systems in a visual representation.

The threat system is designed to keep us safe, and the feelings that are evoked when this system is activated include anger, anxiety, and disgust. Threat behaviors can activate our fight/flight responses; these behaviors may also include freeze and deactivation, which can be associated with a sense of defeat, helplessness, and despair (Gilbert, 2014). While the threat system is meant to protect us from harm and becomes activated to do just that, over a longer period of time, it can interfere with our ability to be open to opportunities for healing, including sharing pain and receiving support from others. Significant losses threaten the attachment system/assumptive world, creating a sense of heightened vulnerability, and in so doing, activate the threat system. The grieving process itself may also feel threatening. Other threats to our safety and security may also activate this system, such as threats to finances, health, and relationships, which are common in non-death loss experiences.

The drive system enables us to seek out and acquire necessities that support our well-being. This system also engages readily when we are concerned about lacking something essential for life or something that is considered a necessity. Our "survival instinct" kicks in, and we take stock of what we must have and what we need to get through a time when there is concern over lack. The drive system may be manifest in the grief response through common attachment-oriented behaviors such as yearning, seeking, and protest that are frequently described in bereaved individuals (Harris & Winokuer, 2021). It is common to unconsciously search for the lost loved one in places where they have previously been found, or to seek out linking objects and reminders of the loved one as a form of proximity-seeking.

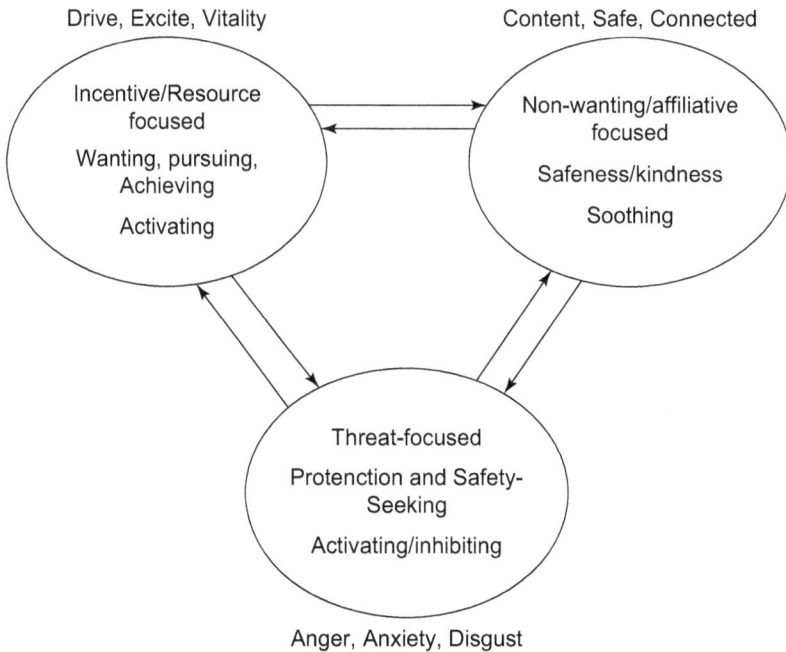

Figure 12.1 Emotion Regulation Systems as Proposed in Compassion-Focused Therapy (CFT). Adapted from *The compassionate mind* (Gilbert, 2009), reprinted with permission from Little, Brown Book Group

These types of behaviors are also commonly present in non-death losses. For example, an individual who has lost their homeland may crave and seek out familiar foods from their country of origin.

The soothing system is frequently not readily accessible for people who come to therapy for various reasons. This system is sometimes referred to as the "rest and digest" system, and as discussed earlier, is also tied into the parasympathetic nervous system (Tindle & Tadi, 2020). The ability to soothe provides an opportunity for resting, reflecting, and slowing down, allowing for reparative and restorative processes to occur. Engaging the soothing system helps us to connect with ourselves and others, and to balance our threat and drive systems in a way that opens the door for conscious choices about how we need to respond to the events in our lives. Certainly, for grieving individuals, activating this system can offer a much-needed respite from the threat and drive system over-activation that is often associated with a significant loss. The therapeutic relationship can act as a link to the soothing system, functioning as a secure base that allows for social connection that feels safe, and for healing the wound that has been created by loss. It would also make sense that if grief presents as a wound to our attachment system, being able to activate the soothing system opens the door for more affiliative encounters and support being offered by those close to us. At times when there is a large amount of uncertainty and an overarching sense of threat, we need to find ways to balance the threat and drive systems with the soothing system. It is important to recognize that each of these systems serves an important purpose, and they have evolved in humans over time to allow for greater chances of survival. However, the key message here is the need to foster balance between them, especially when significant loss and grief skew us toward feeling threatened, vulnerable, and painfully alone.

ADDRESSING SHAME WITH SELF-COMPASSION

Two important issues arise related to shame and grief. The first pertains to the social rules and expectations that are experienced by grieving individuals. These rules may apply to aspects of the loss itself that are disenfranchised, such as the death of a lover who is married, or they may relate to the unspoken but readily identified 'shoulds' about grief, such as how bereaved individuals are expected to grieve, or if their grief is falling within socially expected gender and cultural norms. The second aspect of shame in grief relates to an internalized sense of self-deprecation, feelings of unworthiness, or negative views of self that perpetuate isolation in grief. Shame creates a need to withdraw, making it difficult to connect with others in a meaningful way at a crucial time when support is most needed (Harris, 2016).

Recent research has explored the impact of self-compassion upon grieving individuals who struggle with negative internalized messages. Vara and Thimm (2019) found a significant relationship between low self-compassion and the severity of complicated grief symptoms, indicating that low self-compassion is a vulnerability factor for developing complicated grief. Lenferink et al. (2017) examined the associations between self-compassion and emotional distress in the context of ambiguous loss and grief in families of long-term missing persons, where relatives of missing persons with higher self-compassion scores experienced less emotional distress as they navigated the ambiguity of their loved ones' absence. In another study, Bussolari et al. (2021) demonstrated that participants who were more oriented toward self-compassion reported less intense grief, less frequency of dismissive or negative social interactions, more frequent positive access to a continuing bond, and had better overall psychosocial functioning.

COMPASSIONATE RE-FRAMING

As discussed earlier, the relationship that the therapist establishes with the client is foundational to the development of a secure, compassionate base from which the client can explore their loss and engage with their grief. The therapist also models a compassionate approach to the client's process, re-framing messages of shame and self-disenfranchisement in ways that position grief within the broader context of the human experience. The messaging in the re-frame acknowledges the pain associated with significant losses and recognizes that the difficulties associated with the grief are understandable and appropriate in the situation. In short, the therapist re-frames by pointing out what is 'right' (e.g., the grief response) in the midst of what is 'wrong' (e.g., feeling weak or having difficulties functioning). In the course of therapy, the therapist may gently offer a compassionate interpretation to help counter many of the negative messages that can compound grief. Examples of compassionate re-framing can be found in Table 12.1.

Table 12.1 Learning a New Language of Compassion

If You Are Thinking…	*Compassionate Re-Frame…*
I feel so stupid right now.	Sometimes, my grief makes it hard to focus.
I need to stop wallowing in self-pity.	My grief reminds me of how much I have lost.
I hate feeling so weak.	How I am feeling makes sense given what has happened.
I need to get a grip and just get over this.	My grief affects me so much because I loved so much.

IMAGERY

Compassion-Focused Therapy often utilizes guided imagery to assist clients in their process. Almost all imagery starts with awareness of and grounding in the body through the breath. Once there is familiarity with soothing rhythm breathing, the imagery exercises can be introduced. Common forms of imagery might include creating a safe place, envisioning the compassionate self, the compassionate other, and directing the flows of compassion that were discussed earlier—to self, to others, and from others. These imagery exercises can readily be adapted to loss and grief. A helpful grounding exercise is the safe place exercise. The client is asked to bring to mind a safe space, where they feel comforted, grounded, or where they can imagine spending time with their deceased loved one. During this exercise, it is important that the client not feel rushed, and that there is a sense of the therapist "walking alongside" by asking the client to describe what they see, hear, and sense in the imagined space.

Another imagery exercise involves imagining the compassionate self. The client may be asked to bring to mind someone or something that signifies compassion to them. They may choose an animal, color, or object as well. The therapist then asks the client to identify the compassionate attributes that are present in this image, and how these compassionate ways of being might relate to their experience of grief in the present moment. (For a fuller exploration of compassion-focused imagery techniques, see Tirch et al., 2014.)

CHAIR WORK

Although many different schools of therapy utilize some form of chair work, compassion-focused chair work invites clients to visualize parts of the self or a compassionate other (such as a person, a being, an animal, or even a color) and to dialogue with these parts from a compassionate stance (Bell et al., 2020). Engaging in the dialogue can be a way of identifying how even difficult aspects of the self may be serving an important purpose or function, and the client can begin integrating these "split off" aspects of themselves. This is a really good way to enfranchise aspects of grief that the client identifies as troublesome, but which also may be serving an important purpose. (For a deeper exploration of the use of compassion-focused chair work in grief therapy, see Chapter 22.)

CONCLUSION

Compassion-focused grief therapy emphasizes the importance of cultivating the compassionate base of the therapist, modeling a compassionate way to journey through the grieving process, and fostering greater self-compassion within the client during a time of deep pain and difficulty related to significant losses. The relational component of the therapy serves as a secure base/safe haven and link to the soothing system during a time when the threat and drive systems may be overly engaged and creating further problems for the client. Key components of the application of compassion-focused grief therapy involve enhancing clients' abilities to self-soothe, cultivating greater self-compassion and distress tolerance in the midst of the grieving process, and embracing the full range of emotions associated with significant loss experiences in compassionate awareness.

NOTES

1 For ideas about contemplative practices that support the development of focus and presence, see the Tree of Contemplative Practices, https://www.contemplativemind.org/practices/tree
2 A link to several exercises used in CFT, including soothing rhythm breathing, can be found at https://positivepsychology.com/compassion-focused-therapy-training-exercises-worksheets/

REFERENCES

Bell, T., Montague, J., Elander, J., & Gilbert, P. (2020). "A definite feel-it moment": Embodiment, externalization and emotion during chair-work in compassion-focused therapy. *Counselling and Psychotherapy Research, 20*(1), 143–153.
Bussolari, C., Habarth, J. M., Phillips, S., Katz, R., & Packman, W. (2021). Self-compassion, social constraints, and psychosocial outcomes in a pet bereavement sample. *OMEGA: Journal of Death and Dying, 82*(3), 389–408.
Geller, S. M., & Greenberg, L. S. (2012). *Therapeutic presence: A mindful approach to effective therapy.* American Psychological Association.
Geller, S. M., & Porges, S. W. (2014). Therapeutic presence: Neurophysiological mechanisms mediating feeling safe in therapeutic relationships. *Journal of Psychotherapy Integration, 24*(3), 178.
Gilbert, P. (2009). *The compassionate mind.* Constable.
Gilbert, P. (2014). The origins and nature of compassion focused therapy. *British Journal of Clinical Psychology, 53*(1), 6–41.
Gilbert, P. (2020). Compassion: From its evolution to a psychotherapy. *Frontiers in Psychology, 11,* 3123. https://doi.org/10.3389/fpsyg.2020.586161
Gilbert, P., & Choden. (2013). *Mindful compassion.* Constable-Robinson.
Greenberg, L. S., & Geller, S. (2001). Congruence and therapeutic presence: Rogers' therapeutic conditions. *Evolution, Theory into Practice, 1,* 131–149.
Halifax, J. (2009). *Being with dying: Cultivating compassion and fearlessness in the presence of death.* Shambhala.
Harris, D. L. (2016). Social expectations of the bereaved. In D. Harris & T. Bordere (Eds.), *Handbook of social justice in loss and grief: Exploring diversity, equity, and inclusion* (pp. 165–175). Routledge.

Harris, D. L. (2020). Non-death loss and grief: Laying the foundation. In D. Harris (Ed.), *Non-death loss and grief: Context and clinical implications* (pp. 7–16). Routledge.

Harris, D. L., & Winokuer, H. R. (2021). *Principles and practice of grief counseling.* Springer.

Kolts, R., Bell, T., Bennett-Levy, J., & Irons, C. (2018). *Experiencing compassion-focused therapy from the inside out: A self-reflection workbook for therapists.* Guilford.

Lenferink, L. I., Eisma, M. C., de Keijser, J., & Boelen, P. A. (2017). Grief rumination mediates the association between self-compassion and psychopathology in relatives of missing persons. *European Journal of Psychotraumatology, 8*(Suppl 6), 1378052.

Tindle, J., & Tadi, P. (2020). Neuroanatomy, parasympathetic nervous system. *StatPearls* [Internet].

Tirch, D., Schoendorff, B., & Silberstein, L. R. (2014). *The ACT practitioner's guide to the science of compassion: Tools for fostering psychological flexibility.* New Harbinger.

Vara, H., & Thimm, J. C. (2019). Associations between self compassion and complicated grief symptoms in bereaved individuals: An exploratory study. *Nordic Psychology.* https://doi.org/10.1080/19012276.2019.1684347

CHAPTER 13

THE GRACE MODEL OF COMPASSIONATE RESPONSE

Darcy L. Harris

INTRODUCTION

With the burgeoning interest and research in compassion, clinicians often wonder how they can begin to implement compassion into their work. This task was undertaken by Roshi Joan Halifax, the abbot of the Upaya Zen Center in Santa Fe, New Mexico. On a fellowship to study at the Library of Congress as a Distinguished Visiting Scholar, she used this time to develop her insights into compassion and how it could be more readily applied in clinical settings. Her interest in this area stemmed from her engagement with healthcare providers who worked in various clinical settings with patients at the end of their lives (Halifax, 2009). The outgrowth of her work, the Being with Dying Training Program, is regularly offered through the Upaya Zen Center in Santa Fe, New Mexico. This program is an eight-day residential training for healthcare professionals who work in end-of-life care contexts. Through the training, emphasis is placed upon the ethical, spiritual, existential, and social aspects of end-of-life care delivery. In conjunction with the training, various contemplative practices are incorporated for clinicians to learn how to regulate attention and emotion and develop a meta-cognitive perspective on the suffering of their patients as well as themselves. The training also integrates research in neuroscience as it relates to the clinical, contemplative, and conceptual content of the training (Halifax, 2013). The program has been taught in hundreds of medical and educational institutions around the world, providing important tools for work with people who have a serious illness, as well as dying people and their families. From her research and work, the ABIDE model of compassion was explicated, along with a clinical application of compassion, described as the GRACE model of compassionate response (Halifax, 2011, 2012, 2014). This chapter will explore both of these models.

THE ABIDE MODEL OF COMPASSION

In her work, Halifax cites two large categories of compassion. The first is referential compassion (i.e., compassion directed toward an object), and the second is non-referential or unbiased compassion (i.e., compassion that is objectless and pervasive; Halifax, 2011). These terms are similar to the earlier descriptions in previous chapters of this book, where referential compassion describes a compassionate response that is enacted in a situational context, and non-referential compassion can be equated with earlier descriptions of a compassionate stance, which is a way of being that forms a base from which to respond. Both of these types of compassion are important for clinicians to actualize in their interactions with patients. Halifax describes non-referential compassion as the integration of compassion deep into the life of an individual, "where compassion pervades the mind of the experiencer as a way of being" (Halifax, 2013, p. 212). Her writings indicate that there is a growing awareness of the importance of referential compassion, including the development of many compassion training programs; however, she expresses concern that many of these

DOI: 10.4324/9781003204121-17

programs focus mostly on the outward expression of compassion and not upon the overall cultivation of compassion as a way of being in the world (non-referential compassion).

The ABIDE model of compassion describes compassion as relational, mutual, reciprocal, and asymmetrical (Halifax, 2013). Drawing from neuroscience, social psychology, ethics, and contemplative perspectives, this model identifies compassion as an emergent process primed by non-compassion elements, including attention and affect, intention and insight, as well as embodiment and engagement. Compassion is viewed as a natural extension of several specific elements that come together to create the ability to respond with intention and attention, for the purpose of relieving the suffering of others (and oneself). Each of the individual elements of compassion are amenable to development through training; the model identifies key areas that, when cultivated through practice, will lead to personal resilience and a sense of balance, as well as the ability to respond in any given situation with compassion and equanimity. Training in the cultivation of compassion necessitates that there is clarity in what compassion entails and the processes that nourish and enhance it. In relation to clinicians, it is also important to determine what sustains compassion while providing care to those whose pain and suffering are potentially overwhelming for both the client and the clinician.

Halifax describes compassion as the emergent process when cultivated through training that involves the development of attentional, cognitive, somatic, and affective states, as demonstrated in Figure 13.1.

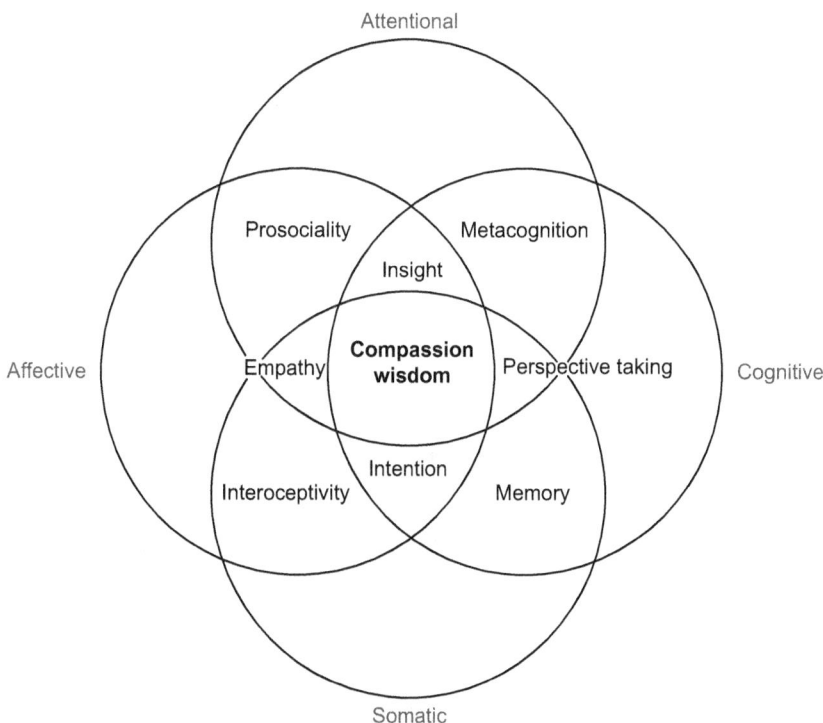

Figure 13.1 The Intersection of the Four Aspects of Compassion in the ABIDE Model. Halifax, J. (2012). A heuristic model of enactive compassion. *Current Opinion in Supportive and Palliative Care*, 6(2), 228–235

The acronym ABIDE stands for the specific components of compassion, that can be cultivated with practice through compassion training.

A—attention.
B—affectual balance.
I—intention and insight.
D—discernment.
E—ethical engagement and embodiment.

Each of these components will be described briefly. Halifax groups the acronym topics into three axes:

Axis A/A—includes attention and affectual balance.
Axis I/I—incorporates insight and intention.
Axis E/E—comprises ethical engagement and embodiment.

ATTENTION AND AFFECTUAL BALANCE

These two key areas involve the ability to hold your attention without distraction or loss of your sense of grounding, and the ability to regulate emotions in the face of distressing or intense experiences. Attention refers to allocating mental processing resources to a selected object or situation. Halifax suggests that cultivating attention through contemplative practices such as mindfulness enhances our ability to perceive the reality of suffering more accurately, without being overwhelmed by the magnitude or intensity of that suffering (Halifax, 2013). In the context of care delivery, the cultivation of attention and attunement is necessary to be able to focus and look broadly with compassion upon the many sources of suffering—both internal and external. For example, the ability to remain focused and open in situations where clients are experiencing intense emotions can be difficult for clinicians, especially if it is not possible to alleviate or address the source of the pain that the client is experiencing, which often occurs in scenarios of end-of-life care and bereavement. Affective balance involves engaging with prosocial elements, such as empathy, kindness, and receptivity, and allowing these elements to inform your perceptions and responses.

INTENTION, INSIGHT, AND DISCERNMENT

In the cognitive domain, the cultivation of intention and insight supports discernment in difficult situations. An important aspect in the cognitive domain is the ability to let go of one's attachment to outcome, which is often very difficult for clinicians. Compassion aspires to transform or end suffering; however, the cognitive dimension provides us with the reasoned realization that our primary focus is upon our intention to relieve suffering without attaching to a specific or desired outcome that may or may not occur. Insight provides us with the discernment to decide how to respond to suffering in a realistic and intentioned manner. As clinicians in helping professions, we diligently strive to alleviate pain and suffering, but, at the same time, it is important to approach those in our care with 'therapeutic humility,' which reminds us that we must accept that the eventual course of events that may be swayed by influences beyond our control.

As discussed earlier, the intention to relieve suffering is one of the main features that distinguishes compassion from empathy. Key to the concept of compassion is that if we wish to enact compassion to others, we must not exclude ourselves from the practice of self-compassion (Fulton, 2018). For example, the heart must pump blood to the entire body, but in order to do this, it must first supply blood to itself. Insight helps us to override habitual responses, to appraise realistically, and to down-regulate our emotions, increasing our ability to tolerate difficult and potentially activating scenarios more readily. Developing our insight through self-awareness and staying focused on our intention, we can more readily shift away from thoughts and behaviors that are counterproductive, and we develop distress tolerance that allows us to remain fully present, even in the midst of very painful circumstances. We are less likely to emotionally pull away from our patients or clients because we are overwhelmed or feel powerless in their presence, less inclined to engage in moral outrage that is not channeled in a healthy way, and we have the ability to be more fully present, both to those in our care, and those who work alongside us. This type of insight provides us with a broader, more open perspective, nurturing hardiness and resilience.

EMBODIMENT, ENGAGEMENT, AND EQUANIMITY

Once we are aware of the suffering around us, we often experience inter-subjective resonance, where another person's experience feels as if it is happening in our own body. (Think of a time when you've seen a cut or wound on another person's body and then felt a sense of resonance from your own body in the same place.) Compassionate action arises from the foundation of a mind that is focused and aware of the reality of suffering, has the ability to attune to self and others, and is able to acknowledge our interconnectedness with others. One of the key mental features that arises when all these components are activated is equanimity. Equanimity is characterized by a balanced state of mind; it is also supported by the realization of the truth of impermanence and the recognition that we cannot control many things that have a profound impact upon our daily lives. We can waste precious reserves of energy trying to achieve an outcome that is not possible or attempting to control what is out of our hands. See Table 13.1 for a summary of Halifax's model mapped out onto each axis.

Halifax (2013, 2014) notes that compassion in its truest sense does not lead to fatigue. Rather, it can become a wellspring of resilience to allow our natural impulse to care for another to become a source of nourishment rather than depletion. Robin Youngson (2013), an anesthesiologist who founded Hearts in Healthcare, an organization dedicated to the cultivation of compassion in healthcare contexts, speaks of his revelation about compassionate care:

> There is a widespread belief among doctors that we need to limit our emotional connection with patients because all of our compassion will run out. This one-sided view of compassion is a peculiarly Western belief. In the Buddhist world, every act of compassion is seen as providing compassion equally for the caregiver as the receiver. This has been my recent experience; the more I bring open-hearted compassion to the care of my patients, the more love I have to give. It is a mutually sustaining practice.

(p. 335)

Table 13.1 Summary of the Halifax Heuristic Model of Modes Priming and Optimizing Enactive Compassion

A/A (Attentional and Affective) Axis: > Balance	**Attentional Balance: Mental Stability through Grounding > Recognize Suffering** (Interoceptivity: Visceral awareness priming empathy) Affective balance: Prosociality: Positive regard for others, kindness Affective attunement; affective resonance with suffering
I/I (Cognitive) Axis: > Discernment	**Intention; Ethical Perspective Priming Intention (Recollection of Vows)** Prosocial motivation to transform suffering Insight: Metacognition > pliancy Self-awareness (inc. memory) > insight for down-regulation Perspective taking (cognitive attunement) and self/other distinction Moral ground; moral imperative, moral sensitivity, moral character Recognizing: Impermanence, interconnectedness, all beings want happiness No attachment to outcome
E/E (Physical) Axis > Ethike; Ethical Behaviors That Are:	**Embodied: Grounded** Engaged: Readiness to act > potential action

Source: Used with permission. Halifax, J. (2012). A heuristic model of enactive compassion. *Current Opinion in Supportive and Palliative Care, 6*(2), 228–235.

GRACE MODEL OF COMPASSIONATE RESPONSE

The GRACE process was developed as an outgrowth of the principles set forth in the ABIDE model. Clinicians working in stressful situations can utilize this process as a simple and efficient intervention, to remind themselves to be open to their client's experience and to stay centered in the presence of suffering in order to enact principled, healthy compassion. The process begins with a pause to focus attention (gathering attention) and then to briefly recall your compassionate intention and motivation (recalling intention). This brief pause is then followed by a quick self-assessment (attune to self) in three interrelated domains of experience: Noticing briefly what your body is experiencing, your emotional tone, or if there is any cognitive bias present. This is followed by the clinician sensing into what the client might be experiencing (attuning to other), which incorporates empathy and perspective taking, and then moving to a short internal prescriptive process (considering what will serve) before engaging more actively with the client. The GRACE acronym is very easy to remember and to recall quickly in a five-step process (see Figure 13.2). Some practitioners use their five fingers as a reminder for recalling the process.

The practice offers a simple and efficient way to open to the experience of suffering, to stay centered in the midst of difficult situations and environmental stresses, and to develop the capacity to respond with compassion (Halifax, 2013, 2014). This internal process might happen very rapidly, even automatically with practice. Clinicians often do not take a "reflective pause," sometimes immediately jumping into a session or encounter

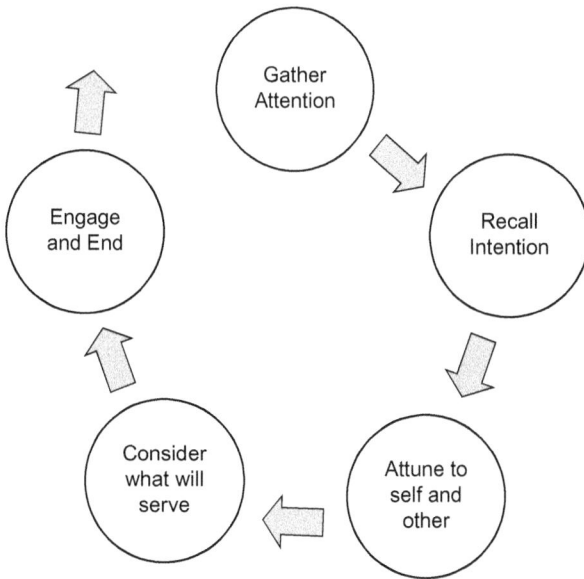

Figure 13.2 The GRACE Model of Compassionate Response (Halifax, 2014)

before being attentionally and ethically grounded and taking a few moments to sense into the client's experience before forming a clinical assessment or engaging in an intervention. The GRACE process can be a guide into that moment (or moments) of reflection that can provide the base for healthy, grounded, and principled compassion once clinicians are in the presence of their client. When this process is followed, engagement with the client comes from a base of focused attunement and intentioned presence in the interaction.

The steps of the GRACE process are directly related to the components of compassion as set out in the **ABIDE** model:

G—gathering attention: A/A Axis: Attentional Domain; focus, grounding, balance.
R—recalling intention: A/A Axis, I/I Axis: Affective/Cognitive Domain; motivation/intention.
A—attuning to self/other: A/A Axis: Affective Domain; somatic, affective, cognitive attunement.
C—considering what will serve: I/I Axis: Cognitive Domain; insight/discernment.
E—engage: E/E Axis: Somatic Domain; ethical enactment, ending.

The following is a guided script to facilitate familiarity with the GRACE process (Halifax, 2014):

Gather your attention:
• Pause, breathe in, give yourself time to get grounded by gathering your attention.

- Be fully in this present moment; focus your attention on the breath, or on a neutral part of the body, like the soles of your feet or your hands as they rest on each other.
- You can use this moment of grounding to set aside your assumptions and expectations.

Recall your intention:
- Remember your intention to relieve suffering wherever possible and to act with integrity.
- Recall the felt-sense of why you have chosen to relieve the suffering of others and to serve in this way. This "touch in" can happen in a moment. This is why you are here right now, in this situation.
- Allow this motivation to keep you focused, morally grounded, and connected to the others in this space, and to your highest values.
- First notice what is going on in your own mind and body. Then sense into the experience of your client(s). This is an active process of bearing witness and inquiry, first involving yourself, then others who are present.
- Give attention to your own somatic state, what your body is experiencing at this moment. Shift your attention to your affective stream, and what emotions are present for you. Then shift to your cognitive stream, and notice what thoughts are present. Your insight into your internal experience can help you regulate biases or defenses that might be present in your perception of and attitude toward your client(s).
- Now, sense into what your client might be experiencing. Sense without judgment. Sense into not only what they are experiencing, but also how they might be seeing their situation, and experiencing you.
- Open a space in which the encounter can unfold, in which you are present for whatever may arise, for both you and your client(s). How you notice and acknowledge your client(s), and how they notice and acknowledge you all constitute a kind of mutual exchange. The richer you make this mutual exchange, the more there is the capacity for unfolding.

Consider what will serve:
- Be open and as fully present as possible, letting insights arise.
- As the encounter unfolds, notice what your client might be offering in this moment. What are you sensing, seeing, learning? Ask yourself: What will really serve here?
- Draw on your expertise, knowledge, and experience, and at the same time, be open to seeing things in a fresh way.
- This is a diagnostic step, and the insights you have may fall outside of standardized categories. Be careful not to jump to conclusions too quickly. Notice that this step does not indicate what you "do," as much as it focuses on your intention to serve, which may be more about 'being with' than 'doing.'

Engage, enact ethically, and then end:
- Compassionate action emerges from the sense of openness, connectedness, and discernment you have created. This action might be a recommendation, an open question about values, or even a proposal for how to spend the remaining time with this individual.

- What emerges is principled compassion: Mutual, respectful of all persons involved, and practical. These aspirations may not always be realized; there may be deeply rooted conflicts in goals and values that must be addressed from this place of stability and discernment.
- End: Mark the end of the interaction; release, let go, breathe out. It might be helpful to consider a ritual that helps you to mark the ending, such as moving something in your room, washing your hands, or using your breath to signal that the encounter is done.
- While this encounter might have been more than you expected or disappointingly small, notice that, and acknowledge your work. Without acknowledging your own work, it will be difficult to let go of this encounter and move forward.

CONCLUSION

The ABIDE model of compassion presents another way to explore compassion, especially as it relates to clinical contexts. The model focuses on the cultivation of the ability to focus attention, balance affect, and gain insight and discernment in order to engage fully and deeply with ourselves and those in our care. The GRACE model of compassionate response is an outgrowth of the ABIDE model, providing an easily remembered acronym for engaging with the components of compassion in order to enact a response to suffering that is ethical, balanced, and sustainable.

REFERENCES

Fulton, C. L. (2018). Self-compassion as a mediator of mindfulness and compassion for others. *Counseling and Values*, *63*(1), 45–56.

Halifax, J. (2009). *Being with dying: Cultivating compassion and fearlessness in the presence of death*. Shambhala.

Halifax, J. (2011). The precious necessity of compassion. *Journal of Pain and Symptom Management*, *41*(1), 146–153.

Halifax, J. (2012). A heuristic model of enactive compassion. *Current Opinion in Supportive and Palliative Care*, *2*(6), 228–235.

Halifax, J. (2013). Understanding and cultivating compassion in clinical settings: The A.B.I.D.E. Compassion model. In T. Singer & M. Bolz (Eds.), *Compassion: Bridging practice and science ebook* (pp. 208–226). Max Planck Society.

Halifax, J. (2014). Grace for nurses: Cultivating compassion in nurse/patient interactions. *Journal of Nursing Education and Practice*, *4*(1), 121.

Youngson, R. (2013). Anesthesiology: Personal reflections. In C. R. Figley, P. K. Huggard, & C. Rees (Eds.), *First do no self-harm* (pp. 331–338). Oxford University Press.

CHAPTER 14

COMPASSIONATE SELF-CARE IN LOSS AND GRIEF

Mindful-Compassion Art-Based Therapy

Geraldine Tan-Ho and Andy H. Y. Ho

INTRODUCTION

Caring for the dying and the bereaved places complex and multifaceted demands on professional end-of-life (EoL) caregivers such as physicians, nurses, social workers, counselors, and allied health workers. These include the necessity for excellent responsiveness, efficiency, and clinical capability as well as emotional competence (Vachon, 1995). In addition to these daily demands, repeated encounters with loss and grief, insufficient support, lack of self-care, and mounting spiritual distress are some of the most common strains EoL professionals struggle with (Koh et al., 2015), despite organizational and personal efforts at mitigating these burdens. Such stressors, when prolonged, can result in burnout, which if not properly managed, can prove detrimental to the physical and mental health of professionals, with effects trickling down to patients, colleagues, family, and friends, posing threats to both quality of patient care and personal life. This chapter will first provide an overview on the impact on burnout, and delineate the important role that emotional regulation supported though expressive arts and mindfulness practices can play in reducing work-related stress. Thereafter, it will introduce a novel, integrative, multimodal arts-and-mindfulness based intervention as a professional imperative parallel to clinical training and supervision, to equip EoL professionals with the necessary resilience and emotional regulation for reducing and coping with work-related stress.

EFFECTS OF BURNOUT ON EOL CAREGIVING

According to Maslach et al. (1996), burnout is defined as "a state of exhaustion in which one is cynical about the value of one's occupation and doubtful of one's capacity to perform" (p. 20). It is a psychophysiological reaction to chronic work-related stress, causing caregivers to lose concern for the people whom they are caring for, and resulting in a 'literal collapse of the human spirit' (Storlie, 1979). While research has found that up to 65% of physicians, 33% of nurses, and 67% of psychosocial care professionals suffer from burnout every year (Genly, 2016), more recent studies have found that healthcare workers, especially those working in community-based and in-patient geriatrics and hospice care, are facing additional significant burdens due to the COVID-19 pandemic. For example, a 2021 survey with geriatric and hospice care workers in Ireland reported that 92% of respondents agreed that their workload had greatly increased due to the pandemic, 72.8% agreed that their responsibility had also increased significantly, and 78.4% agreed that they had experienced much higher levels of work-related stress (Nestor et al., 2021). Similar findings on the detrimental impacts of burnout among healthcare worker being compounded by COVID-19 are emerging across the globe (e.g., Goncalves et al., 2021; Lum et al., 2021; Pastrana et al.,

DOI: 10.4324/9781003204121-18

2021). The reason for such high prevalence of burnout among those immersed in EoL care is the intense emotional and existential nature of their work. Having established trust and relational bonds to competently support terminally ill patients, EoL care professionals eventually need to face the death of their patients with little support for their experience of grief and loss. As Kubler-Ross (1970) and many others have observed, professional EoL caregivers often withdraw from the bedsides of dying patients due to the lack of capacity to cope with the emotions that precede death (i.e., Hanson et al., 1997; Teno et al., 2004; Back et al., 2009).

The effects of burnout can come in many forms. Psychological morbidity including depression, anxiety, and low self-esteem are all potential consequences of burnout and work-related stress (Maslach et al., 2001). Burnout affects physical health as well, correlating to cardiovascular disease and musculoskeletal disorders (Honkonen et al., 2006). Perhaps the most worrisome of these negative consequences is the potential harmful effect on the quality and safety of patient care. A recent study conducted in the United States found that 10.5% of 6,586 physicians surveyed reported having made a major medical error in the previous 3 months, with burnout (54.3%) and fatigue (32.8%) being the principal culprits of safety-related quality of care concerns (Tawfik et al., 2018). Wilkinson et al. (2017) postulate that burnout negatively impacts quality of patient care because of a decreased ability among professional caregivers in expressing empathy. Dill and Cagle (2010) further report that due to stress and burnout, the turnover rate of in-patient hospice workers stands at an alarming 30% and reaches as high as 60% for homecare workers, thus posing great disruption in care continuity as well as a threat to care quality.

RESOLVING BURNOUT THROUGH SUPERVISION AND SELF-CARE INTERVENTIONS

Professional EoL caregiving, by its very nature, necessitates strong levels of psycho-socio-emotional competence. Adequately supporting professional EoL caregivers to better cope with work-related stress would entail clinical supervision and/or self-care interventions that aim to enhance emotional regulation, thereby increasing one's sense of autonomy and empathic capacity (Rushton et al., 2013). Such interventions would also need to provide avenues to cultivate resilience and achieve meaning-making (Ablett & Jones, 2010). Of particular importance is establishing a communal platform for EoL care professionals to periodically reflect on their own attitudes, feelings, and anxieties related to death and loss (Bluck et al., 2008), while being able to express and share their thoughts with team members to build mutual respect, compassionate understanding, and support (Chan & Tin, 2012).

ART-BASED CLINICAL SUPERVISION TO ENHANCE EMOTIONAL REGULATION

While supervision has been shown to be effective in reducing fatigue among hospice workers (Pereira et al., 2011), specific attention to emotion-focused coping skills has proved more effective in reducing burnout than problem-focused strategy skills (Sardiwalla et al., 2007). Emotion-focused supervision requires professionals to consider and communicate feelings and experiences that may be difficult to verbalize. As art provides the means to express oneself through images and metaphors that transcend the barriers of language (McNiff, 2007), emotion-focused supervision that incorporates expressive art techniques for self-reflection and self-expression can promote and enhance the understanding of one's emotions and stress (Lahad, 2000). In other words, supervised art therapy allows art-making and creativity to take central roles in clinical supervision for empowering healthcare workers (Nainis, 2005).

To better support professional EoL caregivers with work-related stress, Potash et al. (2015) designed a novel art-therapy-based supervision model that aimed at alleviating burnout, nurturing emotional awareness, increasing collegial connections, and allowing a safe space to reflect on death and loss. The efficacy of this intervention model was tested through a quasi-experimental design, with 69 participants enrolled in a 6-week, 18-hour art-therapy-based supervision group, and another 63 participants enrolled in a 3-day, 18-hour standard skills-based supervision group (n = 132). Pre- and post-intervention assessments on participants' levels of burnout, emotional regulation, and death attitudes revealed significant reductions in exhaustion and death anxiety, as well as significant increases in emotional awareness for those enrolled in the art-therapy supervision group. This study provides strong evidence that art-therapy-based supervision is effective in enhancing emotional regulation, fostering meaning-making, and promoting self-reflection (Potash et al., 2014).

INTEGRATING MINDFUL SELF-COMPASSION PRACTICE WITH ART-BASED SUPERVISION

In recent decades, both researchers and clinicians have become increasingly interested in mindfulness practice as studies continue to reveal its beneficial effects. Jon Kabat-Zinn (2003) defines mindfulness as "the awareness that emerges through paying attention on purpose, in the present moment, and nonjudgmentally to the unfolding of experience moment by moment" (p. 145). Bishop et al. (2008) delineate two main elements of mindfulness: Paying attention to one's present moment experience as it transpires, and relating to this experience with curiosity, openness, and acceptance. As such, mindfulness practice enables individuals to tune into their emotionality and immediate experiences with a much-deepened understanding of self, together with the potential for developing self-kindness and self-compassion toward painful experiences that are often hidden in our subconscious. Neff (2003) postulates that self-compassion involves being touched by one's own suffering, generating the desire to alleviate that suffering and to treat oneself with understanding and concern. Neff and Germer (2012) further elucidate that self-compassion comprises three interacting components: Self-kindness versus self-judgment, a sense of common humanity versus isolation, and mindfulness versus overidentification when confronting painful thoughts and emotions. A wealth of literature has provided a robust pool of evidence supporting the efficacy of mindfulness practice and self-compassion in promoting psychological well-being (Allen et al., 2012) and reducing depression and anxiety (Krieger et al., 2013), as well as enhancing health and overall physical functioning (Magnus et al., 2010).

Despite these positive findings, relatively little research has attempted to integrate mindfulness practice with art-based therapy to investigate their combined effects for health elevation and stress reduction, an endeavor that warrants much greater attention (Rappaport, 2014). The introspective and intuitive foundation of mindfulness practice can complement and facilitate the expressive and creative foundation of art therapy, and vice versa. A unique amalgamation of these two modalities in the context of supportive intervention for EoL care professionals has immense potential to aid them in coping with and rising above the trauma of loss and grief that they regularly encounter. Mindful-Compassion Art-based Therapy (MCAT) was developed for this purpose (Ho & Tan-Ho, 2018).

MINDFUL-COMPASSION ART-BASED THERAPY (MCAT)

MCAT is a highly structured, multimodal, group-based intervention that aims to create a supportive platform for EoL care professionals to deeply reflect and creatively express their experiences of stress and self-care, caregiving competences and challenges, and the emotionality of their grief, as well as the meaning of their work. These interactive processes serve to foster self-understanding, connectedness, internal strength, and compassion (Potash et al., 2018). The ultimate goal of MCAT is to offer a communal self-care intervention to alleviate burnout and cultivate sustained resilience for professional EoL caregivers.

Table 14.1 Overview of Therapeutic Elements of the MCAT Intervention Model

Session	Weekly Topic	Mindfulness Meditation	Visualization Theme	Art-Based Activities
Week 1	Self-care	Affectionate breathing	Self-kindness	Creation of mandala of self-care/ reflective art observations
Week 2	Stress management	Compassionate body scan	Bodily stress	Creation of symbol of stress/ transformative art-making/reflective writing
Week 3	Inspirational caregiving	Loving-kindness meditation	Strengths and progression in patient care	Creation of symbol of strength/art observation/ creative response writing
Week 4	Challenges caregiving	Loving-kindness meditation	Limitation and stagnation in patient care	Creation of symbol of limitation/ art observation/ creative response writing
Week 5	Loss and grief	Meditation on impermanence	A patient's death	Creation of symbol of grief/collective small group mural/reflective writing
Week 6	Aspiration and meaning reconstruction	Meditation on giving and receiving compassion	Wisdom learnt and meaning of work	Creation of mandala of meaning/ collective large group mural/ reflective writing

MCAT comprises a 6-weekly group-based intervention (18 hours in total) that integrates the reflective power of mindfulness meditation with the expressive power of art-based therapy to support and enhance the psycho-socio-emotional health of professional EoL caregivers (Ho et al., 2019). MCAT is collaboratively delivered by an accredited art therapist and a clinical researcher trained and accredited in mindfulness-based stress reduction. Each MCAT group is heterogeneous and includes participants who may be physicians, nurses, social workers, allied health, and program workers. Each MCAT session covers a unique topic that aims to promote understanding, acceptance, and compassion of self and others for cultivating psychological resilience and shared meaning. The topics are strategically designed to build upon each other week by week, with a scaffolding of brief psychoeducation, themed meditations, guided visualizations, art-based activities, and reflective writing that deepen participants' cognitive awareness and emotionality, empowering them to fully experience and appreciate the authenticity and immediacy of their self-reflection, creative expressions, and group insights. Table 14.1 provides a summary of the topics and activities of the six-week MCAT intervention model.

MCAT PROTOCOL

In Week 1, MCAT participants gain insight into how mindfulness and creative expression can be useful forms of self-care, and reflect on what self-care means to them.

"We need to live not in the past or the future, but in the present."
—Palliative care doctor.

Figure 14.1 Mindful Mandala of Self Care (Week 1)

In Week 2, participants contemplate their stressors at work in relation to their bodily sensations, and practice creative problem-solving as well as experiencing change in perspectives through transformative art-making.

"Stress may not be a bad thing … It can bring out the brilliance in people."
—Palliative care social worker.

Figure 14.2 Symbols of Stress and Transformative Stress (Week 2)

In Weeks 3 and 4, participants reflect on their experiences of strength and limitations through positive and challenging patient interactions respectively, bonding through shared emotions and encounters.

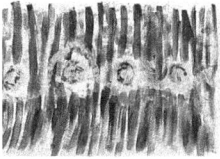

"Illness journeys are long and waving, there are many ups and downs … many struggles to find peace and hope … I wish them safety and calm."—Palliative care nurse.

"While I want to hold on to the hands of the vulnerable, I also recognize that I myself am a vulnerable being who needs love and support."—Palliative care doctor.

Figure 14.3 Caregiving Competencies (Week 3) and Caregiver Challenges (Week 4)

In Week 5, participants delve into their experiences with loss and grief specific to patient death, providing support to each other and finding comfort in expressing their vulnerabilities.

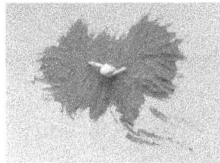

"When all is drowning and sinking in adversity, we need to be still and persevere, to embrace the trapping moves and see them as a dance of life."—Palliative care nurse.

Figure 14.4 Symbols of Grief (Week 5)

In Week 6, participants are invited to consolidate all of their experiences and learnings from the past five weeks to reflect on and solidify the meaning and purpose of their chosen work.

"We are often fixated on looking at things at horizon level. But what we see is not all that there is. Deep down in the blue sea lie beautiful fishes. High up in the heavens there is a beautiful paradise. It is up to you to find meaning of it all."—MCAT participants.

Figure 14.5 Mural of Meaning (Week 6)

Table 14.2 MCAT Weekly Session Plan

MCAT Activity	Time Allocation	Interventionist
Check-in and brief thematic psychoeducation	10 minutes	AT and MP
Mindfulness meditation with guided visualization	20 minutes	MP
Facilitated art-making	50 minutes	AT
Break	15 minutes	—
Mindful breathing	5 minutes	MP
Reflective art-based activities (e.g., transformative art)	30 minutes	AT
Small group discussion	20 minutes	AT and MP
Large group discussion	25 minutes	AT and MP
Mindful breathing and check-out	5 minutes	MP

Note: AT = art therapist; MP = mindfulness practitioner.

MCAT SESSION PLAN

Each weekly session lasts three hours and comprises an integrative alignment of experiential activities that aim to foster self-reflection, creative expression, authentic sharing, and perspective widening (Ho & Tan-Ho, 2019). Table 14.2 provides a summary of the intervention procedures of a three-hour MCAT session.

FINDINGS FROM A RANDOMIZED CONTROL TRIAL

To examine the efficacy of MCAT and supported by the Nanyang Technological University Start-Up Grant [ref no.: M4081570.100], an open label waitlist randomized control trial with two arms was conducted between 2016 and 2018. Fifty-six professional EoL caregivers including physicians, nurses, and social workers were recruited from the largest home-care hospice in Singapore, and allocated to either the immediate-treatment immediate (n = 29) or the waitlist-control (n = 27) condition. All MCAT participants completed a set of standardized psychometric assessment tools that measured: (a) 'burnout' using the 16-item Maslach Burnout Inventory (Maslach et al., 1996); (b) 'resilience' using the 14-item Ego-Resilience Scale (Block & Kremen, 1996); (c) 'emotional regulation' using the 39-item Five-Facets Mindfulness Questionnaire (Baer et al., 2006); (d) 'self-compassion' using 12-item Self-Compassion Scale Short Form (Raes et al., 2011); and (e) 'quality of life' using the WHO Quality of Life Scale (Power, 2003). Assessments were collected as baseline, post-intervention/post-waitlist, and six-week follow-up.

Results from between group analysis reveal that, compared to those in the waitlist control condition, participants in the immediate-treatment condition experienced significant reductions in burnout and the feeling of exhaustion at post-intervention. Significant improvements in emotional regulation, non-reactivity to negative thoughts, and resilience were also observed for treatment group participants at post-intervention. Treatment gains were maintained at six-week follow-up, with new benefits observed in better quality of life, elevated overall self-compassion, increased ability to observe and engage in non-judgmental inner experience, greater mindful awareness, as well as a deepened sense of connectedness to common humanity. These findings reflect the robust effectiveness and positive residual effects of MCAT for reducing burnout, building resilience, nurturing compassion, and promoting mental wellness among professional EoL caregivers (Ho et al., 2021).

CONCLUSION

Burnout has become a global health concern, particularly among medical and social care professionals working in the fields of EoL care. MCAT integrates mindfulness meditation with art-based therapy to form a unique and highly effective intervention that tackles the urgent problem of burnout, while fostering emotional regulation, resilience, self-compassion, and quality of life. It addresses a critical gap in the self-care and supportive supervision literature for professional caregivers. Further research and development of MCAT will contribute to advancements in both theories and practices for empowering EoL care professionals around the world. Such efforts will also inform policy makers about the feasibility and acceptability of delivering such intervention in real-world community-based settings.

As eloquently put by William Shakespeare, "Our bodies are our gardens to which our wills are gardeners" (Shakespeare, 1603/2016, 1.3.313–314). Such timeless wisdom rings true, as without self-care through self-compassion, our ability to support, protect, and honor the dignity of dying patients and their families facing life's most vulnerable moments is greatly undermined. After all, the quality of care of patients is only as good as the quality of health of their caregivers.

REFERENCES

Ablett, J. R., & Jones, R. S. P. (2010). Resilience and well-being in palliative care staff: A qualitative study of hospice nurses' experience of work. *Psycho-Oncology, 16*(8), 733–740.

Allen, A. B., Goldwasser, E. R., & Leary, M. R. (2012). Self-compassion and wellbeing among older adults. *Self and Identity, 11*(4), 428–453.

Back, A. L., Young, J. P., McCown, E., Engelberg, R. A., Vig, E. K., Reinke, L., Wenrich, M. D., McGrath, B. B., Curtis, J. R. (2009). Abandonment at the end of life from patient, caregiver, nurse, and physician perspectives: Loss of continuity and lack of closure. *Archive of Internal Medicine, 169*(5), 474–479.

Baer, R. A., Smith, G. T., Hopkins, J., Krietemeyer, J., & Toney, L. (2006). Using self-report assessment methods to explore facets of mindfulness. *Assessment, 13*(1), 27–45.

Bishop, S. R., Lau, M., Shapiro, S., Carlson, L., Anderson, N. D., Carmody, J., Segal, Z. V., Abbey, S., Speca, M., Velting, D., & Devins, G. (2008). Mindfulness: A proposed operational definition. *Clinical Psychology: Science and Practice, 11*(3), 230–241.

Block, J., & Kremen, A. M. (1996). IQ and ego-resilience: Conceptual and empirical connections and separateness. *Journal of Personality and Social Psychology, 70*(2), 349–361.

Bluck, S., Dirk, J., Mackay, M. M., & Hux, A. (2008). Life experience with death: Relation to death attitudes and to the use of death related memories. *Death Studies, 32*(6), 524–549.

Chan, W. C. H., & Tin, A. F. (2012). Beyond knowledge and skills: Self-competence in working with death, dying, and bereavement. *Death Studies, 36*(10), 899–913.

Dill, J., & Cagle, J. (2010). Caregiving in a patients' place of residence: Turnover of direct care workers in home care and hospice agencies. *Journal of Health and Aging, 22*(6), 713–733.

Genly, B. (2016). Safety and job burnout: Understanding complex contributing factors. *Professional Safety, 61*(10), 45–49.

Gonçalves, J. V., Castro, L., Rêgo, G., & Nunes, R. (2021). Burnout determinants among nurses working in palliative care during the coronavirus disease 2019 pandemic. *International Journal of Environmental Research and Public Health, 18*(7), 3358.

Hanson, L. C., Danis, M., & Garrett, J. (1997). What is wrong with end-of-life care? Opinions of bereaved family members. *Journal of American Geriatric Society, 45*(11), 1339–1344.

Ho, A. H. Y., & Tan-Ho, G. (2018). *Mindful-compassion art therapy: A handbook for practitioners.* Action Research for Community Health (ARCH), Psychology, School of Social Sciences, Nanyang Technological University.

Ho, A. H. Y., Tan-Ho, G., Ngo, T. A., Ong, G., Cheng, P. H., Dignadice, D., & Potash, J. S. (2019). A novel mindful compassion art therapy (MCAT) for reducing burnout and promoting resilience for EoL care professionals: A waitlist RCT protocol. *Trials, 20*(1), 406.

Ho, A. H. Y., Tan-Ho, G., Ngo, T. A., Ong, G., Cheng, P. H., Dignadice, D., & Potash, J. S. (2021). A novel Mindful Compassion Art-based Therapy (MCAT) for reducing burnout and promoting resilience among healthcare workers: Findings from a waitlist randomized control trial. *Frontiers in Psychology, 12*, 74443.

Honkonen, T., Ahola, K., Pertovaara, M., Isometsa, E., Kalimo, R., Nykyri, E., Aromaa, A., & Lonnqvist, J. (2006). The association between burnout and physical illness in the general population-results from the Finnish health 2000 Study. *Journal of Psychosomatic Research, 61*(1), 59–66.

Kabat-Zinn, J. (2003). Mindfulness-based interventions in context: Past, present and future. *Clinical Psychology: Social and Practice, 10*(2), 144–156.

Koh, M. Y., Chong, P. H., Neo, P. S., Ong, Y. J., Wong, W. C., Ong, W. Y., Shen, M. L., & Hum, A. Y. (2015). Burnout, psychological morbidity and use of coping mechanisms among palliative care practitioners: A multi-centre cross-sectional study. *Palliative Medicine, 29*(7), 633–642.

Krieger, T., Altenstein, D., Baettig, I., Doerig, N., & Holtforth, M. (2013). Self-compassion in depression: Associations with depressive symptoms, rumination, and avoidance in depressed outpatients. *Behavior Therapy, 44*(3), 501–513.

Kubler-Ross, E. (1970). *On death and dying.* Collier Books/Macmillan Publishing Co.

Lahad, M. (2000). *Creative supervision: The use of expressive arts methods in supervision and self-supervision.* Jessica Kingsley.

Lum, A., Goh, Y. L., Wong, K. S., Seah, J., Teo, G., Ng, J. Q., Abdin, E., Hendricks, M. M., Tham, J., Nan, W., & Fung, D. (2021). Impact of COVID-19 on the mental health of Singaporean GPs: A cross-sectional study. *British Journal of General Practice Open, 5*(4), BJGPO.2021.0072.

Magnus, C. M. R., Kowalski, K. C., & McHugh, T. L. F. (2010). The role of self-compassion in women's self-determined motives to exercise and exercise-related outcomes. *Self and Identity, 9*(4), 363–382.

Maslach, C., Jackson, S. E., & Leiter, M. P. (1996). *The Maslach burnout inventory* (3rd ed.). Consulting Psychologists Press.

Maslach, C., Schaufeli, W., & Leiter, M. (2001). Job burnout. *Annual Review of Psychology, 52*, 397–422.

McNiff, S. (2007). *Art as medicine*. Shambhala.

Morita, T., Miyashita, M., Kimura, R., Adachi, I., & Shima, Y. (2004). Emotional burden of nurses in palliative sedation therapy. *Palliative Medicine, 18*(6), 550–557.

Nainis, N. A. (2005). Art therapy with an oncology care team. *Art Therapy: Journal of the American Art Therapy Association, 22*(3), 150–154.

Neff, K. D. (2003). Self-compassion: An alternative conceptualization of a healthy attitude toward oneself. *Self and Identity, 2*(2), 85–102.

Neff, K. D., & Germer, C. K. (2012). A pilot study and randomized control trial of the mindful self-compassion program. *Journal of Clinical Psychology, 69*(1), 28–44.

Nestor, S., O' Tuathaigh, C., & O' Brien, T. (2021). Assessing the impact of COVID-19 on healthcare staff at a combined elderly care and specialist palliative care facility: A cross-sectional study. *Palliative Medicine, 35*(8), 1492–1501.

Pastrana, T., De Lima, L., Pettus, K., Ramsey, A., Napier, G., Wenk, R., & Radbruch, L. (2021). The impact of COVID-19 on palliative care workers across the world: A qualitative analysis of responses to open-ended questions. *Palliative and Supportive, 19*(2), 187–192.

Pereira, S. M., Fonseca, A. M., & Carvalho, A. S. (2011). Burnout in palliative care: A systematic review. *Nursing Ethics, 18*(3), 317–326.

Potash, J. S., Chan, F., Ho, A. H. Y., Wang, X. L., & Cheng, C. (2015). A model for art therapy based supervision for end-of-life-care workers in Hong Kong. *Death Studies, 39*(1–5), 44–51.

Potash, J. S., Ho, A. H. Y., Chan, F., Wang, X. L., & Cheng, C. (2014). Can art therapy reduce death anxiety and burnout in end-of-life care workers? A quasi-experimental study. *International Journal of Palliative Nursing, 20*(5), 233–240.

Potash, J. S., Ho, R. T. H., & Ho, A. H. Y. (2018). Citizenship, compassion, the Arts: People living with mental illness need a caring community. *Social Change, 48*(2), 238–259.

Power, M. (2003). Development of a common instrument for quality of life. In A. Nosikov & C. Cudex (Eds.), *EUROHIS: Developing common instruments for health surveys* (pp. 145–163). IOS Press.

Raes, F., Pommier, E., Neff, K. D., & Van Gucht, D. (2011). Construction and factorial validation of a short form of the self-compassion scale. *Clinical Psychology and Psychotherapy, 18*(3), 250–255.

Rappaport, L. (2014). Integrating focusing with the expressive arts therapies and mindfulness. *Folio journal, 25*, 152–161.

Rushton, C. H., Kaszniak, A. W., & Halifax, J. S. (2013). A framework for understanding moral distress among palliative care clinicians. *Journal of Palliative Medicine, 16*(9), 1074–1079.

Sardiwalla, N., VandenBerg, H., & Esterhuyse, K. G. F. (2007). The role of stressors and coping strategies in the burnout experienced by hospice workers. *Cancer Nursing, 30*(6), 488–497.

Shakespeare, W. (1603/2016). *Othello* (E. Pechter, Ed.). WW Norton & Co.

Storlie, F. J. (1979). Burnout: The elaboration of a concept. *American Journal of Nursing, 79*(12), 2108–2111.

Tawfik, D. S., Profit, J., Morgenthaler, T. I., Satele, D. V., Sinsky, C. A., Dyrbye, L. M., Tutty, M. A., West, C. P., & Shanafelt, T. D. (2018). Physician burnout, well-being, and work unit safety grades in relationship to reported medical errors. *Mayo Clinic Proceedings, 93*(11), 1571–1580.

Teno, J. M., Clarridge, B. R., Casey, V., Welch, L. C., Wetle, T., Shield, R., & Mor, V. (2004). Family perspectives on end-of-life care at the last place of care. *JAMA, 291*(1), 88–93.

Wilkinson, H., Whittington, R., Perry, L., & Eames, C. (2017). Examining the relationship between burnout and empathy in healthcare professionals: A systematic review. *Burnout Research, 6*, 18–29.

Vachon, M. L. S. (1995). Staff stress in hospice/palliative care: A review. *Palliative Medicine, 9*(2), 91–122.

CHAPTER 15

DIGNITY AND COMPASSION IN END-OF-LIFE CARE

Andy H. Y. Ho

INTRODUCTION

The defining principles of palliative care, including symptom control and psychological and spiritual support, aim to optimize quality of life and promote death with dignity (Hall et al., 2011). However, most conventional palliative care interventions are heavily medically oriented, focusing predominantly on symptom management and control of physical pain, without addressing the psychosocial, emotional, and existential pains of dying. The lack of a holistic approach to palliative care can lead to a fractured sense of dignity at the end of life. In fact, a growing body of research consolidated through an integrative review (Guo and Jacelon, 2014) found that an undermining of dignity among dying patients is associated with high levels of depression, anxiety, hopelessness, feelings of being a burden to others, and the loss of will to live; whereas a sense of control, hope, meaning, spiritual peace, self-worth, and strengthened relationships with significant others are deemed some of most important facets of dignity at life's end. These empirical works accentuate an imperative need for individuals to attain a sense of closure, completeness, and acceptance so as to experience integrity rather than despair at the last stage of life. Clearly, palliative intervention must expand beyond the realm of physical care toward 'whole person' psycho-socio-spiritual care in order to fully address the 'total pain' of mortality (Saunders, 1967).

This chapter will provide a concise overview of the empirical foundations of dignity in end-of-life contexts stemming from both Western and Asian literature. It will also introduce two empirically driven and clinically robust therapeutic engagements, namely Dignity Therapy and Family Dignity Intervention, for protecting and enhancing patients' dignity. Finally, it will synthesize dignity-enhancing interventions with compassion-based approaches to advance the practice of dignified and compassionate end-of-life care.

DEFINING AND PROTECTING PATIENT DIGNITY IN WESTERN SOCIETIES

While preserving patients' dignity has long been the overarching goal of palliative care, the construct of dignity remained largely underdeveloped. The emergence of Chochinov et al.'s (2002) Empirical Model of Dignity-Conserving Care brought greater clarity to the conceptual and practical knowledge of dignity. Stemming from an in-depth analysis of the rich narratives of 50 Canadian patients with terminal diagnoses, the model provides an empirical scaffold that illuminates dignity-centered needs and concerns at life's final margin.

THE EMPIRICAL MODEL OF DIGNITY-CONSERVING CARE

The empirical model of dignity-conserving care consists of three major thematic constructs: (a) Illness-related concerns, which pertain to the physical and medical aspects of care;

DOI: 10.4324/9781003204121-19

(b) the Dignity-Conserving Repertoire, which pertains to patients' psychological makeup and spiritual practices; and (c) the Social Dignity Inventory, which refers to the external social influences and interpersonal factors that affect dignity. These three constructs, with each containing several carefully defined themes and subthemes, refer to a broad range of physical, psychological, and interpersonal issues that determine how patients experience dignity during the final chapter of life.

The first part of the model, illness-related concerns, describes issues stemming directly from the disease that are active or eventual threats to patients' dignity. The two larger themes include level of independence and symptom distress. The former considers the presence of aberrant cognitive processes and functional decline in everyday activities, and the latter instances of pain and discomfort, as well as distress stemming from health uncertainty and worries of the dying process.

The second part of the model, the dignity-conserving repertoire, observes the two interrelated major themes of dignity-conserving perspectives and dignity-conserving practices. First, dignity-conserving perspectives comprise eight sub-themes, which describe the encompassing worldview of patients and their internal beliefs. These include: (a) continuity of self, (b) role preservation, (c) generativity/legacy, (d) maintaining pride, (e) maintaining hope, (f) autonomy/control, (g) acceptance, and (h) resilience/fighting spirit. Second, dignity-conserving practices comprise three actionable elements: (a) living in the moment, (b) maintaining normalcy, and (c) seeking spiritual comfort.

The final part of the model, the social dignity inventory, addresses how the quality of interpersonal interactions within the patient's care ecosystem facilitates or harms their subjective sense of dignity. The five identified themes consist of: (a) privacy boundaries, (b) social support, (c) care tenor; attitudinal impacts of caregiving interactions with formal and informal carers, (d) burden to others; feelings of distress in the reliance on another with regards to personal care and self-management, and (e) aftermath concerns; worries about the difficulties loved ones will face once death finally occurs.

The empirical model of dignity has been validated, while its themes are supported through statistical testing and analyses of the key constructs pertaining to patients' subjective dignity experience (Hack et al., 2004; Chochinov et al., 2005; Chochinov et al., 2008). The model further establishes a clear and urgent need for palliation to reach beyond pain reduction and symptom control so as to address the board spectrum of psychosocial and spiritual distress of dying and loss.

DIGNITY THERAPY

Dignity Therapy (DT) is a brief, individualized psychotherapeutic intervention that was naturally built upon the framework of the empirical model of dignity-conserving care (Chochinov et al., 2005). In employing a narrative approach with elements such as life review and reminiscence intervention, it invites patients to find hope and meaning through examination of specific past experiences and achievements with the eventual creation of a generativity document. This 'generativity' document will be bestowed upon the patient's family members and loved ones, with the goal of providing patients with an opportunity to build their legacy and to decrease their suffering by fortifying their sense of meaning, purpose, dignity, and overall quality of life.

Table 15.1 Dignity Intervention Core Questions

1. Tell me a little about your life history, particularly the parts that you either remember most, or think are the most important. When did you feel most alive?
2. Are there specific things that you would want your family to know about you, and are there particular things you would want them to remember?
3. What are the most important roles you have played in life (family roles, vocational roles, community service roles, etc.)? Why were they so important to you, and what do you think you accomplished in those roles?
4. What are your most important accomplishments, and what do you feel most proud of?
5. Are there particular things that you feel still need to be said to your loved ones, or things that you would want to take the time to say once again?
6. What are your hopes and dreams for your loved ones?
7. What have you learned about life that you would want to pass along to others? What advice or words of guidance would you wish to pass along to your (son, daughter, husband, wife, parents, others)?
8. Are there words or perhaps even instructions you would like to offer your family to help prepare them for the future?
9. In creating this permanent record, are there other things that you would like included?

Dignity therapy is conducted in the following manner; a trained therapist provides a patient with a written series of nine core questions based on the dignity model (see Table 15.1), and a DT session guided by these questions is scheduled a few days later. Patients are encouraged to respond to what might elicit meaning in them; this often includes offering final statements and discourse as well as remembrances to family and loved ones. DT can be completed within a 60-minute session. These sessions are audio-recorded, transcribed within 2 to 3 days, and edited over the next 24 to 48 hours. A follow-up session is held shortly thereafter to review the edited transcript with the patient and make any final modifications. Upon final revision, the patient is given a printed version of the "generativity" document, and asked to identify individuals with whom the document should be shared or bequeathed following the patient's death.

An intervention study with 100 terminally ill patients from Canada ($N = 50$) and Australia ($N = 50$) observed that DT was considered highly valuable to most participants (91%), enhancing the dignity of 76% of patients, heightening life meaning in 67% of patients, and increasing the will to live among 47% of patients (Chochinov et al., 2011). Moreover, family members of patients also found dignity therapy helpful, whereby 78% reported that it enhanced patients' dignity, 72% reported it heightened patients' life meaning, 78% said that the generativity document comforted their grief, and 95% recommended dignity therapy for other patients and families. A systematic review by Martinez et al. (2016) observed increasing employment of DT globally, and the results indicate that the intervention was beneficial in a myriad of ways, including lowering clinical levels of psychological distress and improving the end-of-life experience.

RE-EXAMINING AND ENHANCING PATIENT DIGNITY IN ASIAN SOCIETIES

Though the mentioned empirical model of dignity and dignity therapy have growing reception in the West, the subjective meaning and nuances of dignity may differ according to various cultural and ethnic values. Lee (2008) observed that a cross-cultural perspective on human dignity emphasizes the convergence of views over different belief systems; individuals from Asian cultures may borrow from Confucianism or other collectivistic philosophies in the construction of their subjective realizations of dignity.

PATIENT-FAMILY MODEL OF DIGNIFIED CARE

Recognizing the ever-important roles that family and collectivism play in Asian societies, Ho and his colleagues conducted an extensive body of research to re-examine the Western model of dignity through investigating the meaning of 'Living and Dying with Dignity' from the perspectives of older Asian terminally ill patients and their family caregivers in Hong Kong (Ho et al., 2013a, 2013b, Ho and Chan, 2013; Chan et al., 2012). The findings from these studies led to the development of the Patient-Family Model of Dignified Care (Ho, 2014). While this model has largely supported the three major constructs of dignity as identified by Chochinov et al. (2002), it also actively addresses the cultural nuances and collective ideologies surrounding familial relations, dynamics, and processes when considering the larger issue of generativity within constitution of dignity.

The patient-family model of dignified care demonstrates that dying patients in Asia experience great distress as they feel trapped in the liminal space between living and dying, challenged by increasing dependency and limited mobility. Thus, in order to maintain and promote dignity at life's final margin, one must strengthen patients' 'Spiritual Plasticity' through helping them find meaning in their pain and reinforce their virtuous traits; to surrender to life's impermanence; to facilitate moral transcendence and wisdom; and to enhance transgenerational unity and establish continuing bonds. Equally important is bolstering their sense of 'Family Connectedness' through expressing appreciation, achieving reconciliation, fulfilling family obligations, and reaffirming family roles and identity. Findings with family caregivers further revealed that patients' sense of dignity can be enhanced through strengthening 'Family Integrity' and 'Filial Compassion,' where the former involves the cultivation of mutual support, kinship involvement, and family adaptability in the provision of end-of-life care; and the latter the nurturance of compassionate duty, reciprocal relationships, and emotional connection through open and empathic communications between patients and their families.

This body of research has also found that despite the longing to rekindle family bonds at the end of life, Asian patients are often unable or are reluctant to engage in dignity-enhancing family discourses and processes as they feel confined by deteriorating physical and mental conditions, longstanding unresolved family conflicts, or by the cultural taboo of mortality. Furthermore, although family caregivers long for meaningful dialogue to facilitate moral transcendence and continuing bonds with patients, their communications are mostly pragmatic and focus primarily on physical care, as they are not well versed in the expression of love and affection. These findings highlight the imperative need for a highly structured and facilitated family-oriented intervention for upholding the dignity of older Asian patients and families at the end of life (Ho et al., 2014)

FAMILY DIGNITY INTERVENTION

Grounded in the patient-family model of dignified care (Ho, 2014) and building upon the clinical foundation of dignity therapy (Chochinov et al., 2005), Family Dignity Intervention (FDI) was developed to address the psycho-socio-spiritual needs of terminally ill patients and their families in Asia (Ho et al., 2017). The FDI adheres mostly to the DT protocol but deviates by adopting a patient-caregiver dyadic therapeutic modus. This is to facilitate open dialogue between patients and their primary family caregivers, thus reconciling the familial themes of dignity in the Asian context.

FDI comprises four standardized clinical sessions led by a trained therapist. The first session constitutes a framing interview with the patient-caregiver dyad to accurately gauge their aspirations and set the focus of therapy, parameters, and goals. A set of FDI dyadic interview questions are shared with the dyad (see Table 15.2), which focus on the elicitation of the patient's life experiences relating to his or her family, with the caregiver's sharing situated to enrich the patient's narratives. The second session involves the full FDI interview and takes place a few days later. The therapist aids the dyad in the structuring and organization of their thoughts and stories through a balanced use of the interview questions and the cues provided by the dyad. The therapist obtains chronological clarifications, vivid descriptions, emotions, and interconnections of events, with the aims of facilitating the sharing of cherished memories, encouraging the expression of appreciation, assisting in reconciliation, and eliciting wisdom. The FDI interview lasts between 60 and 90 minutes, is audio recorded, transcribed verbatim, and edited by the therapist into a coherent account. A third session is arranged two to three days later to review the edited account. The finalization of the account produces a 'Legacy' document detailing the unique, personalized, and carefully curated narratives and wisdoms of the patient in relation to their family. A concluding session is arranged with the dyad, where the document is read by the therapist to the family and any guests they might wish to invite. The sharing session allows therapeutic catharsis and further legacy building. The whole FDI process and all its constituent sessions are usually completed in the span of two weeks.

Table 15.2 Family Dignity Intervention Dyadic Interview Questions

Questions for Patients and Family Caregivers*

1. Tell me a little about your life history *(with your loved one)*; what are some of the most important and memorable times *(you had together)*? When did you feel most alive *(with your loved one)*?
2. How has your relationship with your loved one influenced your life?
3. What are some things you want your loved one to know about you, or to remember about you?
4. What do you think are your *(your loved one's)* most important and meaningful accomplishments in life (family, career, community)?
5. What do you think your loved one is most proud of you for, or appreciates about you?
6. What do you appreciate most about your loved one?
7. Are there particular things that you want to thank your loved one for?
8. Are there particular things that you would like to ask forgiveness for, or offer forgiveness?
9. What teachings, advice, or words of guidance do you want to pass on to your loved one *(what teaching advice or words of guidance have you received from your loved one and would like to pass on to other family members)*?
10. What are your hopes and dreams for the future, for yourself, your loved one, and your family?
11. In creating this permanent record, are there other things that you would like to include?
12. Before the session ends, are there things that you would like to take time to say again?

* Italics are modified questions intended for family caregivers.

A waitlist randomized control trial with 91 patient-caregiver dyads in Singapore (n = 182) found that compared to those in the control group, patients who completed FDI experienced a significant increase in quality of life, overall hope, positive life outlook, life value, life meaning, and perceived social support at post-intervention and five-week follow-up (Ho, 2020). Family caregivers who completed FDI experienced significant decreases in caregiver stress and depressive symptoms, as well as significant increases in overall hope, positive life outlook, and life value as compared to those in the control group at post-intervention and five-week follow-up. Moreover, intervention evaluation revealed that over 85% of patients and caregivers believed FDI was as helpful as all other aspect of their healthcare; 80% found FDI helpful in improving their sense of dignity, self-worth, and respect from others; and 70% found FDI helpful in reducing burden and suffering, while enhancing their sense of control, purpose in life, and family relationships. These findings highlight the robust and sustainable efficacy of FDI in improving the psych-socio-spiritual wellness of patients and caregivers facing mortality and loss.

SYNTHESIZING DIGNITY-ENHANCING INTERVENTIONS WITH COMPASSION-BASED APPROACHES

The effectiveness of DT and FDI would be greatly diminished if the conducting therapists were to lack a sense of kindness and compassion. While the core interview questions of DT and FDI are strength-focused, they are broad in nature and can result in responses and narratives that are loosely constructed, and filled with sorrows, regrets, and suffering. Therapists who practice DT and FDI must listen to and engage with their patients' stories with genuine empathy, attentiveness, curiosity, sensitivity, and unconditional positive regard. As such, the practice of compassion, which involves the three primary components of mindful awareness, therapeutic presence, and the recognition of common humanity (Gilbert, 2014), is of utmost importance when conducting any form of dignity-enhancing intervention.

Mindful awareness emphasizes the capacity of therapists to notice and become aware of the presence of suffering in their patients and within themselves, without judgment and aversion. Such sensitivity can propagate empathy, sympathy, and genuine care for the well-being of others and self in the immediacy of the present with clarity and intentionality, without feeling overwhelmed or losing focus on what is most important during DT and FDI—to elicit important stories that dignify patients' lives while supporting the emotionality and healing process of patients. Therapeutic presence accentuates the ability of therapists to create a safe and nurturing environment for their patients to face their sorrows, grief, and loss with open hearts and minds, empowering them to examine their life stories and narratives with new perspectives for meaning making and finding hope in the midst of dying. Establishing a therapeutic presence and connecting deeply with patients quickly are especially important when conducting DT and FDI, as the interventions are highly time-sensitive given the unpredictability of advanced illness. To do so necessitates genuineness, authenticity, and acceptance from therapists so that they can create a compassionate holding space for their patients' suffering and vulnerability during every precious therapeutic encounter. Finally, common humanity involves the therapists' understanding and appreciation of the interconnectedness between themselves and their patients, especially those rooted in the experience of suffering and the desire to be freed from suffering. The recognition of common humanity enables therapists to let go of their prejudice and self-interest to offer complete support for their patients. Therapists are further empowered to recognize their own vulnerabilities while practicing self-kindness and self-compassion during challenging therapeutic situations.

CONCLUSION

Dignified palliative care is a basic human right, and its provision needs to expand into psychological, social, and spiritual care. Repeated research has shown that dignity therapy and family dignity intervention can competently address the psycho-social-spiritual needs of dying patients and their families, while complementing existing palliative care provision to fully realize the original hospice ideals of whole person care for supporting the total pain of mortality. Most importantly, the success of such authentic and healing dialogues is contingent on the integration of compassion-based approaches accentuated by mindful awareness, the ability to be fully present, and the recognition of our interconnectedness and common humanity.

REFERENCES

Chan, C. L. W., Ho, A. H. Y., Leung, P. P. Y., Chochinov, H. M., Neimeyer, R. A., Pang, S. M. C., & Tse, D. M. W. (2012). The blessing and curses of filial piety on dignity at the end-of-life: Lived experience of Hong Kong Chinese adult children caregivers. *Journal of Ethnic and Cultural Diversity in Social Work, 21*(4), 277–296.

Chochinov, H. M., Hack, T., Hassard, T., Kristjanson, L. J., McClement, S., & Harlos, M. (2005). Dignity therapy: A novel psychotherapeutic intervention for patients near the end of life. *Journal of Clinical Oncology, 23*(24), 5520–5525.

Chochinov, H. M., Hack, T., McClement, S., Kristjanson, L., & Harlos, M. (2002). Dignity in the terminally ill: A developing empirical model. *Social Science and Medicine, 54*(3), 433–443.

Chochinov, H. M., Hassard, T., McClement, S., Hack, T., Kristjanson, L. J., Harlos, M., Sinclair, S., & Murray, A. (2008). The patient dignity inventory: A novel way of measuring dignity-related distress in palliative care. *Journal of Pain and Symptom Management, 36*(6), 559–571.

Chochinov, H. M., Kristjanson, L. J., Breitbart, W., McClement, S., Hack, T. F., Hassard, T., & Harlos, M. (2011). Effect of dignity therapy on distress and end-of-life experience in terminally ill patients: A randomized controlled trial. *Lancet Oncology, 12*(8), 753–762.

Chochinov, H. M., Kristjanson, L. J., Hack, T. F., Hassard, T., McClement, S., & Harlos, M. (2006). Dignity in the terminally ill: Revisited. *Journal of Palliative Medicine, 9*(3), 666–672.

Gilbert, P. (2014). The origins and nature of compassion focused therapy. *British Journal of Clinical Psychology, 53*(1), 6–41.

Guo, Q., & Jacelon, C. (2014). An integrative review of dignity in end-of-life care. *Palliative Medicine, 28*(7), 931–940.

Hack, T. F., Chochinov, H. M., Hassard, T., Kristjanson, L. J., McClement, S., & Harlos, M. (2004). Defining dignity in terminally ill cancer patients: A factor-analytic approach. *Psycho-Oncology: Journal of the Psychological, Social and Behavioral Dimensions of Cancer, 13*(10), 700–708.

Hall, S., Petkova, H., Tsouros, A. D., Costantini, M., & Higginson, I. J. (2011). *Palliative care for older people: Better practices.* World Health Organization.

Ho, A. H. Y. (2014). *Living and dying with dignity: An interpretive-systemic framework in Hong Kong.* [Doctoral dissertation, The University of Hong Kong. The HKU scholars hub]. http://doi.org/10.5353/th_b5106513

Ho, A. H. Y. (2020, June 30). Family dignity intervention (FDI): Advancing the Psycho-socio-spiritual domains of evidence-based palliative care in Singapore [Keynote presentation]. The International Symposium on Dignified and compassionate end-of-life Care, Singapore. https://www.youtube.com/watch?v=JV4K88dgFIY&t=27s

Ho, A. H. Y., Car, J., Ho, M. H. R., Tan-Ho, G., Choo, P. Y., Patinadan, P. V., Chong, P. H., Ong, W. Y., Fan, G., Tan, Y. P., Neimeyer, R. A., & Chochinov, H. M. (2017). A novel family dignity intervention (FDI) for enhancing and informing holistic palliative care in Asia: Study Protocol for a randomized controlled trial. *Trials*, *18*(1), 587.

Ho, A. H. Y., & Chan, C. L. W. (2013). From obligation to compassion: The transformation of filial piety in Chinese family caregiving at the end-of-life. *Association for Death Education and Counseling Forum*, *39*(3), 26–27.

Ho, A. H. Y., Chan, C. L. W., & Leung, P. P. Y. (2014). Dignity and quality of life in community palliative care. In K. Fong & K. W. Tong (Eds.), *Community care in Hong Kong: Current practices, practice-research studies and future directions* (pp. 319–341). City University Hong Kong Press.

Ho, A. H. Y., Chan, C. L. W., Leung, P. P. Y., Chochinov, H. M., Neimeyer, R. A., Pang, S. M. C., & Tse, D. M. W. (2013a). Living and dying with dignity in Chinese society: Perspectives of older palliative care patients in Hong Kong. *Age and Ageing*, *42*(4), 455–461.

Ho, A. H. Y., Leung, P. P. Y., Tse, D. M. W., Pang, S. M. C., Chochinov, H. M., Neimeyer, R. A., & Chan, C. L. W. (2013b). Dignity amidst liminality: Suffering within healing among Chinese terminal cancer patients. *Death Studies*, *37*(10), 953–970.

Lee, M. Y. K. (2008). Universal human dignity: Some reflections in the Asian context. *Asian Journal of Comparative Law*, *3*, 1–33.

Martínez, M., Arantzamendi, M., Belar, A., Carrasco, J. M., Carvajal, A., Rullán, M., & Centeno, C. (2016). 'Dignity therapy', a promising intervention in palliative care: A comprehensive systematic literature review. *Palliative Medicine*, *31*(6), 492–509.

Saunders, C. (1967). *The management of terminal illness*. Hospital Medicine Publications.

CHAPTER 16

SHAME IN THE CONTEXT OF GRIEF

Marcela Matos and Stan Steindl

INTRODUCTION

Shame is a universal human emotion that influences human psychosocial functioning and development (Fessler, 2007; Gilbert, 1998). Shame can arise in the context of grief, especially when the grieving person has difficult shame memories related to the loss (Barr, 2004; Dellmann, 2018; Kauffman, 2001). In this chapter we will explore shame, its evolutionary origins and functions, associated social, cultural, and psychological factors, and shame memories, how they develop and the form they take. We will explore shame in grief and approaches to assessing shame. We will illustrate the key concepts presented via a clinical vignette.

CLINICAL VIGNETTE

Initial Presentation

Talia,[1] a 50-year-old nurse, presented 1 year after the death of her mother, Lila. Talia, the youngest of five children, described her childhood as "like being an only child." According to Talia, Lila was "sweet and gentle ... very generous ... put everyone else first ... [and] worked hard keeping the house, never complaining." They were close, especially given Talia's father was often at work or the local bar, and it was just the two of them at home.

Talia completed school, studied nursing, and became a surgical nurse. She described her father's death, when she was 36 years old, as "sad, but nothing like when I lost Mum." When Talia was in her early 40s, Lila showed signs of memory loss and confusion. She was eventually diagnosed with Alzheimer's Dementia, and began having difficulty with activities of daily living, such as feeding. At 44 years old, Talia resigned from her job and became full-time carer to her mother, then 82 years old.

Five years later, Lila fell and broke her hip. She was admitted to hospital but developed pneumonia and a few short weeks later she died with Talia holding her hand, offering her kind words and comfort. Talia described this loss as "devastating ... overwhelming." She felt "numb," punctuated with sadness and anger. She said there were moments of relief, but mostly she felt overwhelmingly sad, lost, and empty.

She also described how she began to feel a persistent and eventually overwhelming feeling that she was an inadequate carer to her mother, a bad daughter, and an awful person. She began to feel terribly ashamed.

DOI: 10.4324/9781003204121-20

WHAT IS SHAME?

Shame is a powerful self-conscious, socially focused emotion, often triggered by threats to one's social self and status via put-downs, criticisms, and rejections (Gilbert, 1998). It involves feelings of inferiority, inadequacy, unattractiveness, defectiveness, and/or powerlessness, along with a desire to hide, avoid, escape, or conceal our deficiencies (Gilbert, 2007; Tangney & Dearing, 2002). Shame affects our sense of self, social interactions and moral behavior, and vulnerability to mental health problems (Gilbert, 2007; Tangney & Dearing, 2002). Shame is associated with a range of primary threat emotions, including anger, anxiety, sadness, and disgust, and often comes with a sense of defeat, loneliness, and disconnectedness (Fessler, 2007; Gilbert, 2007; Tangney & Dearing, 2002).

THE EVOLUTIONARY ORIGINS AND FUNCTION OF SHAME

Shame is linked to evolutionary salient concerns of social competition, social reputation, and social acceptance, and evolved behavioral adaptations that assist humans to navigate their social and physical environments, enhancing survival. Shame is thought to be rooted in our evolved socially competitive motives, arising from us being self-aware, identity-forming, and highly social (Gilbert, 2007; Sznycer et al., 2016).

The origins of shame are engrained in the evolution of social hierarchical living, where subordinates need to be responsive to threats from dominant members of the group (Gilbert, 2019). When threatened, subordinates express specific defenses (e.g., eye-gaze avoidance, making the body look smaller, reduced outputs) to reduce conflict or de-escalate attacks from the dominant (Keltner & Harker, 1998). Shame is thought to have evolved to respond to social threats, which encompass the actual or potential loss of social status, acceptance, or esteem (Gilbert, 2007), rendering one at risk of being ostracized, persecuted, or harmed by others, compromising one's access to vital biosocial resources (e.g., food, support, protection), reproductive success, and, ultimately, survival.

Hence, shame entails evolved systems to monitor and respond to these threats to the social self via appeasement strategies designed to limit social damage, restore one's social reputation, de-escalate social conflict, and repair social bonds (Fessler, 2007; Gilbert, 2007; Keltner & Harker, 1998). However, shame experiences also constitute some of the most powerful activators of threat processing systems (Dickerson et al., 2009).

CLINICAL VIGNETTE, CONTINUED

Shame in Grief

Talia described how she became tormented by fears of others' judgments. She worried that her brothers were disappointed in her and how she cared for their mother. She found it painfully difficult to be in their presence, sensing that they were judging her and criticizing her. She said:

> I remember the first Christmas together after we lost Mum. They wanted to honor Mum and some of the Christmas traditions she used to have. But I felt I couldn't cope. I went along, but I was so out of sorts.

I couldn't look them in the eye, so I stayed in the kitchen to avoid everyone. They were telling stories about Mum, remembering her, and I felt so alone.

Talia said she was increasingly self-critical and losing confidence that she could do anything positive in the world. She felt returning to work was impossible. She was unable to resolve her feelings of grief and began to feel anxious and depressed, and constantly worried about being caught out as a fraud or imposter.

EXTERNAL AND INTERNAL SHAME

Shame experiences typically involve external and internal/self-evaluative components. *External shame* is focused on perceiving the self as existing negatively in the minds of others, who see the self as inferior, weak, inadequate, flawed, and may therefore criticize, reject, exclude, or even harm the self. In external shame, one's attention and cognitive processing are attuned to the minds of others, and one's behavior is orientated toward positively influencing one's image in the mind of others by submitting, appeasing, or displaying desirable qualities (Gilbert, 2003, 2007).

Internal shame pertains to the global negative self-evaluations of oneself as inferior, defective, inadequate, unwanted, or weak. In internal shame, one's attention and processing are inwardly directed to one's personal characteristics, emotions, or behaviors, focusing on flaws and shortcomings. Internal shame can be seen as an internalizing defensive response to external shame, identifying with the mind of the other and becoming self-critical in order to monitor and repair/preventing further harm to one's social standing and avert criticism, rejection, or attacks from others (Gilbert, 2003, 2007).

Shame experiences usually involve both external and internal shame, although the salience of each can vary according to the shame experiences, with some individuals being more prone to one than the other (Gilbert, 2007; Kim et al., 2011).

THE INFLUENCE OF SOCIETY AND CULTURE

Shame experiences are shaped by social norms and cultural values (Fessler, 2007), influencing what is considered acceptable, attractive, and esteemed, and what is undesirable and shameful (Fessler, 2007; Gilbert, 2003). Anthropological approaches posit that shame and honor systems, which vary among cultures, are key to social regulation and control (Lindisfarne, 1998). A recent study conducted in community samples from Portuguese, French, Australian, Singaporean, and Japanese populations has offered empirical support for this notion and found differences in levels of global shame, external, and internal shame among these countries, indicating that social ecology (e.g., individualistic versus collectivist values) may regulate and shape the experience of shame (Matos et al., 2021).

These social and cultural processes affect experiences of shame, which in turn influence behavioral responses, and ultimately shape personal identities. Reflected shame is associated with the shame one can bring to others, or others can bring to the self. In cultures where shame and honor systems are intimately linked to the behaviors of one's associates, reflected shame can become prominent, and when this happens the defense and repair of shame can be linked to cultural scripts for the repair of honor (Gilbert, 2007).

PSYCHOLOGICAL IMPACT OF SHAME

Shame can change one's mental state and prompt coordinated threat-related psychobiological and neuronal responses, with lasting consequences to emotion regulation, cognitive processing, and behavior, with a detrimental impact on mental and physiological well-being (Dickerson et al., 2009). Shame is associated with a range of mental health problems, including depression (Kim et al., 2011), anxiety (Fergus et al., 2010), post-traumatic stress (López-Castro et al., 2019), eating disorders (Blythin et al., 2018), personality disorders (Schoenleber & Berenbaum, 2010), and psychotic disorders (Birchwood et al., 2002).

SHAME VERSUS GUILT

Shame has been distinguished from guilt (Gilbert, 2019; Tangney & Dearing, 2002), with guilt linked to a caring motivation and avoiding causing harm to others (Gilbert, 2019). Guilt is a response to having caused harm and involves a desire for reparation, rather than concerns with social reputation (characteristic of shame). Guilt is linked to sadness and remorse, while shame is often linked to anxiety, anger, and disgust.

Contrary to shame, guilt is associated with perspective taking, empathy, and sympathy, and linked to moral behavior and cooperation that encourages prosocial behavior and builds interpersonal relationships (DeHooge et al., 2007; Tangney & Dearing, 2002). The anticipation of guilt and its negative affect seem to motivate individuals toward care and compassion (Gilbert, 2019). In addition, research has established that, unlike shame, guilt is weakly associated with mental health difficulties (Gilbert, 2019; Tangney & Dearing, 2002).

CLINICAL VIGNETTE CONTINUED

Shame Memories Associated with Grief

A terrible collection of memories plagued Talia. She recalled instances where she had become very angry with her mother. Lila had begun to refuse food, and the doctors insisted that she "must eat." Talia felt anxious to feed her mother. As a result, she became verbally abusive, calling her mother "stupid," "pathetic," or "wicked."

When Talia spoke of these incidents, she would sob uncontrollably. Her body would fold forward, her hands clutching her face, and she would wail "I am a terrible person, I can't forgive myself, what sort of daughter would do that to her own mother?" Sometimes, she would become furious with herself, attacking herself viciously. At other times, she would be overcome with dread, fearful that she would be found out and punished.

Images of these incidents intruded into her mind. She avoided thinking about them, had removed photographs of her mother, and rarely spoke of her. She continued to live in the house but tidied it vigorously. She constantly felt anxious and/or angry, and while a year had passed, she had not returned to work. She felt she was undeserving of happiness, and returning to working as a nurse seemed unfathomable, given the way she had treated her mother. She would say, "I am bad, awful, ugly, disgusting."

SHAME MEMORIES

When we are shamed (e.g., put down, criticized, or humiliated, rejected by parents or friends, bullying, rejection, and failure, or being neglected, or sexually or physically abused), our threat system is activated, creating a sense of a threatened social self. Early shame experiences may also inhibit the development of the affiliative-soothing system, inhibiting our ability to down-regulate threat through receiving care and connection from others and through self-soothing. Thus, we see ourselves as vulnerable, defective, weak, inadequate, and unworthy, and we see others as critical, judgmental, unavailable, and dangerous (Matos et al., 2017; Matos et al., 2020).

Early shame experiences can be recorded autobiographically as threat-activating traumatic memories, eliciting intrusions, emotional avoidance, and hyperarousal symptoms (Matos & Pinto-Gouveia, 2010), threatening one's sense of self and psychological integrity, rendering one feeling inferior, defective, powerless, and socially unattractive. This threat to social self may contribute to threat-based attentional, emotional, and cognitive processing (Harman & Lee, 2010). Shame memories can become central to self-identity, structuring the life narrative, and forming salient reference points to give meaning to other events (Pinto-Gouveia & Matos, 2011).

Shame memories are associated with elevated proneness to external shame later in life and can become the basis for derogatory self-evaluations and internal shame (Matos & Pinto-Gouveia, 2010; Matos et al., 2012, 2013). Research has revealed that shame memories with traumatic and centrality features not only increase current shame but also heighten one's vulnerability to psychopathological symptoms, namely depression, anxiety, social anxiety, paranoid ideation, or dissociation (Matos et al., 2020). In addition, shame memories are an important part of the origins of negative beliefs and fears about receiving compassion from others or from oneself, which in turn increase vulnerability to psychological distress (Matos et al., 2017). This is the double-bind of shame and shame memories: They increase the risk of psychological distress, and diminish one's openness to seeking and receiving the social connection and support one needs in times of distress in order to alleviate suffering (Matos et al., 2020).

THE ROLE OF SHAME IN GRIEF

Shame can be important to consider with bereaved individuals (Barr, 2012; Dellmann, 2018; Kauffman, 2001). Grief may be permeated by external and internal shame, shaping how grief is processed and expressed. Reflected shame can also be relevant in the experience of grief, particularly where a loss was preventable or where a death was stigmatized. Furthermore, shame memories may complicate the grieving process via activation of the threat system and blocks to the affiliative-soothing system, increasing psychological distress and prolonging grief.

Despite their critical roles across mental health difficulties, research into shame and shame memories in grief is scarce. Existing research into shame in grief is mainly focused on either stigmatized circumstances of death such as suicide, or the death of a child. A review of 57 studies reported higher shame in bereaved people after the suicide of someone close to them (Pitman et al., 2014). Other studies with bereaved people after suicide found that grief was compounded by a sense of shame, self-blame, and failure (Allen et al., 1994; McMenamy et al., 2008). In perinatal bereavement, shame proneness was found to significantly contribute to both early and late grief in parents (Barr, 2004). Parents were found to experience high levels of omnipotence shame: The belief that they should have done something to save their child's life, even when this was medically impossible (Barr, 2012). In addition, significant social stigma and shame are often attached to deaths through preventable diseases, and through acts of intention or volition (Doka, 2002; Harris, 2010).

Shame has also been proposed as a risk factor for prolonged grief. Based on correlational studies suggesting a link between shame and prolonged grief (Boelen et al., 2010; Golden & Dalgleish, 2012), and clinical experience, Dellmann (2018) proposed a model of trauma and shame in prolonged grief after spousal loss. This emotion-focused attachment trauma model puts shame into a developmental context in its interaction with other risk factors. The model posits that past relational trauma (e.g., sexual, physical, or emotional abuse and neglect, loss of a significant other, usually a parent)—which may be regarded as shame memories—may lead to insecure attachment and be at the root of intense shame and difficulties to self-soothe in prolonged grief. In turn, shame, through its effects on coping styles (e.g., dependence on a partner, avoidance of painful emotions and their triggers, inability to express grief, social withdrawal), aggravates the grief and fosters a vicious cycle of shame and prolonged grief after the death of a spouse (Dellmann, 2018). This model has not yet been empirically tested.

In addition, shame in grief can be embedded in the social context in which the grieving individual identifies and resides. It has been argued that Western societal norms may engender shame for those individuals who have experienced significant loss through death (Harris, 2010, 2016). In such individualistic societies, experiences related to grief or mortality can be difficult to integrate. Death represents a failure and loss of control, and the social rules that govern the expression of grief may serve to stigmatize individuals in their grieving processes (Harris, 2010). A key aspect to how social norms may mediate the experience of the bereaved individual and instigate shame is the concept of disenfranchised grief, which states that an individual's reaction to a loss is not recognized or validated socially, and so the grieving individual can feel disenfranchised and excluded from social support (Doka, 2002). Thus, the societal context of loss is central in grief processes, particularly where it minimizes the healthy and integrative aspects of grief and fosters shame regarding the grief experience instead (Harris, 2010; Kauffmann, 2001).

CLINICAL VIGNETTE CONTINUED

Assessing Shame and Shame Memories

On interview, Talia described one specific shameful memory:

> We were at the dinner table. Mum's dementia was really bad. Sometimes she remembered me, but other times she was unresponsive. I was trying to feed her and she was just sitting there, staring at the ceiling, her mouth shut tight. Before I knew it, I was yelling at her. "Eat for God's sake!" She just sat there and I got worse—I couldn't help it—I wanted her to eat, and so I tried to push the spoon into her mouth. I slammed my hand against the table top and Mum jumped in fright. She still stared at the ceiling, but she looked so scared. I felt devastated and ashamed. How could I do that to her? I pushed the bowl away and felt sick. I was shaking and tears rolled down my face. I kept repeating, "I'm so sorry, I'm so sorry." I hugged her, but she just sat there. I told her "I'll never do that again." But I did. I couldn't control my frustration. I took it out on her even though she was so unwell and so innocent.

ASSESSING SHAME IN THE CONTEXT OF GRIEF

Shame can be assessed with a variety of psychometrically sound self-report instruments. Two main self-report questionnaires have been widely used to assess external and internal shame: The *Other as Shamer scale* (OAS; Goss et al., 1994), an 18-item measure designed to assess external shame, and its brief version, the OAS-2, with 8 items (Matos et al., 2015); and the *Internalized Shame Scale* (ISS; Cook, 1994/2001), a 24-item questionnaire measuring internal shame. Recently, a novel self-report instrument, the *External and Internal Shame Scale* (EISS), was developed to measure global shame, as well as external and internal shame (Ferreira et al., 2020). The eight items of the EISS were designed to assess external and internal shame considering four core domains of shame (inferiority/ inadequacy, exclusion, emptiness, and criticism). The EISS was found to be a valid, reliable, and brief measure of external and internal shame, as well as global shame, across countries (Matos et al., 2021).

Other self-report questionnaires have been adapted to assess the traumatic, centrality, and autobiographical qualities of shame memories: *The Impact of Event Scale–Revised* (IES-R; Weiss & Marmar, 1997; shame memory version by Matos et al., 2011) assesses the traumatic qualities of a shame memory; the *Centrality of Event Scale* (CES; Berntsen & Rubin, 2006; shame memory version by Matos et al., 2010) measures the extent to which a shame memory is construed as central to personal identity; and the *Autobiographical Memory Questionnaire* (AMQ; Rubin et al., 2003; shame memory version by Matos & Pinto-Gouveia, 2011) assesses the autobiographical memory properties of shame memories.

Given the limitations associated with measuring shame and shame experiences using self-report questionnaires (e.g., social desirability bias, sensitive nature of the topic, lack of a clear definition of the construct, limited ecological validity, influenced by mood), a semi-structured interview, the *Shame Experiences Interview* (SEI; Matos, 2012) was designed to assess the phenomenology of shame experiences recalled from childhood and adolescence. It measures contextual, cognitive, emotional, bodily, behavioral, and motivational components of shame experiences, coping strategies, others' reactions, autobiographical and traumatic memory characteristics, frequency of shame experiences, and interference and impact of the shame experience recalled.

CONCLUSION

Shame is a universal, self-conscious human emotion, evolved to enhance survival through awareness and responding to social threats and thereby keeping us safely in the group. However, shame also causes often devastatingly painful social and emotional experiences. Such shame experiences can be retained in the form of shame memories, which can have traumatic qualities and become central to our sense of ourselves and our identity.

Shame and shame memories can then play a complicating role in grieving, leading to barriers to the grieving process, greater and longer lasting distress, and the potential for the development of mental disorders. But, as with all shame, shame in grief is often hidden, secreted away, causing complications outside of the awareness of both the grieving person and the clinician trying to help them. Understanding shame and shame memories, their role in the grieving process, and how to assess them can be a vital part of assisting a person in their grief.

NOTE

1 This fictitious case represents individuals experiencing grief after the death of a family member and the complications associated with shame. More details of the case can be found in Chapter 21 of this volume.

REFERENCES

Allen, B. G., Calhoun, L. G., Cann, A., & Tedeschi, R. G. (1994). The effect of cause of death on responses to the bereaved: Suicide compared to accident and natural causes. *OMEGA: Journal of Death and Dying, 28*(1), 39–48. https://doi.org/10.2190/t44k-l7uk-tb19-t9uv

Barr, P. (2004). Guilt- and shame-proneness and the grief of perinatal bereavement. *Psychology and Psychotherapy: Theory, Research and Practice, 77*(4), 493–510. https://doi.org/10.1348/1476083042555442

Barr, P. (2012). Negative self-conscious emotion and grief: An actor–partner analysis in couples bereaved by stillbirth or neonatal death. *Psychology and Psychotherapy: Theory, Research and Practice, 85*(3), 310–326. https://doi.org/10.1111/j.2044-8341.2011.02034.x

Berntsen, D., & Rubin, D. C. (2006). Centrality of event scale: A measure of integrating a trauma into one's identity and its relation to post-traumatic stress disorder symptoms. *Behaviour Research and Therapy, 44*(2), 219–231. https://doi.org/10.1016/j.brat.2005.01.009

Birchwood, M., Meaden, A., Trower, P., & Gilbert, P. (2002). Shame, humiliation and entrapment in psychosis: A social rank theory approach to cognitive intervention with voices and delusions. In A. P. Morrison (Ed.), *A casebook of cognitive therapy for psychosis* (pp. 108–131). Brunner-Routledge.

Blythin, S. P., Nicholson, H. L., Macintyre, V. G., Dickson, J. M., Fox, J. R., & Taylor, P. J. (2018). Experiences of shame and guilt in anorexia and bulimia nervosa: A systematic review. *Psychology and Psychotherapy: Theory, Research and Practice.* https://doi.org/10.1111/papt.12198

Boelen, P. A., van den Bout, J., & van den Hout, M. A. (2010). A prospective examination of catastrophic misinterpretations and experiential avoidance in emotional distress following loss. *Journal of Nervous and Mental Disease, 198*(4), 252–257. https://doi.org/10.1097/nmd.0b013e3181d619e4

Cook, D. R. (1994/2001). *Internalized shame scale: Technical manual.* Multi-Health Systems, Inc.

De Hooge, I. E., Zeelenberg, M., & Breugelmans, S. M. (2007). Moral sentiments and cooperation: Differential influences of shame and guilt. *Cognition and Emotion, 21*(5), 1025–1042.

Dellmann, T. (2018). Are shame and self-esteem risk factors in prolonged grief after death of a spouse? *Death Studies, 42*(6), 371–382. https://doi.org/10.1080/07481187.2017.1351501

Dickerson, S. S., Gruenewald, T. L., & Kemeny, M. E. (2009). Psychobiological responses to social self threat: Functional or detrimental? *Self and Identity, 8*(2–3), 270–285.

Doka, K. J. (2002). *Disenfranchised grief: New directions, challenges, and strategies for practice.* Research Press.

Fergus, T. A., Valentiner, D. P., McGrath, P. B., & Jencius, S. (2010). Shame- and guilt-proneness: Relationships with anxiety disorder symptoms in a clinical sample. *Journal of Anxiety Disorders, 24*(8), 811–815.

Ferreira, C., Moura-Ramos, M., Matos, M., & Galhardo, A. (2020). A new measure to assess external and internal shame: Development, factor structure and psychometric properties of the external and internal shame scale. *Current Psychology.* https://doi.org/10.1007/s12144-020-00709-0

Fessler, D. M. T. (2007). From appeasement to conformity: Evolutionary and cultural perspectives on shame, competition, and cooperation. In J. Tracy, R. Robins, & J. Tangney (Eds.), *Self-conscious emotions: Theory and research* (2nd ed., pp. 174–193). Guilford Press.

Gilbert, P. (1998). What is shame? Some core issues and controversies. In P. Gilbert & B. Andrews (Eds.), *Shame: Interpersonal behaviour, psychopathology and culture* (pp. 3–36). Oxford University Press.

Gilbert, P. (2003). Evolution, social roles and the differences in shame and guilt. *Social Research*, *70*(4), 1205–1230.

Gilbert, P. (2007). The evolution of shame as a marker for relationship security. In J. L. Tracy, R. W. Robins, & J. P. Tangney (Eds.), *The self-conscious emotions: Theory and research* (pp. 283–309). Guilford.

Gilbert, P. (2019). Distinguishing shame, humiliation and guilt: An evolutionary functional analysis and compassion focused interventions. In C.-H. Mayer & E. Vanderheiden (Eds.), *The bright side of shame* (pp. 413–431). Springer.

Golden, A. M. J., & Dalgleish, T. (2012). Facets of pejorative self-processing in complicated grief. *Journal of Consulting and Clinical Psychology*, *80*(3), 512–524. https://doi.org/10.1037/a0027338

Goss, K., Gilbert, P., & Allan, S. (1994). An exploration of shame measures: I. The "other as Shamer scale". *Personality and Individual Differences*, *17*(5), 713–717.

Harman, R., & Lee, D. (2010). The role of shame and self-critical thinking in the development and maintenance of current threat in post-traumatic stress disorder. *Clinical Psychology and Psychotherapy*, *17*(1), 13–24. https://doi.org/10.1002/cpp.636

Harris, D. L. (2010). Healing the narcissistic injury of death in the context of Western society. In J. Kauffman (Ed.), *The shame of death, grief, and trauma* (pp. 75–86). Routledge.

Harris, D. L. (2016). Social expectations of the bereaved. In D. Harris & T. Bordere (Eds.), *Handbook of social justice in loss and grief: Exploring diversity, equity, and inclusion* (pp. 165–176). Routledge.

Kauffman, J. (2001). Shame. In G. Howarth & O. Leaman (Eds.), *Encyclopedia of death and dying* (pp. 407–408). Routledge.

Keltner, D., & Harker, L. A. (1998). The forms and functions of the nonverbal signal of shame. In P. Gilbert & B. Andrews (Eds.), *Shame: Interpersonal behavior, psychopathology and culture* (pp. 75–98). Oxford University Press.

Kim, S., Thibodeau, R., & Jorgensen, R. (2011). Shame, guilt, and depressive symptoms: A meta-analytic review. *Psychological Bulletin*, *137*(1), 68–96.

Lindisfarne, N. (1998). Gender, shame, and culture: An anthropological perspective. In P. Gilbert & B. Andrews (Eds.), *Shame: Interpersonal behaviour, psychopathology and culture* (pp. 246–260). Oxford University Press.

López-Castro, T., Saraiya, T., Zumberg-Smith, K., & Dambreville, N. (2019). Association between shame and posttraumatic stress disorder: A meta-analysis. *Journal of Traumatic Stress*, *32*(4), 484–495.

Matos, M. (2012). *Shame memories that shape who we are* [Doctoral dissertation, Faculty of Psychology and Educational Sciences, University of Coimbra].

Matos, M., Duarte, J., & Pinto-Gouveia, J. (2017). The origins of fears of compassion: Shame and lack of safeness memories, fears of compassion and psychopathology. *Journal of Psychology: Interdisciplinary and Applied*, *151*(8), 804–819. https://doi.org/10.1080/00223980.2017.1393380

Matos, M., Galhardo, A., Moura-Ramos, M., Steindl, S., Bortolon, C., Hiramatsu, Y., Baumann, T., Xin Qi Yiu, R., & Ferreira, C. (2021). Measuring shame across five countries: Dimensionality and measurement invariance of the external and internal shame scale. *Current Psychology*. https://doi.org/10.1007/s12144-021-02019-5

Matos, M., & Pinto-Gouveia, J. (2010). Shame as a traumatic memory. *Clinical Psychology and Psychotherapy*, *17*(4), 299–312.https://doi.org/10.1002/cpp.659

Matos, M., Pinto-Gouveia, J., & Duarte, C. (2012). Above and beyond emotional valence: The unique contribution of the central and traumatic shame memories to psychopathology vulnerability. *Memory*, *20*(5), 461–477. https://doi.org/10.1080/09658211.2012.680962

Matos, M., Pinto-Gouveia, J., & Duarte, C. (2013). Internalizing early memories of shame and lack of safeness and warmth: The mediating role of shame on depression. *Behavioural and Cognitive Psychotherapy*, *41*(4), 479–493. https://doi.org/10.1017/s1352465812001099

Matos, M., Pinto-Gouveia, J., Gilbert, P., Duarte, C., & Figueiredo, C. (2015). The other as Shamer scale - 2: Development and validation of a short version of a measure of external shame. *Personality and Individual Differences*, *74*, 6–11. https://doi.org/10.1016/j.paid.2014.09.037

Matos, M., Pinto-Gouveia, J., & Gomes, P. (2010). The centrality of shame experiences: Psychometric properties of the Portuguese version of the centrality of event scale. *Psicologia*, *XXIV*(1), 73–95.

Matos, M., Pinto-Gouveia, J., & Martins, S. (2011). The traumatic impact of shame memories: Psychometric properties of the Portuguese version of the impact of event scale-revised. *Psychologica*, *54*(54), 413–438. https://doi.org/10.14195/1647-8606_54_16

Matos, M., Steindl, S., Gilbert, P., & Pinto-Gouveia, J. (2020). Shame memories that shape who we are. In P. Gilbert & J. Kirby (Eds.), *Making an impact on mental health. The applications of psychological research* (pp. 97–126). Routledge.

McMenamy, J. M., Jordan, J. R., & Mitchell, A. N. N. (2008). What do suicide survivors tell us they need? Results of a pilot study. *Suicide and Life-Threatening Behavior*, *38*(4), 375–389. https://doi.org/10.1521/suli.2008.38.4.375

Pinto-Gouveia, J., & Matos, M. (2011). Can shame memories become a key to identity? The centrality of shame memories predicts psychopathology. *Applied Cognitive Psychology*, *25*(2), 281–290. https://doi.org/10.1002/acp.1689

Pitman, A., Osborn, D., King, M., & Erlangsen, A. (2014). Effects of suicide bereavement on mental health and suicide risk. *Lancet Psychiatry*, *1*(1), 86–94. https://doi.org/10.1016/s2215-0366(14)70224-x

Rubin, D. C., Schrauf, R. W., & Greenberg, D. L. (2003). Belief and recollection of autobiographical memories. *Memory & Cognition*, *31*(6), 887–901. https://doi.org/10.3758/BF03196443

Schoenleber, M., & Berenbaum, H. (2010). Shame aversion and shame-proneness in cluster C personality disorders. *Journal of Abnormal Psychology*, *119*(1), 197–205.

Sznycer, D., Tooby, J., Cosmides, L., Porat, R., Shalvi, S., & Halperin, E. (2016). Shame closely tracks the threat of devaluation by others, even across cultures. *Proceedings of the National Academy of Sciences*, *113*(10), 2625–2630.

Tangney, J. P., & Dearing, R. L. (2002). *Shame and guilt*. Guilford.

Weiss, D. S., & Marmar, C. R. (1997). The impact of event scale – Revised. In J. P. Wilson & T. M. Keane (Eds.), *Assessing psychological trauma and PTSD* (pp. 399–411). Guilford.

CHAPTER 17

UNDERSTANDING AND HEALING HOARDING AS A RESISTANCE TO GRIEF

Chia-Ying Chou

INTRODUCTION

Hoarding affects a significant percentage of the human population (Postlethwaite et al., 2019). When we think of hoarding, we may think of people who hold onto an excessive amount of seemingly valueless things. Such behavior may be puzzling, until we start to wonder and learn to understand the emotional root(s) of it.

Over the years, I have asked clients, "What makes it so hard to let the things go?"

- *I want to read the art section of those old newspapers when I have time.*
- *Someone may find this useful, so I'm just keeping it now until it finds a good home.*
- *It's a gift from a friend; it would be disrespectful to discard it.*
- *I can fix it and it will work just fine again.*
- *Donating unworn clothes would admit the mistake of getting them in the first place.*
- *I might regret terribly if I give this away.*
- *My children made these when they were little. I just can't throw them away.*
- *I don't want to add more things to the landfill.*

Almost all of the reasons I've heard make sense, or are at least understandable. What puzzles researchers in the field is the broad range of things to which these reasons apply (Frost et al., 2015). The reasons seem to be so pervasive and apply to most possessions rather than a small number of special items. We have to wonder about "the something bigger" that may underlie the difficulties in letting things go.

A GRIEF WORKSHOP

I recently attended a Five-Rhythms dance workshop on grief held at a retreat center known for its baths filled with sacred hot spring water running down from nearby mountains that lead to the Pacific Ocean. Even though I was not grieving anything in particular at that time (so I thought), the idea of soaking in hot springs and dancing in nature drove me to the workshop! The workshop began on a gray and chilly evening. The leaders invited us to think of a loss we were grieving. I identified something that I have lived with and been so used to that I would not normally consider it a loss. After that opening session, I quickly headed to the hot spring for a relaxing bath before bed. The sounds of the waves of the Pacific Ocean were around me. I had a tub filled with gentle warm water all to myself by candle lights. Everything was just as magical as I was told. However, to my surprise, I found myself getting anxious, and becoming terrified for no apparent reason. I desperately held onto the edges of the tub with my feet, hands, arms, head—everything I could possibly use to hold on. My mind tried to make sense of this, and the next thing I noticed was thoughts and mental images of being drowned in a bathtub or the entire place being destroyed by a tsunami. And, of

DOI: 10.4324/9781003204121-21

course, the secondary emotions and my inner-critic would not miss out on this: I felt embarrassed for having these dramatic ideas, and ashamed for my inability to just relax "like a normal person would." It took a while before I decided to make this an exposure session and stay with the difficult emotions until they subsided—and they did eventually. That night I had one of my deepest sleeps in life. I wonder if this experience in the tub in any way resembles how my clients feel when they are confronted by a situation where letting go is asked.

UNDERSTANDING HOARDING AS RESISTANCE TO GRIEF

Let's come back to the question about what may be the something bigger (and maybe less easy to identify) underneath the apparent reasons people give in response to queries on why they hold on to the things. I aspire for myself and my clients to look deeper. Many times, from multiple clients, I have heard statements along these lines:

- *I thought I wanted to get rid of the clutter, but then I realized I would not know what to do with my life if the clutter were gone!*
- *I don't want any (more) regret, so I freeze and find myself unable to make decisions about keeping or tossing anything.*
- *When I let something go, it feels like I am losing some of my own life.*
- *I find myself wanting to avoid making mistakes by holding onto everything I can possibly be asked about. It's like I can only be loved if I am useful to everyone all the time.*
- *I feel despair and powerless when I see my stuff. When I really see my life, I feel the same.*
- *I don't like most of the shirts in my closet. But somehow when I think about donating any of them, I feel like I am abandoning them. It pains me too much, so I keep them all.*
- *When I see the boxes, I see my late husband, and I just can't bring myself to open them.*
- *I feel deprived if I can't go to the shops. I feel left out and not participating the world, just like how I felt growing up.*

I find it very useful to take time and support clients to fully experience the internal experiences that rise up as we entertain the idea of letting a particular item go. Most times, what shows up initially are the reasons why they will not let go, like the ones described in the beginning of the chapter. As we continue to hold space, without judgment or pressure to make a certain decision, but with persistent and gentle guidance to come back to their feelings imagining letting go, long buried feelings often begin to surface: Deep and almost unbearable sadness, regret, loneliness, anger…, and many more.

Clients and I, again and again, come to realize it is not about the specific items they hold onto. Sometimes it is not even about the reasons why they hold onto the items. There are deeper feelings associated with something(s) bigger and more intangible which were lost or never existed: A life that could have been, a loving parent, a treasured identity or period of life, a significant relationship, a fulfilling life, independence or financial security, a happy family, connection with and respect for oneself.

Holding onto the physical items and the reasons for doing so, in many cases, are a means to gain a sense of control, a way to distract from or fix the pain associated with what is lost, never existed, and a void. Without loss being identified, felt, and talked about, the process of grieving would not flow. I started to consider the holding onto physical things as an embodiment and enactment of this resistance to acknowledging and meeting loss. And I wonder what makes grief seem particularly unbearable for people experiencing hoarding.

WHAT MAKES IT SO HARD TO GRIEVE?

Grief is one of the most difficult experiences in life. Most of us have difficulty experiencing it and going through its multifaceted processes. That said, there may be factors, which are mostly not of our choosing, that contribute to grief being relatively more difficult for some of us than others. Research has shown noteworthy relationships between trauma and hoarding (Chou et al., 2018). A high rate of early-life adversity has also been observed among individuals experiencing hoarding clinically.

This is not to say that trauma or early-life adversities cause hoarding or difficulties grieving. Rather, these unsupportive early environments may hinder the development of the skills and capacities needed to tolerate and process emotions. For example, if one grew up in an unstable, unpredictable, cold, and harsh environment, without guidance or protection, it would not be a surprise for one to "learn" to be emotionally turned off and/or have an intensified need to maintain control. Research has shown heightened sensitivity to anxiety, difficulties in tolerating distress, and difficulties in emotion regulation among people experiencing hoarding (Davidson et al., 2019). Growing evidence has also suggested associations between hoarding and challenges in self-worth, self-relationship, and self-concept (Chou et al., 2018; Kings et al., 2017), as well as in relationships and attachment with others (Yap & Grisham, 2021). Such environmental and psychological factors, and genetic and psychoneurological vulnerabilities are currently identified as contributors to hoarding (Ivanov et al., 2017).

- *When I try to make decisions, I can still hear the exact words my mother would yell at me.*
- *I have tried my whole life to look good. Ironically one of my main ways to look good (having lots of impressive possessions) makes me feel most ashamed.*
- *I feel anxious as if I am losing a part of myself when I clear a small corner in my home.*
- *My "clutter" gives me something to put my mind on. I would not know what to do with myself without it.*
- *I have a hard time saying no, not just to people, but also to things. It is like my life is about serving the things and keeping them happy.*

BACKGROUND ABOUT THERAPY FOR HOARDING

Before getting into this topic, I would like to acknowledge how early of a stage we currently are in understanding the phenomena around hoarding and ways to help alleviate it. Perhaps the first step toward understanding is to keep a beginner's mind. Thanks to the work of a small group of dedicated researchers, the field has an established foundation in understanding the nature of hoarding, and evidence in applying Cognitive Behavioral Therapy-based approaches to address the issue before hoarding was recognized as a psychiatric diagnosis in the Diagnostic and Statistical Manual of Mental Disorders (DSM-5) in 2013 (American Psychiatric Association). A Compassion-Focused Therapy (CFT)-based approach began its development in the mid-2010s, with its first pilot study published in 2019 (Chou et al.). This protocol tailors the CFT theoretical framework and techniques to address transdiagnostic psychological mechanisms, e.g., self- and emotion-regulation-related difficulties, in contexts specific to hoarding. More details about the approach will be published in the years to come, as the protocol continues to be tested and refined.

The points of consideration listed below may be useful in helping individuals experiencing hoarding move along the processes of grieving. Please note that, just like most of the other mental health conditions, clinical presentations and root issues among people with hoarding challenges can vary greatly. Grief and its related difficulties may be core to many, but not everyone's experiences.

HOLDING SPACE FOR SHAME AND SELF-LOATHING

What I value the most to offer in therapy, as cliché as it may seem, is a safe space for tenderness to be. Progress looks like a dried tea leaf gradually softening, a gripping hand slowly opening up. And the first layer of hardness we usually need to work with has to do with shame and self-loathing—associated with an internalized stigma around hoarding as well as an innate feeling of inadequacy as a person (Chou et al., 2018). Many people experiencing hoarding describe themselves as having a secret life. *"I seem normal at work. Nobody knows I am a hoarder." "I make up excuses when people want to visit where I live."* A natural response to shame is to hide. Shame separates our hearts from others'. It also associates with self-loathing, an abusive relationship to oneself, where a seemingly powerful part of the self dominates and shuts down any feeling of vulnerability. *"When I look around, I think what a pathetic life." "I just don't understand what's wrong with me."* In shame and self-loathing, disconnection exists both inter- and intra-personally.

One of the most liberating approaches in CFT is its view about how the human brain as a product of evolution, and how our genes, early environments and experiences, and many other things, which we did not choose, have shaped our strength and vulnerability (Gilbert, 2010). Introducing this concept to clients often opens up two paths: One toward self-compassion and forgiveness, and another leading to resistance: *What do you mean it is not my fault? If it is not my fault it would just all seem random, like my life is this way just because of bad luck? I still think it is my fault because I am responsible for my life.* A good CFT-therapist might address the latter by clarifying the difference between blaming and being responsible. We hope to help our clients understand that it is possible for things to be both not our fault and also our responsibility. This intervention is important. I often find clients feeling reassured by getting their sense of control back knowing they are still responsible.

An alternative and sometimes more powerful approach I would suggest is to slow ourselves and clients down, using this opportunity to practice mindfully being with the emotions that are present in the midst of the resistance. In the grief workshop experience described in the beginning, one of the first healing experiences for me was being unconditionally accepted and embraced by the gentle hot spring water. It held me with no agenda, relaxed my resistance without any force. I aspire to offer such space as a therapist. I notice that when I can hold space for anger, deep sadness often follows; when I can hold resistance, fear is often revealed. When these more tender feelings are seen, loss is often not far from being seen, and that is what we need to acknowledge for the process of grief to flow. In the resistance to let go of self-blame, I often find loss and grief right there.

UNDERSTANDING THE SOURCE OF AVOIDANCE

As the gripping hand continues to open, more fear and resistance will be met, which is absolutely normal. If someone doesn't trust their capacity to float or swim in water, of course they are not likely to let go and jump in. And if we want someone who is afraid of water to swim, we should first give them a buoy. Avoidance, and self-criticism about avoidance, are major sources of suffering among people with hoarding challenges. *"Something more important always comes up when I am supposed to be sorting my things." "Escapism is everywhere, even when I seem to be on task: I would rather plan how I am going to clear my house than actually do it."* It may be puzzling for most people, including those experiencing hoarding themselves, why one would be so compelled to run away from seemingly simple house-keeping tasks. However, if we reflect on our own experiences of grieving, haven't we all done something knowingly or unknowingly to avoid or attempt to control those incredibly powerful and vulnerable feelings? Yes, to people suffering from hoarding, letting things go is saying goodbye. Some goodbyes are as big and concrete as grieving the death of someone. Some are almost unnoticeable but deeply impactful such as grieving the passage of one's own life lived with regrets or unfulfillment.

The most important part of the therapy work is about rebuilding one's relationship with, and skills of being with oneself and one's emotions. As described earlier, most people experiencing hoarding issues did not have an early-life environment that fostered these things well. To help, we need to rebuild a good home within our clients for them to dwell in and rely on, as they work with challenging emotions. Many CFT tools are great for such 'home construction.'

REBUILDING THE FLOWS OF COMPASSION

There are three flows of compassion included in the CFT model (Gilbert, 2010): Giving compassion to others, receiving compassion from others and directing compassion to oneself. Like most of you and I, many people with hoarding challenges report less difficulty giving compassion, but a hard time receiving it. My belief is that when receiving does not flow well, giving cannot be without some sort of bitter aftertaste. I work with fear of compassion by using myself as a compassionate other and adjusting the 'dose' of compassion flowing toward clients according to the strength of their compassion-receiving muscles, and gradually increase it. We all have the capacity to learn how to feel about and relate to ourselves by experiencing how the significant people in our lives relate to us. Over time, I see clients become more sensitive and kinder to their suffering. Their giving starts to come from a place of compassion for both themselves and others, rather than one of self-neglectful people-pleasing. Boundary-setting and assertive-training often come into the picture of therapy as compassion for oneself grows. These skills not only apply interpersonally, they are also relevant to the ways of relating to possessions for people with hoarding challenges.

Like the progression in learning to cook, clients first observe how their therapist relates to them and their emotions, and experience being related to with compassion. Next, they shall be guided to build on their psychological and behavioral repertoire of compassion, and practice being compassionate toward themselves. There is a great body of literature that describes how to help clients build a compassionate-self (Gilbert, 2010). Remember our goal of rebuilding a good home within people with hoarding challenges? As their compassionate-self takes shape, this home starts to have a grounding host. A lot of hand holding and support for the newly shaped compassionate-self is to be expected. I find somatic work a powerful add-on to imagery exercises in helping clients embody the compassionate-self and build a body memory of that experience. As the compassionate-self becomes more accessible, we can begin to train them to hold space for different emotions, and even host conversations between different parts of the self, using chair work. Identifying different emotions or parts of the self that often show up in the context hoarding has proven to be worthwhile. This helps people separate their anxiety, for example, from the self, and see it as a target toward which compassion flows.

WHEN EMOTIONS FLOW, THINGS MOVE

I often find that as the strength of the compassionate-self grows, clients seem to engage in less self-criticism and rationalization, and go more directly and deeply into their emotional experiences. They stop saying how frustrated they are with their avoidant behaviors or explaining why they should hold onto something. Instead, they now can more directly work with their feelings. *"A part of me is really angry and wanting to act out by keeping a mess like this."* *"I feel empty and I'm terrified by it."* *"This feels like death. I feel despair and deeply lonely."* Moments like this are worth celebration because now clients are building trust in their skills to stay afloat in waves of emotions.

If I were to describe the emotional landscape in different phases of therapy for hoarding, I would say, first, it is predominantly anxiety and fear. When we work through this with the compassion-based approaches described above and other chapters in this book, we soften the resistance to something deeper underneath, which, in many cases, is grief. This process releases people from being stuck in the cycles of fear and avoidance, and we can see the buried emotions – anger, deep sadness, regret—starting to appear, flow, release, and transform. In layers and layers of emotional releasing like this, life and lightness come through. Compared to the earlier stages of therapy, releasing of the physical things becomes an authentic act of self-compassion and a natural fruit of emotional healing.

REFERENCES

American Psychiatric Association. (2013). *Diagnostic and statistical manual of mental disorders* (5th ed.). Author.

Chou, C., Tsoh, J. Y., Shumway, M., Smith, L. C., Chan, J., Delucchi, K., Tirch, D., Gilbert, P., & Mathews, C. A. (2019). Treating hoarding disorder with compassion focused therapy. *British Journal of Clinical Psychology, 59*(1), 1–21. https://doi.org/10.1111/bjc.12228

Chou, C., Tsoh, J. Y., Smith, L. C., Bain, D., Botcheva, L. B., Chan, E., Chan, J., Eckfield, M., Howell, G., Komaiko, K., Plumadore, J., Salazar, M., Uhm, S. Y., Luis Vega Vega, E., Vigil, O., Delucchi, K., & Mathews, C. A. (2018). How is hoarding related to trauma? A detailed examination on different aspects of hoarding and age when hoarding started. *Journal of Obsessive-Compulsive and Related Disorders, 16*, 81–87.

Chou, C., Tsoh, J. Y., Vigil, O. R., Bain, D., Uhm, S. Y., Howell, G., Chan, J., Eckfield, M., Plumadore, J., Chan, E., Komaiko, K., Smith, L., Franklin, J., Vega, E., Delucchi, K., & Mathews, C. A. (2018). Contributions of self-criticism and shame to hoarding. *Psychiatry Research, 262*, 488–493.

Davidson, E. J., Dozier, M. E., Pittman, J. O. E., Mayes, T. L., Blanco, B. H., Gault, J. D., Schwarz, L. J., & Ayers, C. R. (2019). Recent advances in research on hoarding. *Current Psychiatry Reports, 21*(9), 1–9.

Frost, R. O., Steketee, G., Tolin, D. F., Sinopoli, N., & Ruby, D. (2015). Motives for acquiring and saving in hoarding disorder, OCD, and community controls. *Journal of Obsessive-Compulsive and Related Disorders, 4*, 54–59.

Gilbert, P. (2010). *Compassion focused therapy*. Routledge.

Ivanov, V. Z., Nordsletten, A., Mataix-Cols, D., Serlachius, E., Lichtenstein, P., Lundström, S., Kuja-Halkola, R., & Rück, C. (2017). Heritability of hoarding symptoms across adolescence and young adulthood: A longitudinal twin study. *PLOS ONE, 12*(6), e0179541.

Kings, C. A., Moulding, R., & Knight, T. (2017). You are what you own: Reviewing the link between possessions, emotional attachment, and the self-concept in hoarding disorder. *Journal of Obsessive-Compulsive and Related Disorders, 14*, 51–58.

Postlethwaite, A., Kellett, S., & Mataix-Cols, D. (2019). Prevalence of hoarding disorder: A systematic review and meta-analysis. *Journal of Affective Disorders, 256*, 309–316.

Yap, K., & Grisham, J. R. (2021). Object attachment in hoarding disorder and its role in a compensatory process. *Current Opinion in Psychology, 39*, 76–81.

CHAPTER 18

COMPASSION IN SITUATIONS OF NONFINITE LOSS AND CHRONIC SORROW

Darcy L. Harris

INTRODUCTION

Most people recognize the grief that follows the death of a loved one, which usually includes a period of painful disequilibrium and adjustment. It is also expected that the intensity of this grief will gradually diminish over time, as the loss and its impact are gradually integrated into the fabric of the lives of the loved ones who are left behind. However, some losses are not related to death, nor are they singular, discrete events that precipitate grief in this way. Sometimes referred to as *living losses* or *nonfinite losses*, these are experiences where the loss itself continues throughout a person's life in various ways without a definable ending in sight, requiring ongoing adaptation and adjustment. The unique form of grief that accompanies nonfinite losses is termed *chronic sorrow*, aptly named because the grief continues and is ongoing in nature due to the chronic, ongoing nature of the loss that gives rise to the sorrow (Harris, 2020a).

Examples of nonfinite losses may include being diagnosed with a degenerative condition that affects functionality or ongoing quality of life, having a loved one go missing without any assurance of their return, the loss of hopes and dreams of having a family when a couple is told that they are infertile, or losing a loved one's ability to connect and remember due to a diagnosis of dementia. This is by no means a definitive list; these are simply examples to illustrate the concept. In each of these experiences, returning back to life as it was before is not possible. Life will never be the same again, and the presence of the loss in the person's life will require ongoing accommodation, adaptation, and adjustment, with no ending in sight. This chapter will discuss the unique features and impact of nonfinite loss and chronic sorrow and explore the potential for compassion-based approaches as a potentially sustainable way to support clients who experience these types of losses.

UNIQUE FEATURES OF NONFINITE LOSS AND CHRONIC SORROW

Nonfinite losses are often not recognized or acknowledged by others. Even though their impact can have profound consequences, there are no rituals to provide meaning, no formal means to offer support for those affected (such as a funeral in death losses), and their invisibility, ambiguity, and chronicity make fulfilling the common social expectation to "get over it and move on" highly unrealistic.

Self-reliance and independence are highly prized and idealized in Western-oriented societies. The messages to people who seem "stuck" in their situation may be overt or covert; typically, there is an underlying sentiment that "You should just pick yourself up and move on" or by trying harder, they can conquer their circumstances or somehow not be affected by the pain and grief that accompany their loss (Harris, 2016). These expectations

DOI: 10.4324/9781003204121-22

are all social constructions that have been internalized from childhood (many people remember being told to stop crying when they were young, and to simply "grow up," equating maturity with hiding feelings and denying vulnerability). The actual reality is that most individuals dealing with ongoing, living losses would do anything to be able to move on or to be free of their painful or debilitating experience.

We like our lives to be predictable, and we expect predictability and routine in everyday life. In many of our assumptions about the world, we have often learned to expect that we have control over our lives and our choices, as long as we (insert here—eat well, get enough sleep, do well in our studies, pick the right friends, get a good job, etc.). However, despite all that we believe about determining our health, happiness, and future, living losses are painful reminders that life is messy, unpredictable, uncontrollable, and rarely what we expect it to be or hope it should be (Harris, 2020b). The ongoing nature of nonfinite losses means that those who experience them often endure a protracted, life-long need to continually accommodate and adjust to the loss and the unpredictability that accompanies it. The chronic sense of grief and anxiety associated with living losses is exhausting for the individual who is affected by the loss; in addition, it can be very difficult for the individual's support system to tolerate the intensity and ongoing grief that lasts over a protracted period of time. Thus, it is common for those experiencing nonfinite losses to become isolated, as friends and family members tire of not seeing "progress" in the person's situation, or the loss is not one that they can see, comprehend, or even acknowledge. For example, a couple going through infertility treatment for many years may look fine on the surface, with their appearances betraying the potential devastation to their relationship, finances, plans, and hopes for their future (Harris, 2017). Many nonfinite losses are difficult to describe, lack clarity, and are not readily observable to others. As a result, their impact is typically not acknowledged by others, compounding a sense of shame, guilt, and the isolation that frequently occurs.

IMPLICATIONS FOR CLINICIANS

Professional training programs tend to emphasize fixing, curing, and treatment with specific outcome objectives, most of which simply don't work for long-term, chronic loss experiences. Gradually, the sense of frustration and failure at not being able to effectively remedy the situation can lead clinicians to react to these clients by withdrawal, avoidance, and at times, stigmatizing and labeling the affected individual as the "problem patient," sometimes questioning if the person is malingering, or "attention-seeking." It is important to be aware that even well-meaning professionals and community supports can make things worse by pushing for resolution or closure in situations where these are not possible. Many individuals with nonfinite losses have experiences with professionals or well-intended but uninformed helpers that have been shaming or unrealistic, causing them to be hesitant to ask for assistance or support to avoid further stigma or judgment (Boss et al., 2016; Harris, 2020a).

Unique issues arise in living loss experiences:

1. *Lack of acknowledgment and validation*—losses that are not readily identified or understood tend to be disenfranchised, leaving those affected without validation of their experience by family, friends, and many professionals.

2. *Emotional intensity*—losses that are ongoing in nature are intensified by the anxiety and uncertainty that are intermingled with the grief. While it is expected that grief will include sadness and anger, individuals with nonfinite loss and chronic sorrow often present as intense, nervous, needing control, and even desperate, which can be overwhelming to the people around them, including professionals.

3. *Stress in the present; uncertainty about the future*—the stress of coping with what has already happened combines with uncertainty about the future, adding another layer to the exhaustion in the present. Both those who are living with loss and their loved ones have to adapt to erratically changing versions of self and of the world, often when it is very difficult to access internal and external resources.

4. *Burnout of supports*—it is hard to find good support that doesn't burn out or tire from the ongoing intensity and lack of apparent resolution. People stop asking, "How are you?" or they don't wait to listen to the answer because they don't want to know if you are still struggling. Watching someone struggle over a long period of time can create a sense of powerlessness and helplessness that, in turn, leads to empathic overload and exhaustion in both professionals and friends/family members. Unrealistic expectations about recovery and closure can create a great deal of stress and pressure to try to fix what can't be changed.

5. *Financial impact*—there are usually limits on insurance coverage for services and equipment that may be required in an ongoing way (i.e., psychological support, assistive devices, in home care providers, etc.). Once limits are exceeded (or if there is no coverage), huge financial strains can occur. Adding to these concerns is the potential financial impact of cutting back work hours, retraining and changing careers (if the loss affects abilities that are required in the workplace), mounting expenses, or having to leave work completely due to the limitations and stress of the experience.

Many years ago, when I was working as a nurse in a busy neurology outpatient clinic, I began noticing a trend with patients who were diagnosed with chronic or treatment-resistant conditions. Often, these patients had pronounced symptoms or intractable, chronic pain that was debilitating to them as they tried to function in their everyday lives. They would frequently present to the clinic, asking for help, and the healthcare providers would try various combinations of medication, physical therapy, biofeedback, counseling, and even surgery to offer relief. When these measures did not work, patients would become more anxious and frustrated, often leading them to either call more often to report their symptoms or come into the clinic for further help. The clinical staff also felt frustration, often blended with a sense of failure for their inability to help these patients to feel better. A cycle of increasing anxiety and expectation from the patients and their families compounded the feelings of failure and frustration by the clinical staff. Calls from these patients and their families were pushed to the end of the day and dreaded. The patients and family members were often aware that the clinical staff put off speaking with them, leading them to feel disenfranchised, with subtle messages that they were complaining too much or expecting too much—or that the real issues were psychosocial and not physiological in nature (which meant they were dismissed). The end result of these scenarios was the difficulties of the patients with these intractable conditions were further compounded by the added stigma of being dismissed and disenfranchised by the medical care team, and the care team defended against feelings of failure and inadequacy by labeling patients and family members as "difficult."

COMPASSIONATELY APPROACHING NONFINITE LOSS AND CHRONIC SORROW

Nonfinite losses can be challenging due to the difficulties in balancing expectations regarding outcome with experiences that are not amenable to standard intervention strategies. This is not meant to say that professional support is unhelpful or unwarranted; however, in these situations, the focus of professionals needs to be redirected toward intention and process and not solely upon outcome (Harris, 2020c). This stance may seem contrary to professional training that is outcome-oriented by nature; the focus on "doing" over "being" and the mandate to meet objectives and to demonstrate positive responses to interventions can become a burden that may hinder effective therapy with individuals who are living with ongoing loss experiences. With the strong focus placed on diagnosis, intervention, and solution-oriented therapies (often driven by funding models for reimbursement of services), there is very little emphasis placed upon the essential act of being fully present to someone, bearing witness to another's experience and struggles, and of holding the intention to make a difference, even in the absence of being able to make things better or demonstrate a positive, measurable outcome (Rousseau, 2010).

At the outset, it is important to keep in mind that by the time many people struggling with nonfinite losses seek help from a therapist, they have probably experienced many of the unhelpful attitudes and expectations about recovery and closure that were described in the previous section. They are, very likely, exhausted, anxious, and struggling with the isolation and mixed messages from those close to them who have been overwhelmed and/or exhausted by the chronicity and intensity of their experience. Thus, the relationship that the therapist forms with the client will provide a lifeline of invaluable human contact and support. Fundamental to this support is the therapist's ability to remain present, stay clear with their intention, and build a foundation for working together with the client from a fundamentally compassionate stance (Harris & Winokuer, 2021). In essence, all the components of compassion training and skill development support the clinician's motivation to relieve suffering, affording both wisdom and discernment regarding expectations for outcome, enhanced distress tolerance, and the ability to focus and be fully present to what the client brings forward.

PRESENCE AND PROCESS

As discussed in Chapter eight, the ability to offer our full attention and empathetic presence to another human being is one of the greatest gifts that we have to offer. One of the most important skills required of a clinician in situations of living, nonfinite losses is the ability to "be with" someone, and not focusing solely on what to "do to" the client or in monitoring the "progress" of the client in limited ways. Techniques and book knowledge are not going to be enough when you have someone sitting in front of you whose world has been shattered by loss, who is experiencing ongoing pain and exhaustion, and afraid that there is more loss and pain in the future. There is a good amount of counseling research indicating that what clients experience as the most important aspect of therapy work is not the techniques that were used or the theoretical orientation of the clinician; rather, feeling heard, understood, and sensing genuine care from the clinician matters far more than is often credited (Geller & Greenberg, 2012). In short, the relationship that you form with your clients/patients and their sense of your attentive, engaged presence provides the foundation from which healing can begin to occur, even in the absence of a cure or remedy for the situation.

INTENTION AND MOTIVATION

In this context, your intention is the underlying motivation for why you do what you do, and it deeply reflects who you are. Being aware of your intention, both in a broader, over-arching view as well as in the context of the present, provides you with the opportunity to have a "home base" where you can return if you are unsure, stressed, or feeling over-whelmed. The focus on intention relieves you from getting caught up on the expectation of a specific outcome. For example, if you were working with someone with a health condition that causes ongoing, chronic physical pain, it would be easy to try different ways to address the pain and to look for relief of the pain as your goal. But what if all of the interventions that were tried to relieve the pain were ineffective and the pain continues unremittingly? Most likely, the person who is struggling with the chronic pain has also endured being shuf-fled from one care provider to another, looking for relief. If the treatment goal is focused only on relieving the pain, then not being able to take away the pain is seen as failure, and the therapeutic relationship becomes centered around the clinician's sense of shame and avoidance. If your goal is to accompany this person in the pain and the angst that accom-panies the pain, whether or not there is lessening of the pain in response to interventions, then at least you are not adding to the sense of isolation, shame, and failure that have probably become frequent companions to this individual. It is these complicating factors to nonfinite losses that create a great deal of the suffering that occurs in these situations, and these sources of suffering are readily amenable to compassionate presence and responding. Thinking, "I may not be able to take this pain away from this person, but I can ensure that they will not have to go through this pain alone" may help to reframe some of the expecta-tions around the role of the clinician in similar contexts (Vachon & Harris, 2016).

In a study of interventions with patients with chronic pain (Penlington, 2019), one group of participants was assigned to a Compassion-Focused Therapy (CFT) oriented group inter-vention over a period of eight weeks. While the other groups that were assigned to other forms of support did not show any significant change related to the intervention to which they were assigned, the majority of participants from the CFT group reported changes in how they viewed their situation, with greater freedom to make choices that could better accommodate their current needs. What is most interesting to note in this study is that the participants in the CFT group reported overall improvement in their well-being, even while their reported pain levels did not change. If the only outcome being measured was level of pain, the study would have missed the actual perceived benefit of the CFT intervention. Similarly, a study by Maratos and Sheffield (2020) investigated the impact of Compassion-Focused Imagery (CFI) on coping with chronic pain. This study found that the use of CFI changed the degree of associated stress in coping with pain, providing participants with relief from the anxiety and vigilance associated with pain, even while the actual reported levels of pain did not change.

Interestingly, in compassionately joining with someone in their painful experience, your intention is to be fully present and connected with that person on a moment-to-moment basis. In this intention, you are not hindered in your relationship by a looming sense of failure or unmet expectations (Harris & Winokuer, 2021). The acronym NATO can be very helpful. In this context, NATO means:

Not
Attached
To
Outcome

(All Acronyms, n.d.)

Adopting this stance means letting go of expectations and not being drawn into trying to change what is not amenable to change. It is important to note that letting go is not the same as giving up, nor is it abandonment of the person who is struggling, and it is not the same as resigning in failure. Learning how to remain present when you can't fix something, can't make it better, and can't change the outcome is hard work and requires a deep awareness of the realities of life and our human limitations. Focusing on the present moment and your choice to be where you are, without needing or expecting a client to respond in a certain way provides the freedom to be fully present and open in a way that is quite rare. So, for example, your intention with someone who is struggling with an ongoing, living loss could be to offer your full, compassionate presence in the time that you are together, instead of being frustrated and feeling powerless in the situation of a painful loss that can't be undone.

What is important to remember is that we cannot remove many of the causes of suffering that occur as a result of significant change and loss that can upend a person's world. Our compassion must contain insight and discernment, recognizing that while we desire to relieve suffering, we will not be able to relieve all the suffering that crosses our path. Far from being a passive process or a "soft and fluffy" superficial niceness, true compassion requires us to actively and courageously "be with" another individual when others may leave quickly or get frustrated because they cannot "fix" things or make them "better." Compassion requires a great deal of inner strength and awareness, and it takes time and practice to cultivate the ability to remain grounded, focused, and fully present in such an engaged and open way, especially in the face of suffering that is not amenable to relief (Vachon & Harris, 2016).

ALLOW FOR POSSIBILITIES

Many people will share about the devastating consequences of their nonfinite loss experiences on their relationships, functionality, hopes, dreams, and lives as they once knew them. However, they may also share their learnings, new perspectives, and appreciation for life. Validating the profound and often unrelenting grief associated with nonfinite losses doesn't close the door to the potential for growth, meaning, and transformation that can also occur from these same experiences. The clinician's goal is to strengthen and reinforce the client's innate resiliency to live with the ambiguity and the reality that are created from these loss experiences.

CONCLUSION

As clinicians, we cannot change the past, reverse a diagnosis, or restore what is permanently lost in the lives of our clients. By focusing on our presence and intention to accompany grieving clients through nonfinite losses and the chronic sorrow that defies conventional expectations of cure or resolution, we open the possibilities for healing that are not contingent upon a specific outcome. Most nonfinite losses will continue as an ongoing presence for the rest of an individual's life in some way, shape, or form. The chronic sorrow associated with losses that are ongoing in nature is often misunderstood and can be debilitating for the person experiencing it. In addition, supporting an individual over the long haul through chronic sorrow can be exhausting for those who care for and about that person. This chapter spends a great deal of time focusing on the clinician's compassionate intention and presence because these create the foundation that will provide sustainability when working with people whose painful loss experiences will permeate the rest of their lives. To be a support for the long haul, it is important to have the wisdom to recognize what is and is not possible and be able to separate the desire to relieve suffering from any expectations or outcomes that may never happen. Because the majority of nonfinite losses have no real resolution or sense of closure, the grief can persist for an indeterminate amount of time. Taking this stance at the outset frees your clients from potentially harmful expectations about their process, allowing them to engage in therapeutic work that will ultimately support their resilience and innate strengths.

REFERENCES

All Acronyms. (n.d.). *NATO means not attached to outcome.* https://www.allacronyms.com/NATO/Not_Attached_To_Outcome

Boss, P., Bryant, C. M., & Mancini, J. A. (2016). *Family stress management: A contextual approach.* Sage.

Geller, S. M., & Greenberg, L. S. (2012). *Therapeutic presence: A mindful approach to effective therapy.* American Psychological Association.

Harris, D. L. (2016). Social expectations of the bereaved. In D. Harris & T. Bordere (Eds.), *Handbook of social justice in loss and grief: Exploring diversity, equity, and inclusion* (pp. 165–176). Routledge.

Harris, D. L. (2017). Grief and loss in infertility. *Grief Matters, 20*(2), 32–36.

Harris, D. L. (2020a). Nonfinite loss: Living with ongoing loss and grief. In D. Harris (Ed.), *Non-death loss and grief: Context and clinical implications* (pp. 139–146). Routledge.

Harris, D. L. (2020b). Non-death loss and grief: Laying the foundation. In D. Harris (Ed.), *Non-death loss and grief: Context and clinical implications* (pp. 7–16). Routledge.

Harris, D. L. (2020c). Supporting people through living losses. In D. Harris (Ed.), *Non-death loss and grief: Context and clinical implications* (pp. 311–323). Routledge.

Harris, D. L., & Winokuer, H. R. (2021). *Principles and practice of grief counseling* (3rd ed.). Springer.

Maratos, F. A., & Sheffield, D. (2020). Brief compassion-focused imagery dampens physiological pain responses. *Mindfulness, 11*(12), 2730–2740.

Penlington, C. (2019). Exploring a compassion-focused intervention for persistent pain in a group setting. *British Journal of Pain, 13*(1), 59–66.

Rousseau, P. (2010). Presence. *Journal of Clinical Oncology, 28*(22), 3668–3669.

Vachon, M. L. S., & Harris, D. L. (2016). The liberating capacity of compassion. In D. Harris & T. Bordere (Eds.), *Handbook of social justice in loss and grief: Exploring diversity, equity, and inclusion* (pp. 265–281). Routledge.

CHAPTER 19

MINDFUL AND SELF-COMPASSIONATE EMBODIED GRIEF PRACTICES

Brad Hunter

INTRODUCTION

I have been practicing and teaching different versions of the following practices for many years. In one sense, I view all meditative work as 'grief work'—the acknowledgment and release of the emotional stress, constriction, and pain held in the body. The 'scripts' for these practices are general guidelines only. You need to follow the lead of your own body's response as to what works and what doesn't, in which circumstances, and to what extent. If a certain practice feels too overwhelming, switch to something else or find a way to adapt it so that overwhelm doesn't result. Practices can also be combined, blended, or conjoined, depending on the mood and situation. Again, much of meditation is directed by intuition and feeling. No one can enter someone else's subjective experience, so flexibility and trusting one's own intuition and intention are important.

Much has been said about the efficacy of loving-kindness (LK) meditations. I tend to work with such meditations in a less intellectual way than some models. I also don't often use the term 'loving-kindness' anymore, because I have found that generating this kind of feeling tone can be a stretch for a lot of people and create more frustration. The self-directed verbal guidance—*may I be at ease, may I be free of suffering, etc.*—is kept to a minimum, and the embodied felt sense of the feeling tones is emphasized.

For someone just beginning their mindful grief journey, it might be important, instructive, and healing, to simply engage in those practices that help you feel lighter, clearer, more grounded, and present. There is nothing wrong with temporarily setting aside the grief itself; we know it won't really *go* anywhere. Discovering a relatively grounded, stable, and peaceful refuge within can be a vital first step before confronting the grief itself.

Since grief is such an embodied experience, learn to trust the guidance of the breath and the body, and the peace and healing that can arise when the grace of present-moment awareness is able to hold the space for the natural unfolding of this universal human experience of loss. All of the practices that follow involve deep embodiment. Most of us have been conditioned to value intellectual prowess over the intuitive wisdom of the body and our somatic presence. Generally speaking, we have also become strangers to our own embodiment, with much of our sense of self *entombed* in the face and skull. Therefore, it is important to undertake these practices slowly and gradually, reintroducing ourselves to our most intimate embodied experience with the patience and kindness one might adopt in approaching a frightened child, or a wounded animal.

For example, even if you focused solely on the first practice of rediscovering the experience of breathing throughout the entire body, for days, weeks, or months, it is possible that you could experience a great deal of relief and release from the pain of grief. You might also discover that it is the *fear* of overwhelm that fuels the sense of overwhelm itself.

DOI: 10.4324/9781003204121-23

REDISCOVERING THE NATURAL HEALING OF BREATH AWARENESS: A SUBSEQUENT PRACTICE

Once you have re-established some basic intimacy with breathing, see if you can notice the different qualities of the breath, throughout the inbreath, throughout the outbreath, and during the pauses between the breaths, and even between the inbreaths and outbreaths. Can you notice that the inbreath can bring the feel of freshness, uplift, gladness, and contentment into the body? Can you notice that the outbreath brings a deep sense of release and letting go?

Experiment with seeing for yourself how the inhalations, exhalations, pauses, and brief holding of the breath feel throughout the body... In the face and head. In the legs and feet. In the arms and hands. In the upper chest and heart space. In the solar plexus, belly, and lower belly. In the back of the body. In the front of the body.

JUST THIS MUCH

'Just this much' is a guiding phrase that comes up periodically in meditation practice, particularly when it comes to exposing, feeling, integrating, and healing painful psychological material. Always begin any practice by attending to grounding, calming, and soothing first. Trying to jump right into a meditation practice from a place of high agitation or deep, crushing depression can often make matters worse. In the case of hypovigilance of deep grief, it would be recommended that you find some traces of uplift and gladness first—like concentrating on the qualities of the inbreath and/or working with Metta practice.

Once the body is feeling relatively calm and grounded, stay with the in- and outbreaths as your basic meditation object for a few more minutes, deepening and steadying the focus of the mind. Now spread awareness throughout the whole of the body and feel the embodied presence as fully as possible... Rest in this fullness, wholeness, and contentment for a time. If there is agitation, dread, or anxiety, don't go any further! Just keep infusing the body with calm breath awareness until there is a steady confidence and contentment.

When you feel ready, take a few moments to scan the body with curiosity, wondering "where am I holding grief feelings?" Don't be surprised if a somatic island of grief is being held in an unanticipated place, or places in the body. Don't overwhelm yourself; just pick one. The first thing to do is mentally hold it and touch it gently with kindness and love. Experiment with breathing into and through this grief point, without expectation, an agenda, a timetable, and definitely *not* with the intention of getting rid of it, or 'getting over it.' Having aversion for our pain, emotional or physical, is a certain way to ensure it endures and increases in intensity. We need to learn how to modulate our experience of emotional and psychological distress. Know when 'enough is enough' (for today). Learn when it feels safe to get closer to it and when you need to back away. That is the spirit behind 'just this much.' You can set your own parameters around time spent 'sitting with' your grief and the levels of intensity that are bearable, recognizing that these parameters are flexible and fluid, as your own experience changes. It can also help to think in terms of sitting *with* rather *sitting in* your grief. You want to be a helpful companion and witness to your grief, not constantly overwhelmed by the pain of it.

Another meditation principle comes into play here: Host and guest. Learn to recognize that you are the receiver, the host of your experience, not the guest(s). When we start believing that all of our painful feelings are *me*, that can become an entrenched identity that is very difficult and painful to relinquish. Keep in mind that 'no feeling is final.'

EMBODYING METTA (LOVING FRIENDLINESS)

First bring attention to the grounding of the body at the contact points. Feel the security, reliability, and support of that grounded sense 'holding you,' wrapping you in safety. View gravity as a gift of grace from the earth. Soak in this sense of safety and caring. (This could be a practice on its own.) You could begin with a few prompting metta phrases: *May I be calm and at ease. May I be free of suffering.* (There are many other words, or you could choose your own.) Try to get in touch with a felt sense of kindness and goodwill. It doesn't have to be anything 'big,' just the absence of hostility and ill-will in the present moment can be the spark that initiates much more light and warmth. If such a feeling tone seems remote, bring to mind the millions of little acts of kindness and goodwill that occur every day with ordinary people. Try to get in touch with the feeling of that goodness and begin to touch into your own sense of goodness as well.

Feel the body surrounded by kindness and goodwill and be open to receiving this. Keep verbalization to a minimum. Soak in the kindness and goodwill... through the skin, into the muscles, organs, bloodstream, nervous system, bones, and marrow. If a soaking image doesn't work for you, try using the breathing model above and adding metta to the breath suffusing the entire body. Stay with a body soaking in kindness as long as you like... At some point, some distress grief may start to arise... Allow the kindness and goodwill to naturally open and deepen into compassion.

Soak and suffusing the body with compassion... You may need or want to stop here for now. If not, if the pain is somewhat eased and released through embodied compassion, you might find a quiet happiness, even joy and contentment arising. Appreciate that and rest into it. Open to receiving this happiness, even though it is likely flavored with the bittersweetness of grief. Allow the goodness and healing of this to suffuse the body... You may need to stop here.

As the grief healing and integration continue over time, you could reach a point where the mudita[1] of appreciative joy and contentment begins to naturally arise, absent the pangs of grief. When this begins to happen, you can simply abide in that space, allowing the joy and contentment to become deep and steady. Without any willful intention, when the time is ripe, this joyful contentment can drop even deeper into the fourth level of metta[2]—the serenity and peace of equanimity. (The other side of metta is of course, 'sending it' to others. And there is nothing about focusing metta on yourself, that keeps you from also offering goodwill, compassion, sympathetic joy, and peace to others. Turning your thoughts of goodness outwards can also be a wonderful aid in your own healing. But again, try using the words of metta as prompts, as you radiate friendliness, compassion, and peace with the entire body. Try to make it more of an embodied, energetic experience as opposed to an intellectual and abstract exercise.)

STEPPING BACK FROM OVERWHELM

The fear of overwhelm can be more problematic and painful than the inevitable pain of loss itself. The vigilance of trying to hold back the waves of painful feelings is not only exhausting; it can also become a state of distress that matches or surpasses the discomfort of the natural emotions of grief. As St. Bartholomew has suggested, we are always "bigger than" any suffering that we experience. It takes practice to learn to mindfully step backwards from being the *receiver* of our own experiencing, to being the *knower* of the impermanent thoughts and feelings that arise and pass away—constantly. This might sound like denial or suppression, but in fact it is the opposite. Stepping slightly back into our knowing faculty is the only way to gain real clarity and intimacy. When we are in the midst of overwhelm, flooded by and entangled in our emotional experience, we hardly have a perspective on what we are feeling moment to moment, other than *dread*.

'IT'S LIKE THIS…'

Much of our suffering is created by our own narratives. We get caught in an endless loop of thoughts, images, memories, stories, and worries, that simply adds to the pain of our grief and produces the feeling of overwhelm. When we are caught like this, it is difficult, if not impossible, to even identify exactly the feelings that we are feeling. We need to first calm body and mind through one of the practices above, even if it is just a matter of taking a few breaths and feeling the body grounded on the earth.

From the relatively grounded, stable, and calm position, try to notice the dominant emotion in the arising experience. This is not a thought experiment. Go to the embodied felt sense of it all. Try to identify and name it. This practice, which is common in the Thai Forest tradition, can be an antidote to overwhelm, holding ourselves in a safe distance from an emotional charge while still maintaining intimacy with it. If we can stay with the direct embodied experience, over time, we develop the skills to open to even our most difficult emotions in a measured way that feels safe. We can learn through our own practice how to navigate this territory, feel whatever arises in a measured way, and let it go.

At first what presents itself in our arising experience might simply be pressure, or heat, or tingling, or queasiness, or ache, or dissociation—many different varieties of amorphous, undefined embodied sense. If we can stay with our grounded breath and body, in a relatively safe space, experiencing the detailed body sensations, we can arrive at the core emotion being expressed. Then we can simply acknowledge: 'Fear is like this…,' 'Longing is like this…,' 'Shame is like this…,' 'Anger is like this…,' 'Unworthiness is like this…,' 'Sadness is like this…,' and so on.

We discover that we don't have to take on any or all of our passing feeling states as an identity. We also intuitively find how much we can tolerate of any powerful emotion and for how long, while at the same time finding creative ways of "storing" the impossibly difficult until we feel more confident and prepared to explore more deeply. We can learn directly, through our own embodied experience, that the ceaseless arising and passing of all experience applies as well to grief itself: Even grief is not fixed and permanent.

NOTES

1 Mudita refers to appreciative joy—feeling joy in one's own goodness and the good qualities of others.
2 Metta refers to universal kindness and goodwill, expressed both inwardly and outwardly.

CHAPTER 20

TALES FROM THE FIELD

Self-Compassion as a Resource for Supporting Grief

Jo Storozinski and Cesar Gonzales

INTRODUCTION

The death of a loved one is only the beginning of what may seem like a tumultuous and unpredictable journey which unfolds for the bereaved. For those left behind, there is value in joining a support group (Mayo Clinic, 2018; Lund & Caserta, 1992). It has been our experience that individuals choosing to join a grief support program do so for several reasons, which typically include gaining skills to cope with their loss, alleviating pain and suffering, and decreasing feelings of isolation. The framework of the nine-week program we have developed addresses the needs of the bereaved by drawing upon different concepts and theories regarding loss and grief (Brach, 2003; Germer, 2009; Gilbert, 2009; Hanson, 2009; Kabat-Zinn, 1990; Kumar, 2005; Neff, 2011; Neimeyer, 2001; Neimeyer et al., 2021; Neimeyer, 2016; Worden, 2018).While narrative therapy is a key component of the program, the predominant focus is on our original curriculum with an infusion of mindfulness-based self-compassion practices adapted to grief. Our core philosophies are:

1) Grief is a normal and natural part of life.
2) Each individual is the expert in their own grief.
3) Participation is open to any adult who has experienced the death of a loved one.
4) Participants decide when they are ready to join.
5) No one is broken, and no one needs fixing.
6) The intention is to help support the grief journey by moving it from the head (intellect) to the heart (making space for feelings and emotions).
7) We acknowledge the courage it takes to walk this path, and we invite participants to set their own pace.

In an attempt to increase group cohesion, we discourage the comparison of losses. We intentionally acknowledge within the group that the most difficult loss is the one the participant is experiencing.

Group discussions normalize, reveal, and reinforce the common humanity of the pain and suffering experienced by the participants. The recognition of common humanity (I am not alone) decreases the sense of isolation and helps to alleviate one's suffering. This is an important component of self-compassion (Neff & Dahm, 2015), and has also been validated by feedback and evaluations from past participants.

Another element that we seek to address early in the program is rumination. We have observed that participants frequently attach themselves to the details of their grief story. For example, regrets over perceived hurts, actions, or inactions that they would have done differently, had they realized the exact moment their loved one was going to die; in essence, ruminating over the things they 'could have, would have, or should have

DOI: 10.4324/9781003204121-24

done differently.' This rumination can be viewed as an act of avoidance, "rumination helps individuals to avoid an aversive environment because it occupies attention and time" (Eisma et al., 2020, p. 550).

Additionally, along with rumination, the voice of the inner critic can intensify the pain and suffering of the grief journey. Research in the field of self-compassion provides evidence showing a reduction in rumination as individuals learn to anchor to the present moment, offering oneself comfort and care, while encouraging one to utilize a kinder, more compassionate voice (Neff & Dahm, 2015; Odou & Brinker, 2014). Self-compassion is the container that provides resilience for those that have experienced the death of a loved one.

While we acknowledge that each and every participant's story of grief is sacred and has a right to be honored, we also acknowledge the importance of living life in the present moment, allowing for what is arising without judgment, and with acceptance. In doing so, the bereaved has the choice on how they can *respond* to the moment versus *react*. They also are able to acknowledge while they may not like what is occurring in the moment, it is just this moment and that the next moment may be different. As a result, they are less likely to become overwhelmed. Furthermore, as participants learn to be with their grief, in a stance of self-compassion, resistance to the pain of the moment decreases.

The remainder of this chapter will focus on lessons learned and future considerations in the offering of our program.

LESSONS LEARNED

BECOMING UNCOMFORTABLE

The topic of death is uncomfortable for most of us in North America, having grown up in a death avoidant society. Being mindfully aware of our discomfort and tending to that discomfort with kindness and compassion can aid practitioners in becoming more comfortable with the uncomfortable.

BEING INTENTIONAL

The delivery of our grief program is intentional in all aspects, beginning with the initial contact with the bereaved. We are explicit in our description of what the program entails and how it may serve to support them in their grief journey. Utilizing an authentic and transparent approach, we are able to gently introduce the idea of the importance of honoring the stories of their grief while trying to move away from the details of the story. This is deliberate, in order to work with the pain and suffering as it arises, so as to reduce rumination. Time is set aside for participants to share in the narrative of suffering with other group members in the first three sessions of the program.

BUILDING RELATIONSHIPS

This allows us to engage with the bereaved in an authentic manner in which we earn their trust and provide a compassionate presence. Building authentic relationships, holding a safe space, and giving clients permission to grieve is sacred work. Clients can then feel heard, feel safe, and feel connected.

WHAT DO I NEED?

One of the hallmarks of mindfulness and self-compassion practices is teaching clients to discern for themselves, 'What is it that I need in this moment?' (Germer & Neff, 2019; Hickman, 2015; Schrader, 2018). This includes recognizing whether the adapted grief program is a good fit for the client, or whether individual counseling or a more traditional grief group may better suit their needs. It provides them autonomy and control and reinforces that this, too, is an act of kindness and compassion toward themselves. Furthermore, it alleviates the pressure that some grief participants may feel by having to learn new skills and practices and prevents any shame if they choose to withdraw or decline participating in the program.

SELF-CARE FOR THE PRACTITIONER

As facilitators, holding space, listening, and bearing witness to the narrative of suffering require a commitment to our own personal and daily practices of mindful awareness, kindness, and self-compassion. This self-care regimen helps to support us in providing a compassionate presence while keeping ourselves fully nourished and balanced, free from burnout, and available to hear the stories of grief.

CO-TEACHING

The co-teaching model for facilitating a grief group is extremely beneficial. It allows us to support one another. It provides the necessary safety in which one facilitator can step away to hold private space with a client who may have become activated by an exercise or practice, while the other continues to facilitate the session.

WARMTH

Providing a warm, inviting, culturally safe atmosphere, in which participants feel welcomed, helps participants to feel more at ease. It facilitates the felt sense of connection to the others within the group along with the common humanity of the shared experience of grief. Setting the environment to include refreshments, dim lighting, an informal seating arrangement, and appropriate room temperature is an essential component that further aids group cohesion.

FINDING THE MIDDLE GROUND

It is imperative, as grief counselors, that we assist participants to connect to their stories of loss and grief, while guiding them to not become overwhelmed or consumed by their stories. It is necessary to strike a proper balance of offering just the right amount of opportunity to share their stories, while also engaging the group to step away from the details of their stories, thus preventing rumination and decreasing the possibility of becoming over-whelmed. Participants learn to respond to the arising pain and suffering, without being hijacked by it.

LANGUAGE MATTERS

Sometimes the soft-flowing and tender language of compassion and kindness, in and of itself, can be foreign and even off-putting. Recognizing that participants come from varied cultures, gender roles, family rules, backgrounds, and emotions, the flowery language can be challenging at times for both the participant and the facilitator.

Unpacking a courageous, strong, and protective side of self-compassion, such as rein-forcing the importance of setting healthy limits and boundaries in healthy relationships while grieving and honoring ones' core values and beliefs, is an example of what is referred to as fierce compassion. Offering examples of fierce compassion and including a healthy mix of research and science behind the practices helps to engage those overwhelmed by the language and/or to support the skeptically inclined. For example, it can be very palat-able and compelling for some participants to learn how the flow of the naturally occurring, nurturing hormone oxytocin can act as an antidote to the rising cortisol levels in response to the stress of grief (Germer & Neff, 2019; Gilbert, 2009).

CHALLENGES AND FUTURE CONSIDERATIONS

HOME PRACTICE

One of the more common and challenging aspects for participants is the time and commitment needed to practice when decreased concentration, focus, and energy frequently occur with grief. In this case, the term home practice refers to both informal and formal mindfulness and self-compassion exercises and meditations. These activities aid participants to become mindfully aware of the arising moment and provide them with an opportunity to practice self-compassion and kindness when experiencing pain and suffering. Home practice typically reinforces the skills and training learned in the weekly group sessions. Inviting participants to reflect upon how they would treat a friend who was struggling versus how they treat themselves (Greater Good Science Center at University of California Berkely; n.d.; see Table 20.1), a self-compassion break (Germer & Neff, 2019; see Table 20.2) that we have adapted for grief, and 'Savoring a Memory' meditation (see Table 20.3)are examples of home practice.

We encourage participants to initially select practices, formal or informal, that resonate with them. They are invited to go at their own pace, gradually gaining more comfort in extend-ing the time engaged in home practice. The provision of regularly offered meditation drop-in sessions and half-day retreats is an opportunity for past participants to deepen their practice. Additional benefits include reinforcing personal practice and building a community of support.

While not a common occurrence, from time to time a past participant resurfaces at a different place and time, with different needs in their grief journey. The option to join a new grief group allows the past participant to reacquaint themselves with the practices. In our experience this has served to help deepen their understanding and attend to their present needs, despite it being the same program they previously attended.

Table 20.1 How Would You Treat a Friend (Five Minutes)

The exercise, "How Would You Treat a Friend?," is introduced in the first session with the grief participants. The intent is twofold. Firstly, it helps participants realize how critical they can be of themselves. The second is to help reinforce that this is a shared experience of grieving individuals (common humanity).

The discussion and inquiry after the activity serve to reinforce these principles of common humanity further emphasizing "you are not alone" and to help participants recognize how hard they can be on themselves.

How to Do It

Take out a sheet of paper or open a blank document on your computer and go through the following steps.

1. First, think about times when a close friend feels really bad about him- or herself or is really struggling in some way. How do you respond to your friend in these situations (if you're at your best)? Please write down what you typically do and say, and note the tone in which you talk to your friend.
2. Now think about times when you feel bad about yourself or are struggling. How do you typically respond to yourself in these situations? Please write down what you typically do and say, and note the tone in which you talk to yourself.
3. Did you notice a difference? If so, ask yourself why. What factors or fears come into play that lead you to treat yourself and others so differently?
4. Write down how you think things might change if you responded to yourself when you're suffering in the same way you typically respond to a close friend.
5. Next time you are struggling with something, try treating yourself like a good friend and see what happens.

UNPACKING THE PARADOX

One of the more common and distressing issues we notice with bereaved clients is the sleep irregularity and insomnia that often coincide with the grief journey. Compassion-based meditation practices can be initially very compelling and provide immediate relief to these unwanted and challenging symptoms. However, the practices can become deceiving if they are used in service to resisting or avoiding the pain and suffering that are contributing to the sleep issues. Unpacking the paradox, in times of pain and suffering, *"we give ourselves compassion not to feel better but because we feel bad"* (Davidson & Neff, 2016, p. 46), is critically important. This paradox helps put into perspective that while the practices may in the short term serve to alleviate sleep issues, the individual may be falling into the subtle nuance of another form of resistance to their pain of grief. Therefore, the practices may not continue to successfully work to absolve sleep irregularity if they are used with the wrong intention. As co-facilitators we have observed this to be a challenging and counter-intuitive concept to grasp for some of our clients.

Table 20.2 Soothing Touch/Self-Compassion Break

This practice is introduced in session two of the grief program. This practice teaches participants to identify and make space for the pain that is arising and develop the resources in order to soothe and comfort themselves. This adaptation merges the practices of anchoring to the breath, Soothing Touch, and Self-Compassion Break.

Instructions:

Time:

- **10-15 minutes for practice**
- **5 minutes inquiry**

For teaching purposes, we have combined three practices that flow one into the other. We begin with anchoring to the breath, followed by Soothing Touch, and leading into a Self-Compassion Break. While we have combined these three practices, each component can stand alone, based on what you need in the moment. Just a gentle reminder to pace yourself as you proceed throughout this practice, always keeping yourself safe, recalling that you have the option of proceeding with the practice, staying with a particular component of the practice(s) introduced, or letting go of the practice(s) altogether.

Inviting you to find a comfortable position, feeling fully supported in your chair, noticing how your feet rest on the floor or wherever you find yourselves—you can close your eyes either fully or partially, or alternatively, softly gaze down at the tip of your nose, whichever feels most comfortable for you. (pause)

Taking a moment to notice the natural, normal rhythm of your breath and now, let's begin by anchoring to a few breaths—taking three intentional breaths. (pause)

- Inhaling peace and calm, exhaling tension and stress.
- Inhaling a nourishing breath to slow and to restore and exhaling any lingering or residual feelings that may be present today. (pause)

Finally, inhaling a felt sense of light and well-being and exhaling all that no longer serves you. (longer pause)

Now, moving on to the Soothing Touch component of the practice—cueing the brain to release oxytocin and finding a way to support ourselves when we are feeling badly. Offering ourselves comforting or soothing touch is an opportunity to comfort ourselves in moments of pain and suffering.

Inviting you now to gently place a hand over your heart, simply feeling the gentle pressure and warmth of your hand. If you wish, placing both hands over your heart. Feeling the natural rising and falling of your chest as you continue to breathe in and as you breathe out, lingering with this feeling for as long as you like. (pause)

Now, taking a moment to discover other possibilities for getting the oxytocin to flow, we are going to explore other supportive gestures which can be comforting.

Inviting you to:

- Place a hand on your cheek, and just simply notice how that feels, warm? Cool? Or comforting?
- Next, try supporting both sides of your cheek with both your hands, so you are now cradling your face in your hands.
- Now, moving your hands to opposite arms in a crossed over fashion and then, gently begin stroking your arms and just noticing how this gesture feels for you. (brief pause)
- Continue with your arms crossed, giving yourself a gentle squeeze, as if your loved one, whom you are missing so much in this moment, were here right now, to hug and to hold you. (pause)
- If this feels right to you, moving one hand over your heart and making it into a fist and then cupping your other hand over the fist on your heart, and holding your hands there as a gentle reminder and as a symbol of compassion with strength. (brief pause)
- Now releasing your fisted and cupped hands and flattening them both so that now two hands are over your heart, and just noticing the support and warmth you might be experiencing here. (pause)
- Then move one hand to the belly and one over the heart, and now try moving both hands to your belly. (brief pause)

(Continued)

Table 20.2 Continued

- Finally, try cupping one hand in the other, in your lap and just taking a moment to reflect upon which hand GESTURE feels most right for you. (pause)

And now with your eyes remaining closed (however that might look like for you) we are going to transition into the last part of this practice—the Self-Compassion Break.

So, taking a moment to bring to mind a situation in which you feel discomfort or stress, something that is mild to moderate in nature. See if you can feel the stress or the emotional discomfort in the body, noticing where you feel it the most and making contact with those sensations as they arise in the body, and as you do so, say to yourself, slowly and softly

1. **"This is a moment of suffering"**
   That's mindfulness, just noticing what is arising without judgment.
   You might also say:
   - This hurts.
   - This is the work of grief, it is really painful.
   - Grief and loss are hard.
   - I am hurting right now!
   - This is loss, and this is difficult.
   Now saying to yourself, slowly and softly
2. **"Suffering is a part of life"**
   That is our reminder of our common humanity
   You might also say:
   - I am not alone.
   - Grief and loss are a natural part of the human journey.
   - May I remind myself, that somewhere else in this world, someone else is grieving the loss of their loved one, just like me.
   And finally, saying to yourself, slowly and softly
3. **"May I be kind to myself or may I give myself what I need in this moment"**
   This is an act of kindness you are giving to yourself
   You might also say things like:
   - May I be kind to myself in this moment.
   - May I give myself permission to grieve and offer myself a supportive and comforting gesture.
   - May I learn to comfort and soothe myself while I feel the intensity of my grief.
   - May I trust that kindness and caring for myself help to heal my grief.
   - May I remind myself that each moment is different and that offering myself kindness is my way of healing my grief.
   - May I be patient with myself as I grieve.
   And if you are having difficulty finding the right words, imagine that a dear friend or loved one is struggling in the same way as yourself in this moment.
   - What would you say to this person?
   - How might you say it to that person?

And if your friend were to leave with just a few words in their mind, what would you like those words to be? (pause)

What message would you like to deliver from your heart to theirs? (pause)

Now see if you can offer the same kind, loving, and compassionate message to yourself.

And as you are ready, returning your attention back to this chair in this room and slowly and gently wiggling your fingers and toes and gently opening your eyes.

Ring bell to bring practice to a close.

Table 20.3 Savoring a Memory

We developed the practice of "Savoring a Memory" specifically for our grief program with the intention of integrating a mindfully compassionate practice with memories. This practice was initially introduced to participants during the half-day retreat portion of the program.

It provides participants with an opportunity to realize that they do not have to fear their memories, that they are an integral part of the grief journey. While memories may be painful, they can also bring a sense of joy and appreciation, all of which encompasses the grief experience.

Instruction:
Time:

- **20 minutes practice**
- **15 minutes sharing**
- **10 minutes inquiry**
- If this activity/exercise feels too overwhelming, consider being kind to yourself, then determining what you need in this moment.
- *If mildly distressing*, I encourage you to continue.
- *If moderate distress* is felt and it is feeling less tolerable, then anchor to a mindfulness activity such as your breath or to the soles of your feet, or something in the room.
- Lastly, if this exercise feels so *overwhelming and intolerable*, then an act of kindness may be:
- Completely stopping the activity.
- Focusing on some way to distract yourself, such as creating your grocery list or even getting up and going for a walk or a snack.

Inviting you to now reflect upon a favorite, cherished memory that you shared with your loved one, before they died. It may be from years ago or one of more recent times. (long pause)

Taking a moment now to really reflect upon that memory you have chosen. Recalling to mind what the details are of that memory.

- What happened in that memory? (pause)
- Why was this moment with your loved one occurring? (pause)
- Were you alone with your loved one, or were others around? (pause)
- When and where did this memory take place? (pause)
- What time of year? (pause)
- Can you remember the weather/the day/the date/the year? (pause)
- Are there sounds or smells that come to mind? (pause)

(Long pause to give participants time to reflect and answer the questions.)

- And if you are able to go just a little deeper into that memory bank, can you fondly recall why this moment touched your heart? (pause)
- What feelings did you experience during that event in which the memory was being created? Did it bring you laughter, joy, tenderness, or love? (longer pause)
- So now noticing what is arising for you in this moment, as you savor this memory and whatever is arising for you, can you make space for it?
- How does it feel to embrace that memory fully?
- Can you feel what is arising in your body?
- And if any emotions are arising for you now, are you able to gently ask yourself "what do I need in this moment?" Perhaps a soothing touch, returning to the breath to anchor you into this awareness or perhaps something in your environment that you can anchor to. (pause)

(Continued)

Table 20.3 Continued

- Taking a moment now to affectionately breathe in calm loving awareness of this moment and releasing any stress or tension as you breathe out. Be nourished as you breathe in and feel cleansed as you exhale, all the while being gentle and kind to yourself as you take the time you need to. (pause)
- When you are ready, slowly and gently returning to this moment.

Sharing:
- Invite participants to share their favorite/cherished memory with the larger group.
- Give participants an opportunity to share what it was like to savor that memory.

Inquiry—Sample Questions:
- What was it like to retrieve a cherished memory?
- What was it like to savor that memory?
- Were you able to identify what was arising for you in that moment?
- How did you work with that?
- What resource did you use?
- If it feels comfortable, can we explore this a little bit further? Are you okay now? What do you need in this moment?

FLEXIBILITY

At times, mid-session, we may feel the energy of the group shift to a place of saturation. If it cannot be brought back with a break or a movement exercise then we shift gears, let go of the planned session, and attend to the needs of the group. Not further burdening them with new skills and strategies to learn, regardless of how beneficial we know them to be, is an act of compassion. Flexibility entails being open to carrying over the intended curriculum into the next week's session if need be. As grief practitioners practicing self-compassion, we do our very best to meet the ongoing needs of the bereaved by frequently reassessing and re-evaluating the program and services we offer.

Finally, we'd be remiss if we failed to acknowledge the role we have as facilitators to meet the growing and evolving needs of the clients we serve. We must stay open to evolving and changing the program, understanding that the need often coincides with the evolutionary shifts seen in society as a whole. The more adept and familiar we become with the practices, the concepts, and the supportive research, the better we are able to apply and adapt these practices, exercises, and concepts to meet the needs of the bereaved.

CONCLUSION

Though loss and grief are a natural and normal part of the life journey, we acknowledge as clinicians how difficult and challenging this can be as it brings inevitable, unwanted change and transformation to one's life. The initial act of seeking out grief resources takes an enormous amount of courage for some and can be overwhelming when one is feeling raw and vulnerable in the midst of one's grief. It is with great reverence and respect that we have learned to tenderly hold the space with a compassionate presence for those who grieve as we walk alongside them in their journey of grief. Guided by the practice of humility, we are reminded that no one is exempt from the pain and suffering of loss, and to that end, 'their story' is 'my story' as we share in the common humanity of this life experience.

The fusion of mindful awareness, kindness, and self-compassion practices into the work of grief allows clients to anchor to the present moment, providing them with the courage to navigate what is arising, and teaches them to respond with comfort and care so that it is more bearable.

REFERENCES

Bantam Davidson, O., & Neff, K. (2016). Self-compassion: Embracing suffering with kindness. In I. Ivtzan & T. Lomas (Eds.), *Mindfulness in positive psychology: The science of meditation and wellbeing* (pp. 37–50). Routledge.

Brach, T. (2003). *Radical acceptance: Embracing your life with the heart of a Buddha.*

Eisma, M. C., Lang, T. A., & Boelen, P. A. (2020). How thinking hurts: Rumination, worry, and avoidance processes in adjustment to bereavement. *Clinical Psychology and Psychotherapy, 27*(4), 548–558. https://doi.org/10.1002/cpp.v27.4

Germer, C. K. (2009). *The mindful path to self-compassion: Freeing yourself from destructive thoughts and emotions.* Guilford Press.

Germer, C., & Neff, K. (2019). *Mindful self-compassion teacher guide.* Center for Mindful Self-Compassion.

Gilbert, P. (2009). *The compassionate mind.* New Harbinger Press.

Greater Good Science Center at University of California Berkeley. (n.d.). *How would you treat a friend?* https://ggia.berkeley.edu/practice/how_would_you_treat_a_friend

Hanson, R. (2009). *Buddha's brain.* New Harbinger Press.

Hickman, S. (2015, July 18). Answering the fundamental question of mindful self-compassion. *LinkedIn.* https://www.linkedin.com/pulse/answering-fundamental-question-mindful-steven-hickman-psy-d-

Kabat-Zinn, J. (1990). *Full catastrophe living: Using the wisdom of your body and mind to face stress, pain, and illness.* Dell.

Kumar, S. M. (2005). *Grieving mindfully: A compassionate and spiritual guide to coping with loss.* New Harbinger.

Lund, D. A., & Caserta, M. S. (1992). Older bereaved spouses' participation in self-help groups. *OMEGA: Journal of Death and Dying, 25*(1), 47–61. https://doi.org/10.2190/0f2e-96vy-419k-kxaa

Mayo Clinic. (2018). *How to choose the right support group.* https://www.mayoclinic.org/healthy-lifestyle/stress-management/in-depth/support-groups/art-20044655

Neff, K. (2011). *Self-compassion: Stop beating yourself up and leave insecurity behind.* HarperCollins.

Neff, K., & Dahm, K. (2015). Self-compassion: What it is, what it does, and how it relates to mindfulness. In B. Meier, B. Ostafin, & M. Robinson (Eds.), *Handbook of mindfulness and self-regulation* (pp. 121–140). Springer. https://self-compassion.org/wp-content/uploads/publications/Mindfulness_and_SC_chapter_in_press.pdf

Neimeyer, R. A. (2001). *Meaning reconstruction & the experience of loss.* American Psychological Association.

Neimeyer, R. A. (2016). *Techniques of grief therapy: Assessment and intervention.* Routledge.

Neimeyer, R. A., Harris, D. L., Winokuer, H. R., & Thornton, G. F. (2021). *Grief and bereavement in contemporary society: Bridging research and practice* (2nd ed.). Routledge.

Odou, N., & Brinker, J. (2014). Self-compassion, a better alternative to rumination than distraction as a response to negative mood. *Journal of Positive Psychology, 10*(5), 447–457. https://doi.org/10.1080/17439760.2014.967800

Schrader, J. (2018, February 2). Be kind to yourself: The wisdom of self-compassion. *Psychology Today.* https://www.psychologytoday.com/ca/blog/between-cultures/201802/be-kind-yourself

Worden, W. J. (2018). *Grief counselling and grief therapy: A handbook for the mental health practitioner* (5th ed.). Springer.

CHAPTER 21

COMPASSION-FOCUSED IMAGERY AND EMBODIMENT PRACTICES

Stan Steindl and Marcela Matos

INTRODUCTION

Compassion-Focused Therapy (CFT; Gilbert, 2014) was developed to work with self-criticism and shame. Through psychoeducation and skills training, CFT helps people cultivate the qualities and skills of compassion found to be helpful in the context of grief. Self-compassion, in particular, predicts reduced severity and longevity of the grieving process, and reduced risk of mental disorders, especially when grief is complicated by shame. In this chapter, we will explore the concept, research, and application of compassion-focused approaches in the context of grief, focusing on grief complicated by shame.

CLINICAL VIGNETTE

Compassion-Focused Psychoeducation and Skills Training

Talia[1] was determined to care for her mother as her mother's dementia worsened. She felt solely responsible for her mother's care, especially with feeding, and her threat system was activated in response. Treatment began with psychoeducation of the evolved human brain, the brain's threat system, associated feelings, thoughts, and physical sensations of anger and anxiety, and the associated urges and behaviors (i.e., fight/flight/freeze/appease). She developed mind awareness and understanding with respect to the final years with her mother, beginning the process of de-shaming. Talia learned about the compassionate mind, the way compassion flows in three directions, and the importance of cultivating the compassionate self. She practiced skills to slow down the body and the mind incorporating body posture, facial expressions, inner voice tones, and soothing rhythm breathing. Imagery exercises helped her cultivate feelings of calmness and safeness, and develop a compassionate motivation, through imagery of an ideal compassionate other and compassionate self.

COMPASSION: CONCEPT, RESEARCH, AND APPLICATIONS IN THE CONTEXT OF GRIEF

Compassion has benefits for emotion regulation, social relationships, and psychophysiological well-being (Gilbert, 2020), can be an antidote to shame and shame memories (Matos et al., 2020), and is especially relevant during grief. CFT conceptualizes compassion as "a sensitivity to suffering in self and others, with a commitment to try to alleviate and prevent it" (Gilbert, 2014, p. 19), and incorporates compassion toward others, compassion from others, and self-compassion (Gilbert et al., 2017). These highly interactive flows of compassion can influence each other (Gilbert, 2014; Gilbert et al., 2017), but can also function independently (Lopez et al., 2018).

DOI: 10.4324/9781003204121-25

According to CFT, compassion is an evolved caring motivation that has stimulus (engagement) and response (action) processes (Gilbert, 2017, 2019). Compassionate engagement involves the competencies to engage with suffering, including courage and determination, attentional sensitivity, sympathetic concern, distress tolerance, empathic bridging, and non-judgment. These competencies are difficult but crucial in the face of loss and grief and can promote well-being even in situations of significant distress (Gilbert, 2010; Gilbert & Choden, 2013).

Compassionate action involves motivation and commitment to wisely and skillfully alleviate or prevent suffering and create helpful feelings and behaviors relevant to the context (Gilbert, 2009, 2017, 2019; Gilbert et al., 2017). Distinguished from mammalian caring, compassion draws on human cognitive competencies of self-awareness, social and emotional intelligence, reasoning, and abilities to predict and monitor consequences of behavior (Dunbar, 2017). Compassion is caring that is purposeful, deliberate, thoughtful, and mindful (Gilbert, 2009, 2017; Gilbert & Choden, 2013).

Self-compassion has been suggested as a protective factor in grief, with lower self-compassion and higher self-criticism linked to more severe grief reactions (Vara & Thimm, 2019), and higher self-compassion in relatives of missing persons associated with less emotional distress (Lenferink et al., 2017). Individuals who were more self-compassionate reported less intense grief and better overall psychosocial functioning (Bussolari et al., 2021). Moreover, self-compassion has been shown to be negatively related to shame and to moderate the relationship between shame and psychological distress (Blackie & Kocovski, 2019; Oliveira et al., 2018).

Self-compassion has been found to mediate the effect of the traumatic qualities of shame memories on depressive symptoms (Steindl et al., 2018), to buffer the association between the traumatic and centrality to identity features of shame memories and eating psychopathology severity in women (Ferreira et al., 2014), and to mediate the association between shame and safeness memories, and depressive symptoms and internal shame in gay men (Matos et al., 2017a). The ability to be open to receiving compassion from others also seems to protect against depressive symptoms and is associated with fewer traumatic and centrality qualities of shame memories (Hermanto et al., 2016; Steindl et al., 2018).

Compassion can be cultivated through interventions such as CFT (for patients) and compassionate mind training (CMT; for the general public; Gilbert & Procter, 2006; Gilbert, 2010), with growing support for their effectiveness in reducing mental health issues (e.g., depression, anxiety, stress, shame, self-criticism; Craig et al., 2020 and Kirby et al., 2017 for reviews; Irons & Heriot-Maitland, 2020; Matos et al., 2017b).

CLINICAL VIGNETTE, CONTINUED

Approaching Shame in Grief with CFT

Talia's shame persisted. "How could I do that to her? She looked after me without ever complaining, and when it was my turn, I abused her! I'm a terrible person." We defined shame as a uniquely human experience, common to us all, that evolved to help humans identify and respond to social threat and remain safely in the group. We differentiated shame (i.e., a global negative sense of self, "I am bad") from guilt (i.e., related to our specific harmful behaviors, "I did something bad"). Guilt arises from the soothing-affiliative system. We experience guilt when we harm another who we care about. Thus, therapy proceeded by working with shame, moving toward guilt, and then to forgiveness. Talia's shame was approached in an experiential way, bringing the shame memory to mind, using imagery to explore her feelings, thoughts, physical sensations, and actions, and how these had incorporated multiple patterns of anxiety, anger, and shame. While cautiously and carefully done, she began to embody her shamed self, that part of her that felt so ashamed of who she had become during those final months of her mother's life.

WORKING WITH SHAME IN GRIEF VIA CFT

CFT is an evolutionary-based psychotherapeutic approach that integrates attachment theory, psychological science, neuroscience, and the wisdom traditions (Gilbert, 2010, 2014). Developed to work with shame and self-criticism (Gilbert & Irons, 2005), CFT uses psychoeducation and skills training to cultivate compassionate engagement and action toward others, from others, and self-compassion (Gilbert & Choden, 2013). CFT psychoeducation incorporates the evolved and complex nature and functioning of the human mind, including three core emotion-regulation systems: (a) the threat system, with a threat protection motive, (b) the drive system, focused on resources and rewards, and (c) the soothing-affiliative system, motivating toward affiliative social relationships and resulting feelings of safeness, contentment, and openness. Shame and self-criticism often arise when we are caught between threat and drive systems (Gilbert, 2014).

CFT psychoeducation and skills training are designed to develop the soothing-affiliative system to cultivate compassion across the three flows and thereby down-regulate the threat system, as well as bring awareness and understanding to other aspects of the human mind, such as self-criticism, worry, and rumination. Such mind awareness allows for de-blaming and de-shaming and setting an intention to try to work compassionately with life's difficulties (Gilbert & Choden, 2013). CFT skills training, incorporating CMT, develops the soothing-affiliative system through body-based (e.g., soothing rhythm breathing) and imagery-based practices (e.g., calm place imagery), and a range of behavioral and embodiment techniques that help cultivate the "compassionate self." With practice, this compassionate self facilitates self-grounding, mind awareness and understanding, a shift to a compassionate orientation across the three flows, and the wisdom, strength, and courage to work with difficult emotions and life experiences. Research is providing increasing support for CFT's effectiveness as a psychotherapeutic approach to working with shame and self-criticism (e.g., Kirby et al., 2017; Leaviss & Uttley, 2014).

BODY-BASED PRACTICES

The parasympathetic nervous system (and vagus nerve in particular) is understood to play an important role in the down-regulation of the threat and drive systems and activation of the soothing-affiliative system, creating a sense of soothing through closeness and connection (Porges, 2017). Body postures, facial expressions, voice tones, and breathing have important physiological regulating effects. It appears that the vagus nerve and parasympathetic nervous system play an important role in prosocial behaviors, specifically compassion (Di Bello et al., 2020). CMT involves body-based practices, incorporating upright yet relaxed body postures, warm and friendly facial expressions, supportive voice tones, and soothing rhythm breathing, designed to activate the parasympathetic nervous system, down-regulate threat and drive systems, develop the soothing-affiliative system, and create a sense of calmness, groundedness, and stability.

CLINICAL VIGNETTE, CONTINUED

Using Imagery and Embodiment to Address Grief and Shame with Compassion

Talia was invited to imagine her compassionate self, connecting with compassionate wisdom, strength, and a caring-commitment, embodying this compassionate self, and begin to explore and understand the experience about which she felt ashamed.

Talia arrived at the following:

> *I was sitting at the dinner table, devastated and ashamed. I felt so sad for me in that moment. I could see and connect with my suffering. Those were such difficult times. I loved my Mum so much, and I desperately wanted to be there for her and care for her. I put a lot of pressure on myself, and I guess my brain just struggled under the weight of it all. It was so wrong what I did. Even my compassionate self knows that. And, at the same time, I get it. Thank goodness I didn't hurt her physically. But I was mean and said terrible things, and for that I am very sorry. I want to make amends, do something in her name, honor her memory, and maybe help others. I can do that now, get back into the world, but I understand how difficult life can be for us all.*

COMPASSION-FOCUSED IMAGERY

Once skills to create physical and mental calmness, groundedness, and stability have been learned and practiced, CFT incorporates imagery to develop safeness and compassion. Compassion-focused imagery involves visualizing compassionate qualities and experiences across the three flows of compassion, and cultivating a compassionate motivation (Gilbert, 2010; Naismith et al., 2019). Such imagery is thought to activate the soothing-affiliative system via the parasympathetic nervous system, as evidenced by increased heart rate variability and reduced cortisol levels (Rockliff et al., 2008) and has been found to increase self-compassion in both clinical and non-clinical populations (Matos et al., 2017b; McEwan & Gilbert, 2015; Naismith et al., 2019), reducing negative emotions, increasing self-esteem, and leading to physiological changes associated with threat system down-regulation (Rockliff et al., 2008).

Compassion-focused imagery may be used to cultivate a connection with the shamed self or the grieving self. A study on depression vulnerability in acne sufferers found CMT imagery components reduced body-shame (Kelly et al., 2009). By visualizing these difficult parts of the self, we can then work with those parts with the compassionate self, offering them validation, reassurance, and encouragement. In this phase of CFT, there is an emphasis on the importance of the therapeutic relationship, the sense of safeness and security the person feels with the clinician, as well as the practiced competency and confidence the person has with activating the soothing-affiliative system and the compassionate self. Therefore, timing and pacing are important considerations; however, when the conditions are right or the person feels ready, it can be equally important to approach these most difficult parts of the self, rather than delay or avoid, given the intention to soothe and soften the shame and grief.

Finally, compassion-focused imagery can be used to approach the shamed self or grieving self with compassion. When the person has a clear sense of their compassionate self and has begun to explore the shamed or grieving self through imagery, then we can bring these together, imagining the compassionate self offering kindness, wisdom, strength, courage, and committed helpful action to the parts of ourselves that feel ashamed or in grief.

EMBODIMENT TECHNIQUES

Following compassion-focused imagery, CFT begins a process of behaving from the compassionate self-identity and embodying the compassionate self in daily life. For example, when faced with a difficult situation, being able to use the body-based practices to slow the body and the mind, the compassion-focused imagery practices to connect with the compassionate self, and then asking oneself, "Given all of this, what could I feel, think, or do now to be helpful to myself and others? How might I embody my compassionate self?"

In CFT, the degree to which one embodies the compassionate self-identity in daily life (i.e., ability to think, feel, and act as one's compassionate self) has been found to be an important aspect of the process of change, helping to foster compassion across the three flows, as well as to promote feelings of safeness, contentment, and calmness (Matos et al., 2018). Embodying the compassionate self prepares us for facing life's difficulties when they inevitably arise, including feelings of grief and shame, anxiety, anger, and sadness.

CLINICAL GUIDELINES

When using CFT with people experiencing grief, especially when shame is present, we recommend the following:

1. *Provide psychoeducation on the evolved nature of the human brain.*
   Psychoeducation provides the groundwork for de-blaming and de-shaming. Include aspects of the evolved human brain, brain functioning, emotion regulation systems, the role of life experiences, and the nature of suffering.
2. *Introduce the key concept of compassion.*
   Introduce the concept of compassion and use guided discovery to help the person discover what compassion means to them. Incorporate key elements of the CFT definition, such as wisdom, strength, and caring-commitment. Introduce the three flows of compassion (i.e., compassion for others, compassion from others, and self-compassion). Explore and validate fears, blocks, and resistances to compassion across the three flows should they arise.
3. *Develop the compassionate self via CMT.*
   Body-based practices, imagery-based practices, and behavioral and embodiment exercises are all aspects of CMT. Fears, blocks, and resistances can arise throughout each stage of CMT, and people may find certain skills more difficult than others, for

example, difficulties closing their eyes, focusing on their breath, creating an image in their mind, or moving about physically during embodiment exercises.

4. *Provide psychoeducation regarding shame and shame memories.*
   Introduce the evolutionary bio-psychosocial model of shame. Discuss the universal and ubiquitous nature of shame, the evolved nature of shame, and its adaptive function.

5. *Explore shame and shame memories associated with grief.*
   Shame is very painful, and shame memories can involve trauma-like symptoms. This can be difficult to approach and sometimes avoided by both client and therapist. In CFT, we approach the shame and shame memories gradually and carefully; the therapeutic relationship and a context of safeness are vital. We recommend graduated exposure, coupled with warmth, safeness, non-judgment, and compassion. Use imagery-based practices and embodiment exercises to explore and understand the experience of shame as it arises in the grieving process.

6. *Use the compassionate self to approach the grieving self and/or the shamed self.*
   Using imagery-based practices, behavioral and acting exercises, and chair work, the compassionate self can interact with the shamed self. A number of key questions can be used to explore how the compassionate self might be helpful to the shamed self:
   - What hopes, aspirations, and wishes does the compassionate self have?
   - What does the compassionate self see and understand in, around, and behind the grief or shame?
   - How might the compassionate self empathize and sympathize with the grieving or shamed self?
   - How might the compassionate self offer validation, reassurance, and encouragement to the grieving or shamed self?
   - How might the compassionate self create a shift from shame to guilt and then move toward reparation and forgiveness?
   - What might the compassionate self say or do to bring compassion to the part that is suffering?

7. *Embody the compassionate self to allow grieving.*
   Having worked with shame and shame memories, embody the compassionate self and bring compassion to the grief and sadness that is experienced, as well as other emotions experienced as a part of grief, providing comfort and consoling, and gradually allowing the grief to move through and resolve.

8. *The ongoing importance of inquiry and reflection.*
   Throughout CFT psychoeducation, skills building, body-based practices, imagery, and embodiment, returning to inquiry and reflection is most important. Use guided discovery, inviting the person to reflect on and explore their experiences at each step:
   - What was that experience like, imagining or embodying the compassionate self?
   - What did you notice, good bits or not so good bits?
   - What does this leave you feeling now?
   - What was it like for you to imagine your grief or shame experience?
   - In terms of your shame memory or memories associated with your grieving, how are you feeling now?
   - In terms of your goals and aspirations, how are you feeling now?
   - What would you like to remember, think about, or put into practice in your daily life?

CONCLUSION

Grief is a painful and difficult process, especially when it becomes complicated with shame or shame memories. CFT offers psychoeducation and skills training that can be brought to these difficult emotional experiences to work with the grief and shame. Understanding the evolved nature of the human mind, as well as the nature and source of our suffering, can begin the process of alleviating grief and de-shaming. Body-based practices help to down-regulate threat system activation and develop the soothing-affiliative system to create a sense of calm and safeness. Imagery techniques help us connect with, and understand, the grieving or shamed selves, and help us develop the compassionate self and bring compassion to those other selves. Embodiment techniques assist with implementing compassion in daily life. A number of considerations are important in terms of managing the therapeutic processes when working with grief and shame.

NOTE

1 This fictitious case represents individuals experiencing grief after the death of a family member and the complications associated with shame. See Chapter 15 of this volume for more details.

REFERENCES

Blackie, R. A., & Kocovski, N. L. (2019). Trait self-compassion as a buffer against post-event processing following performance feedback. *Mindfulness, 10*(5), 923–932.

Bussolari, C., Habarth, J. M., Phillips, S., Katz, R., & Packman, W. (2021). Self-compassion, social constraints, and psychosocial outcomes in a pet bereavement sample. *OMEGA: Journal of Death and Dying, 82*(3), 389–408.

Craig, C., Hiskey, S., & Spector, A. (2020). Compassion focused therapy: A systematic review of its effectiveness and acceptability in clinical populations. *Expert Review of Neurotherapeutics, 20*(4), 385–400. https://doi.org/10.1080/14737175.2020.1746184

Di Bello, M., Carnevali, L., Petrocchi, N., Thayer, J. F., Gilbert, P., & Ottaviani, C. (2020). The compassionate vagus: A meta-analysis on the connection between compassion and heart rate variability. *Neuroscience and Biobehavioral Reviews, 116*, 21–30. https://doi.org/10.1016/j.neubiorev.2020.06.016

Dunbar, R. I. M. (2017). *Human evolution: A pelican introduction.* Penguin UK.

Ferreira, C., Matos, M., Pinto-Gouveia, J., & Duarte, C. (2014). Shame memories and eating psychopathology: The buffering effect of self-compassion. *European Eating Disorders Review, 22*(6), 487–494. https://doi.org/10.1002/erv.2322

Gilbert, P. (2009). *The compassionate mind: A new approach to the challenge of life.* Constable & Robinson.

Gilbert, P. (2010). *Compassion focused therapy: Distinctive features.* Routledge.

Gilbert, P. (2014). The origins and nature of compassion focused therapy. *British Journal of Clinical Psychology, 53*(1), 6–41.

Gilbert, P. (2017). Compassion as a social mentality. In P. Gilbert (Ed.), *Compassion: Concepts, research and applications* (pp. 31–68). Routledge.

Gilbert, P. (2019). Explorations into the nature and function of compassion. *Current Opinion in Psychology, 28*, 108–114.

Gilbert, P. (2020). Compassion: From its evolution to a psychotherapy. *Frontiers in Psychology, 11*, 3123.

Gilbert, P., Catarino, F., Duarte, C., Matos, M., Kolts, R., Stubbs, J., Ceresatto, L., Duarte, J., Pinto-Gouveia, J., & Basran, J. (2017). The development of compassionate engagement and action scales for self and others. *Journal of Compassionate Health Care, 4*(1), 4. https://doi.org/10.1186/s40639-017-0033-3

Gilbert, P., & Choden. (2013). *Mindful compassion.* Constable & Robinson.

Gilbert, P., & Irons, C. (2005). Focused therapies and compassionate mind training for shame and self-attacking. In P. Gilbert (Ed.), *Compassion: Conceptualisations, research and use in psychotherapy* (pp. 263–325). Routledge.

Gilbert, P., & Procter, S. (2006). Compassionate mind training for people with high shame and self-criticism: Overview and pilot study of a group therapy approach. *Clinical Psychology and Psychotherapy, 13*(6), 351–379. https://doi.org/10.1002/cpp.507

Hermanto, N., Zuroff, D. C., Kopala-Sibley, D. C., Kelly, A. C., Matos, M., Gilbert, P., & Koestner, R. (2016). Ability to receive compassion from others buffers the depressogenic effect of self-criticism: A cross-cultural multi-study analysis. *Personality and Individual Differences, 98*, 324–332. https://doi.org/10.1016/j.paid.2016.04.055

Irons, C., & Heriot-Maitland, C. (2020). Compassionate mind training: An 8-week group for the general public. *Psychology and Psychotherapy: Theory, Research and Practice.* Advance online publication. https://doi.org/10.1111/papt.12320

Kelly, A. C., Zuroff, D. C., & Shapira, L. B. (2009). Soothing oneself and resisting self-attacks: The treatment of two intrapersonal deficits in depression vulnerability. *Cognitive Therapy and Research, 33*(3), 301–313. https://doi.org/10.1007/s10608-008-9202-1

Kirby, J. N., Tellegen, C. L., & Steindl, S. R. (2017). A meta-analysis of compassion-based interventions: Current state of knowledge and future directions. *Behavior Therapy, 48*(6), 778–792. https://doi.org/10.1016/j.beth.2017.06.003

Leaviss, J., & Uttley, L. (2014). Psychotherapeutic benefits of compassion focused therapy: An early systematic review. *Psychological Medicine, 45*(5), 927–945. https://doi.org/10.1017/S0033291714002141

Lenferink, L. I., Eisma, M. C., de Keijser, J., & Boelen, P. A. (2017). Grief rumination mediates the association between self-compassion and psychopathology in relatives of missing persons. *European Journal of Psychotraumatology, 8*(Suppl 6), 1378052.

Lopez, A., Sanderman, R., Ranchor, A. V., & Schroevers, M. J. (2018). Compassion for others and self-compassion: Levels, correlates, and relationship with psychological well-being. *Mindfulness, 9*(1), 325–331. https://doi.org/10.1007/s12671-017-0777-z

Matos, M., Carvalho, S., Cunha, M., Galhardo, A., & Sepodes, C. (2017a). Psychological flexibility and self-compassion in gay and heterosexual men: How they relate to childhood memories, shame and depressive symptoms. *Journal of LGBT Issues in Counseling, 11*(2), 88–105. http://doi.org/10.1080/15538605.2017.1310007

Matos, M., Duarte, C., Duarte, J., Pinto-Gouveia, J., Petrocchi, N., Basran, J., & Gilbert, P. (2017b). Psychological and physiological effects of compassionate mind training: A pilot randomized controlled study. *Mindfulness, 8*(6), 1699–1712. https://doi.org/10.1007/s12671-017-0745-7

Matos, M., Duarte, J., Duarte, C., Gilbert, P., & Pinto-Gouveia, J. (2018). How one experiences and embodies compassionate mind training influences its effectiveness. *Mindfulness, 9*(4), 1224–1235. https://doi.org/10.1007/s12671-017-0864-1

Matos, M., Steindl, S., Gilbert, P., & Pinto-Gouveia, J. (2020). Shame memories that shape who we are. In P. Gilbert & J. Kirby (Eds.), *Making an impact on mental health: The applications of psychological research* (pp. 97–126). Routledge.

McEwan, K., & Gilbert, P. (2015). A pilot feasibility study exploring the practising of compassionate imagery exercises in a nonclinical population. *Psychology and Psychotherapy: Theory, Research and Practice, 89*(2), 239–243. https://doi.org/10.1111/papt.12078

Naismith, I., Duran Ferro, C., Ingram, G., & Jimenez Leal, W. (2019). Compassion-focused imagery reduces shame and is moderated by shame, self-reassurance and multisensory imagery vividness. *Research in Psychotherapy: Psychopathology, Process and Outcome, 22*(1). https://doi.org/10.4081/ripppo.2019.329

Naismith, I., Mwale, A., & Feigenbaum, J. (2019). Inhibitors and facilitators of compassion-focused imagery in personality disorder. *Clinical Psychology and Psychotherapy, 25*(2), 283–291. https://doi.org/10.1002/cpp.2161

Oliveira, S., Trindade, I. A., & Ferreira, C. (2018). The buffer effect of body compassion on the association between shame and body and eating difficulties. *Appetite, 125,* 118–123. https://doi.org/10.1016/j.appet.2018.01.031

Porges, S. W. (2017). Vagal pathways: Portals to compassion. In E. M. Seppälä, E. Simon-Thomas, S. L. Brown, M. C. Worline, C. D. Cameron, & J. R. Doty (Eds.), *The Oxford handbook of compassion science* (pp. 189–202). Oxford University Press.

Rockliff, H., Gilbert, P., McEwan, K., Lightman, S., & Glover, D. (2008). A pilot exploration of heart rate variability and salivary cortisol responses to compassion-focused imagery. *Clinical Neuropsychiatry: Journal of Treatment Evaluation, 5*(3), 132–139.

Steindl, S., Matos, M., & Creed, A. (2018). Early shame and safeness memories, and later depressive symptoms and safe affect: The mediating role of self-compassion. *Current Psychology.* Advance online publication. https://doi.org/10.1007/s12144-018-9990-8

Vara, H., & Thimm, J. C. (2019). Associations between self compassion and complicated grief symptoms in bereaved individuals: An exploratory study. *Nordic Psychology.* https://doi.org/10.1080/19012276.2019.1684347

CHAPTER 22

COMPASSION-FOCUSED CHAIR WORK FOR GRIEF

Tobyn Bell and Matthew Pugh

INTRODUCTION

Chair work encapsulates a collection of experiential methods that utilize chairs, positioning, and movement for therapeutic purposes (Pugh et al., 2020). Originating from psychodrama (Moreno, 1948) and further developed in gestalt therapy (Perls, 1973) and emotion-focused therapy (Greenberg et al., 1993), these methods span over 100 years of therapeutic application and innovation. Today, chair work forms an integral part of numerous modalities, not least Compassion-Focused Therapy (CFT) (Gilbert, 2010).

Chair work has long been used to address grief through imaginal interactions with absent, internalized others. Empty-chair dialogues are perhaps the most well-known method for resolving loss and 'unfinished business' (Greenberg et al., 1993). This iconic intervention typically proceeds through a series of stages: The absent other is imaginatively placed in an empty chair, thoughts and feelings toward the other are expressed (e.g., sadness, anger, fear, and appreciation), and primary affects and associated needs are clarified and articulated. Resolution of unfinished business usually takes the form of understanding, forgiving, or holding the other accountable, in addition to affirming one's own needs. Unfinished business may also include role-reversal, whereby the client switches chairs and speaks from the perspective of the other so that a dialogue between both positions is made possible.

A particularly affecting example of unfinished business comes from Fritz Perls' work with a woman experiencing prolonged grief following the loss of her baby during surgery (Stevens, 1970, cited in Kellogg, 2015). This enactment involved the woman speaking to her child, held in the empty chair, and then responding as her preverbal infant. Through dialogue and role-reversal, the mother acquired new perspectives on the decision to operate and was able to say goodbye to her daughter. Capturing the ethos of chair work, Perls (1973) remarked, "It is insufficient to recall a past incident, one has to psychodramatically return to it" (p. 65). For Perls, this "return" required the client to "go to the death bed and face the departure" (1973, p. 65).

As illustrated in this example, the experiential nature of chair work differentiates these interventions from discussion-focused or pen-and-paper methods. Moreover, studies suggest that, when addressing the same material, chair work appears to be advantageous compared to written tasks such as thought diaries (de Oliveira et al., 2012). The effectiveness of chair work has been attributed to various change processes (Pugh, 2017, 2019a). These include emotional evocation and the transformation of pathological affect via adaptive emotion (Greenberg et al., 1993), and the role of enactment and embodiment in generating changes in meaning at both the propositional level ('head-level' belief change) and deeper implicational level ('heart-level' belief change; Teasdale, 1997).

Other practitioners have emphasized the role of dialogue in chair work (Stone & Stone, 1993). By enabling here-and-now interactions between parts of the self (including internalized others), these relationships are concretized, clarified, and made open to change. During chair work, there is an invitation to speak *to* and *respond as* problematic parts of the self, rather than talking *about* a problem in an intellectualized or abstract manner.

DOI: 10.4324/9781003204121-26

Consequently, clients relate to parts of the self in novel ways, recruiting social-relational skills that would usually be applied in external relationships, which has been shown to enhance self-compassion and empathy (Bell et al., 2020a).

A final mechanism of action associated with chair work is decentering: Clients can immerse themselves in roles by moving into a particular chair ('stepping in') and distance themselves by moving back out ('stepping back'). In doing so, an 'observing' perspective is established, helping to enhance clients' ability to self-distance, reflect, reason, and regulate affect (Kross & Ayduk, 2017).

PRINCIPLES AND PROCESSES

Given that chair work is used by multiple modalities and for a myriad of therapeutic purposes, this method might initially appear bewildering. Adopting a process-based approach to chair work, Pugh and Bell (2020) have sought to clarify the unifying principles and processes that underpin these methods (see Table 22.1).

The first principle of chair work relates to *self-multiplicity*: That the mind contains multiple agentic 'parts,' 'modes,' 'subpersonalities,' 'mentalities,' or 'I-positions.' Conceptualizations of the self as multi-minded are common in psychotherapy and broader scientific literature (Hermans, 2001). Certain parts of the self may also represent internalized or introjected 'others,' such as the voice of a deceased parent. Accordingly, the first process of chair work is to determine which parts will form the focus of the exercise before *separating* them into different chairs. Separating parts provides multiple benefits, such as dis-identifying from dominant I-positions (e.g., the angry self) and creating space for the emergence of avoided or painful I-positions (e.g., the anxious or vulnerable self). Chairs containing parts of the self can also be occupied and vacated, thereby increasing clients' sense of agency over their activation. Furthermore, chairs can be rearranged in the room to depict old and new configurations of the self.

The second principle of chair work is that parts of the self are capable of communicating information in the form of dialogical interactions. However, *information exchange* between parts can become problematically restricted, stereotyped, or disordered, leading to the emergence of 'dialogical dysfunctions' within the self (Hermans & Dimaggio, 2004; Pugh & Bell, 2020). For example, conflictual inner dialogues may emerge during grief, wherein one part desires one thing ("I want to stay connected with the deceased") and another does not ("I want to move on"). Alternatively, inner dialogues might be disrupted by parts that block or silence others ("I can't bear to think about the deceased"). Information exchange is facilitated during chair work by *animating* parts of the self through either personification or embodiment. Essentially, personification involves the client imagining that parts of the self are held in the opposite chair, while embodiment involves the client changing seats and 'becoming' the part. Embodiment is preferred in chair work as immersion in the subjective

Table 22.1 Principles and Process of Chair Work

Principles (SIT)	Processes (SAT)
Self-multiplicity	Separation
Information exchange	Animation
Transformation	Talk

'reality' of I-positions can provide new perspectives, 'action insights,' and body-based communication and feedback (Whelton & Greenberg, 2005).

The final principle of chair work is that *transformation* of the dialogical mind can be achieved through new ways of *talking* and relating between parts of the self. Modalities differ in terms of the type of transformation they prioritize. These transformations might include cultivating new, adaptive parts, strengthening existing parts, or reconciling conflicted parts (Pugh & Bell, 2020). Far from homogenizing the self, chair work aims to balance and integrate these disparate aspects of the mind. When addressing grief, dialogues often involve polarities of experience, such as between the past and future self, the self and the other, and conflicted parts entrenched in rank-based relating. Chair work for grief involves validation and expression of the self in all its dynamic complexity, allowing for the renegotiation of both internal and external relating.

Compassion-Focused Therapy (CFT) has been introduced in earlier chapters of this book and is used here as the framework for applying compassion. CFT chair work is distinctive in focusing on "the compassionate chair, and building up the feelings, tolerance, insights and strengths of this part of the self" (Gilbert, 2010, p. 167). When in the compassionate chair, the client might embody their 'compassionate self': A version of themselves that encapsulates and enacts the qualities and attributes of compassion. Alternatively, the client might adopt the role of an ideal compassionate 'other' that personifies compassion. These embodiments are used to engage with other parts of the self (e.g., the 'grieving self') via chair work. Through role-reversal, chair work offers a uniquely powerful medium for both giving and receiving compassion within the same exercise. This allows for the potentiation and practice of the various flows of compassion targeted in CFT: Compassion from self-to-self, self-to-others, and others to self (Gilbert, 2010).

We will now explore how the principles and processes outlined so far can be applied in compassion-focused chair work for grief, with an emphasis on bereavement.

EXAMPLES OF COMPASSION-FOCUSED CHAIR WORK PROCEDURES

TWO-CHAIR PROCEDURES: SELF-OTHER DIALOGUES

Influenced by dialogical self-theory (Hermans, 2001) and emotion-focused therapy (Greenberg et al., 1993), Neimeyer (2012) has extended empty-chair dialogues for bereavement by emphasizing the need "to renegotiate the relationship as a living resource" (Neimeyer, 2012, p. 266). As with many other forms of empty chair work, the relationship with the bereaved is recreated to affirm the ongoing bond or address difficulties in the relationship (i.e., modifying the bond). This is achieved by direct, first-person expressions of feelings and associated needs toward the deceased, held in the opposite chair. Meanwhile, the therapist choreographs role-reversals at opportune moments, such as "when the client has voiced something poignant that calls for the response of the other – much … [like] a family therapy session" (Neimeyer, 2012, p. 268). Honesty and complete expression are emphasized during these encounters. Notably, Neimeyer recommends that a third 'witness' chair is incorporated into these dialogues: A 'meta-position' for processing the material and reflecting on the self, other, and their relationship from a third-person perspective, thereby harnessing the benefits of self-distancing (e.g., the regulation of intense affect; Kross & Ayduk, 2017).

A compassion-focused variation of empty-chair work for resolving grief has been outlined by Bell (2019). Similar to the procedure above, this iteration utilizes a third chair for the inclusion of the compassionate self. During CFT chair work, embodiment of the compassionate self is supported through body-based practices (e.g., soothing-rhythm breathing) and compassion-focused visualizations. As identified in previous CFT chair work literature (Bell et al., 2021), the compassionate self/chair is used to reflect on internal and external relationships with greater empathy and mentalization. The compassionate self is also used to support and validate the client while dialoguing with the deceased. This often involves identifying, understanding, accepting, and symbolizing experiences that are unacceptable or blocked by self-criticism. Consequently, clients are able to dialogue with the other more expressively. In addition, clients may choose to address the deceased from the compassionate self (e.g., speaking *for* aspects of self that feel too hurt or vulnerable to be present) in order to establish healthy, assertive boundaries with the other and their continued influence.

While empty chair work often focuses on resolving conflictual feelings underlying unfinished business, new 'positive' emotions and ways of relating might also arise. For example, Darrow and Childs (2020) suggest that role-reversal during empty-chair work often involves accessing the 'compassionate aspect' of the deceased and acknowledging loving and caring parts of the person and associated memories that exist alongside complex feelings and unresolved issues. By accessing compassionate and wise aspects of the deceased, "transformation in the painful narrative and feelings" is achieved (Darrow & Childs, 2020, p. 13). Gratitude-based chair work (Tomasulo, 2019) is another form of empty-chair work that can be incorporated into work with the bereaved. This involves the client expressing appreciation to the deceased, role-reversing, and responding as the gratitude is received. This process can also be reversed once more, with the deceased reciprocating gratitude. When re-negotiating bonds with the deceased, the bereaved may choose to privilege these positive exchanges and qualities as an ongoing resource. Often, expressions of gratitude will also stimulate other emotions such as sadness (Tomasulo, 2019), which support the grieving process.

TWO-CHAIR PROCEDURES: SELF-SELF DIALOGUES

Two-chair dialogues are also used to cultivate self-directed compassion. The compassionate self (chair one) relates to aspects of the grieving self (chair two) that require care and nurturance. As well as providing supportive responses to feelings such as loneliness, the compassionate self also provides a medium for accessing, amplifying, and containing experiences of rage and resentment.

The compassionate self has been conceptualized as an internal 'secure base' or 'safe haven' from which the client can engage with threat-based experiences (Gilbert, 2020). In chair work for grief, this allows the client to move between the compassionate chair and grieving chair so that emotional processing is paced, and the pain of grieving is modulated and tolerated. The compassionate self also supports the client in engaging with experiences and activities not associated with acute stages of grief. For example, this might involve dialoguing with the guilt that accompanies forming new attachments or enjoying the distraction of hobbies. Prompts that support compassionate relating from the compassionate self/chair are outlined in Table 22.2. From clinical experience, it is helpful to begin by naming and observing the suffering held in the opposite chair. This initial step supports the process of separation whilst also "warming up" the client for increased levels of affiliation and care, which may, in turn, activate fears, blocks, and resistance (FBRs) to compassion (Gilbert, 2010).

Table 22.2 Prompts for Compassion-Focused Chair Work

- Witness/acknowledge (sensitivity to suffering, non-judgment)
  "I can see that you are feeling/thinking…"
- Understand/empathize
  "It makes sense you feel this way because…"
- Clarify motivation
  "What I want for you is…"
- Clarify feeling(s) toward the self
  "I feel… to see you having difficulty…"
- Clarify (unmet) needs
  "Given that you are feeling… what you need is…"
- Key message to the self
  "I want you to know that you can/are…"
- Redirecting and broadening attention, or highlighting memory
  "It might be helpful to remember…"; "It might be helpful to focus on…"
- Predict, understand, and plan for blocks to compassion
  "Hearing this, I imagine you are feeling… But this is understandable, because…"
- Compassionate behavioral responses
  "It might be helpful to try…"

Source: Bell & Pugh, 2020.

FBRs to compassion include cognitions ("I'm undeserving of care") and emotional reactions ("the sadness will be too overwhelming"). Indeed, FBRs are often central to the therapeutic process and stem from the client's early attachments and history of care (Gilbert, 2020). In chair work, specific FBRs to compassion can be personified or embodied in a chair and engaged with directly. For example, the compassionate self might be accessed to dialogue with parts of the self that compulsively attend to others, minimize the need for self-care, or prompt dissociation. Compassion-focused dialogues are then used to understand the origins, adaptive functions, and unmet needs associated with the FBRs. Similarly, the compassionate self can be used to address self-criticism and self-blame that complicate grief. In CFT, a dialogue between the critical self (chair one) and criticized self (chair two) is facilitated first, following which the compassionate self (chair three) is used to address both sides of the dialogue. Typically, the compassionate self is also used to understand the fears and defensive functions of the critic (see Bell et al., 2020b).

The processes described above can also be facilitated through use of a compassionate 'other' during chair work. Rather than embodying the compassionate self, the client changes seats and enacts a compassionate being created in imagination or inspired by individuals in their life. Indeed, some clients find that generating and receiving compassion via 'another's mind' helps side-step entrenched FBRs to self-compassion.

INTERVIEW PROCEDURES

Many two-chair methods can be applied in the form of 'interview' procedures. Rather than facilitating a dialogue between parts of the self, interviews involve the therapist questioning the client as a part or another person (Stone & Stone, 1989). In grief-focused chair work, this might include interviewing the client as the deceased (Moules, 2010). Helpful lines of questioning include how the deceased feels toward the client and their grief, how they would like to be remembered, and how they understand ruptures or difficulties that existed in the relationship. The deceased can also be asked for their wisdom and support to aid grieving. Interviews with the deceased often generate new insights regarding the deceased's actions and attitudes, as well as compassionate reflections on the continued bond between the client and the other.

Interviews can also be conducted with particular aspects of loss (e.g., 'the abandoned part'), parts that generate distress (e.g., the 'inner critic'), or blocks to grieving (e.g., the 'emotional wall'). These procedures support compassionate relating in two ways. First, research suggests that interviews stimulate compassion for parts of the self, including those that cause distress (Ling et al., 2022). Second, the therapist models compassionate relating to aspects of the self that might otherwise be denied or avoided. During interviews, the therapist's stance is one of curiosity and validation, helping to reveal parts' origins, concerns, and motivations. For example, a client's "emotional wall" might reveal its intention to protect the client from past neglect or future losses. Alternatively, interviews might address the client's 'future self' to explore how grief can be integrated into their broader life experiences, continued growth, and the pursuit of values-consistent aspirations.

MULTIPLE-CHAIR PROCEDURES: 'MULTIPLE SELVES'

CFT also incorporates a multi-chair procedure known as "multiple selves" (Gilbert, 2010). The multiple selves exercise explores emotional complexity and conflict within the threat system by locating threat emotions in different chairs and then inviting the client to embody each emotional self. Typically, this will involve processing a situation or stimulus from the perspective of the 'angry self,' 'sad self,' and 'anxious self.' In doing so, the action-impulses, perspectives, and subjective realities of each emotional self are differentiated, and their conflicts and interactions are explored. Finally, the compassionate self is accessed in a new chair to understand, regulate, and integrate the various strands of internal experience and address the external situation.

Research indicates that individuals who participate in multiple selves are better able to differentiate 'negative' emotions (Bell et al., 2021), a capacity which is linked to increased well-being, improved emotional regulation, and reduced sensitivity to rejection (Kashdan et al., 2015). Moreover, the multiple selves method enables clients to explore avoided emotions (by giving each emotion a specific chair), build competency and agency when dealing with strong affect (by vacating and returning to specific chairs), and—through use of the compassionate chair—establish a sense of inner coherence and organization (Bell et al., 2021). These factors can be helpful in grief, where emotions can be complex, dysregulated, or avoided (Eisma & Stroebe, 2021). By exploring their varied emotional responses to loss, bereaved clients can explore and acknowledge a greater granularity of feeling, which, in turn, allows for a more attuned use of the compassionate self to address associated needs.

COMPASSION-FOCUSED PROCESS SKILLS

It is important to emphasize that the procedures described in this chapter should be delivered within a caring therapeutic relationship and supported by the use of process skills. Process skills refer to a variety of facilitative micro-interventions that ensure chair work is immersive and meaningful for clients. Many of these are inherited from psychodrama and gestalt therapy. Examples include roling and de-roling chairs, balancing separation and contact between parts of the self, privileging spontaneity and creativity over procedural steps, and the use of 'doubling' (Pugh, 2019b). Doubling or 'feeding a sentence' refers to instances where the therapist offers empathically attuned, first-person statements to the client to repeat aloud during chair work in order to clarify the implicational messages of each role. For example, if a client (chair one) were to state, "My mother should have taken better care of herself" in reference to the deceased (chair two), the therapist's tentative doubling statement might be, "I'm angry at you for giving up." Doubling statements build empathic connection while also extending and deepening the client's experiencing and understanding. In Moreno et al.'s (2000) words, doubling helps the client "bring height, depth, and width to their problem, over and beyond what they could do by themselves" (p. 90).

Imagery can also enhance contact with the other during chair work. For example, empty-chair dialogues usually begin with the client visualizing and describing how the other appears in the empty chair. Research suggests that picturing oneself in an empty chair also enhances clients' capacity for self-directed compassion, as the self is experienced as a separate 'other' with visible signs of distress (Bell et al., 2020a).

Depending on the modality in which chair work is used, the therapist might also become an active participant in the dialogue by offering their voice. In schema therapy, therapists are encouraged to speak directly to clients' 'modes' during chair work, offering reparative messages and limited reparenting. In compassion-focused chair work, the therapist is similarly active in expressing and modeling the compassionate relating the client may have missed in their own lives. Therapists' expressions of compassion are usually directed to the client's empty chair (with the client sitting alongside the therapist) so that both individuals are able to share the role and voice of compassion. Receiving care from a de-centered position such as this often circumvents blocks to compassion that arise during face-to-face conversations.

CONCLUSION

Chair work is an invitation to safely experience, rather than merely describe, the pain and complexity of grief. In doing so, opportunities for therapeutic self-expression, exploration, insight, and closure are created. CFT has expanded upon previous applications of chair work by emphasizing the importance of compassion when facilitating healing conversations with the self and the deceased. These are demanding conversations, however, both for the client and the therapist (Pugh et al., 2021). For this reason, a strong therapeutic alliance, alongside appropriate training and supervision, is critical when using these methods.

REFERENCES

Bell, T. (2019, February 27). *Compassion-focused therapy chairwork*. Workshop, Manchester, UK.
Bell, T., Montague, J., Elander, J., & Gilbert, P. (2020a). "A definite feel-it moment": Embodiment, externalisation and emotion during chair-work in compassion-focused therapy. *Counselling and Psychotherapy Research, 20*(1), 143–153.

Bell, T., Montague, J., Elander, J., & Gilbert, P. (2020b). "Suddenly you are King Solomon": Multiplicity, transformation and integration in compassion focused therapy chairwork. *Journal of Psychotherapy Integration, 31*(3), 223–237.

Bell, T., Montague, J., Elander, J., & Gilbert, P. (2021). Multiple emotions, multiple selves: Compassion focused therapy chairwork. *Cognitive Behaviour Therapist, 14*(22), 1–7.

Bell, T., & Pugh, M. (2020). *Facilitating compassion focused dialogues: Facilitation guidance.* www.chairwork.co.uk

Darrow, L., & Childs, J. (2020). *Experiential action methods and tools for healing grief and loss-related trauma: Life, death, and transformation.* Routledge.

Eisma, M., & Stroebe, M. (2021). Emotion regulatory strategies in complicated grief: A systematic review. *Behavior Therapy, 52*(1), 234–249.

Gilbert, P. (2010). *Compassion focused therapy: Distinctive features.* Routledge.

Gilbert, P. (2020). Compassion: From its evolution to a psychotherapy. *Frontiers in Psychology, 11*, 586161.

Greenberg, L., Rice, L., & Elliott, R. (1993). *Facilitating emotional change: The moment-by-moment process.* Guilford.

Hermans, H. J. M. (2001). The dialogical self: Toward a theory of personal and cultural positioning. *Culture and Psychology, 7*(3), 243–281.

Hermans, H. J. M., & Dimaggio, G. (2004). *The dialogical self in psychotherapy.* Routledge.

Kashdan, T., Barrett, L., & McKnight, P. (2015). Unpacking emotion differentiation: Transforming unpleasant experience by perceiving distinctions in negativity. *Current Directions in Psychological Science, 24*(1), 10–16.

Kellogg, S. (2015). *Transformational chairwork: Using psychotherapeutic dialogues in clinical practice.* Rowan and Littlefield.

Kross, E., & Ayduk, O. (2017). Social distancing: Theory, research, and current directions. *Advances in Experimental Social Psychology, 55*, 81–136.

Ling, N. C. Y., Serpell, L., Burnett-Stuart, S., & Pugh, M. (2022). Interviewing anorexia: How do individuals given a diagnosis of anorexia nervosa experience Voice Dialogue with their eating disorder voice? A qualitative analysis. *Clinical Psychology and Psychotherapy, 29*(2), 600–610.

Moreno, J. (1948). *Psychodrama* (Vol. 1). Beacon House.

Moreno, Z., Blomkvist, L., & Rutzel, T. (2000). *Psychodrama, surplus reality and the art of healing.* Routledge.

Moules, N. J. (2010). Internal connections and conversations: The internalized other interview in bereavement work. *OMEGA: Journal of Death and Dying, 62*(2), 187–199.

Neimeyer, R. (2012). Chair work. In R. Neimeyer (Ed.), *Techniques of grief therapy: Creative practices for counselling the bereaved* (pp. 266–273). Routledge.

de Oliveira, I. R., Powell, V. B., Wenzel, A., Caldas, M., Seixas, C., Almeida, C., Bonfim, T., Grangeon, M. C., Castro, M., Galvão, A., de Oliveira Moraes, R., & Sudak, D. (2012). Efficacy of the trial-based thought record, a new cognitive therapy strategy designed to change core beliefs, in social phobia. *Journal of Clinical Pharmacy and Therapeutics, 37*, 328–334.

Perls, F. (1973). *The Gestalt approach and eye-witness to therapy.* Science and Behavior Books.

Pugh, M. (2017). Chairwork in cognitive behavioural therapy: A narrative review. *Cognitive Therapy and Research, 41*(1), 16–30.

Pugh, M. (2019a). *Cognitive behavioural chairwork: Distinctive features.* Routledge.

Pugh, M. (2019b). A little less talk, a little more action: A dialogical approach to cognitive therapy. *Cognitive Behaviour Therapist, 12*, E47.

Pugh, M., & Bell, T. (2020). Process-based chairwork: Applications and innovations in the time of COVID-19. *European Journal of Counselling Theory, Research and Practice, 4*, 1–8.

Pugh, M., Bell, T., Waller, G., & Petrova, E. (2021). Attitudes and applications of chairwork amongst CBT therapists: A preliminary survey. *Cognitive Behaviour Therapist, 41,* E21.

Stevens, B. (1970). *Don't push the river.* Real People Press.

Stone, H., & Stone, S. (1993). *Embracing your inner critic: Turning self-criticism into a creative asset.* Harper Collins.

Teasdale, J. D. (1997). The relationship between cognition and emotion: The mind-in-place in mood disorders. In D. M. Clark & C. G. Fairburn (Eds.), *The science and practice of cognitive behaviour therapy* (pp. 67–93). Oxford University Press.

Tomasolu, D. J. (2019). The virtual gratitude visit (VGV): Using psychodrama and role-playing as a positive intervention. In L. E. van Zyl & S. Rothmann Sr. (Eds.), *Positive psychological intervention design and protocols for multi-cultural contexts* (pp. 405–413). Springer.

Whelton, W., & Greenberg, L. (2005). Emotion in self-criticism. *Personality and Individual Differences, 38*(7), 1583–1595.

PART FOUR

Organizational and Structural Approaches

CHAPTER 23

CHALLENGES TO COMPASSION IN HEALTHCARE

A Systems Approach

Alina Pavlova and Nathan S. Consedine

INTRODUCTION

While compassion is an evolved characteristic that is 'common' across carers and contexts, delivering medical care with compassion is not a given. Healthcare contexts might reasonably be considered "challenging" care situations that entail terminal diagnoses, delivering bad news, complex clinical cases with co-morbidities and medically unexplained symptoms, and interactions with patients at the height of emotions. However, even if we might agree that some situations are inherently difficult, it is unclear what about them specifically challenges compassion. Highlighting why compassion in medicine is of crucial importance, this chapter discusses why compassion in healthcare *is* "special" even though it is likely rooted in the same evolved caregiving systems. Critiquing compassion fatigue—a perspective that implies that compassion can (in itself) be challenging—we employ the Transactional Model of Physician Compassion (Fernando & Consedine, 2014a) to organize the factors thought to influence compassion in healthcare. Finally, we discuss the role of the *subjective* experience of these factors. We conclude more positively, arguing that while compassion in healthcare might be challenging, facilitators of compassion also exist; more research and systems-wide interventions can scaffold compassionate care.

IMPORTANCE OF COMPASSION IN HEALTHCARE

Compassion—or noticing the suffering of another and being motivated to alleviate it (Strauss et al., 2016)—is an integral component of healthcare mandated by ethical codes and considered a key clinician competency. Compassion is more than a "soft skill." For patients, the experience of compassion predicts greater treatment efficacy and outcomes (Lown et al., 2015). For physicians, practicing with compassion predicts greater job satisfaction (Sinclair et al., 2016) and lower burnout (Post et al., 2014). However, while benefits for compassion are in evidence, a periodic lack of compassion in healthcare is also consistently documented worldwide (Lown et al., 2011). Beyond patients' disappointment, a lack of compassion can also lead to damaging legal, economic, and public perceptions of healthcare organizations (Trzeciak et al., 2017). This begs the question: If compassionate care has benefits for patients, professionals, and organizations, what challenges compassionate care?

COMPASSION FATIGUE: A CRITICAL LENS

For several decades, the dominant framework for thinking about compassion in healthcare has been "compassion fatigue." Often used interchangeably with secondary traumatic

DOI: 10.4324/9781003204121-28

stress, compassion fatigue implies that there is a 'cost of caring' such that compassion is exhausted following use when confronted by repeated suffering (Sorenson et al., 2016). However, while difficult cases and repeated exposure to suffering may challenge compassion, being compassionate is unlikely to be the primary cause of compassion decline (Fernando & Consedine, 2014a). Logically, if deploying compassion led to the emptying of a 'care reservoir,' compassion fatigue should increase with experience; it does not (Shanafelt et al., 2009). Second, in healthcare, compassion predicts greater job satisfaction (Sinclair et al., 2016), a fact that is obscured in the compassion fatigue perspective. Finally, compassion fatigue has focused research on physician factors rather than the *systemic* problems confronting compassion in healthcare (Fernando et al., 2016), many of which are more intervention-accessible than attempting to change or re-train the workforce.

IS HEALTHCARE AN INHERENTLY CHALLENGING CONTEXT FOR COMPASSION?

Before considering what challenging situations affect compassion in healthcare per se, it is important to understand *why* we have compassion in the first place.

THE EVOLUTIONARY ORIGINS OF COMPASSION

There are three arguments important to understanding why compassion has evolved and thus the types of stimuli the system responds to. Perhaps the most central evolutionary explanation regards the origins of compassion in facilitating care for offspring; caring for children requires sensitivity to distress and the ability/motivation to alleviate it (Gilbert, 2019). Relatedly, compassion may partly have evolved in response to the pressures in adaptive contexts where scarcity of resources required cooperation (Gilbert, 2021). Finally, there might also be incentives for compassion if (future) reciprocity can be expected (Gilbert, 2009) and/or where compassion signals a caregiving ability to prospective mating partners (Regan et al., 2000).

However, while compassion likely evolved in the context of small and familiar groups and with the assumption of reciprocity and furthering one's (biological) success, medical compassion happens in very different environments. Compassion in healthcare is a *professional expectation* that is *remunerated, repeated,* has a distinct *carer to caree ratio,* and occurs in *particular settings.* Thus, even though the capacity for (and operations of) the compassion system are themselves innate, contextual differences are likely important to understanding why compassion in healthcare may be challenging.

COMPASSION IN HEALTHCARE: A CHALLENGING SITUATION?

First, compassion in healthcare is a *professional expectation.* Although the obligation to be compassionate is not uncommon—families and communities typically hold expectations in terms of support and caregiving—being told that you "must" be compassionate in a professional setting might interfere with care via psychological reactance where some would try to restore self-agency by purposefully not behaving in line with obligation (Bessarabova et al., 2013). While reactance to being compassionate seems unlikely in such a highly proso-cial sample (McManus et al., 2006), studies show that compassionate behavior is reduced following expectation (Batson et al., 1979). Empirically, the impact of professional obliga-tion on compassion in healthcare remains unknown.

Second, compassion in healthcare is *part of a remunerated role*. Although it is unknown whether remuneration influences compassion per se, the contingencies of professional remuneration and promotion may de-incentivize compassion. Unlike other elements of professional conduct, compassion is often seen as akin to a *feeling* and is not routinely assessed during performance reviews (Gilligan et al., 2019). Fast discharges, protocol and form completion, and reducing occupancy take priority (Pavlova et al., 2022). Thus, unlike everyday compassion that is recognized and celebrated, compassion in healthcare may be unacknowledged (Singh et al., 2018) or even seen as being unprofessional (Molinsky et al., 2012), a dynamic that contradicts its natural tendency to "work best [when people] feel [that they] can make a contribution that others value" (Gilbert, 2021).

Three, while we are desensitized to suffering in many modern contexts, suffering in medicine is a constant and requires *repeated* compassion. Although the compassion fatigue approach suggests that repeated care leads to fatigue, empirically, the effects of repeated caring remain unknown. On the one hand, practicing with compassion may lead to greater compassion (Bayne et al., 2013). Conversely, humans are "psychologically wired to help only one person at a time" (Cameron, 2017, p. 343) and "keeping tabs" on more than one patient might result in attention fragmentation and a reduction of care.

Four, while suffering in daily life might be assisted by multiple others, healthcare envi-ronments have a *lower carer to caree ratio*. Healthcare practitioners are individually *responsible* for a number of patients where others cannot "take over" (Brown & Brown, 2015) and must operate within cultures that can be competitive and isolating, being unable to share chal-lenging experiences or seek help because of fears of appearing incapable (Singh et al., 2018). Compassion may be impaired in the presence of capable others (Preston, 2013), a common scenario in healthcare. Again, perhaps because we have studied compassion as a value rather than a science, little is known regarding how such dynamics impact care.

Finally, compassion in healthcare occurs in *particular settings* where patients continu-ously arrive in busy waiting rooms with the expectation of care. Consults are frequently time-pressured, lack privacy, and may be interrupted by colleagues or medical emergen-cies. More broadly, while compassion likely evolved to facilitate inclusive fitness via care for kin and the in-group (Endicott et al., 2014), compassion in healthcare is intended for *strangers*. Although compassion toward strangers does happen, perhaps motivated by an altruistic "warm glow" (Ferguson et al., 2012) or even as a Pavlovian response to suffering (Gęsiarz & Crockett, 2015), the lower odds of future reciprocity may challenge compassion (Bereczkei et al., 2010).

THE TRANSACTIONAL MODEL OF PHYSICIAN COMPASSION: A SYSTEMS APPROACH

While differences between the settings in which compassion evolved and those in which it is currently needed are a useful starting point, it does not offer much in the way of interventional guidance. Hence, it is important to consider empirical work describing the factors that may interfere with (or facilitate) compassion. Below, empirical evidence regard-ing the factors that may make healthcare challenging for compassion is presented within the framework offered by the Transactional Model (Fernando & Consedine, 2014a), an approach that organizes the dynamic interplay of these influences as reflecting personal, patient and family, clinical, and organizational or environmental factors. The relevant citations provided in this section may be found in the recent large-scale systematic review by Pavlova (Pavlova et al., 2022), Wang (Wang et al., 2022) and colleagues.

First, *personal factors* may facilitate or hinder compassion in healthcare. For instance, one's spiritual beliefs (Anandarajah & Roseman, 2013) or generally believing that compassion is helpful (Chou et al., 2014) may make compassion feel worthwhile. Extending compassion toward strangers may also be facilitated by emotional intelligence (Kliszcz et al., 2006), prosocial traits (Picard et al., 2016), or having personally experienced illness or caregiving (Brady et al., 2015). Conversely, when practitioners are struggling with burnout or physical fatigue (Rawal et al., 2020) compassion is reduced. Thus, the extent to which compassion is rewarding or valued, combined with changes in compassion "capital" (in the sense of resources, experience, skills, and knowledge), may lower the "cost" of caring, creating contexts in which compassion is more likely.

Second, while research has tended to focus on factors within the carer, *patients' and families'* characteristics may be critical. Just as compassion is a natural response to suffering, fight-or-flight responses to threat—such as angry strangers—are also natural and may inhibit compassion (Gilbert, 2021). Consequently, compassion flows more easily toward patients and families who are thankful and cooperative (Batley et al., 2016) but not toward patients who are "different" (e.g., have a language barrier or a stigmatized illness; Bayne et al., 2013; Butalid et al., 2014). As such, while it seems likely that compassion is withdrawn when safety, reciprocity, or harmony are threatened or where judgments of deservingness are salient (Reynolds, et al., 2019), little is known empirically regarding the patient factors that predict a lack of compassion or how compassion for more challenging "others" might be enhanced.

Third, compassion can be interfered with (or facilitated) by aspects of the *clinical picture*. For example, while compassion is activated by suffering, many patients will present with illnesses (or suffering) that are difficult to diagnose or discern. Evidence suggests that non-acute patients report less compassion than patients requiring urgent care (Bishop et al., 2014); conditions in which the etiology or appropriate treatment is unclear and where suffering is less obvious (e.g., somatic symptoms disorders or patients at the end of life) may also challenge care (Batley et al., 2016; Bishop et al., 2014; Bessen et al., 2019).

Finally, while compassion in care is mandated, it is only intermittently celebrated or recognized. Healthcare cultures of business and efficiency (Kerasidou & Kingori, 2019), with pronounced hierarchy and bureaucracy (Ahrweiler et al., 2014), represent *organizational-level* factors that are at odds with compassionate care. Similarly, stressful clinical environments characterized by high demand and frequent interruptions (Derksen et al., 2015) are likely to challenge care. Conversely, when organizations take steps to establish environments more consonant with care—where compassion is recognized (Gilligan et al., 2019) and is evident in supportive collegial relationships (Charles et al., 2018) and the allocation of resources (Chou et al., 2014)—practitioners may be more likely to relate to patients with compassion.

Overall, in addition to noting that compassion evolved for use in different contexts, it is increasingly clear that compassion is also influenced by a variety of personal, patient, clinical, and environmental influences. However, while such influences might be described as objectively challenging, the *extent* to which they interfere with care is not (Fernando & Consedine, 2014b). Even the cases, environments, and presentations that most seriously challenge care for some clinicians can be experienced as less trying for others.

THE INHERENT SUBJECTIVITY OF THAT WHICH CHALLENGES CARE

The fundamental importance of *subjectivity* in identifying the factors that make care challenging is perhaps most clearly evidenced in the responses different professionals may have to particular patients. Empirically, we know that patient-practitioner similarity can either facilitate care (Kirmayer, 2008) or make interactions feel "too close to home," challenging compassion (Picard et al., 2016). Some practitioners struggle with complicated cases (Zandbelt et al., 2007), while others see them as an opportunity (Batley et al., 2016). End-of-life care can evoke deep compassion for some (Bayne et al., 2013) but overwhelm others (Bessen et al., 2019). Hence, with personal differences in history, disposition, aptitude, and skill, clinicians' reactions to the challenges of healthcare will vary more because of their subjective (rather than objective) importance.

In making this claim, we are not suggesting that there are no systemic challenges as there are many. However, individual variation in what is experienced as a challenge to care is important because the processes by which events are "translated" into subjective clinician responses need to be understood. For example, although challenges vary across providers, situations of conflict and diagnostic uncertainty can trigger anxiety, feelings of isolation, overidentification, activate self-doubt, self-criticism, or even hidden biases. Strong emotional responses can activate defensive responses such as detachment, avoidance, or objectification that likely interfere with compassion (Pavlova et al., 2022). Consequently, understanding the subjective response to challenges is a necessary starting point when seeking to characterize the variety and prevalence of the situations that challenge compassion in healthcare.

CONCLUDING REMARKS

Clinicians operate within *contexts* and in *interactions* that can make compassion in response to suffering more difficult, both objectively and subjectively; the evolutionary origins of compassion (and the way our evolved mechanisms are structured) are often pressured in modern healthcare environments. Yet, there is room for optimism, and many clinicians still practice with compassion, even under conditions that seriously challenge care. Instances in which compassion is experienced as reciprocal, appreciated, or creates group harmony may provide clues to the types of situations we should seek to create in the service of enhancing care. Similarly, personal techniques such as practicing compassion for oneself or setting compassionate intentions are promising (Baguley et al., 2020). Hence, although there can be no exhaustive list of challenging situations that affect compassion, each with an easy intervention to solve it, sustaining care in challenging situations is clearly possible. Our hope is that in providing the reader with recent knowledge and ideas about the factors likely to challenge and facilitate compassion in healthcare, we will spur additional research and that compassion in healthcare will be approached as a science in an evidence-based and systemic way.

REFERENCES

Ahrweiler, F., Neumann, M., Goldblatt, H., Hahn, E. G., & Scheffer, C. (2014). Determinants of physician empathy during medical education: Hypothetical conclusions from an exploratory qualitative survey of practicing physicians. *BMC Medical Education, 14*, 122.

Anandarajah, G., & Roseman, J. L. (2013). A qualitative study of physicians' views on compassionate patient care and spirituality: Medicine as a spiritual practice? *Rhode Island Medical Journal, 97*(3), 17–22.

Baguley, S. I., Dev, V., Fernando, A. T., & Consedine, N. S. (2020). How do health professionals maintain compassion over time? Insights from a study of compassion in health. *Frontiers in Psychology, 11*, 3327.

Batley, N. J., Nasreddine, Z., Chami, A., Zebian, D., Bachir, R., & Abbas, H. A. (2016). Cynicism and other attitudes towards patients in an emergency department in a middle eastern tertiary care center. *BMC Medical Education, 16*, 36.

Batson, C. D., Harris, A. C., McCaul, K. D., Davis, M., & Schmidt, T. (1979). Compassion or compliance: Alternative dispositional attributions for one's helping behavior. *Social Psychology Quarterly, 42*(4), 405–409.

Bayne, H., Neukrug, E., Hays, D., & Britton, B. (2013). A comprehensive model for optimizing empathy in person-centered care. *Patient Education and Counseling, 93*(2), 209–215.

Bereczkei, T., Birkas, B., & Kerekes, Z. (2010). Altruism towards strangers in need: Costly signaling in an industrial society. *Evolution and Human Behavior, 31*(2), 95–103.

Bessarabova, E., Fink, E. L., & Turner, M. (2013). Reactance, restoration, and cognitive structure: Comparative statics. *Human Communication Research, 39*(3), 339–364.

Bessen, S., Jain, R. H., Brooks, W. B., & Mishra, M. (2019). "Sharing in hopes and worries"-A qualitative analysis of the delivery of compassionate care in palliative care and oncology at end of life. *International Journal of Qualitative Studies on Health and Well-Being, 14*(1), 1622355.

Bishop, J.P., Perry, J.E., & Hine, A. (2014). Efficient, compassionate and fractured: Contemporary care in the ICU? *Hasting Centre Report, 44*, 35–43.

Brady, C., Bambury, R. M., & O'Reilly, S. (2015). Empathy and the wounded healer: A mixed-method study of patients and doctors views on empathy. *Irish Medical Journal, 108*(4), 125–126.

Brown, S. L., & Brown, R. M. (2015). Connecting prosocial behavior to improved physical health: Contributions from the neurobiology of parenting. *Neuroscience and Biobehavioral Reviews, 55*, 1–17.

Butalid, L., Bensing, J. M., & Verhaak, P. F. M. (2014). Talking about psychosocial problems: An observational study on changes in doctor-patient communication in general practice between 1977 and 2008. *Patient Education and Counseling, 94*(3), 314–321.

Cameron, C. D. (2017). Compassion collapse: Why we are numb to numbers. In E. M. Seppälä et al. (Eds.), *The Oxford handbook of compassion science* (pp. 261–271). Oxford University Press.

Charles, J.A., Ahnfeldt-Mollerup, P., Søndergaard, J., & Kristensen, T. (2018). Empathy variation in general practice: A survey among general practitioners in Denmark. *International Journal of Environmental Research and Public Health, 15*(3), 433. doi: 10.3390/ijerph15030433.

Chou, C. M., Kellom, K., & Shea, J. A. (2014). Attitudes and habits of highly humanistic physicians. *Academic Medicine, 89*(9), 1252–1258.

Derksen, F., Bensing, J., Kuiper, S., van Meerendonk, M., & Lagro-Janssen, A. (2015). Empathy: What does it mean for GPs? A qualitative study. *Family Practice, 32*(1), 94–100.

Endicott, K., Fry, D. P., & Söderberg, P. (2014). Myths about hunter-gatherers redux: Nomadic forager war and peace. *Journal of Aggression, Conflict and Peace Research, 6*(4), 256–266.

Ferguson, E., Taylor, M., Keatley, D., Flynn, N., & Lawrence, C. (2012). Blood donors' helping behavior is driven by warm glow: More evidence for the blood donor benevolence hypothesis. *Transfusion, 52*(10), 2189–2200.

Fernando, A. T., & Consedine, N. S. (2014a). Beyond compassion fatigue: The transactional model of physician compassion. *Journal of Pain and Symptom Management, 48*(2), 289–298.

Fernando, A. T., & Consedine, N. S. (2014b). Development and initial psychometric properties of the barriers to physician compassion questionnaire. *Postgraduate Medical Journal, 90*(1065), 388–395.

Fernando, A. T., & Consedine, N. S. (2016). Enhancing compassion in general practice: It's not all about the doctor. *British Journal of General Practice, 66*(648), 340–341.

Gęsiarz, F., & Crockett, M. J. (2015). Goal-directed, habitual and Pavlovian prosocial behavior. *Frontiers in Behavioral Neuroscience, 9*, 135.

Gilbert, P. (2009). *The compassionate mind.* Robinson.

Gilbert, P. (2019). Explorations into the nature and function of compassion. *Current Opinion in Psychology, 28*, 108–114.

Gilbert, P. (2021). Creating a compassionate world: Addressing the conflicts between sharing and caring versus controlling and holding evolved strategies. *Frontiers in Psychology, 11*, 3572.

Gilligan, M. C., Osterberg, L. G., Rider, E. A., Derse, A. R., Weil, A. B., Litzelman, D. K., Dunne, D. W., Hafler, J. P., Plews-Ogan, M., Frankel, R. M., & Branch, W. T. (2019). Views of institutional leaders on maintaining humanism in today's practice. *Patient Education and Counseling, 102*(10), 1911–1916.

Kerasidou, A., & Kingori, P. (2019). Austerity measures and the transforming role of A&E professionals in a weakening welfare system. *PLOS ONE, 14*(2), e0212314.

Kirmayer, L. J. (2008, December). Empathy and alterity in cultural psychiatry. *Ethos, 36*(4), 457–474.

Kliszcz, J., Nowicka-Sauer, K., Trzeciak, B., Nowak, P., & Sadowska, A. (2006). Empathy in health care providers-validation study of the Polish version of the Jefferson Scale of Empathy. *Advances in Medical Sciences, 51*, 219–225.

Lown, B. A., Muncer, S. J., & Chadwick, R. (2015). Can compassionate healthcare be measured? The Schwartz center compassionate care scale™. *Patient Education and Counseling, 98*(8), 1005–1010.

Lown, B. A., Rosen, J., & Marttila, J. (2011). An agenda for improving compassionate care: A survey shows about half of patients say such care is missing. *Health Affairs (Project Hope), 30*(9), 1772–1778.

McManus, I., Livingston, G., & Katona, C. (2006). The attractions of medicine: The generic motivations of medical school applicants in relation to demography, personality and achievement. *BMC Medical Education, 6*(1), 1–15.

Molinsky, A. L., Grant, A. M., & Margolis, J. D. (2012). The bedside manner of homo economicus: How and why priming an economic schema reduces compassion. *Organizational Behavior and Human Decision Processes, 119*(1), 27–37.

Pavlova, A., Wang, C. X. Y., Boggiss, A. L., O'Callaghan, A., & Consedine, N. S. (2022). Predictors of physician compassion, empathy, and related constructs: A systematic review. *Journal of General Internal Medicine, 37*(4), 900–911. https://doi.org/10.1007/s11606-021-07055-2

Picard, J., Catu-Pinault, A., Boujut, E., Botella, M., Jaury, P., & Zenasni, F. (2016). Burnout, empathy and their relationships: A qualitative study with residents in general medicine. *Psychology, Health and Medicine, 21*(3), 354–361.

Post, S. G., Ng, L. E., Fischel, J. E., Bennett, M., Bily, L., Chandran, L., Joyce, J., Locicero, B., McGovern, K., & McKeefrey, R. L. (2014). Routine, empathic and compassionate patient care: Definitions, development, obstacles, education and beneficiaries. *Journal of Evaluation in Clinical Practice, 20*(6), 872–880.

Preston, S. D. (2013). The origins of altruism in offspring care. *Psychological Bulletin, 139*(6), 1305.

Rawal, S., Strahlendorf, C., & Nimmon, L. (2020). Challenging the myth of the attrition of empathy in paediatrics residents. *Medical Education, 54*(1), 82–87.

Regan, P. C., Levin, L., Sprecher, S., Christopher, F. S., & Gate, R. (2000). Partner preferences: What characteristics do men and women desire in their short-term sexual and long-term romantic partners? *Journal of Psychology and Human Sexuality, 12*(3), 1–21.

Reynolds, L. M., Powell, P., Lin, Y. S., Ravi, K., Chung, C. Y. K., & Consedine, N. S. (2019). Fighting the flinch: Experimentally induced compassion makes a difference in health care providers. *British Journal of Health Psychology*, *24*(4), 982–998.

Shanafelt, T. D., Balch, C. M., Bechamps, G. J., Russell, T., Dyrbye, L., Satele, D., Collicott, P., Novotny, P. J., Sloan, J., & Freischlag, J. A. (2009). Burnout and career satisfaction among American surgeons. *Annals of Surgery*, *250*(3), 463–471.

Sinclair, S., Norris, J. M., McConnell, S. J., Chochinov, H. M., Hack, T. F., Hagen, N. A., McClement, S., & Bouchal, S. R. (2016). Compassion: A scoping review of the healthcare literature. *BMC Palliative Care*, *15*(1), 1–16.

Singh, P., Raffin-Bouchal, S., McClement, S., Hack, T. F., Stajduhar, K., Hagen, N. A., Sinnarajah, A., Chochinov, H. M., & Sinclair, S. (2018). Healthcare providers' perspectives on perceived barriers and facilitators of compassion: Results from a grounded theory study. *Journal of Clinical Nursing*, *27*(9–10), 2083–2097.

Sorenson, C., Bolick, B., Wright, K., & Hamilton, R. (2016). Understanding compassion fatigue in healthcare providers: A review of current literature. *Journal of Nursing Scholarship*, *48*(5), 456–465.

Strauss, C., Taylor, B. L., Gu, J., Kuyken, W., Baer, R., Jones, F., & Cavanagh, K. (2016). What is compassion and how can we measure it? A review of definitions and measures. *Clinical Psychology Review*, *47*, 15–27.

Trzeciak, S., Roberts, B. W., & Mazzarelli, A. J. (2017). Compassionomics: Hypothesis and experimental approach. *Medical Hypotheses*, *107*, 92–97.

Zandbelt, L. C., Smets, E. M. A., Oort, F. J., Godfried, M. H., & de Haes, H. C. J. M. (2007). Patient participation in the medical specialist encounter: Does physicians' patient-centred communication matter? *Patient Education and Counseling*, *65*(3), 396–406.

CHAPTER 24

COMPASSION IN ORGANIZATIONS AND POLITICAL STRUCTURES

June Allan

INTRODUCTION

A community organization in which I worked provided specialist support to refugees experiencing major loss and trauma. Practitioners provided counseling and support with empathy, kindness, and compassion, and routinely advocated to external organizations and bureaucracies. Yet the practitioners and refugees would become frustrated and disillusioned. Their efforts were regularly thwarted by unremitting bureaucratic requirements as the organization labored to meet fiscal constraints and obstructive governmental regulations and practices. Advocacy that was successful—even small 'wins'—was greeted with joy and gratitude. Inhumane policies accompanied by damaging attitudes served to create significant barriers to their efforts, a stark reminder of the organizational and political challenges that can be faced when attempting to exercise compassion.

In this chapter, I delve into the organizational and political factors that thwart or enable the delivery of a compassion-based approach to care. I consider the benefits of compassionate care offered by organizations, and people's experiences when it is lacking. I then investigate organizational and political barriers to enacting compassion and suggest ways to counter these barriers. Although much of the work I draw on has been undertaken in healthcare settings, I also utilize research concerning the grieving and bereaved in non-healthcare settings. The chapter will show that the delivery of compassionate care cannot be solely reliant on skills of frontline staff in exercising compassion. It must be systemically addressed across all levels.

WHEN COMPASSION IS LACKING

A consistent picture emerges from the research of what compassionate care entails (for example, Christiansen et al., 2015; de Zulueta, 2016; Kreitzer et al., 2020; Sinclair et al., 2016). It requires sensitivity of practitioners and organizations to people's suffering, along with freedom to act—with kindness, competence, and timeliness—to alleviate that suffering. Recipients of services feel heard and understood; they have increased trust in their practitioner, and increased hope. Their spiritual, psychological, and physical needs are attended to in safety and with dignity. Being treated compassionately by their organization positively affects practitioners' well-being and increases job satisfaction and sustainment.

Despite compassionate care being regarded as critical to the delivery of healthcare, especially for vulnerable people encountering poor health outcomes and end-of-life care, we are confronted on a regular basis in the media and elsewhere with examples to the contrary. A number of studies from the perspectives of service recipients in a variety of

DOI: 10.4324/9781003204121-29

organizational settings and locations identify experiences of 'a lack of compassion.' For example, during patients' illness and end-of-life care at the Dana-Farber Cancer Institute in Boston, family members found impersonal communication and lack of contact by the team, along with a lack of honest and direct information about end-of-life care and death to be unhelpful (Morris et al., 2020). Similarly, in a scoping review exploring the experiences of staff and bereaved relatives of deaths in prison custody across four European countries and the USA, distress was caused for families by poor communication, a feeling of not being treated with respect, and inaccurate and untimely information (Roulston et al., 2020).

The above examples primarily relate to the action or inaction of frontline staff who are typically seen as the enactors of compassionate care. Yet the impact of institutions, organizational policies, and government legislation on the bereaved is significant, highlighted in a study involving bereaved participants from palliative care services across rural Western Australia (Blackburn & Bulsara, 2018). Struggling with bureaucratic processes and rigid policies and protocols, the bereaved participants felt angry, offended, shamed, and despairing. As negative experiences of service recipients often derive from organizational and wider political influences, it is important to identify these systemic barriers.

THE 'EFFICIENCY CULTURE': BARRIERS TO THE PROVISION OF COMPASSIONATE CARE

SOCIETY AND NEOLIBERALISM

The difficulties with compassion and its provision in care services go deep, and according to Paul Gilbert (2021) are underpinned by our evolution as a human species toward a society in which democracy has become compromised, and the mode of organization once characterized by cooperation, caring, and sharing for the common good has been superseded in Western societies by competitive and narcissistic self-interest. This has contributed to fractured governmental leadership, mistrust, racism, and social injustices of many kinds.

These circumstances are linked to the now dominant political ideology of neoliberalism, a political philosophy and set of practices of late capitalism that focuses on economic rationalization, and individual responsibility. It fosters privatization, commodification (where, for example, care 'packages' are bought and sold in many countries), a commitment to minimal governmental or collective activity, and materialistic attitudes that prioritize economic wealth over other sources of well-being. Promoting managerialism and a target-driven approach to public policy, neoliberalism thwarts critical thinking, thereby risking the perpetuation of existing problems (Borgstrom & Walter, 2015; Brown, 2021; Gilbert, 2021; Kreitzer et al., 2020; Morley & O'Bree, 2021; Thompson, 2016). Furthermore, structural barriers that prohibit compassion from flourishing in formal health and social care systems include the shaping of public and professional behavior in Western countries by strict legal and regulatory codes that have led to anxiety about litigation on health and safety grounds, a cultural preoccupation with health and safety, and limited scope for public participation in the highly institutionalized health systems (Zaman et al., 2018).

This ideology has spawned the popular model of healthcare delivery that we see today, especially in Western society. Its dominance has led to the proliferation of healthcare and other organizations establishing business models of delivery, resulting in a range of effects that have seriously impacted the capacity of organizations to deliver compassionate care.

IMPACT ON ORGANIZATIONS

A growing critique of neoliberalism has coined the notion of organizational culture as "efficiency culture" (Morley & O'Bree, 2021, para. 6). Numerous studies report that with an emphasis on efficiencies, cutbacks in services, and a target-driven culture, staff experience time pressure, excessive paperwork, heavy workloads, and staff shortages, leaving less time to work with those they are seeking to support. Negative role models and a business culture at odds with their own values, along with inadequate remuneration and a lack of acknowledgment of their role, result in staff feeling undervalued and unappreciated. These factors can result in a climate of fear, all of which undermines the capacity for compassionate, relational care (for example, Christiansen et al., 2015; Kreitzer et al., 2020; Sinclair et al., 2016; Valizadeh et al., 2018).

This erosion of relationship-building in the workplace is associated with a lack of respect between team members and a lack of communication between frontline workers and managers who have inadequate knowledge and understanding of the complexity of the work of their staff (Kreitzer et al., 2020). The lack of time for staff to critically reflect on their work is a significant issue, given that compassionate care requires headspace to reason and reflect, and can prevent staff from recognizing how unhelpful and unjust ideologies become embedded in everyday situations and practices (Morley & O'Bree, 2021; Tierney et al., 2017).

Quality and type of leadership is a central issue. Noting the depressingly repetitive outcomes of healthcare inquiries held in the UK and elsewhere, de Zulueta (2016), for example, names poor hierarchical leadership as one of the biggest barriers to compassionate care. Similarly, in the three-year research study on the impact of the Leadership in Compassionate Care (LCC) Program in Scotland, explicitly designed to strengthen organizational capacity to deliver compassionate care, MacArthur et al. (2017) found leadership to be the most significant factor influencing the sustainability of the program. Problems identified included instability or change of leadership, and a lack of interest and support of the LCC Program by managers.

The recently completed Australian Royal Commission into Aged Care Quality and Safety (RCAC) was established in response to growing concerns about the quality of aged care in Australia. A glaring example of systemic effects and barriers, it illustrates the impact of neoliberalism and all its foibles. The Royal Commission found that "[s]ubstandard care and abuse pervades the Australian aged care system" (Australia RCAC, 2021, p. 68), with the Australian Government often focusing on funding requirements of aged care providers rather than on the care needs of older people. Ageist attitudes and assumptions about older people and aged care, massive underfunding, absence of a strong consumer voice, and deficiencies in governance and leadership were all found to contribute to the alarming deficits in the quality and safety of care.

Barriers to the provision of compassionate care are many, shaped by the organizational culture and the prevailing political ideology, which severely impact the capacity of staff to be sufficiently "present," with time and appropriate role models and support, to deliver compassionate care consistent with their professional values. How can this disturbing situation be changed to one in which it is possible for care to be provided in more compassionate ways?

MOVING TOWARD COMPASSIONATE CARE

To create environments that allow compassionate care to flourish in organizations and the wider society is hugely challenging, given the power of neoliberal discourses and associated pressures of the 'efficiency culture.' This situation creates an even greater imperative to advocate for compassionate cultures. While there is not the space here to explore the matter in detail, I cannot ignore the broader context that inhibits the enactment of compassion in organizations.

There are many positive indications that a move toward greater compassion in society is possible. Gilbert (2021), for example, provides hope through tracing the enormous capacity of humans to be compassionate in the face of powerful resistance, especially witnessed through the acts of many around the world during the ongoing COVID-19 pandemic. Adding to this hope is a renewed focus on compassionate care, advocacy, and social equity, along with a growing emphasis in health professional education on critical approaches rather than competency-based education (Halman et al., 2017).

We have already seen the far-reaching consequences of political action and inaction in the examples of the treatment of older people, cancer, and palliative care patients, and family members bereaved from deaths in custody. To push back against this and move toward greater compassion, it is firstly necessary for citizens at large to value compassion, care, and dignity, and have awareness and understanding of the causes of suffering (Gilbert, 2021; Haslam, 2015). To help counter the social inequalities and top-down leadership promoted by materialism and neoliberal ideology, suggested endeavors include committing to social justice, reaffirming a spirituality for all, and developing value-based conversations and approaches that emphasize doing things *with* people rather than to people (Cislaghi et al., 2019; Thompson, 2016).

But to encourage citizens to want to even look at the causes of suffering, education is necessary. The provision of education for 'compassionate citizenship' through the humanities and the arts, education in schools, and independent and well-financed public media can all nurture people's capacity to empathize and imagine the suffering of others (Slawinski, 2018). The use of critical consciousness in health professional education to promote social justice, appreciate the social and cultural context, and question and reflect on existing power structures in healthcare rather than accept systems that may be complicit in maintaining existing problems, can also foster more socially conscious health professionals (Halman et al., 2017).

Other 'big picture' ways of encouraging and sustaining a spirit of compassion include, as Gilbert (2021) suggests, promoting compassionate and respectful leadership at the global level, establishing forms of regulation that ensure fairer resource distribution, influencing the tone and content of media reporting, and advocating for cooperative activities at the global level. An example of this cooperation is the donation of COVID-19 vaccines by wealthy countries to poorer nations.

Thus, education and advocacy play key roles in promoting a more compassionate cultural context. What, then, are possible ways to foster compassionate care at the organizational level, at a time when many organizations are at breaking point due to fiscal constraints and huge workloads, with pressure to deliver care in a cost-effective manner? Two factors are critical: Organizational culture—the shared values, assumptions, and beliefs within an organization—and compassionate organizational leadership, with person-centered care at the core.

The earlier discussion revealed that all people within an organization—service recipients and staff alike—value being treated with respect and compassion. Given this, the organizational culture should attend to the needs of all staff, not just recipients of services. A positive example of changes in organizational culture is demonstrated in the Scottish LCC Program mentioned earlier (MacArthur, 2018; MacArthur et al., 2017).

The program was conducted within a local Scottish Health Board in the context of the National Health Service that had shifted toward a more market-driven and bureaucratic culture often dominated by achieving targets and efficiencies. An organizational culture that showed compassion for staff was adopted, with relation- or person-centered care at the heart of the approach. In the LCC Program, the development of techniques that strongly influenced organizational capacity to provide compassionate care included having a values-based approach that required the articulation and demonstration of values, and agreement about ways of working. Giving patients, relatives, and staff a voice to express their experiences and emotions was instituted, a strategy reinforced by Bolt et al. (2021), who argue about the need for nursing leadership to acknowledge the grief and moral distress among nursing staff who provided palliative care for patients with dementia during the COVID-19 pandemic. Introducing effective feedback mechanisms was another important strategy in the LCC Program. Key outcomes of these strategies included the personalization of patient care, an increased sense of involvement for relatives, and caring conversations as an accepted part of practice (MacArthur et al., 2017).

In other research, undertaken in New Hampshire, USA, with physicians providing end-of-life care in an interdisciplinary team, key strategies for delivering compassionate care were an emphasis for the normalizing of end-of-life conversations between staffs and patients, and shared-decision-making with patients. Critically, another necessary strategy involved facilitating an environment in which staff could dedicate time to team-based strategies, such as sharing patient experiences with co-workers, to establish strong inter-disciplinary relationships (Bessen et al., 2019).

Such relation-centered and inclusive strategies help shape an organizational culture in which staff share common values and approaches to the provision of compassionate care. But to both create and sustain this culture, compassionate leadership is necessary. In their study of leadership in the context of staff from a range of healthcare organizations providing end-of-life and palliative care in the West Midlands in England, Hewison et al. (2019) importantly demonstrated that apart from personal competences in providing compassionate care, enactment of leadership through organizational relations, connectedness, interventions into the organizational system, and changing organizational practices and processes were necessary.

An emphasis on leadership fostering organizational relationships and system-level intervention and change is also central to the LCC Program in which leadership strategies were embedded across all four key levels of the organization. *Support from the top* was implemented through a strongly committed strategic and compassionate leadership, underlined by the LCC Program being included as a corporate objective of the Board. *Leadership at middle management level* advocated for local resourcing and dealt with barriers to change, reinforced through the program becoming a standing agenda item at meetings and regular reporting on processes and outcomes of the program to managers and peers. *Leadership skills at the local level* were developed and enacted to nurture a positive local team ethos, support teams, and role model compassionate behaviors toward patients, families, *and* colleagues. And *facilitation skills of senior nurses* were developed and used to support teams by developing partnerships with others based on inclusivity and approachability, and to provide local ownership of program delivery (MacArthur, 2018; MacArthur et al., 2017).

It is clear, then, that supportive leadership, positive role models, and a collaborative team with a collective identity are all crucial in promoting a compassionate environment. For person-centered compassionate care to be actualized, it must be seen as a responsibility of every person in the system, from societal leadership to the front-line.

CONCLUSION

The capacity for developing and enacting compassionate care in organizations is inter-twined with enhancing compassion in the society at large. Despite the entrenched political philosophy associated with the business models of service delivery and efficiency cultures that now predominate, possibilities for transforming compassion deficits at a societal level require education and advocacy for more compassionate ways of being. To embed compassionate care at an organizational level requires a culture that embeds compassion-oriented principles and practices in the fabric of the organization through the strategic action of compassionate leadership. Worthy challenges for us all, if we are to push back against the damaging impact of organizational and political barriers and deliver more socially just and compassionate care.

REFERENCES

Australia. Royal Commission into Aged Care Quality and Safety (RCAC). (2021). *Final report: Care, dignity and respect*. Vol. 1- Summary and recommendations, 1 March 2021, Commonwealth of Australia. https://Agedcare.royalcommission.gov.au/Publications/Final-Report

Bessen, S., Jain, R., Brooks, W., & Mishra, M. (2019). "Sharing in hope and worries" - A qualitative analysis of the delivery of compassionate care in palliative care and oncology at end of life. *International Journal of Qualitative Studies on Health and Well-Being, 14*(1), 1622355. https://doi.org/10.1080/17482631.2019.1622355

Blackburn, P., & Bulsara, C. (2018). "I am tired of having to prove that my husband was dead." Dealing with practical matters in bereavement and the impact on the bereaved. *Death Studies, 42*(2), 627–635. https://doi.org/10.1080/07481187.2017.1415392

Bolt, S., van der Steen, J., Mujezinovic, I., Janssen, D., Schols, J., Zwakhalen, S., Khemai, C., Knapen, E. P. A. G. M., Dijkstra, L., &Meijers, J. (2021). Practical nursing recommendations for palliative care for people with dementia living in long-term facilities during the COVID-19 pandemic: A rapid scoping review. *International Journal of Nursing Studies, 113*, 103781. https://doi.org/10.1016/jnurstu.2020.103781

Borgstrom, E., & Walter, T. (2015). Choice and compassion at the end of life: A critical analysis of recent English policy discourse. *Social Science and Medicine, 136–137*, 99–105. https://doi.org/10.1016/jsocscimed.2015.05.013

Brown, C. (2021). Critical clinical social work and the neoliberal constraints on social justice in mental health. *Research on Social Work Practice, February*, 1–9. https://doi.org/10.1177/1049731520984531

Christiansen, A., O'Brien, M., Kirton, J., Zubairu, K., & Bray, L. (2015). Delivering compassionate care: The enablers and barriers. *British Journal of Nursing, 24*(16). https://doi.org/10.12968/bjon.2015.24.16.833

Cislaghi, B., Bukuluki, P., Chowdhury, M., Miranda, A., Kenny, L., Kohli, A., Kusumaningrum, S., Brah, B. H., Love, C., Mathpati, M. M., Nkwi, P., Ona, F., Porter, J., Ruiz-Casares, M., Saldanha, N., Sulaiman, M., & Wessells, M. (2019). Global health is political; can it also be compassionate? *Journal of Global Health, 9*(2). https://doi.org/10.7189/jogh.09.020306

de Zulueta, P. (2016). Developing compassionate leadership in health care: An integrative review. *Journal of Healthcare Leadership, 8*, 1–10. https://doi.org/10.2147/jhl.s93724

Gilbert, P. (2021). Creating a compassionate world: Addressing the conflicts between sharing and caring versus controlling and holding evolved strategies. *Frontiers in Psychology, 11*, 582090. https://doi.org/10.3389/fpsyg.2020.582090

Halman, M., Baker, L., & Ng, S. (2017). Using critical consciousness to inform health professions education: A literature review. *Perspectives on Medical Education, 6*(1), 12–20. https://doi.org/10.1007/s40037-016-0324-y

Haslam, D. (2015). More than kindness. *Journal of Compassionate Health Care, 2*(6). https://doi.org/10.1186/s4639-015-0015-2

Hewison, A., Sawbridge, Y., & Tooley, L. (2019). Compassionate leadership in palliative and end-of-life care: A focus group study. *Leadership in Health Services, 32*(2), 264–279. https://doi.org/10.1108/lhs-09-2018-0044

Kreitzer, L., Brintnell, S., & Austin, W. (2020). Institutional barriers to healthy workplace environments: From the voices of social workers experiencing compassion fatigue. *British Journal of Social Work, 50*(7), 1942–1960. https://doi.org/10.1093/bjsw/bcz147

MacArthur, J. (2018). Embedding compassionate care: A leadership programme in the national health service in Scotland. The organizational context of nursing practice. In P. Van Bogaert & S. Clarke (Eds.), *The organizational context of nursing practice* (pp. 139–159). Springer. https://doi.org/10/1007/978-3-319-71042-6_6

MacArthur, J., Wilkinson, H., Gray, M., & Matthews-Smith, G. (2017). Embedding compassionate care in local NHS practice: Developing a conceptual model through realistic evaluation. *Journal of Research in Nursing, 22*(1–2), 130–147. https://doi.org/10.1177/1744987116678901

Morley, C., & O'Bree, C. (2021). Critical reflection: An imperative skill for social work practice in neoliberal organizations? *Social Sciences, 10*(3), 97. https://doi.org/10.3390/socsci10030097

Morris, S., Nayak, M., & Block, S. (2020). Insights from bereaved family members about end-of-life care and bereavement. *Journal of Palliative Medicine, 23*(8), 1030–1037. https://doi.org/10.1089/jpm.2019.0467

Roulston, R., McKeaveney, C., Anderson, M., McCloskey, P., & Butler, M. (2020). Deaths in prison custody: A scoping review of the experiences of staff and bereaved relatives. *British Journal of Social Work*. https://doi.org/10.1093/bjsw/bcaa095

Sinclair, S., Norris, J., McConnell, S., Chochinov, H., Hack, T., Hagen, N., McClement, S., & Bouchal, S. (2016). Compassion: A scoping review of the healthcare literature. *BMC Palliative Care, 15*(6). https://doi.org/10.1186/s12904-016-0080-0

Slawinski, M. (2018). Can institutions be compassionate? On Martha Nussbaum's theory of political compassion. *Psychology Research, 8*(5), 204–213. https://doi.org/10.17265/2159-5542/2018.05.003

Thompson, N. (2016). Compassion in a materialist world. In D. Harris & T. Bordere (Eds.), *Handbook of social justice in loss and grief: Exploring diversity, equity, and inclusion* (pp. 40–49). Routledge.

Tierney, S., Seers, K., Reeve, J., & Tutton, L. (2017). Appraising the situation: A framework for understanding compassionate care. *Journal of Compassionate Health Care, 4*(1). https://doi.org/10.1186/s40639-016-0030-y

Valizadeh, L., Zamanzadeh, V., Dewar, B., Rahmani, A., & Ghafourifard, M. (2018). Nurse's perceptions of organizational barriers to delivering compassionate care: A qualitative study. *Nursing Ethics, 25*(5), 580–590. https://doi.org/10.1177/0969733016660881

Zaman, S., Whitelaw, A., Richards, N., Inbadas, H., & Clark, D. (2018). A moment for compassion: Emerging rhetorics in end-of-life care. *Medical Humanities, 44*(2), 140–143. http://doi.org/10.1136/medhum-2017-011329

CHAPTER 25

COMPASSIONATE CITIES FOR END-OF-LIFE CARE

Allan Kellehear

INTRODUCTION

Compassionate cities are public health experiments that aim to support people living with advanced aging, life-threatening illness, caregiving, and grief and loss. The ideas behind these practices emerged from the field of palliative care in the early 2000s. Compassionate cities are designed to promote cooperative civic actions to support these kinds of populations, usually within a city or town-wide area. These cities develop local policies and actions to help with these aims—in their workplaces, schools, faith groups, local government, cultural centers and festivals, and in local neighborhoods.

My aim in this chapter is to provide a brief introduction to compassionate cities. I will argue that compassionate cities are historically important because they extend traditional public health discussions about citizenship and the health of each citizen to a level that positively embraces the end of life. Compassionate cities accomplish this extension of vision by addressing three shifts identified by public health approaches to palliative care: (a) that healthcare must aim to be *social care* if it is to be truly effective; (b) that public health must include the living experiences of those aging, dying, caregiving, and grieving because these populations have associated troubles that are preventable and modifiable; and (c) that the end of life journey is also commonly characterized by positive experiences such as social support, courage, growing intimacy, resilience, meaning-making, and increased personal and social empathy that can and should be foundations upon which to build health promotion in these kinds of populations.

The following sections in this chapter will trace the origins of compassionate cities in both the formal public health and palliative care movements. I will then reproduce the compassionate city charter. This charter is a widely distributed guideline that maps the civic sectors of the city that should be targeted for social action and policy development. It has also been the planning basis for many international compassionate city developments. I will then provide two examples of existing compassionate cities and provide an outline of their activities and development. I will end with some final comments on the future of these kinds of social experiments.

WHAT ARE COMPASSIONATE CITIES?

Compassionate cities are academically derived from both a critique and a corrective to the WHO health cities literature and movement (Kellehear, 2005). Both healthy cities and compassionate cities are part of the 'new' public health movement, also known as the health promotion movement, established and enshrined in the Ottawa Charter of 1986.

The health promotion movement was a public health policy and practice development that recognized that modern epidemiological and demographic shifts were moving from infectious diseases to chronic diseases; that the world's population was rapidly aging; that a sole focus on 'cure' needed to co-exist with a new focus on 'management' of long-term

DOI: 10.4324/9781003204121-30

illness; that promoting health was the best method for the prevention of disease; that a focus on individual patients must co-exist with an equal attention to the health-enhancing or health-eroding aspects of a local setting (Waddington, 1973; Starr, 1982; Beaglehole & Bonita, 1997).

Furthermore, although genetics may play a limited role in health it is the social determinants of health and illness—occupation, age, social class, gender, or ethnicity among other factors—that play a pivotal role in who gets sick but also who gets treatment. In this way, a revised understanding of bioethics turns into a public health ethics concerned with access, equity, and social justice (Childress et al., 2002). Finally, there emerged from these shifts in the current global public health data a policy and planning realization that there are obvious limits to professional service provision in terms of quality, continuity, and reach of care.

In recognition of these observations and insights, the Ottawa Charter for Health Promotion advocated: Building public policies that support health, creating supportive environments, strengthening community action, developing personal skills, and re-orienting health services. These recommendations promoted, encouraged, and sometimes legislated for greater responsibility for health to be taken by workplaces, schools, or neighborhoods. Businesses and industry developed more health and safety guidelines, and local and national governments were encouraged to enforce them. Marketing campaigns focused not just on products but social conduct. For example, schools or local communities were encouraged to exercise more, eat better, and abstain from smoking or excess drinking. People everywhere were asked to learn more about their own nutrition or hazardous risks in the environment, or to wear sunscreens, condoms, or bicycle helmets, and hundreds of other ways of promoting their own health and well-being.

Soon after the Ottawa Charter was established and promoted the psychiatrist Leonard Dahl coined the term "health cities" (Aicher, 1998). This was part of a broader discussion in health promotion circles to promote a holistic and systemic approach to the promotion of health. However, the problem with the early formulations of health promotion, and the subsequent development of the healthy cities movement was that death and dying remained 'the enemy' and the symbol of public health failure. This was an ironic persistence of an old public health idea built around a past view of human epidemiology and demography.

In the past, societies were characterized by high infant mortality and short life expectancies; dying was frequently sudden or of short duration (e.g., infectious diseases, trauma, deaths in childbirth). However, since the Second World War, middle- and high-income countries have dramatically moved away from this epidemiological and demographic profile and have subsequently witnessed high life expectancy and low infant mortality. Dying, as an experience taking days or weeks, now became an experience spanning months and even years. Caregiving was equally extended for professionals, families, and the social networks of those with short life expectancies. The gentrification that accompanied and fueled the growth of affluent societies also meant a certain sequestering of the experience of death and bereavement that often led to long, protracted, sometimes difficult, and sometimes disenfranchised, experiences of grief. Healthy cities, and the health promotion movement more broadly, remained silent about these changes and this growing population.

Health promoting palliative care (1999) and the compassionate cities/community movements (2005) were academic and social correctives for this oversight. The policies and actions of compassionate cities were designed to alert the major players within the civic sector—from schools and workplaces to neighborhoods and faith groups—that end-of-life care, like healthcare, was everyone's responsibility.

Similar to healthy cities, compassionate cities advocated a settings approach—the local environment needed to change to support people's health or end of life care, wherever they may find themselves in their usual day or weekly cycle (Dooris, 2006, see also: https://www.who.int/healthy_settings/about/en/). Because a single individual will crisscross a variety of social institutions in any one day—at work, school, shopping centers, churches or temples, or on the TV set or social media, their dealings with local government, health services, or local neighbors—any program to change behavior must target those very settings. Policy development was key to promoting those changes. However, the history of health promotion shows that programs that do not involve the people for whom they are designed are among the least effective. Therefore, a participatory approach was essential to any methodology employed by health promotion programs (McClosky et al., 2011).

End of life care services would remain important, but they would be partnerships with communities. Most of palliative care provision, for example, attempts to offer not only medical and nursing support but also social, psychological, and spiritual care. However, a fixed geographical service, that largely keeps business hours, and that has a large clientele, always struggles to provide 24/7 social, psychological, or spiritual support. Enter here the civic domain. Compassionate cities and communities could be seen as an 'asset' to be explored and used in the service of just these kinds of support functions. Not only would health become everyone's business but also the business of compassionate care at the end of life (Kellehear, 2013).

For compassionate cities and communities inside a public health narrative, the term "compassion" would stress its social meaning—consistent with health promotion as a social model of healthcare. The social meaning of compassion was the idea of sharing with and in another's suffering. The emphasis is on mutual care and not a one-way idea of care as something one *does on* or *to another*. This style of mutuality demands a compassion-in-action approach as a civic dimension of life (Kellehear, 2005, pp. 41–42, Abel & Clarke, 2020). At the core of all compassionate cities are the ideas of mutual responsibility and care, partnership working, local social action, and local policy development to support those undergoing the universal human experiences of death, dying, grief, and caregiving. How might this be achieved?

THE COMPASSIONATE CITY CHARTER AND ITS MEANING

Figure 25.1 reproduces the Compassionate City Charter.

This charter is designed to identify the different civic sectors in towns and cities that should be targeted for social actions and policy developments. In this way, the charter acts as a sociological map for activists in end-of-life care. The charter has two further purposes. The charter may be employed as a talking device or a discussion topic, or used as a starting point for developing a more locally relevant charter for social actions in end-of-life care for any community; it may serve as an illustrative model. Finally, the charter acts as an intellectual or social alert for overlooked sectors and social groups. In this way, the charter advocates for a systematic, and systemic, approach to civic care and cooperation.

- A CHARTER OF ACTIONS -

Compassionate Cities are communities that recognize that all natural cycles of sickness and health, birth and death, and love and loss occur everyday within the orbits of its institutions and regular activities. A compassionate city is a community that recognizes that care for one another at times of crisis and loss is not simply a task solely for health and social services but is everyone's responsibility. Compassionate Cities are communities that publicly encourage, facilitate, supports, and celebrates care for one another during life's most testing moments and experiences, especially those pertaining to life-threatening and life-limiting illness, chronic disability, frail ageing and dementia, grief and bereavement, and the trials and burdens of long term care. Though local government strives to maintain and strengthen quality services for the most fragile and vulnerable in our midst, those persons are not the limits of our experience of fragility and vulnerability. Serious personal crises of illness, dying, death and loss may visit any us, at any time during the normal course of our lives. A compassionate city is a community that squarely recognizes and addresses this social fact.

Through auspices of the Mayor's office a compassionate city will - by public marketing and advertising, by use of the cities network and influences, by dint of collaboration and co-operation, in partnership with social media and its own offices – develop and support the following 13 social changes to the city's key institutions and activities.

1.   Our schools will have annually reviewed policies or guidance documents for dying, death, loss and care
2.   Our workplaces will have annually reviewed policies or guidance documents for dying, death, loss and care
3.   Our trade unions will have annually reviewed policies or guidance documents for dying, death, loss and care
4.   Our places of worship will have at least one dedicated group for end of life care support
5.   Our city's hospices and nursing homes will have a community development program involving local area citizens in end of life care activities and programs
6.   Our city's major museums and art galleries will hold annual exhibitions on the experiences of ageing, dying, death, loss or care
7.   Our city will host an annual peacetime memorial parade representing the major sectors of human loss outside military campaigns – cancer, motor neuron disease, AIDS, child loss, suicide survivors, animal companion loss, widowhood, industrial and vehicle accidents, the loss of emergency workers and all end of life care personnel, etc.
8.   Our city will promote compassionate communities programs to engage neighborhoods and local streets in direct care activities for their local residents living with health crisis, ageing, caregiving, and grief.
9.   Our city will create an incentives scheme to celebrate and highlight the most creative compassionate organization, event, and individual/s. The scheme will take the form of an annual award administered by a committee drawn from the end of life care sector. A 'Mayors Prize' will recognize individual/s for that year those who most exemplify the city's values of compassionate care.
10. Our city will publicly showcase, in print and in social media, our local government policies, services, funding opportunities, partnerships, and public events that address 'our compassionate concerns' with living with ageing, life-threatening and life-limiting illness, loss and bereavement, and long term caring. All end of life care-related services within the city limits will be encouraged to distribute this material or these web links including veterinarians and funeral organizations
11. Our city will work with local social or print media to encourage an annual city-wide short story or art competition that helps raise awareness of ageing, dying, death, loss, or caring.
12. All our compassionate policies and services, and in the policies and practices of our official compassionate partners and alliances, will demonstrate an understanding of how diversity shapes the experience of ageing, dying, death, loss and care – through ethnic, religious, gendered, and sexual identity and through the social experiences of poverty, inequality, and disenfranchisement.
13. We will seek to encourage and to invite evidence that institutions for the homeless and the imprisoned have support plans in place for end of life care and loss and bereavement.

Our city will establish and review these targets and goals in the first two years and thereafter will add one more sector annually to our action plans for a compassionate city – e.g. hospitals, further & higher education, charities, community & voluntary organizations, police & emergency services, and so on.

This charter represents a commitment by the city to embrace a view of health and wellbeing that embraces social empathy, reminding its inhabitants and all who would view us from beyond its borders that 'compassion' means to embrace mutual sharing. A city is not merely a place to work and access services but equally a place to enjoy support in the safety and protection of each other's company, even to the end of our days.

Figure 25.1 The Compassionate City

The Compassionate City Charter was first introduced inside a 'toolkit' for social action as part of a commissioned report for Public Health England (2014). It was then revised and published internationally (Kellehear, 2016, Abel & Clarke, 2020). The version here has been reproduced with an additional modification and is publicly available in the UK by accessing the Compassionate Communities UK website (a registered UK charitable trust—www.compassionate-communitiesuk.co.uk) or internationally through the Public Health Palliative Care International website (www.phpci.info). (This charter must be distinguished from the similarly titled US Charter for Compassion which is a religious/philosophical set of principles based on the Golden Rule and that encourages personal and social affirmations. That charter is not specifically associated with end-of-life care or public health social action and advocacy.)

TWO EXAMPLES

The Compassionate City Charter is currently used in flexible ways by different organizations and in different contexts. Some employ the charter literally as a guide; some encourage the local or municipal government to lead on the charter. Some organizations choose to lead with the charter themselves. Some organizations apply the charter to significant size cities, and yet others apply these principles to the civic sectors in their much smaller towns. Some organizations employ the charter to create one of their own, and others simply employ the "spirit" of the charter to reach out and inspire civic changes in end-of-life care.

PLYMOUTH, ENGLAND

Plymouth in England is a compassionate city with a population over 260,000. In this case, the local hospice has taken the leadership role and has employed the charter as a specific guide for their civic actions and partnerships (see https://www.stlukes-hospice.org.uk/plymouth-a -compassionate-city/). An initial large public conference, organized by St Luke's Hospice— the local hospice—brought most of the interested future partners together and this led to further talks, agreements, and planning. Out of these initial talks emerged a partnership with the elected members of the local government and some of their public health officers in 2018. A series of compassionate city working groups were formed around the different sections of the charter. Each of the groups took particular responsibilities for generating new partnerships and cooperative actions and policies in their designated areas—schools or workplaces, community neighborhood support, or faith groups and prisons.

Publicity and marketing of the working groups attracted some 700 community volunteers, over 500 action pledges, 13 social networks, and 10 compassionate cafes (to increase public discussion and end of life literacy in the community). These different groups, networks, and individual local volunteers ensure the policy changes and social actions are made inside the different civic organizations and institutions within the city. End of life care has become integrated into many workplace health and safety policies or school cultures. Marginal groups, such as found in local prisons, have been engaged to develop internal resources and networks that address the formerly overlooked problems of their aging, and hence dying, caregiving and grieving populations.

SEVILLE, SPAIN

Seville in Spain is a compassionate city with a local population of over half a million people with this increasing to 1.5 million in the larger sprawling metropolitan area. In this case, a small non-government, not-for-profit organization (New Health Foundation) led by public health workers took the leadership role and used the charter as an inspirational guide—not a literal guide. Entitled "All with You," Seville's compassionate city program was designed as a model of social networking and innovations (Librada et al., 2018).

Eight methods were deployed to create the changes in the broad areas relevant to the charter's visions. This included networking with the city council and mayor's office and creating a public function covered by the local media. Other interested civic organizations were identified and enlisted to this vision of civic participation in end-of-life care. These early members created a board of advisors and first networks. One of the first functions of this board was to create a series of agreements and memoranda of cooperation with private companies, professional associations, churches, brotherhoods, schools, and cultural organizations. Beneficiary organizations in health and social care were identified and enlisted. These were health or social care services that could benefit from civic actions and support for those people in their care—the very elderly, those living with life-threatening or life-limiting illness, those living with long-term caregiving and loss and grief.

Other actions included creating agreements with universities and schools for policy development around death, dying, and end of life care; connecting with volunteer organizations to encourage them to integrate a compassionate civic vision of end-of-life care within their own; linking with and involve end of life care professionals; and creating a working map of potential centers and organizations with whom the Health Foundation might work in the future. Crucial to the spread, strengthening, and sustenance of community energy, commitment, and widening capacity was publicity and marketing. Of further importance to the Seville compassionate city operation was the willingness and capacity to attract basic funding support from partners and the provision of information and training sessions for those partners and subsequent volunteers and civic allies.

WHAT IS THE FUTURE FOR COMPASSIONATE CITIES?

Examples of compassionate cities similar to Plymouth and Seville are spreading rapidly. *Public Health Palliative Care International* documents some ten further cities who are adopting these models or who are employing the charter as a way to help them to broker and then navigate civic participation at the end of life. Other excellent examples can be examined in the long-term work of Koshikode in South India (Kumar, 2007, and also http://compass ionatekozhikode.in), or the more recent innovative work in the city of Ottawa in Canada (https://compassionateottawa.ca). Many more are applying the charter's principles from earlier experiments in compassionate communities that have their beginnings in smaller villages or suburbs of a city such as the case in Taipei in Taiwan. (https://www.shennong .org.tw). All of these are part of the civic and professional desire to make compassionate care a practical as well as a felt reality for modern end of life care efforts.

Although the compassionate cities/communities movement is comparatively new, it represents an attempt to create a healthy settings approach that is inclusive of those at the end of life irrespective of diagnosis, age, or institutional circumstance. In this way, the idea of compassionate care offered by and to all—and not merely health services—becomes an extended, extensive, and open-ended civic movement. In sociological terms, compassion slowly but practically evolves from the belly of the social system that ordains it.

REFERENCES

Abel, J., & Clarke, L. (2020). *The compassion project: A case for hope & humankindness from the town that beat loneliness*. Aster.

Aicher, J. (1998). *Designing healthy cities: Prescriptions, principles, and practice*. Krieger.

Beaglehole, R., & Bonita, R. (1997). *Public health at the crossroads: Achievements and prospects*. Cambridge University Press.

Childress, J. F., Faden, R. R., Gaare, R. D., Gostin, L. O., Kahn, J., Bonnie, R. J., Kass, N. E., Mastroianni, A. C., Moreno, J. D., & Nieberg, P. (2002). Public health ethics: Mapping the terrain. *Journal of Law, Medicine and Ethics, 30*(2), 170–178.

Dooris, M. (2006). Healthy settings: Challenges to generating evidence of effectiveness. *Health Promotion International, 21*(1), 55–65.

Karapliagou, A., & Kellehear, A. (2014). *Public health approaches to end of life care: A toolkit*. Public Health England & National Council for Palliative Care.

Kellehear, A. (1999). *Health-promoting palliative care*. Oxford University Press.

Kellehear, A. (2005). *Compassionate cities: Public health and end of life care*. Routledge.

Kellehear, A. (2013). Compassionate communities: End of life care as everyone's responsibility. *Quarterly Journal of Medicine, 106*(12), 1071–1076.

Kellehear, A. (2016). The compassionate city charter: Inviting the cultural and social sectors into end of life care. In K. Wegleitner, K. Heimerl, & A. Kellehear (Eds.), *Compassionate communities: Case studies from Britain and Europe* (pp. 76–87). Routledge.

Kumar, S. (2007). Kerala, India: A regional community-based palliative care model. *Journal of Pain and Symptom Management, 33*(5), 623–627.

Librada, S., Herrer, A. E., Boceta, J., Mota, R., & Nabal, M. (2018). All with you: A new method for developing compassionate communities and cities at the end of life. Experiences in Spain and Latin-America. *Annals of Palliative Medicine, 7*(Suppl 2), S15–S31.

McCloskey, D., Aguilar-Gaxiola, S., Michener, J., Akintobi, T. H., Bonham, A., Cook, J.,… & White-Cooper, S. (2011). *Principles of community engagement* (2nd ed.). (NIH Publication No. 117782). National Institute of Health, Department of Health and Human Services, USA.

Ottawa Charter for Health Promotion. (1986). *Health Promotion, 1*, iii–v. https://www.canada .ca/en/public-health/services/health-promotion/population-health/ottawa-charter-health -promotion-international-conference-on-health-promotion.html

Starr, P. (1982). *The social transformation of American Medicine*. Basic Books.

Waddington, I. (1973). The role of the hospital in the development of modern medicine: A sociological analysis. *Sociology, 7*(2), 211–224.

CONCLUSION

Compassion and Grief as Companions

Darcy L. Harris and Andy H. Y. Ho

Throughout the chapters of this book, a common theme is evident: Compassion and grief are both entwined with our need and desire for connection. When we train in compassion and set our intention to act in ways that are compassionate, we are acknowledging the threads of our common experiences and interconnectivity with each other. As Gilbert (2009) eloquently explains, our potential for compassion has emerged with the growth and evolution of humanity over thousands of years. We need each other. We are social beings, born with an innate need to form attachments and to feel that we belong with others in a meaningful way. The irony is that our need for attachment and relational anchoring is juxtaposed with a world where the only constant is impermanence. The very relationships that anchor us will not last forever, whether they end by dissolution or by death. Life does not unfold the way we had planned. All of us will experience suffering, pain, and loss at various times in our lives. There are no exceptions; no form of clinical training or spiritual practice can alter this foundational aspect of life.

Compassion is a choice that requires courage to turn towards suffering rather than away from it. Discerning a response that is compassionate requires wisdom that is cultivated by reinforcement through the everyday practice of navigating through complexities with mindful awareness and intentioned presence. It is not about doing or being as much as it is about intention and motivation. We cannot bring back a loved one who has died. We cannot reverse a diagnosis that completely upends the life trajectories of ourselves and those we love. Relationships that dissolve cannot be readily renewed. The glass shatters, and we are left to pick up the shards with our bare hands, risking deeper cuts each time we want to wipe the slate clean.

In the chapters that have been included in this volume, there are examples and descriptions of compassion as a way of being in the world and of compassion as a consciously enacted process in specific situations that involve loss and grief. These writings demonstrate that there is not one way to compassionately respond to grief. Rather, our practice and compassionate intention allow us the ability to "take in" the entirety of the loss and to journey alongside those who are doubled over in their grief without the additional burden of expectation for a specific outcome.

Similar to compassion, grief is also a reminder of our shared humanity. We grieve because we have engaged and invested in an aspect of life that suddenly is no more. We lose those that we love. We must leave places and careers that formed our core sense of identity. We lose our younger selves to our mature selves as we age. We must accept the inevitable loss of our health and increased limitations as we enter the golden years of our lives. No matter our ethnicity, sexuality, political orientation, or religious beliefs, we all share the common language of loss. There is something "right" about grief. It is painful and messy, similar to when a major renovation project is undertaken. When we are in the midst of the renovation process, all that we can see is the mess and the gaping holes left behind when old boards and walls have been pulled out. In the end, we can appreciate new colors, patterns, and changes that have emerged from the calamity—but this result only came about from the removal and destruction of what had been in place that was familiar before.

DOI: 10.4324/9781003204121-31

What can we say about compassion and grief? They are partners to us in our life's journey. They accompany us and our clients in both painful and profound ways. Compassion
acknowledges the presence of suffering and the desire to relieve that suffering in whatever
ways are possible. Grief reminds us that some wounds must be carefully tended, with a
shared sense of presence in the midst of tremendous pain. Both grief and compassion point
us toward healing and wholeness; the key is understanding that neither is about fixing or
arriving at a specific endpoint. Grief rips the fabric of our lives, leaving behind the loose
threads of our hopes and dreams that dangle in mid-air; compassion is the loom that allows
us to re-weave these loose threads slowly and mindfully, perhaps adding different colors
and textures to create a tapestry that reflects a new world into which we now venture.

It is our deepest wish that this book will foster dialogue about our common shared experiences of grief and loss in the context of compassion as a sustainable, healing approach. We
look forward to continuing discussions about compassionate ways to respond to the grief
that occurs from all types of loss experiences. May all beings be at peace. May all beings be
free of suffering. And may we always remember our intention to be instruments to relieve
suffering wherever and whenever possible.

REFERENCE

Gilbert, P. (2009). *The compassionate mind: A new approach to the challenges of life.* Constable &
    Robinson.

INDEX

Page numbers in **bold** indicate tables and page numbers in italics indicate figures

For Product Safety Concerns and Information please contact our EU
representative GPSR@taylorandfrancis.com
Taylor & Francis Verlag GmbH, Kaufingerstraße 24, 80331 München, Germany

www.ingramcontent.com/pod-product-compliance
Lightning Source LLC
Chambersburg PA
CBHW050636280326
41932CB00015B/2667